NUMBER TWO HUNDRED AND EIGHTEEN

The Old Farmer's Almanac

CALCULATED ON A NEW AND IMPROVED PLAN FOR THE YEAR OF OUR LORD

2010

BEING 2ND AFTER LEAP YEAR AND (UNTIL JULY 4) 234TH YEAR OF AMERICAN INDEPENDENCE

Fitted for Boston and the New England states, with special corrections and calculations to answer for all the United States.

Containing, besides the large number of Astronomical Calculations and the Farmer's Calendar for every month in the year, a variety of

NEW, USEFUL, & ENTERTAINING MATTER.

Established in 1792 by Robert B. Thomas (1766–1846)

*Go forth under the open sky, and list
To Nature's teachings.*

–William Cullen Bryant, American poet (1794–1878)

Cover T.M. registered
in U.S. Patent Office

Copyright © 2009 by Yankee Publishing Incorporated
ISSN 0078-4516

Library of Congress
Card No. 56-29681

Original wood engraving by Randy Miller

THE OLD FARMER'S ALMANAC • DUBLIN, NH 03444 • 603-563-8111 • ALMANAC.COM

No Contract

Bigger, Brighter screen. Larger, backlit numbers.

NEW and IMPROVED

It doesn't play music, take pictures, or surf the Internet.

Introducing the NEW Jitterbug®. It's the cell phone that offers simplicity for everyone.

The new Jitterbug cell phone makes calling simple!

- Bigger, Brighter LCD screen... easier to see even in daylight
- Comes pre-programmed and ready to use right out of the box
- No contract required
- Live, 24-hour Jitterbug Operators greet you by name, connect calls and update your Phone Book[1]
- Soft ear cushion and louder volume for better sound quality
- Comfortable keypad designed to make dialing easy
- Hearing aid compatible – top ratings in this category
- Familiar dial tone confirms service (no other cell phone has this)
- Service as low as $14.99* a month

U.S.-Based Customer Service

Why pay for minutes you'll never use!

Monthly Minutes[‡]	50	100 New
Monthly Rate*	$14.99	$19.99 New
Operator Assistance	24/7	24/7
911 Access	FREE	FREE
Long Distance Calls	No add'l charge	No add'l charge
Voice Dial	FREE	FREE
Nationwide Coverage[††]	Yes	Yes
Trial Period	30 days	30 days

Other plans available. Ask your Jitterbug expert for details.

FREE Gift
Order now and receive a free Car Charger.
A $24 value![5]

Service as low as $14.99 a month* and a friendly 30-day return policy.** If you've ever wanted the security and convenience of a cell phone, but never wanted the fancy features and minutes you don't need... Jitterbug is for you. Like me, you'll soon be telling your friends about Jitterbug. Call now.

*first*STREET
for Boomers and Beyond
brought to you by
1998 Ruffin Mill Road
Colonial Heights, VA 23834

Jitterbug Cell Phone
Call now for our lowest price.
Please mention promotional code 38026.

1-888-763-5158
www.firststreetonline.com

47349

Contents

The Old Farmer's Almanac • 2010

32

98

148

152

SPECIAL REPORT

(continued on page 6)

There's more of everything at Almanac.com.

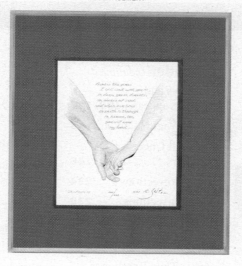

A Most Unusual Gift of Love

THE POEM READS:

"Across the years I will walk with you—
in deep, green forests; on shores of sand:
and when our time on earth is through,
in heaven, too, you will have my hand."

Dear Reader,

The drawing you see above is called *The Promise*. It is completely composed of dots of ink. After writing the poem, I worked with a quill pen and placed thousands of these dots, one at a time, to create this gift in honor of my youngest brother and his wife.

Now, I have decided to offer *The Promise* to those who share and value its sentiment. Each litho is numbered and signed by hand and precisely captures the detail of the drawing. As a wedding, anniversary or Christmas gift or simply as a standard for your own home, I believe you will find it most appropriate.

Measuring 14" by 16", it is available either fully framed in a subtle copper tone with hand-cut mats of pewter and rust at $110, or in the mats alone at $95. Please add $14.50 for insured shipping and packaging. Your satisfaction is completely guaranteed.

My best wishes are with you.

The Art of Robert Sexton, 491 Greenwich St. (at Grant), San Francisco, CA 94133

MASTERCARD and VISA orders welcome. Please send card name, card number, address and expiration date, or phone (415) 989-1630 between noon-8 P.M. EST. Checks are also accepted. *Please allow 3 weeks for delivery.*

The Promise is featured with many other recent works in my book, *Journeys of the Human Heart.*
It, too, is available from the address above at $12.95 per copy postpaid. Please visit my Web site at
www.robertsexton.com

Contents

(continued from page 4)

42

56

68

192

Local Solutions for Local Problems

The More Things Change . . .

In 1792, when Robert B. Thomas founded this Almanac, life was different. Then, most people lived on a farm and used traditional methods to grow the fruit and vegetables that stocked their larders and filled their root cellars. The growing cycle dominated life. Community members helped each other to sow and harvest, and schools closed to allow students and teachers to help with farmwork. (For 118 years, this Almanac, then available only in the Northeast, published the dates of such college "vacations.") Even the livestock contributed to the endeavor as workers, breeders, fertilizers, and, ultimately, sustenance. Autumn's bounty was shared with neighbors and friends, sometimes for sale, sometimes in trade, often in celebration.

Eventually, though, the increased demands of our burgeoning population led to the megafarms of agribusiness, the "wonders" of modern preservation and packaging, and the thousands of giant supermarkets and fast-food outlets built to deliver food to consumers.

So today, in many ways, we live in a different world—or do we?

In recent years, individually and collectively, in spirit if not in fact, we have moved our lives closer to the land. We have a seemingly insatiable appetite for growing our own food, in pots or plots, in cities and in suburbs. There is even a vegetable garden at the White House—the first since 1943. Sales of vegetable seeds are breaking records, and farmers' markets have replaced malls as weekend destinations. Grocery stores boast about their organically grown produce. And an increasing number of people are taking shares in community-supported agriculture (CSA).

Chefs, many of whom tend kitchen gardens, create menus around just-picked or -butchered ingredients. In the United States, "grazing"—dining on different courses at different restaurants—has given way to "farm feast" meals inspired by the harvest and served in the field. In Canada, "feasts of fields" tastings, where patrons meet providers, are proliferating.

It has been the good fortune and pleasure of this Almanac to witness and support such close-to-the-earth activities through the centuries. From the start, Mr. Thomas intended nothing less. In his 1794 edition, he wrote to his predominantly agrarian readership: "My greatest ambition is to make myself useful to the community."

We continue Mr. Thomas's mission and embrace that charge with an eye to gardeners as well as farmers. Just as the seasons, the Sun, and the Moon cycle through their phases, this humble Almanac links the past with the present and portends the future.

We also try to make ourselves useful to the community through our Web sites. Almanac.com, the complement to this

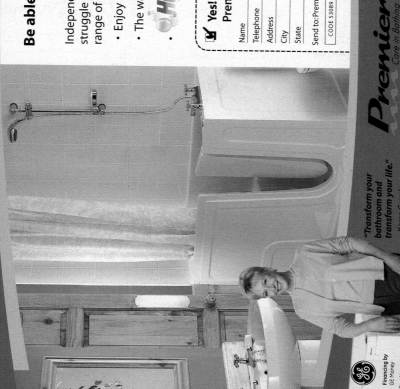

Ease of use, peace of mind.

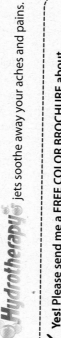
Premier Guarantee
WALK-IN
Premier
SHELL
BATH

Be able to bathe safely, without worry with a Premier Walk-In Bath.

Independence and security are only a phone call away. If you struggle taking your bath, talk to us at Premier about our extensive range of walk-in baths.

- Enjoy a relaxing bath again, without the fear of slipping or falling.
- The walk-in door feature allows easy access and exiting.
- *Hydrotherapy* jets soothe away your aches and pains.

☑ **Yes! Please send me a FREE COLOR BROCHURE about Premier Walk-In Baths.**

Name

Telephone

Address

City

State   Zip

Send to: Premier Bathrooms Inc., 2330 South Nova Rd., South Daytona, Florida 32119

CODE 53089

"Transform your bathroom and transform your life."
~ Karen Grassle

Premier
Care in Bathing

CALL NOW • TOLL FREE
1-800-578-2899

SOURCE CODE 53089

publication, has been redesigned and now offers many free new features. To accompany the release of Volume 3 of *The Old Farmer's Almanac for Kids,* we've also added lots of new pages to Almanac4kids.com, its companion site.

Finally, as we present to you our 218th edition, we note the achievements of two of our valued contributors:

Artist Beth Krommes, whose scratchboard illustrations grace our Astronomy pages, has been awarded the 2009 Caldecott Medal for creating "the most distinguished picture book of the year." She adapted the scratchboard technique to create her illustrations in *The House in the Night* (Houghton Mifflin, 2008), written by Susan Marie Swanson.

Also, this edition of the Almanac marks writer Tim Clark's 26th consecutive turn as composer of the weather doggerel that appears on the Right-Hand Calendar Pages. In these quasi-poems that run vertically down the center of the page (in italics), he pens a tune that we love to dance to in sunshine, showers, sleet, or snow.

We are grateful to Beth and Tim—indeed, to all of our contributors—for bringing to our pages the same commitment to quality that farmers and gardeners bring to their fields and plots every day.   J. S., June 2009

However, it is by our works and not our words that we would be judged. These, we hope, will sustain us in the humble though proud station we have so long held in the name of

Your obedient servant,

Robt. B. Thomas.

Time for a change? A new career? Supplemental income?

Work at Home!

BE A MEDICAL BILLING SPECIALIST

Take the first step to earning up to $40,000 a year and more!

Now you can train in the comfort of your own home to work at home or in a doctor's office, hospital or clinic making great money...up to $40,000 a year and more as your experience and skills increase! It's no secret, healthcare providers need Medical Billing Specialists.

Absolutely No Previous Medical Experience Required.
We make it easy to learn how to prepare medical claims for Medicare, Medicaid and private patients. And since every medical procedure must be properly billed, there's plenty of work available. You'll make great money working with doctors as a vital part of the medical team...and really helping people, too.

10 Years	
5 Years	**Increase In Demand!***
Now	

*The U.S. Department of Labor projects a significant increase in demand for specialists doing billing for doctors' offices!

We make it easy and affordable to start a new career! You can be ready to work in as little as four months. Get FREE FACTS on Medical Billing— the perfect work-at-home career!

TRAIN AT HOME

Learn at your own pace –when you want and where you want!

You Get Toll-Free Support!

You are never alone with USCI training. Just call our toll-free hotline if you ever need help from our expert instructors.

Nationally accredited training... be ready to work in as little as four months!

Our experts train you step by step to perform the job of a qualified Medical Billing Specialist. Everything is explained in easy-to-understand language. You learn exactly what to do and how to do it! Graduate in as little as four months and be ready to work! **Approved for V.A. education benefits, too!**

Get FREE Facts! Call 1-800-388-8765 Dept. FMAB2A99

- -

U.S. Career Institute, Dept. FMAB2A99
2001 Lowe Street, Fort Collins, CO 80525
www.uscareerinstitute.com

Or mail this coupon today!

Be a Medical Claims & Billing Specialist!

SENT FREE!

Yes! Rush me my free information package with complete details about training at home to be a Medical Billing Specialist. I understand there is absolutely no cost and no obligation.

Name: _____ Age: _____
Address: _____ Apt: _____
City: _____ State: _____ Zip: _____
E-mail: _____

CL298

Tastes & Trends

AROUND THE HOUSE

Less is more

Homes are shrinking . . .

▓ In mid-2008, the average size of a new home was 2,629 square feet. By the end of that year, it was 2,438 square feet.

We want . . .

LED **lighting** in bathrooms

radiant-heat **flooring**

solar panels

water reclamation systems

water-saving **toilets**

water-purification products (tap water is replacing bottled)

multipurpose rooms (for entertainment, fitness, gatherings, and more)

colored **walls** and white **equipment** in offices

We don't want . . .

double-sink **vanities**

game **rooms** and home **offices**

granite **countertops**

high **ceilings**

towel-warming **drawers**

whirlpool baths

fireplaces

People Are Talking About . . .

▓ artwork depicting homeowners' own DNA

▓ a combined washer and dryer appliance

▓ basement karaoke bars where performances are filmed and scored on Web sites

▓ disposable oven- and freezer-safe dishes made from palm leaves

▓ smiley faces on energy bills to inspire neighborhood competitions to reduce usage

▓ high-quality craftsmanship by Amish woodworkers and builders

▓ food-related colors: eggplant purples, artichoke greens, and pomegranate reds

▓ subdivisions featuring organic farms

2010

A chronicle of the fads, fashions, and farsighted ideas that define our life and times.

compiled by Anastasia Kusterbeck

By the Numbers

35.5 percent of Americans' garbage is recycled (double the 1990s rate).

$30,000 will buy a flame-retardant, typhoon-resistant, termite-repellent, premolded Styrofoam dome house.

670,000 U.S. households are without indoor plumbing.

Tops on kitchen wish lists

- walk-in pantry (86 percent)
- island work area (80 percent)
- built-in microwave (72 percent)

IN THE GARDEN

We are going back to basics

People are . . .

doing their own **yard work**

growing food instead of flowers, especially new varieties not generally available in supermarkets

turning backyards into habitats for birds and butterflies; green, serene retreats from technology; or low-energy environments, with solar lighting or shade plantings

EXTRA!

■ Birds and butterflies love the ornamental seed heads on these two tough natives:
- yellow *Echinacea* 'Mac 'n' Cheese'
- red *Echinacea* 'Tomato Soup'

■ Hummingbirds crave this drought-tolerant, July-to-September bloomer:
- pink *Agastache* 'Cotton Candy'

(continued)

Echinaceas 'Mac 'n' Cheese' and 'Tomato Soup'

People Are Talking About . . .

- using "push" lawn mowers
- matching outdoor flowers to indoor room colors
- architectural effects: containers, arbors, and plants as sculpture

EXTRA!

These veggies and fruit are tops as container crops:

'Honey Bear' acorn squash *(right),* for its compact squashes

'Baby Belle' pepper, for its red and yellow bite-size fruit

'Ruby' & 'Emerald' Duet, a tasty, colorful lettuce combination

'Neon Glow', a sweet, mild chard with hot pink and gold stalks and green leaves

Calamondin orange, for its small, juicy, sour oranges (use in preserves or cooking) and its variegated forms

What the pros are planting

New varieties of variegated agave: "They survive blazing heat and cold, need very little water, and look like living sculptures."

—Jimmy Turner, senior director of gardens, Dallas Arboretum

Small gardens in one or two bold colors: "The days of tapestry plantings of many different colors are over."

—Jimmy Turner

Plants that "fade with dignity" through the seasons:

- ***Heuchera x villosa 'Tiramasu'*** *(right),* with golden yellow foliage and red veins in summer and purplish fall foliage with a lime-green edge

- ***Heuchera* 'Georgia Peach',** peach-pink in spring and deep rose in autumn

- **'Fatal Attraction'** and **'Green Jewel' echinaceas,** with seed heads for floral arrangements or to feed goldfinches

—Sonia Uyterhoeven, gardener for public education, The New York Botanical Garden

By the Numbers

600 small-scale farms/large-scale vegetable gardens are within New York City.

38 percent of people grill year-round.

20 percent is the average increase in sales at seed companies recently—mostly due to a surge in vegetable growing.

(continued)

—squash photo, All-America Selections

Get the **Tempur-Pedic**® **advantage** at an unmatched **value**...

20 YEAR LIMITED WARRANTY

The
AdvantageBed
by Tempur-Pedic™

The AdvantageBed makes it possible to enjoy all the benefits of **better sleep** and **better health** at an unmatched value! Unlike traditional spring mattresses that push against you causing painful pressure points, Tempur-Pedic beds are made of our proprietary TEMPUR® material.

TEMPUR material absorbs pressure, cradling your body with customized support and providing deep, rejuvenating sleep giving you **renewed daytime energy**.

Tempur-Pedic delivers all the life-improving benefits of body conforming support. Invest in more than simply a new mattress, make an investment in your health with guaranteed better sleep night after night! Rest assured...**Every Tempur-Pedic bed is backed by our 20 year Limited Warranty!**

You spend 1/3 of your life sleeping, you deserve the highest level of comfort available...**you deserve a Tempur-Pedic!**

Which would you rather sleep on?

Traditional Steel Spring Mattress

Pressure-Absorbing TEMPUR® Material

Value a Tempur-Pedic...

"*Because of the stress that people feel you're not getting enough sleep. If you're not **resting and feeling good** you're going to have a harder time during your day. The person that values sleep, they'll **value a Tempur-Pedic**.*"

Luci & Barry *Tempur-Pedic owners since January 2005*

Call today for your FREE Information Kit with FREE DVD / FREE Sample / FREE Tryout Certificate

888-702-8557

or visit us online at www.TempurPedic.com to find a retail location near you!

⚕ **TEMPUR**-PEDIC

© 2009 Tempur-Pedic Management, Inc.

SIGNS OF THE TIMES

The going is getting greener

Bike-pedaled rickshaws — **"pedicabs"** — are rolling out in U.S. cities.

Pedal- and electric motor–powered **"ecocabs"** use their small motor only when going up hills.

Groups of suburban kids are pounding the pavement as **"walking school buses"** under adult supervision.

Electric scooters go up to 62 mph (up from 30 mph) and on highways.

Teardrop-shape cars with only a driver's seat expand in the rear for passengers and thus use extra energy only when needed.

People Are Talking About . . .

- comparing heredity at DNA parties

- jousting competitions, with fully armored, horse-mounted combatants

- nighttime cycling on bikes with laser lights that project red "lane" lines onto the road

- using discarded Christmas trees to create underwater habitats in man-made lakes

We are changing our ways:

- "Green" bibles have nature-related verses printed in green ink.

- Nightclubs are turning customers' dance-floor stomping into electricity.

- Kindergarten classes are being held in the woods, where kids are more attentive and imaginative.

- Advertisements are appearing on GPS systems in automobiles.

By the Numbers

4.7 million people belong to Meetup.com, a worldwide network of local groups.

28,716,407 passengers rode on Amtrak trains in 2008—the most since the National Railroad Passenger Corporation started in 1971.

69 percent of Canadians who live in small towns and rural areas (more than twice the percentage of urban dwellers) know some or all of their neighbors.

32,000 horses roam free in western states.

9 percent of U.S. adults are compulsive buyers.

23 percent of Americans say that the place where they live isn't their "true home."

40 pounds of junk mail are sent to each American annually (new companies will end its delivery—for a fee).

(continued)

THE DUKE

A Hand-painted, Fully Sculpted Holster and Revolver Replica Inspired by the One John Wayne Carried in his Classic Westerns

Take hold of frontier justice, John Wayne style, with a sculpted collectible inspired by the holstered revolver carried by Duke in his unforgettable movie roles. Hanging by leather straps from a sculpted sheriff's badge, this nearly 12-inch long sculpture features a faux ivory gun handle and vivid images of Duke.

An exceptional value; satisfaction guaranteed "The Duke" is hand-cast and hand-painted, and comes with a 365-day guarantee. Strong demand is expected, so act now to acquire yours in three easy installments of $16.65 each, for a total of $49.95*. Send no money now. Just return the Reservation Application today, and set your sights on this classic tribute to John Wayne! Don't miss out!

Reserve Today!
www.bradfordexchange.com/dukepistol

Shown smaller than actual height of 12 inches.

©2009 BGE 01-07202-001-DI

RESERVATION APPLICATION

THE BRADFORD EXCHANGE
—HOME DECOR—

9345 Milwaukee Avenue · Niles, IL 60714-1393

YES. Please reserve "The Duke" Sculpted Replica Holster for me as described in this announcement.
Limit: one per order. Please Respond Promptly

Signature _____

Mrs. Mr. Ms, _____
Name (Please Print Clearly)

Address _____

City _____

State _____ Zip _____

01-07202-001-E63591

*Plus $8.99 shipping and service. Limited-edition presentation restricted to 295 crafting days. Please allow 4-8 weeks after initial payment for shipment. Sales subject to product availability and order acceptance. For decorative use only; not a firearm.

ON THE FASHION FRONT

Low cost is high style

There's no pride in overpaying

THE BEST BUYS IN . . .	ARE AT . . .
authentic vintage garments	secondhand shops
attire and accessories from attics and closets	online stores
status-brand men's watches	auctions and thrift stores

Ladies are looking for . . .

eco-conscious **dresses** made from recycled materials

men's **V-neck t-shirts**, vests, motorcycle jackets, baggy jeans, and fedoras

surprisingly comfortable **4-inch stiletto heels**

sandals with designs on foot beds and linings or soles in contrasting fabrics

blousons and windbreaker shapes for gym or office

loose trousers

hooded sweaters for the workplace and tunic-length knits and wovens

Men are dressing in . . .

pajama-inspired jackets with colored piping, spread-open shirt collars, and loose drawstring pants

plaid shirts, especially the block pattern "buffalo" plaid in red/black

slim-fitting gray, traditional dark, and faded blue **jeans**

moccasins and boat shoes in navy blue, red, and green

replicas of vintage outdoor clothing: construction boots, 1940s-era denims, and chambray shirts

EXTRA!

- **Single-purpose or one-season items are out:** Summer fabrics and colors are suitable for winter wear.

- **Bags with bling are in:** Handbags have appliquéd stones, grommets, tassels, logo charms, and lots of zippers.

(continued)

GET MORE AFFECTION WITH ATHENA PHEROMONES

Dr. Winnifred Cutler co-discovered human pheromones in 1986 (TIME 12/1/86; NEWSWEEK 1/12/87)

Add to your fragrance. These odorless additives contain synthesized human pheromones. Vials of 1/6 oz., added to 2 - 4 oz. of fragrance, **should be a 4 to 6 mos. supply,** or use straight. Athena Pheromones increase your attractivness.

♥ **Chloe (WI)** "I need to order 2 more vials of Athena Pheromone 10:13. **Everybody treats me differently.** It's wonderful. Before, it was like I didn't exist; now everyone is so nice to me. **They notice me, pay attention, act courteous. I am ecstatic with it."**

♥ **Larry (NY)** "This stuff is like catnip. **Too many women come after me.** I am looking for a woman my own age, but **the 10X attracts them all."**

♥ **Gene (TX)** "Both my wife and I use your products and **feel we are starting a new relationship** with each other."

ATHENA PHEROM♥NES: The Gold Standard since 1993™

- **Casual Fridays are over:** For men, three-piece suits in matching fabrics are standard office attire.

The hot hues

- **Blue:** "It's all about clean skies and water."

  –James Martin, president, Color Marketing Group

- **Bright yellow:** In small doses, it "has power."

  –James Martin

- **Varying values of complementary colors** (e.g., soft apricot with strong yellow-green and a touch of wine)

  –Lee Eiseman, executive director, Pantone Color Institute

People Are Talking About . . .

- "cloning" a favorite pair of jeans
- bulletproof clothing, with stab-proof lining
- "no wash" clothing, with stain-resistant lamination on the front
- shirts with low armholes so that smells don't accumulate

PET-ICULARS

We love to pamper our pets

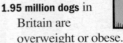

1.95 million dogs in Britain are overweight or obese.

69 percent of dog owners would cut back on holiday spending for friends or family to afford gifts for their pet.

People Are Talking About . . .

- putting identifying microchips in pets, due to increasing thefts of purebreds
- fitness contests for plump pets

Finally: Why dogs are man's best friend

- **Dogs have an innate sense of what's fair.** When researchers at the University of Vienna's "Clever Dog Lab" rewarded only one of two dogs playing, the unrewarded dog quit the game.

- **Canines display empathy.** Dogs refused to look at a person if they noticed that person ignoring another dog.

(continued)

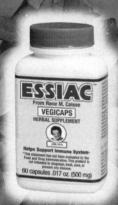

ON THE FARM

Freshness matters

Farmers are working harder . . .

creating Web sites with video tours, contact info, and blogs

visiting elementary schools to teach kids where food comes from

going to speed dating–like events where they quickly chat with local chefs and food buyers about supplying locally grown produce

offering produce with longer growing/keeping seasons (greens, root crops, herbs, gourds, apples) in winter

Thank God, I'm a country boy (or girl)

92 percent of young farmers and ranchers worry about . . .

- land and facility availability
- profitability
- urbanization and loss of farmland

By the Numbers

98 percent of U.S. farms are owned by individuals, family partnerships, or family corporations.

52 percent of nonfarming Canadians think positively of Canadian agriculture.

42 percent of U.S. farmers believe that the public thinks positively about them.

436 percent is the increase in commercial chicken meat production since 1970.

1 poultry breed is used in industrial egg production today.

People Are Talking About . . .

- microwave heaters that prevent frost damage by heating crops rather than the air around them

- "edible optical sensors" made of silks spun by spiders and silkworms and put into produce bags to detect harmful bacteria

- package bar codes that when scanned display the faces of the ranchers/ farmers who produced the food

(continued)

A PICTURE OF HEALTH

Life is good and getting better

Sound sleep is healthier. People who get less than 7 hours a night are three times more likely to get sick, while people who toss and turn are five times more likely.

Quitting smoking is contagious. People in a social network are 20 percent more likely to quit if someone else does, even if they don't know that person.

Doctors will be checking **"brain fitness"** (memory and reasoning), along with blood pressure and weight.

Church basements are hosting **"gospel aerobics"** classes.

Fit or fat?

- The fittest city: **Salt Lake City, Utah**
- The fattest city: **Miami, Florida**

–*Men's Fitness* magazine

By the Numbers

4.8 months is the increase in average American life expectancy over the past 10 years, thanks to cleaner air.

$639 million was the value of vitamin/supplement retail sales in 2008 (up 10 percent from 2007).

(continued)

FOR THE TOUGHEST JOBS ON PLANET EARTH.®

Incredibly strong and ideal for indoor and outdoor applications. Bonds wood, stone, metal, ceramic, foam, glass and much more!

CASH & COLLECTIBLES

Haggling has reached retail

Hot items

"Niche-specific" collectibles: concert posters, animation art, marbles. "Record prices were set this past year in these categories."

–Gary Sohmers of AllCollectors.com

Furniture and fixtures from the mid–20th century on, at all price levels

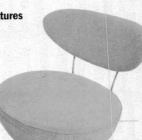

Past their peak

- refinished **oak furniture**, middle-market Victorian, **Depression-era glass**
- **historical newspapers** (John F. Kennedy's assassination, the first Moon landing)
- **memorabilia** of deceased important people (but only items from during their lifetime)

(continued)

The simplest, most accurate watch on the planet!

You never have to set this watch...
in fact you never even have to look at it.

This new Talking Atomic Watch is the ultimate in simplicity, accuracy, and practicality. It's accurate to within a billionth of a second... and it talks!

**Whether you travel or not...
this watch is a necessity.**

This Talking Atomic Watch from *first*STREET maintains its phenomenal accuracy because it is designed to receive a signal from the US Atomic Clock in Fort Collins, Colorado. This clock is the standard for time measurement worldwide... it can go 20 million years without gaining or losing a second! It never needs to be set, because it automatically adjusts itself for daylight savings time and leap years.

"Ten-ten AM, Thursday, August 27th, 2009"

FREE Shipping

Easy to read, even easier to hear.

The most accurate watch in the world is of no use if you can't read it. This timepiece is designed to tell you the correct time... anytime. It features a clear, uncluttered analog display that you won't need reading glasses to see. Best of all, you can press a button and it will tell you the time in a clear, easy-to-understand voice. So whether you're driving to an appointment or dining in a candle-lit restaurant ... you are sure to know the exact time. Press the button again and it will even tell you the day and date if you want. There's even an automatic hourly chime.

Try it for yourself... it's risk-free.

The US Atomic Clock cost billions to build and maintain, but you can have the next best thing for less than one hundred dollars. Thanks to a special arrangement with the manufacturer, we can offer you this watch at a special price with our exclusive home trial. Call now, and we'll give you a $10 INSTANT DISCOUNT and FREE SHIPPING. If you are not completely amazed by the accuracy and quality of this product, simply return it within 90 days for a full "No Questions Asked" refund.

Talking Atomic Watch ~~$99.95~~ **$89.95***
*After $10 Instant Rebate Call now for free shipping.

1-877-665-6358
Please mention code 38027 when ordering.
www.atomictimedirect.com

Senior Approved Services

*first*STREET®
for Boomers and Beyond®
1998 Ruffin Mill Road • Colonial Heights, VA 23834

50062

Top-dollar items

- pink Beach Bomb **Hot Wheels** 1969 VW bus with a surfboard ($70,000)

- original *Peanuts* Sunday comics strip art, signed by Charles Schulz ($67,400)

- Marx **Wagon Train** Playset with plastic cowboys and Indians ($15,255)

- 1954 **Superman** lunchbox ($11,500)

By the Numbers

10.6 million Internet coupons were redeemed in 2008.

400 "giving circles," where people pool funds and vote on a recipient charity, exist in the United States.

1 percent is the amount that charitable giving declines in recession years.

People Are Talking About . . .

- young, single people buying houses together

- towns printing their own "currency" to be spent locally

- e-coupons in cell phones or frequent-shopper cards

- teaching kids how to save, with pretend checkbooks and ATMs

INCREDIBLE EDIBLES

Everybody's home cooking

We're loving . . .

- homemade bread
- broth made from scratch
- cooking grass-fed meats

We're leaving . . .

- expensive frozen dinners
- takeout coffee and meals
- bottled water

By the Numbers

399 million pounds of specialty cheese are produced by Wisconsin factories—triple the output of a decade ago.

367,000 U.S. kids are vegetarians.

$104,700 was paid for a 282-pound Japanese bluefin tuna at a Tokyo fish auction.

.04 percent of milk is delivered to homes.

Favorite foods

frosting "shots" (blobs of frosting in small cups) at bakeries

savory "sweets": blue cheese cupcakes and bacon ice cream

sorghum syrup, a Southern staple, on French toast and in vinaigrettes and sauces

(continued)

"Americanized" sushi (cream cheese and salmon rolls)

heirloom-breed pork and ham from acorn-fed pigs in southwestern Spain

the taste of umami in Parmesan cheese, dried mushrooms, tomatoes, and seaweed

People Are Talking About . . .

- "flexitarians"—occasional vegetarians
- restaurant menus that list the farms that supply the meats
- sweet and salty aromatic crystals that trick us into eating less
- "head to hoof" dining (eating all animal parts—pig tails, bone marrow, duck hearts)
- classes in butchering
- the "small [10-inch-diameter] plate movement" toward small portions

SCIENCE AND TECH

From the lab to life

- Electronic paper and e-book pages are getting whiter, more colorful, and faster.
- Sensors in wind turbine blades will allow the blades to adjust to changes in the wind for increased efficiency.
- Cars will monitor weather conditions, warn drivers of road hazards (black ice, fog), and suggest alternate routes.

By the Numbers

71 percent of Americans are trying to reduce their use of energy and goods whose production creates greenhouse gases.

43 percent of people say that weather in their county has been more unstable during the past 3 years than they can remember at any other time.

People Are Talking About . . .

- edu-vacations with research scientists
- jets powered by oil from the jatropha tree, a plant native to the Caribbean
- materials that bend light to make an object appear where it is not
- robotic helicopters that map out hot spots in wildfires
- trash dryer technology: Astronauts remove water from garbage and purify it to drink
- robots doing civic duty, taking photos of speeding cars and raising/lowering flags

☐☐

Anastasia Kusterbeck, a frequent contributor to *The Old Farmer's Almanac*, writes about popular culture from New York State.

Mrs. Nelson's
CANDY HOUSE
"Your house for all occasions"

Candies! For over 51 years we have
used only the finest ingredients in
our candies—cream, butter, honey,
and special blends of chocolates.
Call for a FREE brochure. Long famous
for quality candies mailed all over the
world. Treat yourself or someone
special today.

Come visit us today!

**292 Chelmsford Street
Chelmsford, MA 01824
For Free Brochure Call:**

978-256-4061

Maine Goodies

Explore our website and select from hundreds of
delicious gourmet foods and unique Maine-made
gifts. Think of us for a taste of home or that
something special from your recent vacation.
Birthdays, weddings and the holidays, we have
something for everyone on your gift list.

Order on-line from our Web site:
MaineGoodies.com
5 Winslow Road • Albion, ME 04910
1-866-385-6238

Smart Mower
for Small Lawns!

The **Neuton® Battery-Powered Mower** uses no gas or oil,
so it's quiet, clean, and starts instantly — every time!
It is lightweight, so it's easy for anyone to use.
So economical it costs about 10¢ to mow your
lawn and never needs a tune-up. It's the
only lawn mower that will also TRIM
around trees and EDGE along your
walk or driveway.

FREE DVD!
see it in action!

America's #1-selling
battery-powered
mower!

neuton®

66001X © 2009

FREE Neuton DVD & Catalog
1-888-212-0740
www.neutonmowers.com

CHIPS OFF THE OLD BLOCKS

by Kelly Koepke

Chain saws are loud, dangerous, and a little scary, yet in the right hands, they are ideal tools for creating works of art. Smaller, lighter saws and the appeal of quickly turning a block or log of wood into a bear, eagle, or just about anything have made chain saw carving increasingly popular among both men and women.

The origins of the craft are as old and grand as the timber that inspires it. "Chain saw art was evolutionary," says Liz Boni, of Ridgway, Pennsylvania, whose husband and daughter practice the art. "If there was a logging camp, then there was someone doing carving."

Although the identities of these early enthusiasts as well as their efforts have been lost, modern-day artists—whether they create cute but crudely cut tourist bears in a "quick-carve" performance or sculpt intricate, museum-quality pieces in a studio—are carving out names for themselves.

Ray Murphy, the "Wild Mountain Man," of Hancock,

Ray Murphy, the "Wild Mountain Man," of Hancock, Maine, stands behind his lobster and ice cream sculpture at Hampton Beach, New Hampshire.

Maine, is generally acknowledged as an originator of the contemporary craft. He started sawing in the 1950s (Murphy doesn't "carve"), using his father's chain saw to cut designs and messages on logs and fence posts.

Ray inspects one of his sawed alphabet pencils.

Since then, he has sawed over 50,000 pieces, including dime-size ladybugs, 7-foot-tall angels, numbers on toothpicks, and his trademark alphabet pencils. During the summer, he puts on a 90-minute show in which he demonstrates techniques he has invented as well as other feats.

Carver Don Colp, of Oakridge, Oregon, is credited with the idea of a narrow-tipped guide bar, introduced in the 1970s. Shorter carving bars, some with tips as small as a dime, can accommodate smaller carving chains and enable ever more intricate cuts.

Canada's best-known—and most modest—chain saw carver is probably Pete Ryan from Hope, British Columbia. "To me, it's just a tool for removing wood," he says of the chain saw. His large-scale (up to 13 feet), lifelike sculptures of wildlife and mining pioneers take hundreds of hours to create. Visitors to Hope can see 27 of Ryan's carvings on a self-guided walking tour in and around town.

Canada's Pete Ryan with one of his large-scale chain saw sculptures

CONTINUED

Women are not new to the craft, but more are taking it up all the time. Octogenarian Lois Hollingsworth of Miranda, California, is known for her abstract carving. Judy McVay of Deming, Washington, once dubbed "queen of the chain saw–carved sign," has been wielding a chain saw for more than 40 years. Susan Miller from Mist, Oregon, has carved out a reputation for carousel and rocking horses. Zoe Boni (Liz's daughter) began carving when she was 22; now, at 30, she is a formidable contender in competitive events.

From **TIMBER** to **ART**

As interest in the art has increased, so have the number and scales of shows or competitions where carvers work in front of live audiences. The artists' task is to carve their vision of an assigned theme. They must complete the work within a limited time, usually from 45 minutes to 20 hours. The art and the artist are judged according to theme, difficulty of design, and craftsmanship. Some competitive events have thousands of dollars in prizes at stake, and almost all contests have a people's choice award that results from spectators voting for their favorite.

The medium —the wood—is chosen and provided by the contest organizers. Soft woods such as

Zoe Boni, of Ridgway, Pennsylvania, poses with her carving "Dream Launcher" at the 2008 ECHO Chain Saw Carving Series Championship in Albuquerque, New Mexico.

Bob King, of Edgewood, Washington (top), begins carving "Innocent Dreams" (left), the winner of the 2008 ECHO Chain Saw Carving Series Championship.

–photos this page, ECHO, Inc.

34

Imagine examining artifacts in the Smithsonian Institution and finding a never-before-seen sketch for the largest and highest denomination American coin ever proposed? That's just what happened as one coin expert recently explored the

America's Lost Masterpiece

Discovered...Historic Coin Design!

THE $100 UNION™

Original sketches found at the Smithsonian

collection at this celebrated public institution. But as this numismatist discovered, it has more to share than he could ever imagine.

To his own surprise, he had found the original design concept for a hundred dollar denomination created by George T. Morgan, arguably the greatest American coin designer. These sketches, hidden within an original sketchbook for nearly a century, represent perhaps the grandest American coin ever proposed—the $100 Union.

George T. Morgan will always be remembered for his most famous coin—the Morgan silver dollar. Until recently, the world knew nothing of Morgan's larger sized and higher denomination $100 Union concept design.

The secret's out! For a limited time, you can secure the world's first and only $100 Union Proof struck in pure .999 Silver at our special price of only $99 (plus S&H). CALL TODAY!

Call now to secure your reservation for this exceptional collector's treasure!

$100 Union™ Silver Proof
Only $99

This is not a reproduction...this is the first time ever Morgan's $100 Union™ design has been struck as a silver proof.

 Smithsonian Institution®

A portion of the sales proceeds from your purchase of this licensed product supports the chartered educational purposes of the National Numismatic Collection, housed in the Smithsonian's National Museum of American History.

1-800-585-9240 ext. 4397

New York Mint, 5577 West 78th Street, Edina, MN

©2009 New York Mint, Ltd. New York Mint is a private company and is not affiliated with the United States Mint. This Silver Proof is not legal tender and the U.S. Mint has not endorsed it nor the New York Mint.

Carving
CAVEATS

- **Use the proper saw.** Carvers' chain saws are designed for the craft. Regular chain saws are made to cut with the long sides of the guide bar (the blade around which the toothy chain travels), not with the tip. Forcing the tip of a regular chain saw into wood causes "kick-back": The machine thrusts wildly back and up toward the operator—and possible injury. Chain saws with carving bars have anti–kick-back and chain-braking safety features.

- **Be certain that the wood contains no metal.**

- **Make sure that your saw and chain are in tip-top condition and that your chain tension is correct.**

- **Avoid handling power tools if you are fatigued or under the influence of drugs, alcohol, or other inhibiting substances.**

pine are the most common. Western U.S. and Canadian artists prefer cedar and redwood; carving them is said to be like cutting through cake. Many artists in the southern states use cypress and spruce pine. In England, woods such as yew and oak are the materials of choice. The harder the wood (such as black cherry and hard maple), the greater the strain on the saws and the arms, shoulders, and backs of the carvers.

The wood, as well as the size and shape of a log, can make or break a design. In competition, carvers choose their wood in a lottery, but they will often swap with other carvers to ensure that they get a piece that will enable them to fully realize their idea. If the log they draw will not work for their concept, they'd better have a plan B.

Purists in the craft use only the chain saw—the tip, the sharp (top) side of the chain, and the side of the chain. Depending on the size of the bar and chain and the part of the bar used, an artist can achieve surfaces that are sander-smooth. "With practice, you can remove something as small as the size of a piece of sawdust," says Zoe Boni.

Many artists also use sanders, power drills, and rotary tools such as Dremels. Some burn detail or color into the wood with handheld torches or use paint to enliven their sculptures. Almost all craftspeople varnish or apply protective coatings to enhance the shine and ensure the weather fastness of their finished pieces.

"Make a Wish," carved by Terry Ahola of Grants Pass, Oregon, claimed second prize at the 2008 ECHO Chain Saw Carving Series Championship.

—ECHO, Inc.

CONTINUED

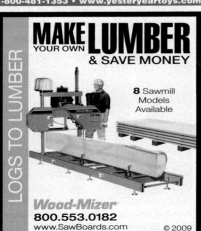

The **BUZZ**

A chain saw is an inherently dangerous power tool. According to the Centers for Disease Control and Prevention, approximately 32,000 people were injured from using chain saws in 2004, with the average chain saw injury requiring 110 stitches. To reduce your chances of winding up in the emergency room, use this equipment:

- Hard hat and safety goggles, or safety helmet with face shield

- Steel-toed boots that cover the ankle

- Hearing protection

- Cut-resistant chaps and pants made with chain saw–protective fibers (UL rated)

- Gloves with chain saw–protective padding on the back

□□

Kelly Koepke is a freelance writer who explores the quirky side of life from her home in Albuquerque, New Mexico.

If you can hold a saw, you can be a chain saw artist. Learn more about classes in the art at **Almanac.com/ChainSaw**.

A student at the Appalachian Arts Studio displays the work he completed in 3 days.

Summon Emergency Help Immediately

"This pendant saved my life."

Exclusive *Designed For Seniors™* MedicalAlarm is a life-changing, lifesaving solution. Help when you need it *most*:
Medical Emergency – Accident – Fire – Burglary

NEW

FREE Shipping

3 FREE adapters for pendant, belt, or wrist

Simple
- No contract
- Large buttons
- Easy 5 minute setup

Reliable
- 48 hour battery backup
- 24/7 monitoring
- Lifetime warranty
- Waterproof pendants

Affordable
- Free equipment
- Free activation
- Lowest monthly rate
- Ask about adding a second user – FREE

Dear Friends,

At Designed For Seniors™ MedicalAlarm, we have the simple notion that it's possible to provide great care, great service, and peace-of-mind --- affordably --- for Seniors all across America. Unlike other companies we've eliminated all the up front costs related to our service… no equipment to buy/rent, no activation fee, and no contract. Our monthly fee is the lowest available – – plus ask about adding a second user in the same household.

How it Works. In an emergency, push your button, which sends a wireless signal to your medical unit allowing it to contact us toll free. Within seconds you will hear the reassuring voice of a member of our highly trained monitoring staff through the "whole house" two-way intercom unit attached to your home phone. We check on your status and dispatch your local Emergency Medical Services and/or the needed assistance of a nearby friend, neighbor, or family member. And, because no one likes to be alone in an emergency, we maintain voice contact with you until someone arrives!

"Peace-of-mind" that is always on! We believe our policies and concerns for our clients set us apart from other companies. We provide you with the highest rated equipment on the market today, combined with the reliability and precision of our state-of-the-art monitoring center. You will even have a personal Life Safety Representative that you can call with any questions or concerns. We provide a service that is unparalleled and we NEVER compromise when it comes to your safety! Our entire staff from the sales team to technical assistance will treat YOU as if you were their own loved one… and that's a promise!

"Hello, this is the monitoring center. Is everything okay?"

*first*STREET
for boomers and beyond

1998 Ruffin Mill Road
Colonial Heights, VA 23834

Call now for more information on how the Designed For Seniors™ MedicalAlarm can keep you safe, and save you money!

1-877-459-4550

Please mention promotional code 38028 for FREE Shipping.

www.DFSmedicalalarm.com

New advanced portable heater can cut your heating bill up to 50%

Heats a large room in minutes with even heat wall to wall and floor to ceiling

Does not get hot, cannot start a fire and will not reduce humidity or oxygen

By John Whitehead, Media Services

A new advanced quartz infrared portable heater, the EdenPURE®, can cut your heating bills by up to 50%.

You have probably heard about the remarkable EdenPURE® as heard on radio and television features across the nation.

The EdenPURE® can pay for itself in a matter of weeks and then start putting a great deal of extra money in your pocket after that.

And that's just the start of the benefits for the new EdenPURE® Quartz Infrared Portable Heater.

A major cause of residential fires in the United States is portable heaters. But the EdenPURE® cannot cause a fire. That is because the quartz infrared heating element never gets to a temperature that can ignite anything.

The outside of the EdenPURE® only gets warm to the touch so that it will not burn children or pets. Pets can sleep on it when it is operating without harm.

The EdenPURE® will also make you healthier. That is because, unlike other heating sources, it will not reduce humidity or oxygen in the room. Typical heating sources reduce humidity which dries out your sinuses, makes you more susceptible to disease and makes your skin dry. With other heating sources, you'll notice that you get sleepy when the heat comes on because they are burning up oxygen.

The advanced space-age EdenPURE® Quartz Infrared Portable Heater also heats the room evenly, wall-to-wall and floor-to-ceiling. Other heating sources heat rooms unevenly with most of the heat concentrated high in the room and to the center of the room. And, as you know, portable heaters only heat an area a few feet around the heater. With the EdenPURE®, the temperature will not vary in any part of the room.

Unlike other heating sources, the EdenPURE® cannot put poisonous carbon monoxide into a room or any type of fumes or any type of harmful radiation.

For more details on the amazing EdenPURE® Quartz Infrared Portable Heater, here is my interview with Julius Toth, Director of Product Development for BioTech Research®.

Q. What is the origin of this amazing heating element in the EdenPURE®?

A. This advanced heating element was discovered accidentally by a man named John Jones. He had a large old farmhouse that was impossible to heat. Jones had a coal furnace in his basement. Jones placed a sheet of cured copper near the furnace to store it. Cured copper is a type of copper that goes through an extensive heating process to give it special properties.

After the fire went out in the coal furnace, Jones noticed that the sheet of copper was heating his entire basement evenly, even though the furnace was no longer putting out heat. He also was amazed as to how long the heat stayed in the copper and continued to warm the room.

Jones was so taken back by this that he started to experiment. He formed a company to develop a heating source out of this cured copper. But Jones had a number of children and he did not want a heating source that would cause a fire or create other hazardous situations like creating carbon monoxide or radiation. He also did not want his children to get burned.

To make a long story short, through a great deal of research and development, Jones developed a heating source that utilized commercial infrared quartz tubes.

Q. What advantages does infrared quartz tube heating source have over other heating source products?

A. John Jones designed his heating source around the three most important consumer benefits: economy, comfort, and safety. The final development of this infrared quartz heat source cannot be matched by any other heating system in the world.

In the EdenPURE® system, electricity is used to generate infrared light which, in turn, creates a very safe heat. Infrared is the safest form of heat because it does not create carbon monoxide or harmful radiation. And, most importantly, infrared heat does not reach a burning temperature.

After a great deal of research and development, very efficient infrared heat chambers were developed that utilize three unique patented solid copper heat exchangers in one EdenPURE® heater. Over 5 years of research, development and real life field testing stand behind this heat source. It has now worked in residential and commercial applications worldwide for over 25 years.

Q. Why is it that this quartz infrared heating source uses less ener-

Never be cold again

Cannot start a fire; a child or animal can touch or sit on it without harm

gy to create heat than other sources?

A. Actually, there is more than one reason. One of the primary reasons is that heat at combustion level, which is what all other heat sources use, causes the heat to instantly rise to the ceiling. Therefore, the heat is not evenly distributed, causing a very inefficient and uncomfortable heat source.

The EdenPURE® Quartz Infrared Portable Heater does not use burning heat. Once the heat exchanger absorbs the infrared heat, it exhales the heat into the living area which is carried by the existing humidity in the air. This causes the heat to travel rapidly and evenly throughout a room.

In actual studies, photos using infrared lighting demonstrated that the heat was almost perfectly even from floor-to-ceiling and wall-to-wall. The EdenPURE® Quartz Infrared efficiency is based on the distribution of energized air, not on just fan movement. This heat is coined as "soft heat" due to how comfortable it is.

Q. What are the other disadvantages of combustion heat sources?

A. Heat sources that are above the burning level have many unhealthy side effects. One of these is that it creates dry, irritating indoor air. It also burns a great deal of oxygen in the air. If you remember, when you sit in front of a fireplace or a portable heater or close to a heat source, you will remember yawning. This is because you are not getting enough oxygen.

This dry irritating heat and lack of oxygen dries out sinuses and mucus in the throat, and makes people susceptible to disease. The lack of oxygen causes fatigue.

There's more of everything at Almanac.com.

Also, many combustible heat sources produce carbon monoxide, static cling, and some produce radiation.

Q. So you're saying that children or pets can come up to this unit and touch it and not be harmed?

A. That is absolutely correct. As a matter of fact, pets are actually drawn to this heat because it is a natural source of heat, just like the sun heats the earth. Animals are much more instinctive than humans. This heat not only heats the air, but it also heats the objects in the room. It is a perfectly balanced heat.

Q. How can a person cut their heating bill by up to 50% with the EdenPURE®?

A. First, the EdenPURE® uses less energy to create heat than other sources, but that is just part of why it will cut a person's heating bill. The EdenPURE® will heat a room in minutes. Therefore, you can turn the heat down in your house to as low as 50 degrees, but the room you are occupying, which has the EdenPURE®, will be warm and comfortable. The EdenPURE® is portable. When you move to another room, it will quickly heat that room also. This can drastically cut heating bills, in some instances, by up to 50%.

Q. I also understand that the EdenPURE® produces clean fresh air without furnace filters. How can it do that?

A. A furnace generates a lot of dust due to the combustion. By lowering the furnace temperature, you are using your furnace less and therefore reducing the requirement for the furnace filters. Also, when there's no combustion, there are no harmful fumes.

Q. So, the EdenPURE® is totally safe to use?

A. It absolutely is. Tests prove the unit does not transmit any energy into the atmosphere that will burn or harm anyone regardless of distance between the person and the EdenPURE®.

The EdenPURE® will pay for itself in weeks. It will put a great deal of extra money in a users pocket. Because of today's spiraling gas, oil, propane, and other energy costs, the EdenPURE® will provide even greater savings as the time goes by.

The EdenPURE® comes in 2 models. GEN3 Model 500 heats a room up to 300 square feet and GEN3 Model 1000 heats a room up to 1,000 square feet.

End of interview.

Readers who wish can obtain the EdenPURE® Quartz Infrared Portable Heater at a $75 discount if they order in the next 10 days. Please see the Special Readers Discount Coupon on this page. For those readers ordering after 10 days from the date of this publication, we reserve the right to either accept or reject order requests at the discounted price.

How it works:

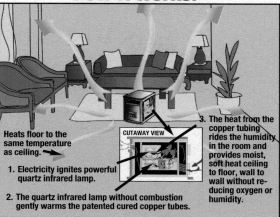

Heats floor to the same temperature as ceiling. ➜

CUTAWAY VIEW

1. **Electricity ignites powerful quartz infrared lamp.**

2. **The quartz infrared lamp without combustion gently warms the patented cured copper tubes.**

3. **The heat from the copper tubing rides the humidity in the room and provides moist, soft heat ceiling to floor, wall to wall without reducing oxygen or humidity.**

SPECIAL READER'S DISCOUNT COUPON

The price of the EdenPURE® GEN3 Model 500 is $372 plus $17 shipping for a total of $389 delivered. The GEN3 Model 1000 is $472 plus $27 shipping and handling for a total of $499 delivered. People reading this publication get a $75 discount with this coupon and pay only $297 delivered for the GEN3 Model 500 and $397 delivered for the GEN3 Model 1000 if you order within 10 days. The EdenPURE® comes in the decorator color of black with burled wood accent which goes with any decor. There is a strict limit of 3 units at the discount price - no exceptions please.

Check below which model and number you want:
- ☐ GEN3 Model 500, number _____
- ☐ GEN3 Model 1000, number _____

- To order by phone, call TOLL FREE **1-800-588-5608 Ext. EHS1078**. Place your order by using your credit card. Operators are on duty Monday - Friday 6am - 3am, Saturday 7am - 12 Midnight and Sunday 7am - 11pm, EST.
- To order online, log on to www.edenpure.com
- To order by mail, by check or credit card, fill out and mail in this coupon.

This product carries a 60-day satisfaction guarantee. If you are not totally satisfied, your purchase price will be refunded. No questions asked. There is also a three year warranty.

NAME _____

ADDRESS _____

CITY _____ STATE _____ ZIP CODE _____

Check below to get discount:

☐ I am ordering within 10 days of the date of this publication, therefore I get a $75 discount and my price is only $297 for GEN3 Model 500 and $397 for GEN3 Model 1000 delivered.

☐ I am ordering past 10 days of the date of this publication, therefore I pay shipping and handling and full price totaling $389 for GEN3 Model 500 and $499 for GEN3 Model 1000.

Enclosed is $_____ in: ☐ Cash ☐ Check ☐ Money Order
(Make check payable to BioTech Research) or charge my:

☐ VISA ☐ MasterCard ☐ Am. Exp./Optima ☐ Discover/Novus

Account No. _____ Exp. Date ___/___

Signature _____

MAIL TO: BioTech Research Dept. EHS1078
7800 Whipple Ave. N.W.
Canton, OH 44767

Ghosts in Your Garden?

"If you do not know the names of things, the knowledge of them is lost, too."
–Carl Linnaeus, *Philosophia Botanica*

Most flowers have at least two names: common and botanical. Often, a flower's botanical name once belonged to a human being. During the heyday of international plant exploration, it became customary to honor famous botanists, naturalists, or gardeners by naming plants after them. Here are a few.

Nicotiana

French politician **Jean Nicot** (1530–1600) served as ambassador to Portugal. In Lisbon, botanist Damião de Goes introduced him to tobacco, considered to be an effective cure-all. In 1561, Nicot sent samples to the French court. Soon, the plant was decreed to be "the queen's herb," and Nicot was appointed Lord of Villemain. In self-congratulatory fashion, Nicot gave his name to the genus, a member of the nightshade family. Today, we smoke *Nicotiana tabacum* and grow several species of fragrant ornamentals—tall *N. sylvestris*, sticky *N. langsdorffii*, and night-scenting *N. alata*.

Nicotiana

by Cynthia Van Hazinga

Begonia

Frenchman **Michel Bégon** (1638–1710) was governor of Haiti and Barbados under Louis XIV. While there, Bégon became acquainted with Charles Plumier (see *"Plumeria,"* page 44) and invited him to share the bounty of his wine cellar. In return, Plumier named a tropical plant genus after Bégon. *Begonia* (family Begoniaceae) now has 1,300 species and numerous cultivars.

Begonia

Magnolia

Pierre Magnol (1638–1715) was a French physician, professor of botany at the University of Montpellier, and director of the Royal Botanic Garden in an age when most cures were botanical. An expert organizer, Magnol was the first to publish the concept of plant families as we know them. In recognition of his work, in 1703 Charles Plumier (see *"Plumeria,"* page 44) named the family and genus of a flowering tree from the island of Martinique for Magnol. Today, there are about 125 species of *Magnolia.*

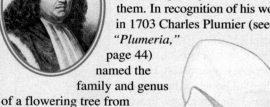

Magnolia

–Kristin Kest

CONTINUED

43

-Kristin Kest

Plumeria

French Franciscan monk, botanist, and explorer **Charles Plumier** (1646–1704) classified and named more than 4,300 plants after specialists of his day. On a trip to the Caribbean in the 1690s, Plumier found a fragrant, showy, white-

Plumeria

flowering tree and sent samples home. In 1704, prior to embarking on his fourth journey, to Peru, he fell ill with pleurisy and died. Soon after, botanists Joseph Pitton de Tournefort and Carl Linnaeus gave the genus name *Plumeria* to the tree with the five-petaled flowers from the dogbane family now also known as frangipani, Pagoda Tree, and West Indian jasmine.

Camellia

Georg Joseph Kamel (1661–1706), born in Moravia (now part of the Czech Republic), entered the Jesuit order and became a pharmacist. His superiors sent him to the Philippines, where he established a pharmacy and studied plants, lizards, and insects. Kamel sent many plant samples to Europe and became known for his ornamental herbarium. In 1735, Carl Linnaeus named a genus of evergreen flowering trees and shrubs after

Camellia

Kamel, using his name's feminine Latinized form, *Camellia*. Ironically, the camellia, a member of the tea family and a garden treasure in Japan and China, was unknown to Kamel.

Kalmia

In the 1740s, Finnish botanist **Pehr Kalm** (1716–69) was a pupil of Carl Linnaeus. The Swedish government sent Kalm on a plant expedition to Britain's North American colonies. During forays into the

Erase Spider & Varicose Veins Without Surgery!

Once only available by prescription in Europe, all-natural formula noticeably reduces the appearance and embarrassment of varicose & spider veins.

A friend told me about Venacura™, a new product she's been using that just became available here in the U.S. that reduces the appearance and embarrassment of varicose veins *naturally* without surgery. Venacura contains Diosmin 95, which has been used for years in Europe to promote healthy veins. This ingredient has been proven in clinical trials to help significantly reduce the appearance of varicose and spider veins by increasing the metabolic activity in the veins which helps to bring new life and vitality to tired legs.

Visible Results You Will See and Feel

Needless to say, I couldn't wait to try Venacura™ for myself. I started taking it once a day and within 30 days my spider and varicose veins began to actually fade. I even noticed the swelling in my lower legs was better especially on the days when I was on my feet all day.

Now I Can Show My Legs Again

After taking Venacura™ now for a few months, my legs look and feel great. Even my husband (who doesn't notice anything) suggested maybe now with the warmer weather we should go to our community pool again sometimes …*which means exposed legs!* (he was even more embarrassed then I was). I said YES because now that I've got these smooth, younger-looking legs again, I want to show them off. Maybe this year I will get to the beach. I only wish I had heard about Venacura sooner!

*These statements have not been evaluated by the FDA. This product is not intended to treat, diagnose, cure, mitigate or prevent any disease. * Does not provide surgical results. Results may vary.*

Available For the First Time in U.S.

Venacura™ contains the powerful ingredient Diosmin 95, a naturally occurring flavonoid that can be isolated from various plant sources. Diosmin 95 has been used in Europe for decades as an all-natural treatment for veins and the venous system. It has undergone 20 years of clinical testing and is currently used by doctors throughout Europe. After further refinement by Venacura, Diosmin 95 is now available as a once-a-day dietary supplement and for a limited time on a risk free trial basis.

Trouble Finding Venacura™?

Venacura™ is the only oral supplement containing Diosmin 95 currently available in the U.S. that you can try for FREE. Venacura is not available in stores and you can only order directly from the manufacturer while limited supplies are available. The manufacturers are so confident that Venacura will make your legs look and feel significantly younger and healthier, they are offering a 30 day risk free trial offer…because seeing is believing.

To get your supply of Venacura risk free for just a small shipping and processing fee, call today. Try one of the greatest breakthroughs in reducing the appearance of varicose and spider veins without spending hundreds of dollars on lasers or surgery.

Call 888-321-3799 today to get your 30-Day Supply of Venacura™ Risk-Free!

Mention Promotional code VN100009 for express shipping!

wilderness, he admired the ever-green shrub that Native Americans called spoonwood (aka mountain laurel and calico bush), which was used to make spoons and trowels. In 1751, he returned to Sweden with 90 plant species, 60 of them new. In appreciation, Linnaeus gave the name *Kalmia* to a genus of evergreen laurels that includes the mountain laurel species.

Kalmia

Gardenia

Scottish-born physician and amateur botanist **Alexander Garden** (1730–91) was brilliant and opinionated. From his indigo plantation near Charleston, South Carolina, he carried on correspondence and plant exchanges with William Bartram, Carl Linnaeus, and John Ellis, among others. When Ellis got hold of a fragrant, long-flowering, showy specimen from China, he named the genus *Gardenia,* after his friend. (This plant was actually *Gardenia jasminoides,* or Cape jasmine, which, although originally from Asia, is so called because it was first thought to have come from the Cape of Good Hope in Africa.)

Gardenia

CONTINUED

Frequent
BATHROOM TRIPS?

Bell Prostate Ezee Flow Tea #4a

Within 3-5 days most men can lead a normal life again. A majority of men over 50 suffer day and night. This mix of 13 herbal teas stops dribbling, burning and rushing to the toilet every half hour or hour night and day. 99% success rate. Helps virtually everybody quickly. The only prostate remedy that works so well that it comes with **a money-back guarantee**.

True Testimonials: ■ **Had to get up every hour** at night. Now I get
up once a night. What a relief. *Joseph Whittaker, Sewell, NJ* ■ **Doctor said keep on taking the tea** Prostate drugs did not help. *Leonard Pearcey, Wassis, NB* ■ **I cancelled my prostate surgery!** Get up just once a night now. Prostate Tea really works. I'm so happy not to face the torment of prostate surgery and possibly incontinence or impotency. *Albert E. Blain, 74, Schumacher, ON* ■ **Even after TURP prostate surgery** and microwave therapy had to get up many times a night. Down to 1-2 times. Tea is 100% better. *Robert G. Stocker, Eustis, FL* ■ **After 1st year drinking the tea** my PSA went down to 4.5; after 2nd year to 2.9; after 3rd year to 2.3. I highly recommend this tea. A real life saver. *Thomas M. Thurston, Forsyth, GA.* ■ **Literally hundreds more testimonials with full names on our web site**. *If you are considering prostate surgery, try this tea first.*

WOMEN suffering with incontinence, frequency and bladder infections ask for **Bell Bladder Control Tea for Women #4b**. Guaranteed to get complete relief usually within days. Over 100 true testimonials on our web site saying "amazing and quick relief", "better than antibiotic drugs", "tea really works" and many others. Go shopping & travelling with confidence.

ARTHRITIS Pain free in 2 weeks!

This is what happened to me personally. After suffering for years I desperately tried everything, drugs, natural products, physiotherapy, acupuncture, magnets and nothing was of any real help. Finally I had relief in 2 weeks by taking shark cartilage **that was specially processed to preserve the natural active ingredients.** This is the kind we are now promoting. I realized then that there are over *50 million* men and women that are battling the same illness and getting treatments that are not working well, otherwise we would not have this ongoing huge health problem. In the last 10 years we have helped tens of thousands of men and women to have less pain or no pain at all. This is a by-product of the food industry. No sharks are caught because of their bones/cartilage. *Nick A. Jerch, President*

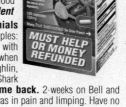

We have real **EVIDENCE** that it works. On our web site you find over **100 testimonials** with full names and towns. All 100% true. Skeptics may call them. Here are some examples: ■ I recommend it to those **millions suffering needlessly** like I did for 40 years with arthritis in my knees. It's a shame that I was given drugs and injections all these years when a natural medicine could have spared me the endless torture day and night. Pat Laughlin, Coldwater, ON ■ **My hip is 95% pain free.** Pain killing drugs mask and Bell Shark Cartilage heals. Rebecca Hite, Oroville, CA ■ **I tried another brand and pain came back.** 2-weeks on Bell and pain is gone again. Gert Dupuis, Hanmer, ON ■ **Cancelled knee replacement.** I was in pain and limping. Have no more pain now. Can square dance for hours. Anton Melnychuk, Porcupine Plain, SK.

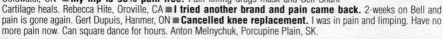

BELL 50 PRODUCTS THAT REALLY WORK

Available in 7,000 health food stores and pharmacies in U.S.A. and Canada. Look up your local store on our web site **www.BellLifestyleProducts.com** "Where to buy" or call us at **1-800-333-7995**. If there is no local store listed, place your order by telephone or order on our web site with VISA or Mastercard. Or send us your check, add $9.95 S&H per order. Bell Lifestyle Products Inc., 07090 68th Street, South Haven MI, 49090.

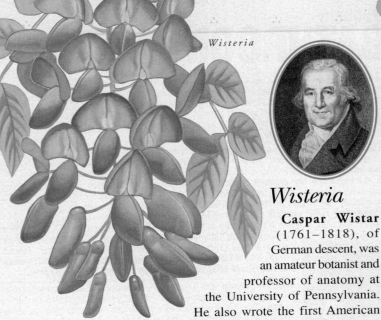

Wisteria

Wisteria

Caspar Wistar (1761–1818), of German descent, was an amateur botanist and professor of anatomy at the University of Pennsylvania. He also wrote the first American textbook on anatomy. Soon after the professor's death, American naturalist Thomas Nuttall named the genus of woody twining vines from the pea family for him (the misspelling, *Wisteria* instead of *Wistaria*, caused confusion for centuries).

Forsythia

Scotsman **William Forsyth** (1737–1804) served as Royal Gardener at London's Kensington and St. James's Palaces and founded the Royal Horticultural Society. He built the first rock garden in England, using lava from Iceland and 40 tons of stone from the Tower of London. Later, he invented "Forsyth's Plaister" (sic) to heal tree wounds. (A scandal erupted when the plaster was revealed to consist of cow dung, wood ashes, powdered lime, and sand mixed with soapsuds and urine.) Forsyth's plant honorarium, the bushy yellow *Forsythia* (in the olive or Oleaceae family), was awarded posthumously in 1804 by Danish botanist Martin Vahl.

Forsythia

CONTINUED

Kerria

In 1804, wealthy British naturalist and explorer Sir Joseph Banks sent Scottish-born botanist and gardener **William Kerr** plant-hunting in China on a meager salary. Kerr succumbed to evil habits (probably opium addiction) but returned with many plants, including a shaggy-headed, orange-yellow shrub. Banks then sent Kerr to Ceylon to supervise a new botanical garden; in 1814, he died on the island. In 1818, Swiss botanist Augustin Pyramus de Candolle named the shrub *Kerria japonica* for Kerr; it is the only species in the genus *Kerria*, which is in the rose or Rosaceae family.

Kerria

Poinsettia

Gardener and amateur botanist **Joel Roberts Poinsett** (1779–1851) was the first U.S. minister to Mexico. While there in 1828, he found a shrub with large red bracts and sent cuttings to his greenhouse in South Carolina. The plant was shown at the 1829 Philadelphia Flower Show. In 1836, German botanist Karl Ludwig Wilenow found the dazzling red plant growing through a crack in his

Poinsettia

greenhouse and assigned it the botanical name *Euphorbia pulcherrima* ("the most beautiful *Euphorbia*"). In 1843, historian William Prescott was asked to give the plant a common name, and he chose to honor Joel Poinsett.

A Short Tour of the Plant Kingdom

■ The accepted way of naming plants is the Latin binomial system, which follows specific rules and has been modified only slightly from Linnaeus's original. Most gardeners today are interested in only family, genus, and species, the latter two of which are italicized when written.

Sometimes a third name in italics is present. This means that the plant is a subspecies (ssp.) or naturally growing variety (var.). An "X" indicates a hybrid, the result of crossing two genera, species, or

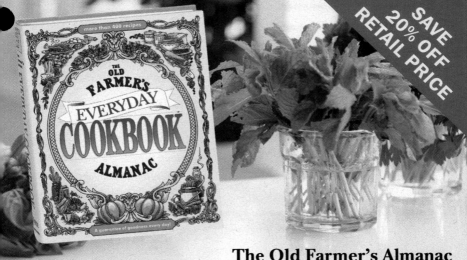

cultivars. A capitalized name in roman type with single quotation marks indicates a cultivar, or cultivated variety.

FAMILY: *a group of one or more genera that share a set of underlying features, commonly grouped on the basis of the flower (the reproductive organ). Family names end in "aceae."*

GENUS *(or type; pl. genera): a group of related species of plants; designated by* a capitalized noun, always in italics, *appears before the species name.*

SPECIES: *the basic unit of plant classification; an adjective, always in italics, describes the plant. Species are groups of plants capable of breeding together to produce offspring similar to themselves; often, the species name will refer to its color, the shape of its leaves, or the place where it was found.*

The Legendary Linnaeus

Sweden's Carl Linnaeus (1707–78) may be the world's most famous botanist and first plant information architect. In 1753, his book *Species Plantarum* revolutionized plant classification as well as nomenclature. His system, known as binomial classification, tagged every plant known with two Latin words—a generic name (genus) followed by a specific qualifier (species). For example, *Helianthus annuus* (Latin for "sunflower, annual") neatly describes the plant. Until then, plants were identified with whole phrases; in the case of the sunflower: "annual, much-branched with strongly angled, glabrous branches and leaves with saw-toothed edges." Linnaeus held that every plant could be assigned to one of 24 classes based on its reproductive parts, the pistils (female) and stamens (male).

Linnaeus named hundreds of plants, often with humor. At his request, his own name became attached to the pan-arctic *Linnaea borealis,* or twinflower, which he described as "a plant of Lappland, lowly, insignificant, disregarded, flowering but for a brief space." ☐☐

Cynthia Van Hazinga, a regular contributor to Almanac publications, divides her time between Hillsborough, New Hampshire, and New York City.

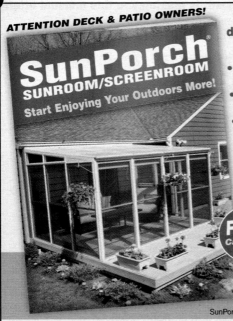

Maria Duval, the famous clairvoyant, is making you this unusual offer:

Choose from the 33 wishes below those you'd most like to see come true in your life NOW!

I'll try to realize them for you, FREE

Maria Duval

Holder of the highest honorary awards and degrees

More than 30 years of accurate and verifiable predictions

More than 10,000 TV appearances and radio programs, and featured in over 700 newspaper articles.

Has predicted hundreds of major events all around the world

Has never failed to telepathically locate missing persons (more than 20 to date)

Ability to predict the future confirmed in experiments by the greatest scientific authorities

Consulted by many international celebrities

Maria Duval, the famous clairvoyant and medium, is making you this strange and truly amazing offer. She is ready to help you to realize your Secret Wishes, the wishes you cherish most, FREE OF CHARGE. All you have do is choose from the list of 33 Secret Wishes below those you'd most like to see come true in your life, and then leave the amazing "powers" of Maria Duval to do their work…

Please note: offer limited to only 7 Secret Wishes per person.

Then what will happen?

As soon as Maria Duval is in possession of your "Special Form for Fulfilling Your Wishes", she is going to perform, on your behalf, a ritual known only to her which should allow your Secret Wishes to come true. You will have absolutely nothing special to do, other than to follow the very simple instructions that she is going to send you in a large, discreet envelope.

Only a few days after receiving your big white envelope, you should see the first beneficial effects of this special help. Then your life will take a new and quite astonishing turn!

You can expect some real "MIRACLES!"

That's right, "miracles" are

Nothing to pay, everything is FREE!

Yes, Maria Duval wants to help you free of charge, and that's why she doesn't want any money in return for the help she's going to give you. All you need to do to benefit from Maria Duval's free help and to see your Secret Wishes coming true in your life is to simply indicate on your "Special Wish Fulfillment Form" the 7 Secret Wishes that you'd like Maria Duval to realize for you, and then return it as soon as possible to the address indicated.

going to occur in your life once Maria Duval has performed (free of charge) this very special ritual that should allow your Secret Wishes – whichever they may be – to become a reality in your life. You probably won't be able to believe your eyes, but each of the wishes you have asked for should come true.

Please, don't hesitate. Remember, you have nothing to lose, and EVERYTHING TO GAIN!

Got POTS?

by Marty Ross

"In the solitude of garden labor, one gets into a sort of communion with the vegetable life."

—Charles Dudley Warner, American editor (1829–1900)

he ingredients for a simple salad—lettuce, peppers, cucumbers, and tomatoes—all thrive in containers, and your options for pots are almost infinite. Here are some pointers and a few ideas for getting started.

POT-TICULARS

- Grow lettuce in baskets, window boxes, a wine crate, a trough—even a little red wagon. Its roots require only a few inches of soil.

- Plant tomatoes, peppers, and cucumbers in tubs, pots, or buckets. All need depth to support their roots. Use an 18-inch pot or a 5-gallon bucket, at minimum.

- Vegetables in containers generally need 6 hours of sun; 8 hours is better. If necessary to get adequate sunlight, choose pots that will fit into a wheelbarrow or wagon and thus can be moved into the sun easily.

- All plants in pots need more attention to watering than plants in the ground. Plastic pots retain moisture better than unglazed terra-cotta pots.

- To achieve consistent moisture, add moisture pellets to your potting mix according to the package directions.

- Make sure that every container has adequate drainage holes.

- Use fresh, sterile, soil-less potting mix for perfect drainage.

- Position mature, top-heavy plants out of the wind even if they are well staked.

- Fertilize tomatoes, peppers, and cucumbers with a slow-release formula or use a water-soluble fertilizer every 2 weeks.

Grow SALADS!

LETTUCE

'Green Ice'

"Lettuce is like a conversation: It must be fresh and crisp, so sparkling that you hardly notice the bitter in it."

A t the Chicago Botanic Garden's fruit and vegetable demonstration garden, enormous hanging baskets densely planted with three or more kinds of loose-leaf lettuce steal the show. To make one, line a wire hanging basket with sphagnum moss (sold in "sheets" and available at garden shops) and then fill it with potting mix. Use several varieties of lettuce seedlings grown in six-packs or flats. Baby spinach, mesclun, mustard, arugula, orach, and other greens add interesting flavor to the salad bowl. Snip through the moss with scissors to plant the seedlings on the bottom, sides, and top of the basket, in that order.

Lettuce thrives in the cool days and nights of spring, so plant it 4 weeks before the last frost. (To get a fall harvest, plant 4 weeks before the first frost.) If you're starting with seeds, sprinkle them directly on top of the soil in spring when its temperature reaches 50°F.

Fertilizer is unnecessary with lettuce, because the crop usually matures before the days are warm enough to trigger its

-S. Ulloa

ROWS OF PROSE. The gardening quotations cited here are from Charles Dudley Warner's collection of humorous essays titled *My Summer in a Garden*, which is based on his experiences at Nook Farm in Hartford, Connecticut, in 1870.

release. Experts recommend an occasional drenching with fish emulsion.

Harvest your lettuce with scissors, taking the outer leaves first—and often. In hot weather, lettuce turns bitter and bolts.

FOR STARTERS

Loose-leaf lettuces work best in containers. For the prettiest pots, choose lettuces with different colors, shapes, and textures, such as . . .

'Green Ice' (green)
'Red Sails' (red)
'Salad Bowl' (green)

You can also buy seed packets with a mix of lettuce varieties. Experiment: Try growing greens that are unfamiliar to you or are expensive to buy in the supermarket. One seed packet is more than enough for one pot. Gardeners in the South should look for heat-tolerant mixes.

■ ■ ■

"Nothing makes one feel more complacent, in . . . July days than to have his vegetables from his own garden."

Peppers are among the easiest and most satisfying salad crops for containers: Their size is manageable, and healthy plants produce bright fruit nearly all summer long.

Bell peppers and sweet peppers are the best choices for salads; hot peppers can overpower a summer salad, and the plants generally grow too lanky for pots.

Start your peppers as transplants. One per 18-inch pot is sufficient. Stake any

PEPPERS

'Bulgarian Carrot'

'Merlot Hybrid'

pepper plants that are placed in windy areas. A sturdy bamboo cane and a length of twine (or strips of laundered, worn-out nylon stockings) or a small, two- or three-ring cage works well.

Peppers set fruit when temperatures are

between about 60° and 80°F. Keep the plants watered and healthy during heat waves, and they'll set fruit again once temperatures drop. If your growing season is short, look for varieties that mature in 50 days or less.

FOR STARTERS
Choices abound for pepper lovers:

'Ace' (sweet bell, red at maturity)
'Blushing Beauty' (sweet bell, ivory to red fruit)
'Bulgarian Carrot' (medium to spicy, orange fruit)
'Cherry Pick' (sweet salad, red at maturity)
'Fruit Basket' (orange bell; great for hanging baskets)
'Karma Hybrid' (sweet bell, red fruit)
'Merlot Hybrid' (sweet bell, purple fruit)

■ ■ ■

"Then there is the cool cucumber, like so many people—good for nothing when it is ripe and the wildness has gone out of it."

With a lot of enemies, cucumbers are among the most challenging vegetables to grow. Fungus, wilt, and mildew can cause problems, and then there are cucumber beetles. To minimize difficulties, choose disease-resistant varieties, plant seeds at the appropriate time, and water frequently. When the beetles arrive, pick them off by hand. Cucumber plants resent transplanting, stubbornly refuse to grow until air and soil temper-

—www.parkseed.com

'Diva'

atures are in the 70°F range, and demand consistent moisture—or else their fruit will develop a bitter taste. Despite all of this, they are worth the trouble.

To compensate for the problems and secure a good harvest, overplant. Choose a large container, such as half of a whiskey barrel, plant ten seeds in it, and then snip off weak seedlings to leave seven healthy plants. (Don't pull the weak ones; you'll disturb the roots of the others.)

Your choices are (1) bush cucumbers

FOR STARTERS
The first three cukes are All-America Selections.

'Diva' (vine)
'Fanfare' (vine)
'Salad Bush' (bush)
'Spacemaster' (bush)

ITALIAN TREE TOMATO

Rush Industries, Inc.
Quality Products Since 1977
© Rush Industries, Inc. 2009

PRODUCE OVER 50 Lbs OF TOMATOES

FOR LESS THAN **1¢** each

Tomato Variety:
Italian Tree

EASY TO GROW!
• No Trimming • No Pruning • No Effort

✓ **Zooms up to 15 Feet in One Season!**
✓ Fruits are Rich, Red, Meaty and Large - Up to 2 Lbs Each
✓ Guaranteed to Produce Bushels of Delicious Tomatoes
✓ Easy to Plant & Grow Prize Winning Tomatoes

Imagine, each plant can produce up to 2-3 bushels of large and luscious mouth-watering tomatoes in less than 90 days. Fruit is incredibly sweet and juicy, full of old fashioned gourmet tomato flavor weighing up to 2 lbs. each. Practically no effort...No pruning... No trimming. Simply sit back and watch them grow "Prize Winning" giant-size gourmet tomatoes. It's that simple.

IT'S LIKE A TOMATO FACTORY IN YOUR OWN BACKYARD!!!

Grows indoors or outdoors. A showpiece for patio orgarden. You'll receive Nurseryman's Starter Pots containing everything you need to grow your Italian Tree Tomatoes ... pre-treated... ready to sow with easy-to-follow instructions. Absolutely guaranteed to grow or your money back! ORDER NOW!!!

30 DAY MONEY BACK GUARANTEE (less S&H)

Send to: Rush Industries, Inc.   263 Horton Highway, Mineola, NY 11501   Dept. TP223KA

SPECIAL! ☐ 2 For Only $6.98 + $2.95 **S&H**   SALE! ☐ 4 For Only $9.98 + $3.95 **S&H**
SAVE! ☐ 8 For Only $17.98 + $4.95 **S&H**   SUPER SAVER! ☐ 10 For Only $19.98 + $5.95 **S&H**

Enclosed is $_____   Or Charge it! ☐ VISA ☐ MasterCard ☐ AMERICAN EXPRESS ☐ DISCOVER Date _____

Acct. #_____   Name_____

Address_____   City_____   State_____ Zip_____

Order by Phone: 1-516-741-0346 or www.RushIndustries.com/TP223KA

that are relatively compact, set fruit close to the center of the plant, and have a tidy habit in a container; or (2) vining varieties, which love to wander and can be grown up a tepee or trellis or allowed to sprawl.

Expect to harvest your cucumbers for about 4 weeks in midsummer. Enjoy them while they last, in a salad or on their own with a bit of salt and vinegar.

■ ■ ■

— Thompson & Morgan Seedsmen Inc.

TOMATOES

'Ildi'

"Sitting in the sun amid the evidences of a ripe year is the easiest part of gardening."

Tomatoes thrive in containers, and they like heat, especially early in the summer. Since the soil in a pot warms up faster than soil in the ground, you can set transplants out a little early, before the competition (you may need to protect plants from frost if a cold night sneaks up on you).

Many experts recommend determinate

tomatoes, which grow to about 3 feet tall are thus more manageable in pots. Indeterminate tomatoes keep on growing—and producing—until frost. They're gangly plants, but they can be pruned to be kept in proportion to the pot. Cherry tomatoes, which produce prodigious quantities of fruit in beautiful clusters, are also excellent in pots. They'll all require staking.

Tomatoes need lots of room for their roots and require plenty of moisture, so plant them in large (18-inch-diameter or bigger) containers.

Tomato plants adapt to hanging pots. They look odd growing upside down in bags or buckets and hanging from a porch or pergola, but they are said to produce an enviable harvest. At minimum, such a display will secure your reputation as a gardener of great versatility and talent.

FOR STARTERS
Try these tomatoes in pots:

'Container Choice' (bushy, red fruit, determinate)

'Flamme' (French heirloom, orange fruit, indeterminate)

'Green Zebra' (heirloom, green fruit with green stripes, indeterminate)

'Ildi' (yellow, grape-clustered, indeterminate)

'Razzleberry' (pink fruit, determinate)

'Sun Sugar' (orange cherry tomato, indeterminate)

Try these in hanging baskets:

'Tumbling Tom' (trailing, red or yellow fruit, indeterminate)

'Yellow Canary' (low-growing, yellow fruit, determinate)

(continued)

The Old Farmer's Almanac
2010 Engagement Calendar

It's easy to stay organized with this charmingly illustrated hardbound, lay-flat, desk calendar. The week-at-a-glance format provides ample space for appointments and notes, and each day offers a bit of useful advice, quirky history, or folklore. There are also pages to record addresses, birthdays and anniversaries, and plans for the future.

Name_____

Street_____

City_____State_____ Zip_____

☐ Check/MO   Charge my: ☐ Visa ☐ MasterCard ☐ AmEx ☐ Discover

Acct. No._____Exp._____

Signature_____
required for credit card orders

2010 Engagement Calendar	
Price $14.99 each	$_____
Add MA or IL sales tax (MA 5.0%, IL 6.25%)	$_____
+ S&H $4.95 each*	$_____
Total enclosed	$_____
SKU: OF10CEB / Promo: A90AEC	

THREE EASY WAYS to order! MAIL *this form with payment to:* The Old Farmer's Almanac Products, P.O. Box 370, Mt. Morris, IL 61054 **ONLINE** *visit:* Shop.Almanac.com **PHONE** *call toll-free:* 1-800-ALMANAC (1-800-256-2622) and mention code A90AEC.
*$4.95 s/h valid only in the U.S. Canadian residents, please add $5.00 additional s/h, for a total of $9.95 each.   A90AEC

APPETIZING ACCENTS

Plant 'Lemon Gem' marigolds, nasturtiums, pansies, and calendulas among your vegetables. All have edible flowers that will add a touch of color to the containers and spice to your salads. ☐☐

Get Growing

Salad is only the beginning! To get more advice and watch videos about growing vegetables, go to **Almanac.com/Gardening.**

Marty Ross, who gardens in both Kansas City, Missouri, and Gloucester, Virginia, has been writing about the subject since 1976.

The Easiest-Ever Container Garden

Anyone can turn an ordinary bag of potting soil into a "grow bag": Lay the bag of soil flat. Poke a few drainage holes in the top surface. Roll the bag over. Cut a few holes in the new top surface. Insert seedling plants into the holes. Water and fertilize as you would a bed. For best results, set this sack into a wheelbarrow or child's wagon and move it into and out of the sunlight as needed.

There's more of everything at Almanac.com.

Maine Goodies
Your one stop on
the Internet for
Maine products.
Over 1,500
Maine-made or
inspired items.
MaineGoodies.com
1-866-385-6238

The Illuminator
Patented house numbering display

Displays your
house number by
day, and lights
up automatically
for 6 hours at
sundown. Price
$39.95 + $5 S&H.
5-year warranty. Money-back guarantee.
Call **617-742-2900**. Or send for more details:
20 Parsons Dr., Swampscott, MA 01907

Thompson & Morgan

*Quality English
Seeds Since 1855*
Over 1,700 unique and
unusual flowers and
vegetables for your
garden – all GMO free.
50 new varieties for 2010.
Money Back Guarantee.
Reserve Your Free
Catalog Today!
Mention Code 1001
1-800-274-7333 ~ www.tmseeds.com

FREE Catalog

**San Francisco
Herb &
Natural
Food Co.®**
*Wholesale Herbs,
Spices and Teas
Since 1969*
All spice blends
are prepared
in-house, salt-free. NO additives, MSG &
non-irradiated. ALL NATURAL!
510-770-1215   www.herbspicetea.com

**Country
Carpenters, Inc.**
Fine New England
style post & beam
carriage houses,
garden sheds, and
country barns.
860-228-2276

Or visit our Web site: **countrycarpenters.com**

Barn House Lighting
Colonial Reproduction &
Rustic Lighting for your Home
Outdoor Lanterns
Chandeliers • Sconces
Solid Cedar Wood Lamp Posts.
503 Suncook Valley Road
Alton, NH 03809
1-800-481-4602
*We offer a wide selection of
American-made manufacturers*
www.barnhouselighting.com

Bug Baffler, Inc.
Concerned about
bug bites?
The essential bug
protection clothing
for all outdoor
activities. To order:
1-800-662-8411
or secure
www.bugbaffler.com
Wholesale inquiries
invited.

Mantis Tiller/Cultivator
The world's favorite small tiller.
Lightweight and powerful.
Breaks through hard
soil, even clay!
Choose from
three models.
One-year money-back
guarantee and 5-year warranty.
1-800-366-6268
www.mantis.com

What Is

"NORMAL" WEATHER?

. . . or, is "average" only in the eye of the beholder?

by Peter N. Spotts

L isten to almost any TV or radio weather forecast or read the predictions in this Almanac, and you'll notice the terms "normal" or "average" used to describe current conditions. These averages are based on 30 years' worth of data, and this year marks one bookend of a new 30-year period. The National Climatic Data Center (NCDC) in Asheville, North Carolina, is shifting the base period from 1971–2000 to 1981–2010. This involves sweeping up the period's daily temperature, precipitation, and other weather information from more than 7,000 sites around the country and computing new statistics to be rolled out in 2011.

This may sound simple enough. But these days, a growing number of people say that the normals, used as a tool for forecasting conditions months ahead, aren't working for them anymore.

Arguments over how official calculations are made get aired decade after decade, says Nolan Doesken, Colorado's state climatologist, and the outcomes of these discussions matter to more than just weather experts. Normals are used to determine how much you pay to heat your home, whether you may face water restrictions this summer, and even when it's best to plant your vegetables or annuals.

(c o n t i n u e d)

-John Lund/Getty Images

Many weather and climate experts say that the 30-year period—updated each decade—is long enough to average out the effects of natural climate swings, to help meteorologists to smooth out discrepancies in readings, and to place weather and climate activity in a common historical context. But despite the label "normal," these numbers may not really represent what you could expect to experience today.

Increasing demands by energy, agricultural, insurance, investment, and other interests for "normals" are leading the NCDC to seek additional techniques for calculating normal, or average, conditions.

Anthony Arguez, a scientist at NCDC working on calculating the new base numbers, believes that it's "a stretch" to presume that the 30-year base formula represents current conditions. Because the calculations for normals are in reality mathematical averages, the results best represent conditions that exist around the midpoint of the base period (e.g., 1985 for the period 1971–2000). Robert Livezey, former chief of the climate-service branch of the U.S. National Weather Service (NWS) and a proponent of greenhouse gas–induced global warming, considers the traditional 30-year base "essentially worthless . . . as a benchmark for decision-making" in today's world. "When the convention was decided upon, rapid climate change was not an important consideration," he says.

Other experts chafe, even scoff, at the use of the word "normal" at all when talking about weather and climate. They cite the formula's incompatibility with Mother Nature. Chuck Doswell, a severe-weather scientist at the University of Oklahoma, has argued that since extremes are a feature of weather, the normals would be more useful if they also addressed how often or how frequently weather departs from the average.

Such viewpoints, as well as the increasing demand by energy, agricultural, insurance, investment, and other interests for "normals" that better represent today's conditions, are leading the NCDC and other agencies to seek additional techniques for calculating normal, or average, conditions. At last count, a dozen methods, some with highly specialized uses and several involving shorter base periods, have been proposed or are in development.

Expect the grumbling and the traditional calculations to continue. As new methods are added, the 30-year statistics will remain as reference for research.

"When it's all said and done," says Doesken, "for most applications we revert back to those 30-year averages."

(c o n t i n u e d)

HOME LIGHTING *Breakthrough*

A floor lamp that spreads sunshine all over a room.

The Balanced Spectrum® floor lamp brings many of the benefits of natural daylight indoors for glare-free lighting that's perfect for a variety of indoor activities.

1. Sunshine indoors. Balanced Spectrum® lamps replicate the full spectrum of natural sunlight and its many benefits. The dual brightness switch features two light levels.

2. Glare-free light. Unlike the harsh glare of incandescent or fluorescent light, full spectrum light helps prevent eyestrain from reading or computer use.

3. Save Money. *Compared to a regular 100-watt incandescent bulb, our 27-watt bulb saves you about $0.0076 per hour. Over the 8,000 hour life of the bulb, you'll save almost $61 in electricity costs.

Technology revolutionizes the light bulb
- *8,000 hours bulb life*
- *Energy efficient*
- *Shows true colors*

Try the Balanced Spectrum® floor lamp for the best value ever! Now more than ever is the time to add sunshine to every room in your home at this fantastic low price! The Balanced Spectrum® floor lamp comes with *first*STREET's exclusive guarantee. Try this lamp for 90 days and return it for the product purchase price if not completely satisfied.

Balanced Spectrum® floor lamp

Item# BB-3589 . . . . was $59.95

Call now for $10 instant savings!

Only $49.95 each + S&H

*Order two Balanced Spectrum® floor lamps and get **FREE shipping** on both lamps.

*Free shipping within the contiguous 48 states only.

Please mention promotional code 38029.

For fastest service, call toll-free 24 hours a day.

1-888-649-6827

We accept all major credit cards, or if you choose, you can pay by check over the phone. To order by mail, please call for details.

www.balancedspectrum.com

*first*STREET
for Boomers and Beyond®

1998 Ruffin Mill Road
Colonial Heights, VA 23834

41472

Weather

Strengths and Weaknesses of Normal Numbers

The process of calculating weather statistics starts with collecting data from weather stations. The NCDC has to make sure that the data each station records come from changes in the weather and not from other factors that just *look* like changes in the weather. **(c o n t i n u e d)**

A Pretty Normal Picture

■ Although climate change has received a great deal of attention in recent years, the actual change in the normals in each decade is very small compared with the day-to-day variation in the weather. For example, in Boston, the largest change in the 30-year normal temperature in the past century has been only 0.5 degree F. In contrast, the annual average temperature has increased by as much as 3.3 degrees (1888 to 1889) and decreased by as much as 3.2 degrees (1991 to 1992), and it is not unusual for temperatures to vary by 20 degrees or more from day to day.

–Michael Steinberg,
Old Farmer's Almanac *meteorologist*

Years	Normal Temp. in Boston, Mass. (°F)
1881–1910	49.4
1891–1920	49.9
1901–1930	50.4
1911–1940	50.7
1921–1950	50.9
1931–1960	51.1
1941–1970	51.1
1951–1980	51.3
1961–1990	51.2
1971–2000	51.6
1981–2008	51.6

Fund Raising

Your non-profit club, team, church or school works directly with the manufacturer to make great profits. Your customers receive a tremendous value on kitchen knives, utensils and gift sets while supporting your cause.

Rada Cutlery's reputation for Made in the USA quality is well known. Our proven fund raising system guarantees your success.

Request your **FREE** catalog
and information packet:
1-800-311-9691
or **www.RadaCutlery.com**
NOTE: Dept **A10OFA**

*Find out why our
customers say that
"Rada knives sell themselves!"*

RADA CUTLERY
"A Cut Above The Rest"

Viyella

Viyella is, as always, an intimate blend of natural fibers. It is soft, warm, light, and supremely comfortable. Its fine blend of 80% long staple cotton and 20% merino wool affords the unique combination of luxury and practicality. Viyella is produced solely by William Hollins & Company Ltd., world-famous for superb British textile craftsmanship since 1784. Reg. sizes Small-XXL. Tall sizes L-3XL. Robes also available.

MILLER BROS. NEWTON
Fine Men's Clothier for 150 Years

www.mbnmenswear.com
105 Main St., Keene, NH • 888-256-1170

STOP ANIMAL DAMAGE!
Messina Wildlife's Animal Stopper Line - <u>Now Available Nationwide!</u>

55 Willow Street, Washington, NJ 07882
Tel: 908-320-7009 Fax: 908-320-7088
www.StopAnimalDamage.com

SAFE & ORGANIC
RAIN RESISTANT
PLEASANT ODOR

This is especially true for data supplied by volunteer "cooperative" stations. Although rigorous NWS standards apply, volunteers move. They may shift their daily observing times, or they may cease running their stations due to medical or other problems. (In the mid-1990s, the U.S. government replaced many human-tended stations with stations in an automated surface-observing system, or ASOS, to gain uniformity.)

Weather stations also move. For instance, in the early 1960s, Denver authorities built a reservoir in the Rockies, filling a valley that had long hosted a weather station. The state moved the station to its current location along the shore of the reservoir—a compatible move by NWS standards.

"Lo and behold, there was an immediate and significant change in temperature and precipitation," says Nolan Doesken, Colorado's state climatologist. Days became cooler, nights were warmer, and precipitation dropped. Among the reasons: The station sat in the lee of a small ridge that blocked snowfall from the north.

Similarly, wildfires, which change vegetation cover, and sub/urban development, which brings pavement and heat-absorbing materials, can

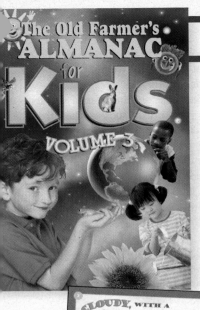

It's Better Than Ever!

The Old Farmer's Almanac for Kids • VOLUME 3

ALL NEW!

Do you know . . .

Why all stars are not white, and some can shrink and grow?

Which part of its body a cricket uses to listen?

How many billion plastic bags are used around the world each year?

Find the answers to these questions and much more:

✦ "green" pages, featuring energy alternatives, a trash trail

✦ articles on stars, weird weather, pets that work, sports heroes, the history of pizza, desert-dwelling animals

✦ how to grow a loofah sponge, make a wind chime, and create a sunflower house—plus more!

■ **$9.95** 5⅝" x 8¼"
Item: OF09KIDS • 192 pages

FUN AND FACTS FOR KIDS!

−photos, NOAA's National Weather Service Collection

introduce changes in the records that do not reflect actual changes in weather patterns or climate trends.

To provide a background of measurements untainted by phenomena such as the urban heat-island effect, the U.S. government is establishing a network of automated "reference stations" around the country in locations far from human encroachment. The program's annual report for fiscal year 2008 noted 114 stations in the contiguous 48 states, with plans afoot to expand into Alaska with the addition of 29 more.

A cooperative weather station at Granger, Utah, circa 1930, where volunteers observed temperature, precipitation, and other weather conditions

A Normal Start

■ Attempts to set common standards for weather and climate data records cropped up in the early 1870s through the International Meteorological Committee (IMC). For the next 60 years or so, countries simply arithmetically averaged the weather data that they had on record. In 1935, the global meteorological community set three decades as the basis for comparison on the belief that climate conditions were fairly stable and were likely to reoccur every 30 years. Today, the World Meteorological Organization, which evolved from the IMC, continues that practice, updating every 30 years.

The weather station at Cape Henry, Virginia, circa 1900

In the mid-1950s, the U.S. National Weather Bureau (now Service) adopted the 30-year base but advanced it a decade every 10 years. The thinking was that with decadal advances the calculations stood a better chance of representing current conditions. Many national weather services, including those of Canada and the United Kingdom, use this standard today.

(**c o n t i n u e d**)

Psoriasis? Dermatitis? Dandruff? Dry, Itchy Skin?

Now you can relieve the itching and restore your skin to its clear healthy state!

Introducing Soravil™, the scientifically advanced skin therapy system whose active ingredients are clinically proven to provide immediate relief from Psoriasis, Dermatitis, Dandruff, and other bothersome skin disorders.

If you suffer from an irritating skin disorder, you must try Soravil™! Unlike anything you may have tried in the past, Soravil™ is guaranteed to provide immediate relief from the redness and irritation associated with chronic skin disorders. Our clinically tested formulas soothe, moisturize and heal dry, damaged skin...leaving it feeling smooth, supple, and healthy again! Even better, the power of Soravil™ is available in the form of Shampoo and Body Wash, so you can treat your condition as part of your daily routine. There is also easy to apply (and invisible) Body Gel and Skin Spray to take care of those stubborn flare ups. Soravil™ makes it easy for you to relieve yourself from that bothersome skin disorder.

What are you waiting for? If you want to relieve yourself from the suffering and rejuvenate your dry, itchy skin, it's time you tried Soravil™! This highly effective formula is guaranteed to work for you. So don't suffer any longer, call today for your risk-free trial, 1-800-711-0719, Offer # 909.

Success Stories:

"Right away it cleared my arms up. I think your product is wonderful. Thanks so much!"
-Judy K.

"I am amazed at the improvement that Soravil has made to my scalp! To say I'm delighted would be putting it lightly."
-David L.

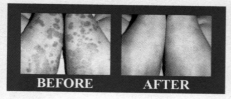

BEFORE   AFTER

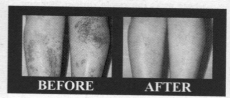

BEFORE   AFTER

Call now and get your risk-free trial!
1-800-711-0719

Mention Offer # 909 and ask how you can get a **FREE SUPPLY** of our Soravil Skin Hydration Formula.

Active Ingredient FDA Approved • Results Guaranteed
Steroid-Free Formula • Provides Immediate Relief
Works On All Skin Types • Easy Application-No Mess

Average vs. Normal

■ **The "average" temperature** (or precipitation) is the numerical average (e.g., the average of 50, 70, and 90 degrees is 70 degrees).

■ **The "normal" temperature** (or precipitation) is generally defined as the adjusted average over the most recent 30-year period ending in zero.

Two kinds of adjustments are made to the 30-year average to determine the "normal": The first is done to maintain consistency throughout any changes in site location or instrumentation, and the second is to fit the daily normals to a curve (cubic spline interpolation) to smooth out any statistical anomalies. *–Steinberg*

This Almanac's Formula

■ **In forecasting the "deviations from average,"** this Almanac uses the official 30-year normals for temperature and precipitation, averaged across each of our designated regions. Technically, we use the normals rather than the averages. (Although the spline-curve modifications affect the daily normals, they have no discernible effect on the monthly normals that we use—so in this case, the normals and averages are actually the same.) For more, see "How We Predict the Weather."

–Steinberg

Have It Your Way

In 2006, the NCDC set up a Web page (www7.ncdc.noaa.gov/CDO/normals) where users can create custom "dynamic normals" for a location. One utility in Florida uses it to calculate 5-year normal periods to estimate demand for electricity.

Peter N. Spotts is the science reporter for *The Christian Science Monitor* (www.csmonitor.com). He has written extensively on astronomy, earth science, climatic and atmospheric science, and more.

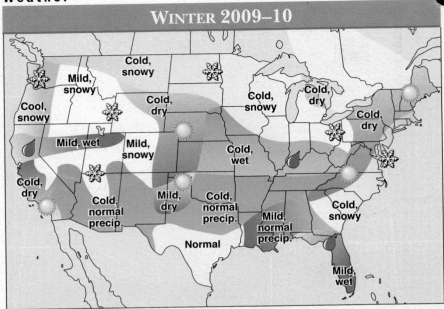

WINTER 2009–10

These weather maps correspond to the winter (November through March) and summer (June through August) predictions in the General Weather Forecast (opposite).

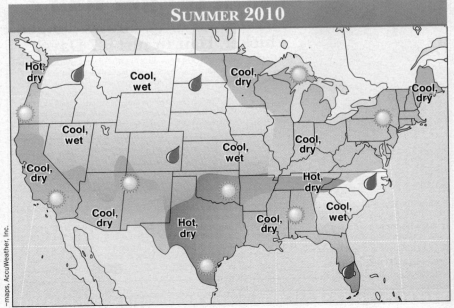

SUMMER 2010

—maps, AccuWeather, Inc.

General Weather Forecast and Report

For regional forecasts, see pages 205–221.

The prolonged low level of sunspot and space weather activity in the early stage of Solar Cycle 24 reinforces our belief that we are at the beginning of a period of significant change. Over the coming years a gradual cooling of the atmosphere will occur, offset by any warming caused by increased greenhouse gases. We expect that the El Niño Southern Oscillation (ENSO) will be neutral during the winter of 2009–10, with neither a strong El Niño nor La Niña. Most of the nation will have below-normal winter temperatures, on average. Snowfall will be above normal in most areas along the Atlantic coast, in the northern tier of states, and in the Intermountain Region.

Spring will be warm in the east but cool in the west. Summer will be relatively cool in most of the country, with Texas and the Pacific Northwest the chief exceptions. Although the hurricane season will not have a high number of storms, there may be major hits in Florida near Labor Day and in the Deep South later in September.

November through March temperatures will be above normal, on average, in Florida, the Deep South, the Texas Panhandle, and the Intermountain Region, with near-normal temperatures in southern Texas, the Pacific Northwest, and northern California. Elsewhere, temperatures will be below normal, with especially brutal cold in the High Plains and Upper Midwest. Precipitation will be below normal from North Carolina through New England and in Texas, Oklahoma, Washington, and southern California. Precipitation will be at or above normal elsewhere. Snowfall will be above normal along the Atlantic seaboard from Georgia to southern New England, from the western Great Lakes through the northern High Plains, and in most of the Intermountain Region. Snowfall will be below normal in most other areas that normally receive snow.

April and May will be cooler than normal in the Northeast, in Minnesota, in the Desert Southwest, and in much of the Pacific states and warmer than normal elsewhere. Rainfall will be above normal from California northeastward to the Upper Midwest and near or below normal in other regions.

June through August will be hot and dry in most of Texas, Oklahoma, the Tennessee Valley, and the Pacific Northwest. Cooler- and drier-than-normal weather will prevail from the Great Lakes and Ohio Valley northeastward, in the Deep South, and from the Desert Southwest through most of California. Elsewhere, expect below-normal temperatures and above-normal rainfall.

September and October will be warmer than normal in most of the country. Rainfall will be above normal from Florida and the Deep South through much of the Mississippi, Ohio, and Missouri Valleys and near or below normal elsewhere.

How accurate was our forecast last winter? We predicted that La Niña conditions would prevail in the winter of 2008–09 and, after weakening in summer 2008, the La Niña peaked in early 2009. We were also correct in our predictions of below-normal snowfall in much of the southern two-thirds of the nation and above-normal snowfall in New England and the northern Intermountain region. In between, the axis of above-normal snowfall was north of where we forecast, extending from the Dakotas to New York's Finger Lakes. Overall, our monthly regional forecasts were 88 percent accurate in predicting the direction of change in precipitation from the previous winter, and we were within 1.2 degrees F, on average, in our winter temperature forecasts using a city selected from each region. See the table below.

Region/City	Winter Temp. Variations From Normal (degrees)		Region/City	Winter Temp. Variations From Normal (degrees)	
	PREDICTED	ACTUAL		PREDICTED	ACTUAL
1/Caribou	–0.3	–0.5	9/Marquette	+2.3	–0.7
2/New York	–0.5	–0.6	10/Des Moines	+0.1	+0.2
3/Scranton	–0.7	–0.7	11/Houston	–1.3	+2.2
4/Columbia	–2.1	–0.2	12/Rapid City	–0.6	–0.6
5/Orlando	–1.0	–1.4	13/Pendleton	–2.4	–2.2
6/Syracuse	–0.3	–0.5	14/Las Vegas	–3.2	+2.0
7/Pittsburgh	–0.9	–0.8	15/Portland	+0.5	–0.6
8/Nashville	–1.5	0.0	16/Los Angeles	–1.1	+0.1

The Old Farmer's Almanac

Established in 1792 and published every year thereafter

ROBERT B. THOMAS (1766–1846), *Founder*

YANKEE PUBLISHING INC.

EDITORIAL AND PUBLISHING OFFICES

P.O. Box 520, 1121 Main Street, Dublin, NH 03444
Phone: 603-563-8111 • Fax: 603-563-8252

EDITOR *(13th since 1792):* Janice Stillman
ART DIRECTOR: Margo Letourneau
COPY EDITOR: Jack Burnett
SENIOR RESEARCH EDITOR: Mare-Anne Jarvela
SENIOR EDITOR: Heidi Stonehill
ASSOCIATE EDITOR: Sarah Perreault
WEATHER GRAPHICS AND CONSULTATION:
AccuWeather, Inc.

DIRECTOR, PRODUCTION AND NEW MEDIA:
Paul Belliveau
PRODUCTION DIRECTORS:
Susan Gross, David Ziarnowski
SENIOR PRODUCTION ARTISTS:
Lucille Rines, Rachel Kipka

WEB SITE: ALMANAC.COM

WEB EDITOR: Catherine Boeckmann
WEB DESIGNER: Lou S. Eastman
INTERNET PROJECT COORDINATOR: Brenda Darroch
ONLINE MARKETING MANAGER: David Weisberg
PROGRAMMING: Reinvented, Inc.

CONTACT US

We welcome your questions and comments about articles in and topics for this Almanac. Mail all editorial correspondence to Editor, The Old Farmer's Almanac, P.O. Box 520, Dublin, NH 03444-0520; fax us at 603-563-8252; or send e-mail to us at almanac@yankeepub.com. *The Old Farmer's Almanac* can not accept responsibility for unsolicited manuscripts and will not acknowledge any hard-copy queries or manuscripts that do not include a stamped and addressed return envelope.

Thank you for buying this Almanac! We hope you find it new, useful, and entertaining. Thanks, too, to everyone who had a hand in it, including advertisers, distributors, printers, and sales and delivery people.

OUR CONTRIBUTORS

Bob Berman, our astronomy editor, is the director of Overlook Observatory in Woodstock and Storm King Observatory in Cornwall, both in New York. In 1976, he founded the Catskill Astronomical Society. Bob will go a long way for a good look at the sky: He has led many aurora and eclipse expeditions, venturing as far as the Arctic and Antarctic.

Bethany E. Cobb, our astronomer, earned a Ph.D. in astronomy at Yale University and was awarded a National Science Foundation postdoctoral fellowship. She is currently conducting independent research at the University of California, Berkeley. Her passion for the heavens has led to her involvement in numerous astronomy programs, including Alien Earths at New Haven's Peabody Museum. When she is not scanning the sky, she enjoys playing the violin, figure skating, and reading science fiction.

Castle Freeman Jr., who lives in southern Vermont, has been writing the Almanac's Farmer's Calendar essays for more than 25 years. The essays come out of his longtime interest in wildlife and the outdoors, gardening, history, and the life of rural New England. His latest book is *All That I Have: A Novel* (Steerforth Press, 2009).

Celeste Longacre, our astrologer, often refers to astrology as "the world's second-oldest profession." A New Hampshire native, she has been a practicing astrologer for more than 25 years: "It is a study of timing, and timing is everything." Her book, *Love Signs* (Sweet Fern Publications, 1999), is available on her Web site, www.yourlovesigns.com.

Michael Steinberg, our meteorologist, has been forecasting weather for the Almanac since 1996. In addition to having college degrees in atmospheric science and meteorology, he brings a lifetime of experience to the task: He began making weather predictions when he attended the only high school in the world with weather Teletypes and radar.

THE 2010 EDITION OF

The Old Farmer's Almanac
Established in 1792 and published every year thereafter

Robert B. Thomas (1766–1846), *Founder*

YANKEE PUBLISHING INC.
P.O. Box 520, 1121 Main Street, Dublin, NH 03444
Phone: 603-563-8111 • Fax: 603-563-8252

PUBLISHER *(23rd since 1792):* Sherin Pierce
PUBLISHER EMERITUS: John B. Pierce Jr.
EDITOR IN CHIEF: Judson D. Hale Sr.

FOR DISPLAY ADVERTISING RATES
Call 800-729-9265, ext. 215
Bob Bernbach • 914-769-0051
Steve Hall • 800-736-1100, ext. 320
Go to Almanac.com/Advertising

FOR CLASSIFIED ADVERTISING
Call Gallagher Group • 203-263-7171

AD PRODUCTION COORDINATOR: Janet Grant

PUBLIC RELATIONS
Quinn/Brein • 206-842-8922

TO BUY OR INQUIRE ABOUT ALMANAC PUBLICATIONS
Call 800-ALMANAC (800-256-2622)
or go to Shop.Almanac.com

TO SELL ALMANAC PRODUCTS
RETAIL: Cindy Schlosser, 800-729-9265, ext. 126,
or Stacey Korpi, ext. 160

FUND-RAISING WITH ALMANAC PRODUCTS
Sherin Pierce, 800-729-9265, ext. 137

DISTRIBUTORS
NATIONAL: Curtis Circulation Company
New Milford, NJ
BOOKSTORE: Houghton Mifflin Harcourt
Boston, MA

The Old Farmer's Almanac publications are available for sales promotions or premiums. Contact Beacon Promotions, info@beaconpromotions.com.

YANKEE PUBLISHING INCORPORATED

Jamie Trowbridge, *President;* Judson D. Hale Sr., *Senior Vice President;* Jody Bugbee, Judson D. Hale Jr., Brook Holmberg, Sherin Pierce, *Vice Presidents.*

Embarrassed By
THIN HAIR?

My mother's hair was extremely thin. She was terribly embarrassed by it. You could look right through the hair and see large spots of exposed scalp; and she had split ends. She tried everything available but nothing worked, until we found Neutrolox™. Today, my mother's hair looks thick and gorgeous; she looks years younger and she was able to donate her wigs for use by cancer patients.

Neutrolox™ is not just a hair thickening cream; its effective ingredients are the answer to the embarrassing problem of thinning hair and it lets your hair grow fast and naturally. My name is John Peters and I was balding at an extreme rate. After using Neutrolox™ we both are getting compliments on our hair for the first time in our lives. It is great for men and women and can be used on color-treated, permed or processed hair. There is nothing like Neutrolox™ and it is not yet available in stores. Neurolox™ is in a class of it's own.

We honestly believe in Neutrolox™ and know you will too! Try Neutrolox™, if you don't agree you get every penny of your money back—no one can beat a 100% no-risk money-back guarantee. To order send $16.95 (plus $4.00 S&H) for a medium, or the most SAVINGS come with the large (you save $9.95) send only $26.95, plus $4.00 S&H for each order to:

NEUTROLOX™, Dept.FA-N2010, BOX 366, Taylor, MI 48180

RINGING in the EARS?
GREAT NEWS for YOU!

If you ever experience ringing in the ears, buzzing, hissing or any other annoying sounds that may be interfering with your life, you should know about Dr. John's Special Ear Drops™. The drops are truly remarkable; for example: 79-year-old Gloria Gains of Richmond, VA writes: "I tried everything available and my doctor told me I would have to live with my trouble. I had trouble sleeping at night and the sounds were driving me out of my mind. Thank God, I seen your ad. I hardly notice anything at all anymore and I'm sleeping like a baby. Your drops have been a God-Send." Thousands of users like Gloria have written to us regarding Dr. John's Special Ear Drops™. If your doctor has not been able to help you, I strongly urge you to give Dr. John's Special Ear Drops™ a try. You won't be sorry!

The drops are guaranteed to be better for you than anything you have tried or you will get every cent of your money back, no questions asked. You can't beat that!

Send $16.95 plus $4.00 S&H (that's only $20.95) for 1 bottle. Or better yet save $10.00 by ordering 2 bottles for only $26.95 plus $4.00 S&H (a total of $30.95). Send payment with your name and address to:

Dr. John's Research, Dept. FA-DJ2010, Box 637, Taylor, MI 48180

Dr. John's Research is celebrating its 35th anniversary this year providing only the best products. Results may vary. A testimonial reflects the opinion of that person. The FDA does not review claims made on herbal products and the drops are not intended to diagnose, treat, cure or prevent any disease. You should see a doctor if you think you have a disease. If you suffer from ringing in the ears, don't wait a minute longer. Order Today!

Write Children's Books

By Patricia Pfitsch

I f you've ever dreamed of writing for publication, this may be your best chance to turn that dream into a reality. If you qualify and show promise, we'll teach you—the same way I was taught—how to break into one of the most rewarding of all markets for new writers.

The $3 billion children's market

The continued success of publications for young people has led to a growing *need* for new writers to help create the $3 billion worth of children's books published each year, plus stories and articles for more than 600 magazines.

"But am I good enough?"

My dream of writing professionally while raising three kids on a farm was once bogged down in the same kind of uncertainty you may have experienced.

Then, an ad for the Institute seemed to offer the writing and selling skills I needed. I passed its test and entered into a richly rewarding relationship with an author-instructor, which was a major turning point in my life—as I hope it will be in yours.

The at-home training that has launched more successful children's authors than any other school

The Institute of Children's Literature has successfully trained more new writers to meet the needs of this market than any other school. Its unique program turned my dream into reality, and I became one of more than 11,000 Institute graduates who have published children's stories, articles, and books, including prestigious award winners. Now I'm using my skills at the Institute to train promising new writers.

The promise that paid off

The Institute made exactly the same promise to me that it will make to you if

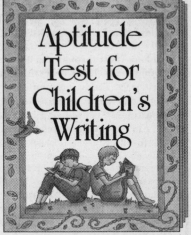

Aptitude Test for Children's Writing

Our test and professional evaluation are free

you demonstrate basic writing aptitude:
You will complete at least one manuscript suitable to submit to editors by the time you finish the course.

With skill, empathy, and tough love when needed, my Institute instructor helped me complete and sell three of my course assignments, which, I later discovered, was not unusual.

Now, as a nationally published author of 7 children's books and over 500 stories and articles, I enjoy helping aspiring writers—as *I* was helped—to change their dreams into bright reality.

A nationally published author or editor is your one-on-one writing and selling coach

If you are accepted, you will be assigned a personal instructor who is a successful author or experienced editor—and who becomes your energizing spark plug and deeply committed writing and selling coach. We all work the same way.

Patricia Pfitsch, a graduate of our course, has published 552 stories and articles, plus 7 books, including 3 award-winning novels and an Edgar nominee. She is also an instructor at the Institute.

When you've finished an assignment at *your* pace, you send it to me. I edit it line-by-line and send you a detailed letter explaining my edits.

I point out your strengths, help eliminate weaknesses, and even show you how to turn bits of your everyday life into saleable writing. You push and I pull, and between us both, you learn how to write—and how to sell what you write.

From "wannabe" to published author

What I got from my instructor at the Institute changed me from a "wannabe" into a nationally published writer. While there's no guarantee that every student will have the same success, we're praised by students and publishers alike.

"I just wanted to let you know how pleased we are with the work and professionalism of your students, Michelle Barone and Dorothy Heibel," writes Joanne Deitch, editor and former President of Discovery Enterprises. "We just launched a new series entitled Adventures in History. Our first two books were *Out of the Ordinary* by Michelle Barone and *Message for a Spy* by Dorothy Heibel.

"We want to congratulate the writers on their work. Often we read of the struggle to get published, but not so often of the successes, so we just thought you'd like to know how well prepared these students were. Keep up the good work."

Dorothy Heibel, who lives in Wessington Springs, South Dakota, also sent us a note. "I graduated from the Institute 20 years ago. The help I received from your course proved to be a wonderful foundation for writing. You planted the seeds that took root and are now producing the results I had hoped for. In addition to *Message for a Spy*, I currently have two mysteries out making the rounds of publishers."

We also talked to Michelle Barone of Denver, Colorado. She applied to the Institute 25 years ago, was accepted, then "forgot about it." Her careers as a medical worker, real estate agent, curriculum writer, and adoptive mother (before she started teaching 5th grade English and math) came first. She finally enrolled in 2000. "Now," she says, "I grab time for my writing when I can find it. Besides my stories and articles, I've had five books published. You've opened up a whole new world to me."

Don't let your dream die— send for your free test today!

If a writing life is the one you long for, here's your chance to test that dream. The Institute offers a revealing aptitude test for children's writing based on its 40 years of experience, and it's free.

If you pass, it's because you have the aptitude to make it in the world of writing for children. It takes work, it takes commitment, it takes courage—but you can do it.

Just fill out and mail the coupon below to receive your free test and 32-page introduction to our course, *Writing for Children and Teenagers,* and 80 of our instructors.

There is no obligation.

Eclipses

■ There will be four eclipses in 2010, two of the Sun and two of the Moon. Solar eclipses are visible only in certain areas and require eye protection to be viewed safely. Lunar eclipses are technically visible from the entire night side of Earth, but during a penumbral eclipse, the dimming of the Moon's illumination is slight.

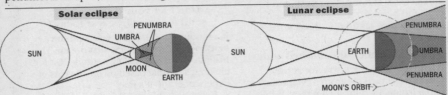

JANUARY 15: Annular eclipse of the Sun. This eclipse will not be visible from North America. It will be visible from Africa, India, and China, while a partial solar eclipse will be visible from Europe, the Middle East, and Asia.

JUNE 25–26: Partial eclipse of the Moon. This eclipse will be fully visible only from Hawaii. The Moon enters penumbra at 10:56 P.M. HAST on June 25 and leaves penumbra at 4:21 A.M. on June 26. It will be partially visible from western and central North America. The Moon enters penumbra at 1:56 A.M. PDT on June 26 and enters umbra at 3:17 A.M. PDT. However, the Moon will have set before the eclipse exits umbra at 6:00 A.M. PDT. Only a penumbral eclipse will be visible from most of the East Coast, starting on June 26 at 4:56 A.M. EDT before the Moon sets. **See page 124** for Moon set times.

JULY 11: Total eclipse of the Sun. This eclipse will not be visible from North America. It will be visible only from the South Pacific Ocean and parts of South America.

DECEMBER 21: Total eclipse of the Moon. This eclipse will be fully visible from North America. The Moon enters penumbra at 12:28 A.M. EST on December 21 and leaves penumbra at 6:06 A.M. EST on December 21.

Full-Moon Dates (Eastern Time)

	2010	2011	2012	2013	2014
Jan.	30	19	9	26	15
Feb.	28	18	7	25	14
Mar.	29	19	8	27	16
Apr.	28	17	6	25	15
May	27	17	5	25	14
June	26	15	4	23	13
July	25	15	3	22	12
Aug.	24	13	1 & 31	20	10
Sept.	23	12	29	19	8
Oct.	22	11	29	18	8
Nov.	21	10	28	17	6
Dec.	21	10	28	17	6

The totality phase begins at 2:40 A.M. EST on December 21 and ends at 3:54 A.M. EST on December 21.

The Moon's Path

The Moon's path across the sky changes with the seasons. Full Moons are very high in the sky (at midnight) between November and February and very low between May and July.

Next Total Eclipse of the Sun

November 13, 2012: visible from northern Australia and the South Pacific Ocean.

Why wait ten months?

Now you can have rich, dark compost *in just 14 days!*

With the amazing ComposTumbler, you'll have bushels of crumbly, ready-to-use compost — *in just 14 days!* (And, in the ten months it takes to make compost the old way, your ComposTumbler can produce *hundreds of pounds* of rich food for your garden!)

Say good-bye to that messy, open compost pile (and to the flies, pests, and odors that come along with it!) Bid a happy farewell to the strain of trying to turn over heavy, wet piles with a pitchfork.

Compost the Better Way

Compost-making with the ComposTumbler is neat, quick and easy!

Gather up leaves, old weeds, kitchen scraps, lawn clippings, etc. and toss them into the roomy 18-bushel drum. Then, once each day, give the ComposTumbler's *gear-driven* handle a few easy spins.

The ComposTumbler's Magic

Inside the ComposTumbler, carefully positioned mixing fins blend materials, pushing fresh mixture to the core where the temperatures are the hottest (up to 160°) and the composting bacteria most active.

After just 14 days, open the door, and you'll find an abundance of dark, sweet-smelling "garden gold" — ready to enrich and feed your garden!

NEW SMALLER SIZE!

Now there are 2 sizes. The 18-bushel original ComposTumbler and the NEW 9.5-bushel Compact ComposTumbler. Try either size risk-free for 30 days!

See for yourself! Try the ComposTumbler risk-free with our 30-Day Home Trial!

Call Toll-Free 1-800-880-2345

Visit us at
www.compostumbler.com

ComposTumbler®

The choice of more than 250,000 gardeners

❏ YES! Please rush FREE information on the ComposTumbler, including special savings and 30-Day Home Trial.

Name _____

Address _____

City _____

State _____ ZIP _____

MAIL TO:
ComposTumbler
1834 Freedom Rd., Dept. 420110C
Lancaster, PA 17601

© 2010 PBM Group

Bright Stars

Transit Times

■ This table shows the time (EST or EDT) and altitude of a star as it transits the meridian (i.e., reaches its highest elevation while passing over the horizon's south point) at Boston on the dates shown. The transit time on any other date differs from that of the nearest date listed by approximately four minutes per day. To find the time of a star's transit for your location, convert its time at Boston using Key Letter C.*

Star	Constellation	Magnitude	Time of Transit (EST/EDT) Bold = P.M. Light = A.M.						Altitude (degrees)
			Jan. 1	Mar. 1	May 1	July 1	Sept. 1	Nov. 1	
Altair	Aquila	0.8	**12:50**	8:58	5:59	1:59	**9:51**	**5:51**	56.3
Deneb	Cygnus	1.3	**1:41**	9:49	6:49	2:49	**10:41**	**6:42**	92.8
Fomalhaut	Psc. Aus.	1.2	**3:57**	**12:05**	9:05	5:05	1:01	**8:58**	17.8
Algol	Perseus	2.2	**8:07**	**4:15**	**1:15**	9:15	5:11	1:12	88.5
Aldebaran	Taurus	0.9	**9:34**	**5:42**	**2:42**	10:43	6:39	2:39	64.1
Rigel	Orion	0.1	**10:13**	**6:21**	**3:21**	11:21	7:17	3:17	39.4
Capella	Auriga	0.1	**10:15**	**6:23**	**3:23**	11:23	7:20	3:20	93.6
Bellatrix	Orion	1.6	**10:23**	**6:31**	**3:31**	11:32	7:28	3:28	54.0
Betelgeuse	Orion	var. 0.4	**10:53**	**7:01**	**4:01**	**12:02**	7:58	3:58	55.0
Sirius	Can. Maj.	−1.4	**11:43**	**7:51**	**4:51**	**12:51**	8:48	4:48	31.0
Procyon	Can. Min.	0.4	12:41	**8:45**	**5:45**	**1:45**	9:42	5:42	52.9
Pollux	Gemini	1.2	12:47	**8:51**	**5:51**	**1:51**	9:48	5:48	75.7
Regulus	Leo	1.4	3:10	**11:14**	**8:14**	4:14	**12:10**	8:10	59.7
Spica	Virgo	var. 1.0	6:26	2:34	**11:30**	7:30	**3:27**	11:27	36.6
Arcturus	Boötes	−0.1	7:16	3:24	**12:24**	**8:21**	**4:17**	**12:17**	66.9
Antares	Scorpius	var. 0.9	9:30	5:38	2:38	**10:34**	**6:30**	**2:31**	21.3
Vega	Lyra	0	11:37	7:45	4:45	12:45	**8:37**	**4:37**	86.4

Rise and Set Times

■ To find the time of a star's rising at Boston on any date, subtract the interval shown at right from the star's transit time on that date; add the interval to find the star's setting time. To find the rising and setting times for your city, convert the Boston transit times above using the Key Letter* shown at right before applying the interval. The directions in which the stars rise and set, shown for Boston, are generally useful throughout the United States. Deneb, Algol, Capella, and Vega are circumpolar stars—they never set but appear to circle the celestial north pole.

Star	Interval (h. m.)	Rising Key	Rising Dir.**	Setting Key	Setting Dir.**
Altair	6 36	B	EbN	E	WbN
Fomalhaut	3 59	E	SE	D	SW
Aldebaran	7 06	B	ENE	D	WNW
Rigel	5 33	D	EbS	B	WbS
Bellatrix	6 27	B	EbN	D	WbN
Betelgeuse	6 31	B	EbN	D	WbN
Sirius	5 00	D	ESE	B	WSW
Procyon	6 23	B	EbN	D	WbN
Pollux	8 01	A	NE	E	NW
Regulus	6 49	B	EbN	D	WbN
Spica	5 23	D	EbS	B	WbS
Arcturus	7 19	A	ENE	E	WNW
Antares	4 17	E	SEbE	A	SWbW

*The values of Key Letters are given in the Time Corrections table (page 234). **b = "by"

Delicious fruit relieves arthritis pain better than most drugs.

Reduce blood pressure with beans and bananas!

"When You Should Never Eat Strawberries!"
(or nuts or spinach or chocolate)

(By Frank K. Wood)

If you want to put prescription dollars back in your pocket, feel better than ever, and reduce the symptoms of heart disease, arthritis, diabetes, and more — without risky drugs, you need *1,001 Prescription Secrets for Seniors*.

You'll be amazed at all the natural ways you can treat and manage today's most common ailments, helping you slam the lid on rising healthcare costs, lower the risk of dangerous side effects, and more! Plus you'll learn how to save on prescriptions you really do need and how to use them safely.

▶ Is it possible to lower blood pressure, cholesterol, and blood sugar without expensive drugs? The experts say yes. Learn more.

▶ The artery-cleaning fruit juice so powerful doctors are recommending it in lieu of drugs. No side effects!

▶ Team up to fight cholesterol! A dynamic food duo lowers your LDL better together than either one can do alone.

▶ Lose those extra inches around your middle and lower your risk for heart disease and diabetes — even surgery! No-fail ways to do it safely, easily.

▶ Free prescription drugs — virtually every brand name available!

▶ Help stay healthy and cancer free, improve your chances, without drugs. Find an alternative.

▶ The arthritis treatment that does what no other medication can do: It actually restores damaged cartilage!

▶ The lowest rate of Alzheimer's in the world: It could be because people there use so much of one spice, which can stop brain plaques from forming, and even break them down!

▶ Fuzzy thinking? Memory slipping? Slow reactions? It may not be Alzheimer's, but an easily reversible condition instead!

▶ They lowered their risk of hardened arteries, heart attack, and stroke just by drinking one glass of juice a day. And it just might work for you!

▶ Simple vitamin that can lower LDL cholesterol by 20% and raise the "good kind" by a whopping 35%!

▶ Have extra pounds crept onto your body over the years? Use 7 no-nonsense tips to take off the excess weight — and keep it off!

Learn all these amazing secrets and more. To order a copy, just return this coupon with your name and address and a check for $9.99 plus $3.00 shipping and handling to: **FC&A, Dept. XR-3028**, 103 Clover Green, Peachtree City, GA 30269. We will send you a copy of *1,001 Prescription Secrets for Seniors.*

You get a no-time-limit guarantee of satisfaction or your money back.

You must cut out and return this coupon with your order. Copies will not be accepted!
IMPORTANT — FREE GIFT OFFER EXPIRES IN 30 DAYS

All orders mailed within 30 days will receive a free gift, *117 Natural Health Secrets for a Longer, Healthier Life,* guaranteed. Order right away!   ©FC&A 2009

The Twilight Zone

Twilight is the time preceding sunrise and again following sunset, when the sky is partially illuminated. The three ranges of twilight are defined according to the Sun's position below the horizon. Civil twilight occurs when the Sun is between the horizon and 6 degrees below the horizon (visually, the horizon is clearly defined). Nautical twilight occurs when the Sun is between 6 and 12 degrees below the horizon (the horizon is indistinct). Astronomical twilight occurs when the Sun is between 12 and 18 degrees below the horizon (sky illumination is imperceptible). When the Sun is at 18 degrees (dawn or dark) or below, there is no illumination.

Length of Twilight (hours and minutes)

LATITUDE	Jan. 1 to Apr. 10	Apr. 11 to May 2	May 3 to May 14	May 15 to May 25	May 26 to July 22	July 23 to Aug. 3	Aug. 4 to Aug. 14	Aug. 15 to Sept. 5	Sept. 6 to Dec. 31
25°N to 30°N	1 20	1 23	1 26	1 29	1 32	1 29	1 26	1 23	1 20
31°N to 36°N	1 26	1 28	1 34	1 38	1 43	1 38	1 34	1 28	1 26
37°N to 42°N	1 33	1 39	1 47	1 52	1 59	1 52	1 47	1 39	1 33
43°N to 47°N	1 42	1 51	2 02	2 13	2 27	2 13	2 02	1 51	1 42
48°N to 49°N	1 50	2 04	2 22	2 42	—	2 42	2 22	2 04	1 50

TO DETERMINE THE LENGTH OF TWILIGHT: The length of twilight changes with latitude and the time of year. Use the **Time Corrections** table, **page 234,** to find the latitude of your city or the city nearest you. Use that figure in the chart above with the appropriate date to calculate the length of twilight in your area.

TO DETERMINE WHEN DAWN OR DARK WILL OCCUR: Calculate the sunrise/sunset times for your locality using the instructions in **How to Use This Almanac, page 106.** Subtract the length of twilight from the time of sunrise to determine when dawn breaks. Add the length of twilight to the time of sunset to determine when dark descends.

EXAMPLE:

Boston, Mass. (latitude 42°22')

Sunrise, August 1	5:36 A.M. EDT
Length of twilight	−1 52
Dawn breaks	3:44 A.M.
Sunset, August 1	8:03 P.M. EDT
Length of twilight	+1 52
Dark descends	9:55 P.M.

Principal Meteor Showers

SHOWER	BEST VIEWING	POINT OF ORIGIN	DATE OF MAXIMUM*	NO. PER HOUR**	ASSOCIATED COMET
Quadrantid	Predawn	N	**Jan. 4**	25	—
Lyrid	Predawn	S	Apr. 22	10	Thatcher
Eta Aquarid	Predawn	SE	May 4	10	Halley
Delta Aquarid	Predawn	S	July 30	10	—
Perseid	**Predawn**	NE	**Aug. 11–13**	50	**Swift-Tuttle**
Draconid	Late evening	NW	Oct. 9	6	Giacobini-Zinner
Orionid	Predawn	S	Oct. 21–22	15	Halley
Taurid	Late evening	S	Nov. 9	3	Encke
Leonid	Predawn	S	Nov. 18	10	Tempel-Tuttle
Andromedid	Late evening	S	Nov. 25–27	5	Biela
Geminid	**All night**	NE	**Dec. 13–14**	75	—
Ursid	Predawn	N	Dec. 22	5	Tuttle

*May vary by one or two days   **Moonless, rural sky   **Bold**=most prominent*

WORLD'S 1ˢᵗ SELF-FEEDING CHIPPERS FOR HOMEOWNERS!

FREE DVD! SEE IT IN ACTION!

...ust load a DR® RAPID-FEED™ CHIPPER, step ...ack, and watch it chip branches up to 5½" thick!

...ELF-FEEDING saves time and energy. Most ...anches can be dropped into the hopper and will ...lf-feed, instead of you having to force-feed them.

...ARNESS YOUR TRACTOR'S POWER!
...e 3-Point Hitch DR® CHIPPER transforms up to ...5 HP of tractor power into raw chipping power!

...RO-SPEC™ CHIPPER KNIFE is made of ...rged alloy tool steel, making it exceptionally strong ...th an excellent edge-holding ability. Far more ...urable than stamped steel knives.

...O TRACTOR? NO PROBLEM! ➡
...lf-Powered Models with engines
... to 18 HP available!

The Visible Planets

■ Listed here for Boston are viewing suggestions for and the rise and set times (EST/EDT) of Venus, Mars, Jupiter, and Saturn on specific days each month, as well as when it is best to view Mercury. Approximate rise and set times for other days can be found by interpolation. Use the Key Letters at the right of each listing to convert the times for other localities **(see pages 106 and 234).** *For all planet rise and set times by zip code, visit* **Almanac.com/Astronomy.**

Venus

Venus starts the year invisibly behind the Sun. It slowly climbs higher in the evening twilight to first become visible in March and floats near Mercury in early April. Venus increases its height above the sunset until June, when it starts getting brighter but lower, and is below Saturn during August 6–8. Its brilliance peaks in late September, but it vanishes well ahead of its inferior conjunction on October 28. Speedily entering the eastern predawn sky, Venus climbs rapidly in November in both elevation and brightness and is a superb morning star in December at magnitude –4.9, when it comes up nearly 3 hours ahead of the Sun.

Jan. 1	rise	7:07	E	Apr. 1	set	8:48	D	July 1	set	10:43	E
Jan. 11	set	4:27	A	Apr. 11	set	9:13	E	July 11	set	10:30	D
Jan. 21	set	4:51	B	Apr. 21	set	9:39	E	July 21	set	10:14	D
Feb. 1	set	5:19	B	May 1	set	10:03	E	Aug. 1	set	9:53	C
Feb. 11	set	5:45	B	May 11	set	10:24	E	Aug. 11	set	9:33	C
Feb. 21	set	6:11	C	May 21	set	10:41	E	Aug. 21	set	9:10	C
Mar. 1	set	6:31	C	June 1	set	10:52	E	Sept. 1	set	8:43	B
Mar. 11	set	6:56	C	June 11	set	10:55	E	Sept. 11	set	8:16	B
Mar. 21	set	8:20	D	June 21	set	10:52	E	Sept. 21	set	7:46	B

Oct. 1	set	7:11	A
Oct. 11	set	6:29	A
Oct. 21	set	5:43	A
Nov. 1	rise	7:03	E
Nov. 11	rise	4:54	D
Nov. 21	rise	4:04	D
Dec. 1	rise	3:35	D
Dec. 11	rise	3:22	D
Dec. 21	rise	3:20	D
Dec. 31	rise	3:25	E

Mars

Mars is the opposite of Venus, at its best early and gone late in the year. The Orange World comes closest in January and has its opposition on the 29th at magnitude –1.2, in Cancer, outshining every star except Sirius. It remains bright throughout the spring, losing half of its light each month. Binocular users can observe Mars passing very near Cancer's Beehive star cluster from April 16–19; it strikingly meets Leo's blue star, Regulus, during the first ten days of June. Much lower and fainter, Mars skims below Saturn during July 28–August 1, is near Venus from August 15–22, and then vanishes from sight in October.

Jan. 1	rise	7:11	B	Apr. 1	set	4:01	E	July 1	set	11:35	D
Jan. 11	rise	6:19	A	Apr. 11	set	3:28	E	July 11	set	11:08	C
Jan. 21	rise	5:20	A	Apr. 21	set	2:57	E	July 21	set	10:41	C
Feb. 1	rise	4:13	A	May 1	set	2:27	E	Aug. 1	set	10:11	C
Feb. 11	set	6:29	E	May 11	set	1:58	E	Aug. 11	set	9:45	C
Feb. 21	set	5:40	E	May 21	set	1:30	E	Aug. 21	set	9:19	C
Mar. 1	set	5:02	E	June 1	set	1:00	D	Sept. 1	set	8:52	B
Mar. 11	set	4:19	E	June 11	set	12:32	D	Sept. 11	set	8:28	B
Mar. 21	set	4:40	E	June 21	set	12:05	D	Sept. 21	set	8:04	B

Oct. 1	set	7:42	B
Oct. 11	set	7:22	B
Oct. 21	set	7:03	B
Nov. 1	set	6:44	A
Nov. 11	set	5:30	A
Nov. 21	set	5:18	A
Dec. 1	set	5:08	A
Dec. 11	set	5:02	A
Dec. 21	set	4:57	A
Dec. 31	set	4:55	A

☞ **Bold = P.M.** ☞ Light = A.M.

–illustrations, Beth Krommes

Jupiter

24 Jupiter has a truly extraordinary year. On September 21, it comes closer to Earth than at any time since 1963, achieving a stunning brilliance of magnitude –2.9 against the faint stars of Pisces. Beginning the year low in the southwest, it is lost in the Sun's glare until emerging in the predawn east in April. It rises 2 hours earlier each month thereafter, coming up at midnight in July and nightfall in September. In mid-September, it hovers near blue-green Uranus, visible with binoculars. Jupiter continues to dominate the night sky for the rest of the year.

Jan. 1	set	8:07	B	Apr. 1	rise	5:39	D	July 1	rise	12:17	C	Oct. 1	set	5:49	C
Jan. 11	set	7:39	B	Apr. 11	rise	5:05	C	July 11	rise	11:35	C	Oct. 11	set	5:04	C
Jan. 21	set	7:11	B	Apr. 21	rise	4:31	C	July 21	rise	10:56	C	Oct. 21	set	4:19	C
Feb. 1	set	6:41	B	May 1	rise	3:56	C	Aug. 1	rise	10:13	C	Nov. 1	set	3:32	C
Feb. 11	set	6:13	B	May 11	rise	3:21	C	Aug. 11	rise	9:33	C	Nov. 11	set	1:51	C
Feb. 21	rise	6:51	D	May 21	rise	2:46	C	Aug. 21	rise	8:52	C	Nov. 21	set	1:11	C
Mar. 1	rise	6:24	D	June 1	rise	2:07	C	Sept. 1	rise	8:07	C	Dec. 1	set	12:33	C
Mar. 11	rise	5:50	D	June 11	rise	1:31	C	Sept. 11	rise	7:25	C	Dec. 11	set	11:53	C
Mar. 21	rise	6:16	D	June 21	rise	12:54	C	Sept. 21	set	6:35	C	Dec. 21	set	11:19	C
											Dec. 31	set	10:46	C

Saturn

ħ With its rings nearly on edge, Saturn has an opposition on March 21 that will prove to be its dimmest of the next 14 years. Still, after beginning the year as a moderately bright "star" rising due east at 10:30 P.M. in Virgo, it rises at 8:30 P.M. in mid-February and at nightfall in March, when it's out all night. At magnitude 0.5, Saturn outshines all but four of the night's stars. Remaining visible through the summer during the first half of the night, it floats above the Moon on May 22, hovers above Mars during the last days of July and on August 1, and is too low to be seen after September. In November, it returns low in the southeast just before sunrise.

Jan. 1	rise	11:13	C	Apr. 1	set	6:22	C	July 1	set	12:19	C	Oct. 1	set	6:33	C
Jan. 11	rise	10:35	C	Apr. 11	set	5:41	C	July 11	set	11:37	C	Oct. 11	rise	6:04	C
Jan. 21	rise	9:55	C	Apr. 21	set	5:01	C	July 21	set	10:59	C	Oct. 21	rise	5:31	C
Feb. 1	rise	9:10	C	May 1	set	4:20	C	Aug. 1	set	10:18	C	Nov. 1	rise	4:54	C
Feb. 11	rise	8:29	C	May 11	set	3:40	C	Aug. 11	set	9:41	C	Nov. 11	rise	3:20	C
Feb. 21	rise	7:46	C	May 21	set	3:00	C	Aug. 21	set	9:04	C	Nov. 21	rise	2:46	C
Mar. 1	rise	7:12	C	June 1	set	2:16	C	Sept. 1	set	8:23	C	Dec. 1	rise	2:12	C
Mar. 11	set	6:48	C	June 11	set	1:37	C	Sept. 11	set	7:46	C	Dec. 11	rise	1:36	C
Mar. 21	set	7:07	C	June 21	set	12:58	C	Sept. 21	set	7:10	C	Dec. 21	rise	1:00	C
											Dec. 31	rise	12:24	C

Mercury

☿ Mercury is best seen when it's at least 7 degrees high in deepening twilight and its brightness exceeds magnitude 0.5. In 2010, these conditions occur 40 minutes after sunset only from March 28–April 11. Look for Mercury low in the west, close to Venus. Its less favorable morning appearances occur during January 16–30 and September 15–29 and at the end of December.

DO NOT CONFUSE ■ *Venus with Mercury in early April. Venus is 15 times brighter.* ■ *Mars with Saturn in late July and early August. Mars is orange.* ■ *Saturn with Virgo's main star, Spica, just before dawn from late November through December. Spica is dimmer and appears blue.*

Astronomical Glossary

Aphelion (Aph.): The point in a planet's orbit that is farthest from the Sun.

Apogee (Apo.): The point in the Moon's orbit that is farthest from Earth.

Celestial Equator (Eq.): The imaginary circle around the celestial sphere that can be thought of as the plane of Earth's equator projected out onto the sphere.

Celestial Sphere: An imaginary sphere projected into space that represents the entire sky, with an observer on Earth at its center. All celestial bodies other than Earth are imagined as being on its inside surface.

Circumpolar: Always visible above the horizon, such as a circumpolar star.

Conjunction: The time at which two or more celestial bodies appear closest in the sky. **Inferior (Inf.):** Mercury or Venus is between the Sun and Earth. **Superior (Sup.):** The Sun is between a planet and Earth. Actual dates for conjunctions are given in the **Right-Hand Calendar Pages, 111–137;** the best times for viewing the closely aligned bodies are given in **Sky Watch** on the **Left-Hand Calendar Pages, 110–136.**

Declination: The celestial latitude of an object in the sky, measured in degrees north or south of the celestial equator; analogous to latitude on Earth. This Almanac gives the Sun's declination at noon.

Eclipse, Lunar: The full Moon enters the shadow of Earth, which cuts off all or part of the sunlight reflected off the Moon. **Total:** The Moon passes completely through the **umbra** (central dark part) of Earth's shadow. **Partial:** Only part of the Moon passes through the umbra. **Penumbral:** The Moon passes through only the **penumbra** (area of partial darkness surrounding the umbra). **See page 88** for more eclipse information.

Eclipse, Solar: Earth enters the shadow of the new Moon, which cuts off all or part of the Sun's light. **Total:** Earth passes through the umbra (central dark part) of the Moon's shadow, resulting in totality for observers within a narrow band on Earth. **Annular:** The

Moon appears silhouetted against the Sun, with a ring of sunlight showing around it. **Partial:** The Moon blocks only part of the Sun.

Ecliptic: The apparent annual path of the Sun around the celestial sphere. The plane of the ecliptic is tipped 23½° from the celestial equator.

Elongation: The difference in degrees between the celestial longitudes of a planet and the Sun. **Greatest Elongation (Gr. Elong.):** The greatest apparent distance of a planet from the Sun, as seen from Earth.

Epact: A number from 1 to 30 that indicates the Moon's age on January 1 at Greenwich, England; used for determining the date of Easter.

Equinox: When the Sun crosses the celestial equator. This event occurs two times each year: **Vernal** is around March 20 and **Autumnal** is September 22 or 23.

Evening Star: A planet that is above the western horizon at sunset and less than 180° east of the Sun in right ascension.

Golden Number: A number in the 19-year cycle of the Moon, used for determining the date of Easter. (Approximately every 19 years, the Moon's phases occur on the same dates.) Add 1 to any given year and divide by 19; the remainder is the Golden Number. If there is no remainder, the Golden Number is 19.

Greatest Illuminated Extent (Gr. Illum. Ext.): When the maximum surface area of a planet is illuminated as seen from Earth.

Magnitude: A measure of a celestial object's brightness. **Apparent** magnitude measures the brightness of an object as see from Earth.

Objects with an apparent magnitude of 6 or less are observable to the naked eye. The lower the magnitude, the greater the brightness. An object with a magnitude of -1, for example, is brighter than an object with a magnitude of $+1$. **Absolute** magnitude expresses how bright objects would appear if they were all the same distance (about 33 light-years) from Earth.

Midnight: Astronomical midnight is the time when the Sun is opposite its highest point in the sky (noon). Midnight is neither A.M. nor P.M., although 12-hour digital clocks typically display midnight as 12:00 A.M. On a 24-hour time cycle, 00:00, rather than 24:00, usually indicates midnight.

Moon on Equator: The Moon is on the celestial equator.

Moon Rides High/Runs Low: The Moon is highest above or farthest below the celestial equator.

Moonrise/Moonset: When the Moon rises above or sets below the horizon.

Moon's Phases: The changing appearance of the Moon, caused by the different angles at which it is illuminated by the Sun. **First Quarter:** Right half of the Moon is illuminated. **Full:** The Sun and the Moon are in opposition; the entire disk of the Moon is illuminated. **Last Quarter:** Left half of the Moon is illuminated. **New:** The Sun and the Moon are in conjunction; the entire disk of the Moon is darkened.

Moon's Place, Astronomical: The actual position of the Moon within the constellations on the celestial sphere. **Astrological:** The astrological position of the Moon within the zodiac, according to calculations made more than 2,000 years ago. Because of precession of the equinoxes and other factors, this is not the Moon's actual position in the sky.

Morning Star: A planet that is above the eastern horizon at sunrise and less than 180° west of the Sun in right ascension.

Node: Either of the two points where a celestial body's orbit intersects the ecliptic. **Ascending:** When the body is moving from south to north of the ecliptic. **Descending:** When the body is moving from north to south of the ecliptic.

Occultation (Occn.): When the Moon or a planet eclipses a star or planet.

Opposition: The Moon or a planet appears on the opposite side of the sky from the Sun (elongation 180°).

Perigee (Perig.): The point in the Moon's orbit that is closest to Earth.

Perihelion (Perih.): The point in a planet's orbit that is closest to the Sun.

Precession: The slowly changing position of the stars and equinoxes in the sky resulting from variations in the orientation of Earth's axis.

Right Ascension (R.A.): The celestial longitude of an object in the sky, measured eastward along the celestial equator in hours of time from the vernal equinox; analogous to longitude on Earth.

Solar Cycle: In the Julian calendar, a period of 28 years, at the end of which the days of the month return to the same days of the week.

Solstice, Summer: When the Sun reaches its greatest declination (23½°) north of the celestial equator, around June 21. **Winter:** When the Sun reaches its greatest declination (23½°) south of the celestial equator, around December 21.

Stationary (Stat.): The brief period of apparent halted movement of a planet against the background of the stars shortly before it appears to move backward/westward (retrograde motion) or forward/eastward (direct motion).

Sun Fast/Slow: When a sundial reading is ahead of (fast) or behind (slow) clock time.

Sunrise/Sunset: The visible rising and setting of the upper edge of the Sun's disk across the unobstructed horizon of an observer whose eyes are 15 feet above ground level.

Twilight: For definitions of civil, nautical, and astronomical twilight, **see page 92.** □ □

GIANT JUPITER PAYS A VISIT

All hail and behold this sky king! In 2010, it's closer than ever.

Mankind has observed Jupiter for millennia; no single person discovered this heavenly body. It was one of five brilliant, moving "stars" (now known to be planets) called "wanderers" by ancient Greeks. In Roman mythology, it was known as Jupiter, or Jove ("father"), ruler of the skies.

This year, we're calling it "simply awesome."

Not since 1963 has Jupiter been so close, so bright, so easily seen—a result of its slow, oval orbit around the Sun that will take nearly 12 Earth years.

Each year, Jupiter visits a different one of the 12 zodiacal constellations (making it the easiest planet to track), and for 1 month each year, the planet appears both opposite (or, in opposition to) the Sun *and* at its

by Bob Berman

position closest to Earth. This combination results in a best-viewing time for us.

Of course, some "bests" are better than others. When Jupiter's orbit traverses the lower, or southern, zodiac constellations (e.g., Scorpius), the view from Earth appears to be through smudgier air because people are gazing through more of Earth's atmosphere. Conversely, when Jupiter is in the higher constellations (Taurus or Gemini), we see the planet with much less distortion. (In the United States and Canada, Hawaii is the only place from which Jupiter can be seen to reach its zenith.) From 2010 through 2015, Jupiter will be in northern constellations, with minimal distorting air.

Jupiter advances a month each year. In recent years (2007, 2008, and 2009), Jupiter was best viewed in June, July, and August, respectively. In 2010, it is at its best in September (its closest approach is on September 20, while its opposition is on September 21). It will hover just 367 million miles away and shine at magnitude –2.5.

If you are busy or Mother Nature fails to provide clear skies on these nights, don't despair. The sky king is out most of the night and visible 2 to 3 months before and after opposition—in this case, the entire last half of the year.

Finding Jupiter should be easy. Beginning in mid-August, look halfway up the southern sky for the night's brightest star. This is Jupiter! Dazzling and astonishingly conspicuous against the faint stars of Pisces, it will stand at its highest at 2:00 A.M. (In July, early birds can catch a glimpse at 4:00 A.M.) *(continued)*

Artists' renditions of the space probe *Galileo*, above, and the Jupiter Polar Orbiter, at right

GO, JUNO!

The National Aeronautics and Space Administration (NASA) has successfully sent a number of probes to Jupiter. One, named *Galileo*, orbited the planet and sent back images of its swirling storms and details on its moons, as well as indications that its moon Europa has liquid water under its mile-thick surface ice.

Next August, NASA's Jupiter Polar Orbiter *(Juno)* will leave Earth and begin a 5-year flight to the Giant Planet, arriving in 2016. *Juno* will orbit Jupiter's polar regions and collect data on the planet's size, structure, atmosphere, temperature, and winds.

—NASA

As the year winds down, Jupiter will be at its best earlier each month: at midnight in September (look for green Uranus hovering nearby in midmonth), at 10:00 P.M. in October, at 7:00 P.M. in November, and at nightfall in December. Want to make an appointment? Get the planet's rise and set times in your zip or postal code at Almanac.com/Astronomy.

No one needs to miss this night show. Even the most inexpensive backyard telescope or steadily braced binoculars will inspire ooohs and ahhhs. Jupiter reveals more detail through amateur instruments than any other planet (60× magnification is ideal). If you are not equipped, contact an astronomy club (www.astronomy-clubs.com) or a university (www.publictele-scopes.com) about getting a look through a lens.

In 2010, the quadricentennial of Galileo's heavenly discoveries, the view—by Jove!—should be nothing short of amazing!

Jupiter

Io

Europa

Callisto

Ganymede

—NASA

Jupiter and four of its moons are shown in relative positions, but not to scale.

Jupiter by the Numbers

Diameter: 11 Earths

Mass (quantity of matter): 318 Earths

Volume: 1,312 Earths

Length of year: 11.86 Earth years

Length of day: 9 hours 56 minutes

Surface temperature: −234°F

Density: $\frac{1}{4}$ of Earth's

Gravity: 2.4 times stronger than on Earth (a 100-lb. person would weigh 240 lbs. on Jupiter)

Magnetic force: 14 times stronger than Earth's

Average distance from the Sun: More than 5 times Earth's

Closest distance to Earth: 367 million miles

Brightness, on average: Magnitude −2.3

Natural satellites (moons): More than 63

King-size
Curiosities

■ Jupiter reigns over a miniature solar system of at least 63 moons, including huge and ever-changing Io, Europa, Ganymede, and Callisto (named the Galilean Satellites in Galileo's honor).

■ Its rotation, which is faster than that of any other planet, creates streaks: dark areas (belts) indicate rising clouds and gases; light areas (zones) indicate where belts sink.

■ It spins fast at its equator and slowly at its poles; where the momentums clash, gaseous layers produce violent eddies, curlicues, swirls, white spots, and the famous Great Red Spot—a hurricane three times the size of Earth. (You can see this on nights when Earth's air is steady.)

(continued)

Galileo's Destiny:
Discovery and Downfall

Exactly 400 years ago, Galileo Galilei (1564–1642) and Jupiter changed the order of the universe.

By around 1608, spyglasses and magnifying devices had become popular. Duplicating one such instrument, Galileo had painstakingly fashioned wood and leather into a tube into which he set one concave and one convex glass lens. The result was a refracting telescope with three-power (3×) magnification. Later models would boast 9×, 20×, and eventually 30× magnification. (Watch informative videos at Italy's Institute and Museum of the History of Science Web site, www.imss.fi.it.)

When Galileo turned his primitive instrument toward the sky, the universe revealed its wonders. The Moon, long thought to be a smooth-surfaced body with seas, appeared pockmarked with mountains and craters. The creamy glow of the Milky Way burst into untold separate stars. The Sun, believed to be a flawless object, could be seen

Galileo's telescope proved that Jupiter's moons orbited the Giant Planet, but this contradiction to church doctrine would later seal his fate.

to have spots, whose changing positions suggested that it rotated.

The most amazing and controversial body viewed through this device was Jupiter, shining brilliantly in Taurus. Galileo's observations revealed that this body was a round disk, not merely a point of light.

All was breathtaking and incredible but incomplete until, on January 7, 1610, he discovered three "stars" alongside Jupiter. Within a week, he had observed the trio change positions, spotted yet another star, and realized that these stars (later determined to be moons) orbited the Giant Planet!

This astounding news contradicted Catholic church doctrine, which insisted that Earth was the center of the universe. Certain that proof would trump perception, Galileo invited some priests to peer through the lens.

The clergymen realized what their fate would be if they admitted the obvious, so they looked—and lied.

"Yes, there it is," the astronomer exclaimed. "Jupiter, with the little moons around it. Look again!"

"No," each priest shrugged in turn. "I can not see a thing."

Despite overwhelming resistance, Galileo bravely published his startling discoveries. Instead of being cheered, he was jeered. Church officials detained him, forced him to recant (or be burned at the stake), and placed him under permanent house arrest, where he eventually died on January 8, 1642, penniless. □□

Bob Berman's most recent book, coauthored with Robert Lanza, M.D., is *Biocentrism* (BenBella 2009). Learn more about Berman's universe at www.skymanbob.com.

How to Use This Almanac

The calendar pages (110–137) are the heart of *The Old Farmer's Almanac*. They present sky sightings and astronomical data for the entire year and are what make this book a true almanac, a "calendar of the heavens." In essence, these pages are unchanged since 1792, when Robert B. Thomas published his first edition. The long columns of numbers and symbols reveal all of nature's precision, rhythm, and glory, providing an astronomical look at the year 2010.

–Beth Krommes

Why We Have Seasons

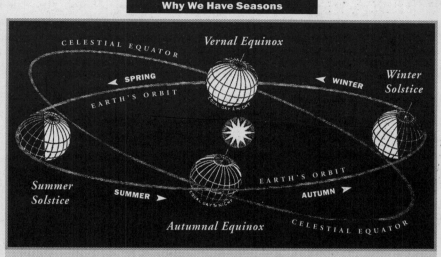

THE SEASONS OF 2010

Spring	March 20, 1:32 P.M. EDT	Autumn. . . . September 22, 11:09 P.M. EDT
Summer.	June 21, 7:28 A.M. EDT	Winter . . . . . . December 21, 6:38 P.M. EST

■ The seasons occur because as Earth revolves around the Sun, its axis remains tilted at 23.5 degrees from the perpendicular. This tilt causes different latitudes on Earth to receive varying amounts of sunlight throughout the year.

In the Northern Hemisphere, the summer solstice marks the beginning of summer and occurs when the North Pole is tilted toward the Sun. The winter solstice marks the beginning of winter and occurs when the North Pole is tilted away from the Sun.

The equinoxes occur when the hemispheres equally face the Sun and receive equal amounts (12 hours each) of daylight and darkness. The vernal equinox marks the beginning of spring; the autumnal equinox marks the beginning of autumn. In the Southern Hemisphere, the seasons are the reverse of those in the Northern Hemisphere. **(continued)**

The Left-Hand Calendar Pages • 110–136

A SAMPLE MONTH

SKY WATCH ☆ *The box at the top of each Left-Hand Calendar Page describes the best times to view celestial highlights, including conjunctions, meteor showers, and planets. (The dates on which select astronomical events occur appear on the Right-Hand Calendar Pages.)*

1 2 3 4 5 6 7 8

Purchase these pages with times set to your zip code at MyLocalAlmanac.com.

Day of Year	Day of Month	Day of Week	☼ Rises h. m.	Rise Key	☼ Sets h. m.	Set Key	Length of Day h. m.	Sun Fast m.	Declination of Sun ° ′	High Tide Times Boston		☾ Rises h. m.	Rise Key	☾ Sets h. m.	Set Key	☾ Place	☾ Age
1	1	Fr.	7:13	E	4:22	A	9 09	12	22 s. 58	11	11¾	5:39	B	7:56	E	GEM	16
2	2	Sa.	7:13	E	4:23	A	9 10	12	22 52	12	—	6:59	C	8:35	E	CAN	17
3	3	C	7:13	E	4:24	A	9 11	11	22 46	12½	12¾	8:18	D	9:08	E	CAN	18

The **Left-Hand Calendar Pages** (detail above) contain daily Sun and Moon rise and set times, the length of day, high tide times, the Moon's place and age, and more for Boston. Examples of how to calculate astronomical times for your location are shown below.

1 To calculate the sunrise/sunset times for your locale: Each sunrise/sunset time is assigned a Key Letter whose value is given in minutes in the **Time Corrections** table on **page 234**. Find your city in the table, or the city nearest you, and add or subtract those minutes to/from Boston's sunrise or sunset time given.

EXAMPLE:

■ To find the time of sunrise in Denver, Colorado, on the first day of the month:

Sunrise, Boston, with Key Letter E (above)	7:13 A.M. EST
Value of Key Letter E for Denver (p. 234)	+ 7 minutes
Sunrise, Denver	7:20 A.M. MST

2 To determine your city's length of day, find the sunrise/sunset Key Letter values for your city on **page 234**. Add or subtract the sunset value to/from Boston's length of day. Then simply *reverse* the sunrise sign (from minus to plus, or plus to minus) and

add or subtract this value to/from the result of the first step.

EXAMPLE:

■ To find the length of day in Richmond, Virginia:

Length of day, Boston (above)	9h. 09m.
Sunset Key Letter A for Richmond (p. 238)	+ 41m.
Reverse sunrise Key Letter E for Richmond (p. 238, +11 to −11)	− 11m.
Length of day, Richmond	9h. 39m.

3 Use the Sun Fast column to change sundial time to clock time in Boston or another location. A sundial reads natural time, or Sun time, which is neither Standard nor Daylight time. To get Boston clock time, *subtract* the minutes given in the Sun Fast column (except where the number is preceded by an asterisk [*], in which case *add* the minutes) and use Key Letter C in the table on **page 234** to convert the time to your city.

ATTENTION, READERS: *All times given in this edition of the Almanac are for Boston, Massachusetts, and are in Eastern Standard Time (EST), except from 2:00 A.M., March 14, until 2:00 A.M., November 7, when Eastern Daylight Time (EDT) is given. Key Letters (A–E) are provided so that you can calculate times for other localities.*

EXAMPLE:

■ To change sundial time to clock time in Boston, or, for example, in Salem, Oregon:

Sundial reading (Boston or Salem)	12:00 noon
Subtract Sun Fast (p. 106)	− 12 minutes
Clock time, Boston	11:48 A.M. EST
Use Key Letter C for Salem (p. 237)	+ 27 minutes
Clock time, Salem	12:15 P.M. PST

Longitude of city	Correction minutes
58°–76°	0
77°–89°	+1
90°–102°	+2
103°–115°	+3
116°–127°	+4
128°–141°	+5
142°–155°	+6

EXAMPLE:

■ To determine the time of moonrise in Lansing, Michigan:

Moonrise, Boston, with Key Letter B (p. 106)	5:39 P.M. EST
Value of Key Letter B for Lansing (p. 236)	+ 53 minutes
Correction for Lansing longitude, 84°33'	+ 1 minute
Moonrise, Lansing	6:33 P.M. EST

Use the same procedure to determine the time of moonset.

4 This column gives the degrees and minutes of the Sun from the celestial equator at noon EST or EDT.

5 This column gives the approximate times of high tides in Boston. For example, the first high tide occurs at 11:00 A.M. and the second occurs at 11:45 P.M. the same day. (A dash indicates that high tide occurs on or after midnight and is recorded on the next day.) Figures for calculating high tide times and heights for localities other than Boston are given in the **Tide Corrections** table on **page 239**.

6 To calculate the moonrise/moonset times for localities other than Boston, follow the example in the next column, making a correction for longitude (see table, above right). For the longitude of your city, **see page 234**. (Note: A dash in the moonrise/moonset columns indicates that rise or set times occur on or after midnight and are recorded on the next day.)

7 The Moon's Place is its *astronomical* placement in the heavens at midnight. (This should not be confused with the Moon's *astrological* place in the zodiac. All calculations in this Almanac are based on astronomy, not astrology, except for those on **pages 229–231**.)

In addition to the 12 constellations of the zodiac, this column may indicate others: Auriga **(AUR)**, a northern constellation between Perseus and Gemini; Cetus **(CET)**, which lies south of the zodiac, just south of Pisces and Aries; Ophiuchus **(OPH)**, a constellation primarily north of the zodiac but with a small corner between Scorpius and Sagittarius; Orion **(ORI)**, a constellation whose northern limit first reaches the zodiac between Taurus and Gemini; and Sextans **(SEX)**, which lies south of the zodiac except for a corner that just touches it near Leo.

8 The last column gives the Moon's Age, which is the number of days since the previous new Moon. (The average length of the lunar month is 29.53 days.) **(continued)**

−Beth Krommes

Purchase the Left-Hand Calendar pages with times set to your zip code at **MyLocalAlmanac.com.**

The Right-Hand Calendar Pages • 111–137

A SAMPLE MONTH

- Weather prediction rhyme.
- Civil holidays and astronomical events.
- Sundays and special holy days.
- The bold letter is the Dominical Letter (from A to G), a traditional ecclesiastical designation for Sunday determined by the date on which the first Sunday falls. For 2010, the Dominical Letter is **C**.
- Symbols for notable celestial events. (See opposite page for explanations.)
- Proverbs, poems, and adages.
- High tide heights, in feet, at Boston.
- Noteworthy historical events, folklore, and legends.
- Religious feasts. A[T] indicates a major feast that the church has this year temporarily transferred to a date other than its usual one. This is to avoid conflict with Sundays, Holy Week, Easter Week, and other observances that take precedence.

Day of Month	Day of Week	Dates, Feasts, Fasts, Aspects, Tide Heights	Weather
1	Th.	Maundy Thursday • All Fools' • Satellite *Tiros I* launched, 1960 • {11.7 / 10.7	*Snow*
2	Fr.	Good Friday • 7.9 earthquake triggered tsunami, Hawaii, 1868 • Tides {11.4 / 10.2	*and*
3	Sa.	First national issue of *TV Guide*, 1953 • Tides {10.9 / 9.6	*showers*
4	**C**	Easter • ☾ RUNS LOW • *If the sun shines on Easter Day, it shines on Whitsunday likewise.*	*bring*
5	M.	Easter Monday • ☌♇☾ • Golfer Elsie McLean made hole-in-one, 2007	*glowers,*
6	Tu.	☾ AT ☊ • ♇ STAT. • Jimmy Dewar invented Twinkies, 1930 • {9.3 / 8.2	*not*
7	W.	John Wayne won Oscar for *True Grit*, 1970 • {8.9 / 8.2	*flowers.*
8	Th.	☾ AT APO. • ☿ GR. ELONG. (19° EAST) • First Lady Betty Ford born, 1918 • {8.8 / 8.3	*Bright*
9	Fr.	☌♆☾ • Jumbo the elephant arrived in U.S., 1882 • Tides {8.9 / 8.6	*but*
10	Sa.	*A promise is a cloud; fulfillment is rain.* • {9.0 / 9.0	*bracing:*
11	**C**	2nd S. of Easter • ☾ ON EQ. • ☌♃☾ • {9.2 / 9.4	*too*
12	M.	☌♅☾ • First U.S. championship billiards game, 1859 • Tides {9.4 / 9.7	*cool*
13	Tu.	Thomas Jefferson born, 1743 • Conservationist Archie "Grey Owl" Belaney died, 1938 • {9.5 / 10.1	*for*
14	W.	New ● • Judge ruled "aspirin" is generic trademark in U.S., 1921 • {9.6 / —	*the pool,*
15	Th.	☌☿☾ • First state entomologist position approved, N.Y., 1854 • {10.3 / 9.6	*just*
16	Fr.	☌♀☾ • Three tornadoes struck Nashville, Tenn., 1998	*right*
17	Sa.	Order of Canada, to honor outstanding contributions to society and country, instituted, 1967 • {10.6 / 9.4	*for*
18	**C**	3rd S. of Easter • ☾ RIDES HIGH • ☿ STAT.	*marathon*
19	M.	*When prosperity smiles, beware of its guiles.* • {10.5 / 9.1	*racing!*
20	Tu.	☾ AT ☋ • Preakness and Kentucky Derby winner Funny Cide born, 2000 • Tides {10.4 / 9.1	*Rain*
21	W.	Astronomer Peter Apianus died, 1552 • Tides {10.2 / 9.1	*fallin',*
22	Th.	☌♂☾ • Albert Einstein Memorial unveiled, Wash., D.C., 1979 • {10.1 / 9.4	*temperature*
23	Fr.	St. George • *Ranger 4* spacecraft launched, 1962 • Tides {10.1 / 9.8	*risin'—*
24	Sa.	☾ ON EQ. • ☾ AT PERIG. • Robert B. Thomas born, 1766 • {10.2 / 10.3	*could*
25	**C**	4th S. of Easter • ☌♄☾ • Tides {10.4 / 10.8	*that*
26	M.	St. Mark[T] • William Shakespeare baptized, 1564 • {10.5 / 11.3	*be*

☞ **For explanations of Almanac terms, see the glossaries on pages 96, 138, and 241.**

Predicting Earthquakes

■ Note the dates in the **Right-Hand Calendar Pages** when the Moon rides high or runs low. The date of the high begins the most likely five-day period of earthquakes in the Northern Hemisphere; the date of the low indicates a similar five-day period in the Southern Hemisphere. Also noted are the two days each month when the Moon is on the celestial equator, indicating the most likely time for earthquakes in either hemisphere.

–Beth Krommes

■ Throughout the **Right-Hand Calendar Pages** are groups of symbols that represent notable celestial events. The symbols and names of the principal planets and aspects are:

⊙	Sun	♆	Neptune
○ ● ☾	Moon	♇	Pluto
☿	Mercury	☌	Conjunction (on the
♀	Venus		same celestial
⊕	Earth		longitude)
♂	Mars	☊	Ascending node
♃	Jupiter	☋	Descending node
♄	Saturn	☍	Opposition (180 de-
♅	Uranus		grees from Sun)

EXAMPLE:

☌♇☾ on the 5th day of the month (see opposite page) means that on that date a conjunction (☌) of Pluto (♇) and the Moon (☾) occurs: They are aligned along the same celestial longitude and appear to be closest together in the sky.

EARTH AT PERIHELION AND APHELION

■ Perihelion: January 2, 2010. Earth will be 91,402,516 miles from the Sun. Aphelion: July 6, 2010. Earth will be 94,508,356 miles from the Sun.

2010 Calendar Highlights

MOVABLE RELIGIOUS OBSERVANCES

Septuagesima Sunday	**January 31**
Shrove Tuesday	**February 16**
Ash Wednesday	**February 17**
Palm Sunday	**March 28**
First day of Passover	**March 30**
Good Friday	**April 2**
Easter	**April 4**
Orthodox Easter	**April 4**
Rogation Sunday	**May 9**
Ascension Day	**May 13**
Whitsunday–Pentecost	**May 23**
Trinity Sunday	**May 30**
Corpus Christi	**June 6**
First day of Ramadan	**August 11**
Rosh Hashanah	**September 9**
Yom Kippur	**September 18**
First Sunday of Advent	**November 28**
First day of Chanukah	**December 2**

CHRONOLOGICAL CYCLES

Dominical Letter	**C**
Epact	**14**
Golden Number (Lunar Cycle)	**16**
Roman Indiction	**3**
Solar Cycle	**3**
Year of Julian Period	**6723**

–Beth Krommes

ERAS

Era	Year	Begins
Byzantine	**7519**	September 14
Jewish (A.M.)*	**5771**	September 9
Chinese (Lunar) [Year of the Tiger]	**4708**	February 14
Roman (A.U.C.)	**2763**	January 14
Nabonassar	**2759**	April 21
Japanese	**2670**	January 1
Grecian (Seleucidae)	**2322**	September 14 (or October 14)
Indian (Saka)	**1932**	March 22
Diocletian	**1727**	September 11
Islamic (Hegira)*	**1432**	December 8

Year begins at sunset the evening before.

NOVEMBER

THE ELEVENTH MONTH • 2009

SKY WATCH ☆ *On the 1st, Mars, now bright at magnitude 0.4 within the Beehive star cluster, rises at around 11:00 P.M. in Cancer. The Moon joins Mars on the 8th and Jupiter on the 23rd. On the 30th, Mars finally cracks magnitude zero, joining the ranks of the top-five brightest sky objects. Meanwhile, Jupiter, in the opposite part of the sky, is highest at nightfall and sets by 10:00 P.M. at month's end. In the predawn east, Venus is now very low and has faded to magnitude –3.9. Its show is over until it returns as a conspicuous evening star next April. Saturn is back and nicely high for early risers, ensconced in Virgo, its new home for the next 3 years.*

○ **Full Moon**	2nd day	14th hour	14th minute
◑ **Last Quarter**	9th day	10th hour	56th minute
● **New Moon**	16th day	14th hour	14th minute
◐ **First Quarter**	24th day	16th hour	39th minute

After 2:00 A.M. on November 1, Eastern Standard Time is given.

Purchase these pages with times set to your zip code at MyLocalAlmanac.com.

Day of Year	Day of Month	Day of Week	☼ Rises h. m.	Rise Key	☼ Sets h. m.	Set Key	Length of Day h. m.	Sun Fast m.	Declination of Sun ° '	High Tide Times Boston		☾ Rises h. m.	Rise Key	☾ Sets h. m.	Set Key	☾ Place	☾ Age
305	1	**D**	6:17	D	**4:37**	B	10 20	32	14 s.37	9½	**10**	**3:37**	B	5:02	E	PSC	14
306	2	M.	6:19	D	**4:36**	B	10 17	32	14 56	10¼	**10¾**	**4:09**	B	6:13	E	ARI	15
307	3	Tu.	6:20	D	**4:34**	B	10 14	32	15 15	11	**11½**	**4:48**	B	7:25	E	ARI	16
308	4	W.	6:21	D	**4:33**	B	10 12	32	15 33	11¾	—	**5:38**	B	8:37	E	TAU	17
309	5	Th.	6:22	D	**4:32**	B	10 10	32	15 51	12¼	**12½**	**6:38**	B	9:43	E	TAU	18
310	6	Fr.	6:23	E	**4:31**	B	10 08	32	16 09	1¼	**1¼**	**7:47**	B	10:40	E	TAU	19
311	7	Sa.	6:25	E	**4:30**	B	10 05	32	16 27	2	**2¼**	**9:01**	B	11:27	E	GEM	20
312	8	**D**	6:26	E	**4:29**	B	10 03	32	16 44	3	**3¼**	**10:17**	C	**12:06**	E	GEM	21
313	9	M.	6:27	E	**4:27**	B	10 00	32	17 02	4	**4¼**	**11:31**	C	**12:37**	E	CAN	22
314	10	Tu.	6:28	E	**4:26**	B	9 58	32	17 18	5	**5¼**	—	–	**1:04**	D	LEO	23
315	11	W.	6:30	E	**4:25**	B	9 55	32	17 35	6	**6½**	12:44	D	**1:29**	D	SEX	24
316	12	Th.	6:31	E	**4:24**	B	9 53	32	17 51	7	**7½**	1:55	D	**1:54**	C	LEO	25
317	13	Fr.	6:32	E	**4:23**	B	9 51	31	18 07	8	**8½**	3:06	E	**2:19**	C	VIR	26
318	14	Sa.	6:33	E	**4:23**	B	9 50	31	18 23	8¾	**9¼**	4:17	E	**2:46**	B	VIR	27
319	15	**D**	6:35	E	**4:22**	B	9 47	31	18 38	9½	**10¼**	5:27	E	**3:18**	B	VIR	28
320	16	M.	6:36	E	**4:21**	B	9 45	31	18 53	10¼	**11**	6:36	E	**3:55**	B	LIB	0
321	17	Tu.	6:37	E	**4:20**	B	9 43	31	19 07	11	**11¾**	7:41	E	**4:38**	A	SCO	1
322	18	W.	6:38	E	**4:19**	B	9 41	30	19 22	11¾	—	8:40	E	**5:29**	A	SCO	2
323	19	Th.	6:40	E	**4:18**	B	9 38	30	19 36	12½	**12½**	9:31	E	**6:25**	B	OPH	3
324	20	Fr.	6:41	E	**4:18**	B	9 37	30	19 49	1	**1¼**	10:13	E	**7:25**	B	SAG	4
325	21	Sa.	6:42	E	**4:17**	B	9 35	30	20 02	1¾	**2**	10:48	E	**8:27**	B	SAG	5
326	22	**D**	6:43	E	**4:16**	B	9 33	29	20 15	2½	**2¾**	11:18	E	**9:29**	C	CAP	6
327	23	M.	6:44	E	**4:16**	B	9 32	29	20 28	3½	**3½**	11:43	E	**10:30**	C	CAP	7
328	24	Tu.	6:46	E	**4:15**	A	9 29	29	20 40	4¼	**4½**	**12:05**	D	**11:31**	D	CAP	8
329	25	W.	6:47	E	**4:15**	A	9 28	29	20 51	5	**5¼**	**12:27**	D	—	–	AQU	9
330	26	Th.	6:48	E	**4:14**	A	9 26	28	21 03	5¾	**6¼**	**12:48**	C	12:33	D	PSC	10
331	27	Fr.	6:49	E	**4:14**	A	9 25	28	21 14	6¾	**7**	**1:10**	C	1:36	E	PSC	11
332	28	Sa.	6:50	E	**4:13**	A	9 23	28	21 24	7½	**8**	**1:35**	B	2:41	E	PSC	12
333	29	**D**	6:51	E	**4:13**	A	9 22	27	21 34	8¼	**8¾**	**2:04**	B	3:50	E	PSC	13
334	30	M.	6:52	E	**4:12**	A	9 20	27	21 s.44	9	**9½**	**2:40**	B	5:02	E	ARI	14

 To use this page, see p. 106; for Key Letters, see p. 234. ☞ **Bold = P.M.** ☞ Light = A.M.

NOVEMBER HATH 30 DAYS • 2009

It's autumn, autumn, autumn late,
'Twill soon be winter now. –William Allingham

Day of Month	Day of Week	Dates, Feasts, Fasts, Aspects, Tide Heights	Weather
1	D	All Saints' • Daylight Saving Time ends, 2:00 A.M. • Tides {10.3 / 9.6	*First*
2	M.	All Souls' • Full Beaver ○ • Frontiersman Daniel Boone born, 1734 • Tides {10.7 / 9.7	*it's*
3	Tu.	Election Day • Dog launched into space on U.S.S.R.'s *Sputnik II*, 1957 • {11.0 / 9.8	*glowing,*
4	W.	♆ stat. • Sergei Rachmaninoff's first piano recital in U.S., Smith College, Northampton, Mass., 1909	*then*
5	Th.	☾ rides high • ☿ in sup. ☌ • Edwin Armstrong first demonstrated FM radio transmission, 1935	*it's*
6	Fr.	NPR announced largest donation in its history, about $200 million, 2003 • Tides {9.6 / 11.2	*snowing!*
7	Sa.	Sadie Hawkins Day • ☾ at ☋ • ☾ at perig. • Boxer Gene Tunney died, 1978	*A*
8	D	23rd S. af. P. • Black bears head to winter dens now. • {9.4 / 10.6	*pause,*
9	M.	☌♂☾ • Architect Stanford White born, 1853 • Astronomer Carl Sagan born, 1934 • {9.3 / 10.3	*then*
10	Tu.	*November take flail / Let ships no more sail.*	*screaming*
11	W.	St. Martin of Tours • Veterans Day • ☾ on Eq. • {9.7 / 9.9	*squalls*
12	Th.	Indian Summer • ☌♄☾ • Lobsters move to offshore waters.	*and*
13	Fr.	"U.S." Gen. Montgomery captured Montreal, 1775	*williwaws.*
14	Sa.	First cabooseless Canadian Pacific train left Winnipeg, bound for Thunder Bay, 1989 • {10.8 / 9.8	*Bright*
15	D	24th S. af. P. • Crab apples are ripe now. • {11.0 / 9.8	*but*
16	M.	New ● • *Skylab 4* launched from Kennedy Space Center, 1973 • Tides {11.0 / 9.7	*bitter,*
17	Tu.	St. Hugh of Lincoln • U.S. Congress met for first time in the Capitol, Washington, D.C., 1800	*then*
18	W.	☾ runs low • *Don't turn up your trousers before you get to the brook.*	*a*
19	Th.	☌♇☾ • John Carpenter first to win $1 million on TV's *Who Wants to Be a Millionaire,* 1999	*thaw.*
20	Fr.	Skunks hibernate now. • Final ride of Pony Express completed, 1861 • {9.0 / 10.1	*Yet*
21	Sa.	☾ at ☊ • Jonathan Jay Pollard arrested for spying, 1985 • Tides {8.8 / 9.8	*again*
22	D	25th S. af. P. • ☾ at apo. • Tides {8.6 / 9.4	*it's*
23	M.	St. Clement • ☌♃☾ • First jukebox installed, San Francisco, 1889 • {8.5 / 9.1	*cold*
24	Tu.	☌♆☾ • Charles Darwin's controversial *Origin of Species* published, 1859 • Tides {8.4 / 8.8	*and*
25	W.	*What's sauce for the goose is sauce for the gander.*	*storming:*
26	Th.	Thanksgiving Day • ☾ on Eq. • ☌♅☾ • Blizzard, N.Dak., 1896	*What ever*
27	Fr.	Spectacular Andromedid meteor storm, 13,000 per hour, 1885 • Tides {9.1 / 8.7	*happened*
28	Sa.	John Lennon's last public performance, N.Y.C., 1974 • {9.5 / 8.8	*to*
29	D	1st S. of Advent • *When friends meet, hearts warm.*	*global*
30	M.	St. Andrew • Celtics' Larry Bird scored his 20,000th point, 1990 • {10.5 / 9.3	*warming?*

The sky is the daily bread of the eyes. –Ralph Waldo Emerson

Farmer's Calendar

■ Indian summer, formerly an anomalous few days of improbably warm, sunny weather fitted in between late autumn and the onset of winter, seems recently to be making a bid for full seasonhood. Often, of recent years, the leaves of the hardwoods turn color, their colors glow, then fade—but the leaves don't fall, or not all of them. Instead, a rear guard of turned leaves decks the woods and roadsides, not with the bright scarlets and lemons of October, but with muted browns and tans. This subdued show of post-autumn color, moreover, lingers for days, then weeks, with mild, sunlit afternoons that can stretch well into December.

On such a day last year, the dogs and I took a walk along the forest road near our place. The sun coming into the fox-colored woods made an amber light. The woods were full of stirrings as squirrels scurried among the fallen leaves. The dogs did the same. They're little, short-legged things, and as they plowed belly-deep through the down leaves beside the road, they might have been swimming in a brown, rustling river of dry foliage. "This is November?" they asked.

Nobody is fooled, however. Indian summer may be bucking for promotion, but in the army of the seasons, promotion is slow. These soft days are borrowed from the winter, and the winter will want its payment, with interest, soon enough.

SKY WATCH ☆ *Mars, in Leo, rises at around 9:30 P.M. on the 1st, just as Jupiter sinks into the west; they remain on exact opposite sides of the sky. Ideal moonless conditions make the Geminids the year's best meteor shower on the 13th. Look in any direction and expect one per minute. Mercury has a low, so-so, evening apparition from the 14th to the 26th and is to the upper left of the crescent Moon on the 17th. The Moon passes through the Pleiades star cluster on the 28th; use binoculars. The 31st brings a second full Moon this month—a so-called "blue Moon"—to adorn the final night of the year. The solstice arrives with winter on the 21st at 12:47 P.M.*

○	Full Moon	2nd day	2nd hour	30th minute
◑	Last Quarter	8th day	19th hour	13th minute
●	New Moon	16th day	7th hour	2nd minute
◐	First Quarter	24th day	12th hour	36th minute
○	Full Moon	31st day	14th hour	13th minute

All times are given in Eastern Standard Time.

Purchase these pages with times set to your zip code at MyLocalAlmanac.com.

Day of Year	Day of Month	Day of Week	☼ Rises h. m.	Rise Key	☼ Sets h. m.	Set Key	Length of Day h. m.	Sun Fast m.	Declination of Sun ° ′	High Tide Times Boston		☾ Rises h. m.	Rise Key	☾ Sets h. m.	Set Key	Place	☾ Age
335	1	Tu.	6:53	E	4:12	A	9 19	27	21 s.53	9¾	10½	3:26	B	6:15	E	ARI	15
336	2	W.	6:54	E	4:12	A	9 18	26	22 02	10½	11¼	4:22	B	7:26	E	TAU	16
337	3	Th.	6:55	E	4:12	A	9 17	26	22 11	11¼	—	5:30	B	8:29	E	TAU	17
338	4	Fr.	6:56	E	4:11	A	9 15	25	22 19	12	12¼	6:46	B	9:22	E	GEM	18
339	5	Sa.	6:57	E	4:11	A	9 14	25	22 26	1	1	8:04	C	10:04	E	GEM	19
340	6	D	6:58	E	4:11	A	9 13	25	22 33	1¾	2	9:21	C	10:39	E	CAN	20
341	7	M.	6:59	E	4:11	A	9 12	24	22 40	2¾	3	10:35	D	11:08	D	LEO	21
342	8	Tu.	7:00	E	4:11	A	9 11	24	22 46	3¾	4	11:47	D	11:34	D	SEX	22
343	9	W.	7:01	E	4:11	A	9 10	23	22 52	4½	5	—	—	11:58	C	LEO	23
344	10	Th.	7:02	E	4:11	A	9 09	23	22 57	5½	6	12:58	E	12:23	C	VIR	24
345	11	Fr.	7:03	E	4:11	A	9 08	22	23 02	6½	7¼	2:07	E	12:49	B	VIR	25
346	12	Sa.	7:04	E	4:11	A	9 07	22	23 07	7½	8¼	3:17	E	1:18	B	VIR	26
347	13	D	7:05	E	4:12	A	9 07	21	23 11	8½	9	4:25	E	1:53	A	LIB	27
348	14	M.	7:05	E	4:12	A	9 07	21	23 14	9¼	10	5:30	E	2:33	A	LIB	28
349	15	Tu.	7:06	E	4:12	A	9 06	20	23 17	10	10¾	6:31	E	3:21	A	SCO	29
350	16	W.	7:07	E	4:12	A	9 05	20	23 20	10¾	11½	7:24	E	4:15	A	OPH	0
351	17	Th.	7:07	E	4:13	A	9 06	19	23 22	11½	—	8:10	E	5:14	B	SAG	1
352	18	Fr.	7:08	E	4:13	A	9 05	19	23 24	12	12	8:47	E	6:16	B	SAG	2
353	19	Sa.	7:09	E	4:13	A	9 04	18	23 25	12¾	12¾	9:19	E	7:18	C	SAG	3
354	20	D	7:09	E	4:14	A	9 05	18	23 26	1½	1½	9:45	E	8:19	C	CAP	4
355	21	M.	7:10	E	4:14	A	9 04	17	23 26	2	2¼	10:08	D	9:20	C	CAP	5
356	22	Tu.	7:10	E	4:15	A	9 05	17	23 26	2¾	3	10:30	D	10:20	D	AQU	6
357	23	W.	7:11	E	4:15	A	9 04	17	23 25	3½	3¾	10:50	D	11:21	D	PSC	7
358	24	Th.	7:11	E	4:16	A	9 05	16	23 24	4¼	4½	11:11	C	—	—	PSC	8
359	25	Fr.	7:11	E	4:17	A	9 06	16	23 22	5	5½	11:34	B	12:24	E	PSC	9
360	26	Sa.	7:12	E	4:17	A	9 05	15	23 20	5¾	6¼	12:00	B	1:30	E	PSC	10
361	27	D	7:12	E	4:18	A	9 06	15	23 17	6¾	7¼	12:32	B	2:38	E	ARI	11
362	28	M.	7:12	E	4:19	A	9 07	14	23 14	7½	8¼	1:12	B	3:50	E	ARI	12
363	29	Tu.	7:13	E	4:19	A	9 06	14	23 11	8½	9	2:02	B	5:01	E	TAU	13
364	30	W.	7:13	E	4:20	A	9 07	13	23 07	9¼	10	3:05	B	6:08	E	TAU	14
365	31	Th.	7:13	E	4:21	A	9 08	13	23 s.03	10¼	11	4:19	B	7:07	E	GEM	15

DECEMBER

DECEMBER HATH 31 DAYS • 2009

The frost is here,
And fuel is dear. –Alfred, Lord Tennyson

Day of Month	Day of Week	Dates, Feasts, Fasts, Aspects, Tide Heights	Weather
1	Tu.	Winnie, real bear after whom Christopher Robin Milne named Pooh, donated to London Zoo, 1919	*Shoppers*
2	W.	**St. Viviana** • **Full Cold** ○ • ☾ rides high • ♅ stat. • { 11.3 / 9.7	*scurry*
3	Th.	Annette Toft was two millionth immigrant to Canada since WWII ended, 1960 • { 11.6 / —	*through*
4	Fr.	☾ at ☋ • ☾ at perig. • Crew of shipwrecked tanker *Kyzikes* rescued, Kill Devil Hills, N.C., 1927	*snow*
5	Sa.	*Well to work and make a fire; It does care and skill require.* • Tides { 9.9 / 11.5	*flurries:*
6	**D**	**2nd S. of Advent** • **St. Nicholas** • ☌♂☾ • { 9.9 / 11.2	*Time*
7	M.	**St. Ambrose** • **Nat'l Pearl Harbor Remembrance Day** • ☌☿♇ • Tides { 9.9 / 10.8	*is*
8	Tu.	☾ on Eq. • Winterberry fruits especially showy now.	*fleeting!*
9	W.	Actress Dame Judi Dench born, 1934 • Tides { 10.0 / 9.8	*Watch*
10	Th.	**St. Eulalia** • ☌♄☾ • Duke Ellington recorded "Mood Indigo," 1930 • { 10.0 / 9.4	*for*
11	Fr.	First public demonstration in U.S. of colored moving pictures, N.Y.C., 1909 • Tides { 10.2 / 9.2	*sleeting,*
12	Sa.	**Our Lady of Guadalupe** • **First day of Chanukah** • { 10.3 / 9.1	*even*
13	**D**	**3rd S. of Advent** • **St. Lucia** • Tides { 10.4 / 9.0	*rime.*
14	M.	Halcyon Days • Scotchguard carpet treatment patented, 1973 • Tides { 10.5 / 9.0	*Snow*
15	Tu.	☾ runs low • *Venera 7* landed on Venus, 1970 • Tides { 10.5 / 9.0	*turns*
16	W.	Ember Day • **New** ● • 7.1 earthquake, Fairview Peak, Nev., 1954 • { 10.5 / 9.0	*rainy,*
17	Th.	Beware the Pogonip. • *One can not help many, but many can help one.* • { 10.4 / —	*then*
18	Fr.	Ember Day • **Islamic New Year** • ☾ at ☊ • ☿ Gr. Elong. (20° East)	*sunshine!*
19	Sa.	Ember Day • Walter Williams, last known Civil War vet, died, 1959 • { 8.9 / 10.1	*Christmas*
20	**D**	**4th S. of Advent** • ☾ at apo. • ☌♃♆ • { 8.8 / 9.8	*will*
21	M.	**St. Thomas** • **Winter Solstice** • ☌♃☾ • ☌♆☾ • ♂ stat. • { 8.8 / 9.5	*be*
22	Tu.	*No matter how long the winter, spring is sure to follow.*	*white,*
23	W.	☾ on Eq. • ☌♅☾ • Jeanne Sauvé appointed governor-general of Canada, 1983 • { 8.8 / 8.9	*we*
24	Th.	☌♇☉ • Reginald Fessenden transmitted the first radio broadcast, from Brant Rock, Mass., 1906	*ken;*
25	Fr.	**Christmas** • *As many mince pies as you taste at Christmas, so many happy months will you have.*	*sing*
26	Sa.	**St. Stephen** • **Boxing Day (Canada)** • **First day of Kwanzaa** • ☿ stat. • { 9.2 / 8.3	*of*
27	**D**	**1st S. af. Ch.** • ☌♇♀ • Chemist Louis Pasteur born, 1822 • { 9.6 / 8.4	*silent*
28	M.	**Holy Innocents** • John Calhoun became first U.S. vice president to resign, 1832 • { 10.0 / 8.6	*nights*
29	Tu.	**St. John**[T] • American Meteorological Society founded, 1919 • Tides { 10.5 / 9.0	*and*
30	W.	☾ rides high • *He who would know what shall be, must consider what has been.* • Tides { 11.0 / 9.4	*then:*
31	Th.	**St. Sylvester** • **Full Long Nights** ○ • **Eclipse** ☾ • { 11.5 / 9.9	*2010!*

Farmer's Calendar

■ Painfully bending my back to shovel the first real snow of the winter, I reflect that the affliction of the aging spine comes not in the bending over, but in the straightening up again; and I recall that this was the year in which I had determined at last to buy a snowblower.

For years I have resisted the step. Another machine, I have thought, another engine, another iron helper requiring thoughtful purchase, intelligent care, frequent repair, and, soon enough, costly replacement. Need I add this one more to the automobiles, mowers, chainsaws, and string trimmers that currently serve, and are served by, me? I have resolved against it, but as the years advance, resolve softens.

Handy outfit, the snowblower. Invented in 1925 by a man in Quebec, it uses a pumplike system of impellers to break up the snow and force it through its stack and out of its path. You don't lift or heave, you don't bend—you don't unbend. You merely saunter along behind the machine and watch the snow fly harmlessly, conveniently, into another jurisdiction.

Well, maybe snowblowing isn't always quite that easy, but these rigs must have something going for them. In my town, following a storm, the village resembles a calm sea on which frolic a pod of whales, playfully spouting their jets of white spray high into the air on every hand.

SKY WATCH ☆ *The new year opens like a Dickens novel: It's the best of times for Mars and the worst for Venus, which hides behind the Sun, crossing from the morning to the evening sky on the 11th. Mars makes its closest approach this year on the 27th and is exactly opposite the Sun two nights later. Highest at midnight at magnitude –1.2, orange Mars outshines every star except blue Sirius. It's a transition time: Mars starts the month in Leo but retrogrades into Cancer. Brilliant Jupiter, low in the southwest at nightfall, starts in Capricornus but crosses into Aquarius. Uranus, in Aquarius, ambles into Pisces. Earth comes closest to the Sun on the 2nd. The year's nearest Moon—a full Moon, to boot—is on the 30th.*

◖ Last Quarter	7th day	5th hour	39th minute
● New Moon	15th day	2nd hour	11th minute
◐ First Quarter	23rd day	5th hour	53rd minute
○ Full Moon	30th day	1st hour	18th minute

All times are given in Eastern Standard Time.

Purchase these pages with times set to your zip code at MyLocalAlmanac.com.

Day of Year	Day of Month	Day of Week	☼ Rises h. m.	Rise Key	☼ Sets h. m.	Set Key	Length of Day h. m.	Sun Fast m.	Declination of Sun ° '	High Tide Times Boston		☾ Rises h. m.	Rise Key	☾ Sets h. m.	Set Key	☾ Place	☾ Age
1	1	Fr.	7:13	E	4:22	A	9 09	12	22 s.58	11	11¾	5:39	B	7:56	E	GEM	16
2	2	Sa.	7:13	E	4:23	A	9 10	12	22 52	12	—	6:59	C	8:35	E	CAN	17
3	3	C	7:13	E	4:24	A	9 11	11	22 46	12½	12¾	8:18	D	9:08	E	CAN	18
4	4	M.	7:13	E	4:25	A	9 12	11	22 40	1½	1¾	9:34	D	9:36	D	LEO	19
5	5	Tu.	7:13	E	4:26	A	9 13	10	22 34	2¼	2½	10:47	E	10:01	C	LEO	20
6	6	W.	7:13	E	4:27	A	9 14	10	22 26	3¼	3½	11:58	E	10:27	C	VIR	21
7	7	Th.	7:13	E	4:28	A	9 15	10	22 19	4¼	4½	—	–	10:53	B	VIR	22
8	8	Fr.	7:13	E	4:29	A	9 16	9	22 11	5	5¾	1:08	E	11:21	B	VIR	23
9	9	Sa.	7:12	E	4:30	A	9 18	9	22 02	6	6¾	2:17	E	11:54	B	LIB	24
10	10	C	7:12	E	4:31	A	9 19	8	21 53	7	7¾	3:23	E	12:32	A	LIB	25
11	11	M.	7:12	E	4:32	A	9 20	8	21 44	8	8¾	4:25	E	1:17	B	SCO	26
12	12	Tu.	7:11	E	4:33	A	9 22	7	21 34	9	9¾	5:20	E	2:09	B	OPH	27
13	13	W.	7:11	E	4:34	A	9 23	7	21 24	9¾	10½	6:08	E	3:06	B	SAG	28
14	14	Th.	7:11	E	4:35	A	9 24	7	21 14	10½	11	6:48	E	4:06	B	SAG	29
15	15	Fr.	7:10	E	4:36	A	9 26	6	21 03	11	11¾	7:21	E	5:08	B	SAG	0
16	16	Sa.	7:10	E	4:38	A	9 28	6	20 51	11¾	—	7:49	E	6:10	C	CAP	1
17	17	C	7:09	E	4:39	B	9 30	6	20 39	12¼	12½	8:13	E	7:11	C	AQU	2
18	18	M.	7:09	E	4:40	B	9 31	5	20 27	1	1	8:35	D	8:12	D	AQU	3
19	19	Tu.	7:08	E	4:41	B	9 33	5	20 15	1½	1¾	8:55	D	9:12	D	AQU	4
20	20	W.	7:07	E	4:42	B	9 35	5	20 02	2	2¼	9:16	C	10:13	E	PSC	5
21	21	Th.	7:07	E	4:44	B	9 37	5	19 48	2¾	3	9:37	C	11:16	E	PSC	6
22	22	Fr.	7:06	E	4:45	B	9 39	4	19 35	3½	3¾	10:01	B	—	–	PSC	7
23	23	Sa.	7:05	E	4:46	B	9 41	4	19 21	4¼	4¾	10:30	B	12:21	E	ARI	8
24	24	C	7:05	E	4:47	B	9 42	4	19 06	5	5¾	11:04	B	1:29	E	ARI	9
25	25	M.	7:04	E	4:49	B	9 47	4	18 51	6	6¾	11:47	B	2:39	E	TAU	10
26	26	Tu.	7:03	E	4:50	B	9 47	3	18 36	7	7¾	12:42	B	3:46	E	TAU	11
27	27	W.	7:02	E	4:51	B	9 49	3	18 21	8	8¾	1:49	B	4:48	E	TAU	12
28	28	Th.	7:01	E	4:53	B	9 52	3	18 05	9	9¾	3:05	C	5:42	E	GEM	13
29	29	Fr.	7:00	E	4:54	B	9 54	3	17 49	10	10½	4:27	C	6:26	E	GEM	14
30	30	Sa.	6:59	E	4:55	B	9 56	3	17 33	10¾	11½	5:49	C	7:03	E	CAN	15
31	31	C	6:58	E	4:56	B	9 58	2	17 s.16	11¾	—	7:08	D	7:34	D	LEO	16

JANUARY HATH 31 DAYS • 2010

No cloud above, no earth below—
A universe of sky and snow! –John Greenleaf Whittier

Day of Month	Day of Week	Dates, Feasts, Fasts, Aspects, Tide Heights	Weather
1	Fr.	**New Year's Day** • **Holy Name** • ☾ at ☋ • ☾ at perig. • { 11.9 / 10.2	*Rain,*
2	Sa.	⊕ at perihelion • 14°F on the summit of volcano Haleakala, Hawaii, 1961 • { 12.0 / —	*snow,*
3	**C**	☌♂☾ • Moscow State Symphony first Soviet orchestra to play in the U.S. (in N.Y.C.), 1960	*Sun*
4	M.	**St. Elizabeth Ann Seton** • ☿ in inf. ☌ • Tides { 10.7 / 11.5	*emerging;*
5	Tu.	Twelfth Night • ☾ on eq. • ☌☿♀ • Tides { 10.7 / 10.9	*flurries,*
6	W.	**Epiphany** • ☌♄☾ • Poet Carl Sandburg born, 1878 • { 10.6 / 10.3	*and*
7	Th.	Distaff Day • Bank of North America, first commercial bank chartered by Congress, opened, Philadelphia, 1782	*the*
8	Fr.	*How swiftly doth time pass away, When happiness completes the day.* • Tides { 10.2 / 9.0	*cold's*
9	Sa.	28.5" snow, Olympia, Wash., 1880 • Tides { 10.0 / 8.6	*resurging.*
10	**C**	**1st S. af. Ep.** • First UN General Assembly met in London, 1946	*Whitening*
11	M.	Plough Monday • ♀ in sup. ☌ • National Ballet of Canada founder, Celia Franca, retired, 1974	*then*
12	Tu.	☾ runs low • Hattie Caraway first woman elected to U.S. Senate, 1932 • { 9.9 / 8.5	*brightening,*
13	W.	**St. Hilary** • ☌☿☾ • ☌♇☾ • Tides { 10.0 / 8.7	*with*
14	Th.	☾ at ☊ • ♄ stat. • General Benedict Arnold born, 1741 • { 10.1 / 8.8	*welcome*
15	Fr.	**New ● • Eclipse ☉** • ☌♀☾ • ☿ stat. • { 10.1 / 8.9	*warming:*
16	Sa.	☾ at apo. • *The opportunity of a lifetime is seldom so labeled.* • { 10.1 / —	*Storming!*
17	**C**	**2nd S. af. Ep.** • ☌♆☾ • Benjamin Franklin born, 1706	*Drifts*
18	M.	**Martin Luther King Jr.'s Birthday (observed)** • ☌♃☾ • Tides { 9.1 / 9.8	*forming!*
19	Tu.	☾ on eq. • Explorer Charles Wilkes claimed discovery of Antarctica, 1840 • Tides { 9.2 / 9.5	*Cold*
20	W.	☌♅☾ • National Hockey League season began after 103-day lockout, 1995 • Tides { 9.2 / 9.2	*and*
21	Th.	First American novel, *The Power of Sympathy*, published, 1789 • Tides { 9.2 / 8.9	*likely*
22	Fr.	**St. Vincent** • *St. Vincent opens the seed.* • Tides { 9.2 / 8.5	*to*
23	Sa.	Calif. vintner Agoston Haraszthy received 100,000 European grape vine cuttings, 1862	*continue; it's*
24	**C**	**3rd S. af. Ep.** • Gold! Sutter's Mill, Calif., 1848 • { 9.4 / 8.2	*comfortable*
25	M.	**Conversion of Paul** • Hot drinks served on frozen Hudson River between N.J. and N.Y.C., 1821 • { 9.6 / 8.2	*for*
26	Tu.	**Sts. Timothy & Titus** • ☾ rides high • Tides { 10.0 / 8.5	*Inuits.*
27	W.	☿ gr. elong. (25° west) • ♂ at closest approach • Tides { 10.5 / 9.0	*More*
28	Th.	**St. Thomas Aquinas** • ☾ at ☋ • Tides { 11.1 / 9.6	*pelting,*
29	Fr.	♂ at ☍ • Charles Steinmetz patented a "system of distribution by alternating currents," 1895	*then*
30	Sa.	**Full Wolf ○** • ☾ at perig. • ☌♂☾ • Raccoons mate now. • { 11.9 / 10.7	*some*
31	**C**	**Septuagesima** • *Apollo 14* launched, 1971	*melting.*

Farmer's Calendar

■ When the modern, rational systems on which we rely fail us, we are quick to fall back on systems that are the opposite of modern, the opposite of rational. For example, every winter at my house, the electricity is knocked out once or twice, sometimes for days. When this happens, I find myself reverting to what is essentially magical thinking.

Magical thinking, related to superstition, is the belief that our actions can produce outcomes with which they have no physical, causal connection. When we knock on wood for good luck, we are thinking magically, as we are when in midwinter we bring into our homes evergreen boughs to replicate the restoration of spring.

During a power failure, the outcome we wish to secure is the speedy return of electric service, and since we ordinarily have no way to bring that about in reality, we seek to do it by magic. But there's a difference, at least for me. Most magical thinking is imitative: We act to imitate the result we hope for—as with our holiday greenery. For my part, however, in a power failure, I seem superstitiously to imitate the outcome I don't want: the power's remaining off. I drive 25 miles to buy lamp oil that I won't use when the lights come back on. I bring in a huge load of firewood that I won't burn when the furnace starts up again. Because I want the power to return, I act as if I know it won't.

THE SECOND MONTH • 2010

SKY WATCH ☆ *Jupiter falls into the Sun's glare at dusk and vanishes for the season. It meets slowly emerging Venus at midmonth, but is too close to the Sun for the pair to be readily seen. Mars has a banner month, still brilliant all night long even while it loses half its brightness as Earth pulls away from it. Saturn enters convenient viewing hours, rising by 8:30* P.M. *at midmonth, due east in Virgo. By midnight, the planet is high enough to appear through thinner air, its rings still very much edge-on. The thin crescent Moon is oriented "on its back," like a smile, in the fading dusk from the 14th to the 17th. It meets Mars when almost full, on the 25th.*

◑ **Last Quarter**	5th day	18th hour	48th minute
● **New Moon**	13th day	21st hour	51st minute
◐ **First Quarter**	21st day	19th hour	42nd minute
○ **Full Moon**	28th day	11th hour	38th minute

All times are given in Eastern Standard Time.

Purchase these pages with times set to your zip code at MyLocalAlmanac.com.

Day of Year	Day of Month	Day of Week	☼ Rises h. m.	Rise Key	☼ Sets h. m.	Set Key	Length of Day h.	m.	Sun Fast m.	Declination of Sun °	'	High Tide Times Boston		☾ Rises h. m.	Rise Key	☾ Sets h. m.	Set Key	☾ Place	☾ Age
32	1	M.	6:57	E	**4:58**	B	10	01	2	16 s.	59	12¼	**12½**	**8:26**	E	8:01	D	SEX	17
33	2	Tu.	6:56	E	**4:59**	B	10	03	2	16	42	1	**1½**	**9:41**	E	8:28	C	LEO	18
34	3	W.	6:55	D	**5:00**	B	10	05	2	16	24	2	**2¼**	**10:54**	E	8:54	C	VIR	19
35	4	Th.	6:54	D	**5:02**	B	10	08	2	16	06	2¾	**3¼**	—	—	9:23	B	VIR	20
36	5	Fr.	6:53	D	**5:03**	B	10	10	2	15	48	3¾	**4¼**	12:06	E	9:55	B	VIR	21
37	6	Sa.	6:52	D	**5:04**	B	10	12	2	15	29	4½	**5¼**	1:14	E	10:32	B	LIB	22
38	7	**C**	6:51	D	**5:06**	B	10	15	2	15	11	5½	**6¼**	2:18	E	11:15	B	SCO	23
39	8	M.	6:49	D	**5:07**	B	10	18	2	14	52	6½	**7½**	3:16	E	**12:05**	A	OPH	24
40	9	Tu.	6:48	D	**5:08**	B	10	20	2	14	32	7¾	**8½**	4:06	E	**1:00**	B	SAG	25
41	10	W.	6:47	D	**5:10**	B	10	23	2	14	13	8½	**9¼**	4:48	E	**1:59**	B	SAG	26
42	11	Th.	6:46	D	**5:11**	B	10	25	2	13	53	9½	**10**	5:23	E	**3:01**	B	SAG	27
43	12	Fr.	6:44	D	**5:12**	B	10	28	2	13	33	10	**10¾**	5:52	E	**4:02**	C	CAP	28
44	13	Sa.	6:43	D	**5:13**	B	10	30	2	13	13	10¾	**11¼**	6:18	E	**5:04**	C	CAP	0
45	14	**C**	6:42	D	**5:15**	B	10	33	2	12	53	11½	**11¾**	6:40	D	**6:04**	D	CAP	1
46	15	M.	6:40	D	**5:16**	B	10	36	2	12	32	**12**	—	7:02	D	**7:05**	D	AQU	2
47	16	Tu.	6:39	D	**5:17**	B	10	38	2	12	11	12¼	**12½**	7:22	C	**8:06**	E	PSC	3
48	17	W.	6:37	D	**5:19**	B	10	42	2	11	50	1	**1¼**	7:43	C	**9:08**	E	PSC	4
49	18	Th.	6:36	D	**5:20**	B	10	44	2	11	29	1½	**1¾**	8:06	B	**10:12**	E	PSC	5
50	19	Fr.	6:35	D	**5:21**	B	10	46	2	11	08	2¼	**2½**	8:33	B	**11:18**	E	PSC	6
51	20	Sa.	6:33	D	**5:22**	B	10	49	2	10	46	2¾	**3¼**	9:04	B	—	–	ARI	7
52	21	**C**	6:32	D	**5:24**	B	10	52	2	10	25	3¾	**4¼**	9:43	B	12:25	E	ARI	8
53	22	M.	6:30	D	**5:25**	B	10	55	2	10	03	4½	**5¼**	10:31	B	1:31	E	TAU	9
54	23	Tu.	6:29	D	**5:26**	B	10	57	3	9	41	5½	**6¼**	11:30	B	2:33	E	TAU	10
55	24	W.	6:27	D	**5:27**	B	11	00	3	9	19	6½	**7¼**	**12:39**	B	3:29	E	GEM	11
56	25	Th.	6:25	D	**5:29**	B	11	04	3	8	56	7¾	**8¼**	**1:56**	B	4:16	E	GEM	12
57	26	Fr.	6:24	D	**5:30**	C	11	06	3	8	34	8¾	**9¼**	**3:16**	C	4:55	E	CAN	13
58	27	Sa.	6:22	D	**5:31**	C	11	09	3	8	11	9½	**10¼**	**4:36**	D	5:29	E	CAN	14
59	28	**C**	6:21	D	**5:32**	C	11	11	3	7 s.	49	10½	**11**	**5:55**	D	5:58	D	LEO	15

 To use this page, see p. 106; for Key Letters, see p. 234. ☞ **Bold = P.M.** ☞ Light = A.M.

FEBRUARY HATH 28 DAYS • 2010

'Tis he! 'Tis he!
The chickadee-dee! –Sidney Dayre

Day of Month	Day of Week	Dates, Feasts, Fasts, Aspects, Tide Heights	Weather
1	M.	St. Brigid • ☾ on Eq. • Tides {11.1 / 11.9	*Punxsatawney*
2	Tu.	Candlemas • Groundhog Day • ☌♄☾ • Tides {11.2 / 11.4	*Phil's*
3	W.	Teddy Roosevelt visited his sweetheart, Alice Lee, Chestnut Hill, Mass., 1880 • {11.2 / 10.8	*befuddled;*
4	Th.	Aviator Charles Lindbergh born, 1902 • Tides {10.9 / 10.0	*rain*
5	Fr.	St. Agatha • First "Don't Walk" automatic signs installed in N.Y.C., 1952 • Tides {10.5 / 9.3	*and*
6	Sa.	*It is better to see a troop of wolves than a fine February.*	*snow*
7	C	**Sexagesima** • ☌♀♆ • Basketball player Steve Nash born, 1974	*are*
8	M.	☾ runs low • Boy Scouts of America incorporated, 1910 • Tides {9.4 / 8.1	*mixed and*
9	Tu.	☌♇☾ • Star of Joanne Woodward first on Hollywood Walk of Fame, 1960 • {9.4 / 8.1	*muddled.*
10	W.	☾ at ☊ • Act of Union merged Upper and Lower Canada, 1841 • Tides {9.4 / 8.3	*With*
11	Th.	*It is the belief in roses that makes them flourish.* • {9.6 / 8.6	*your*
12	Fr.	☾ at apo. • ☌☿☾ • Pres. Abraham Lincoln born, 1809 • Tides {9.8 / 8.8	*valentine*
13	Sa.	New ● • –2°F, Tallahassee, Fla., 1899 • Tides {9.9 / 9.1	*be*
14	C	Valentine's Day • Chinese New Year • ☌♀☾ • ☌♆☾	*cuddled,*
15	M.	Pure Monday • George Washington's Birthday (observed) • ☾ on Eq. • ☌♃☾ • {9.9 / —	*by*
16	Tu.	Shrove Tuesday • ☌♀♃ • ☌♅☾ • Winter's back breaks. • {9.5 / 9.8	*a*
17	W.	Ash Wednesday • Chiricahua Apache leader Geronimo died, 1909 • {9.6 / 9.6	*fireplace*
18	Th.	Auguste Bartholdi granted design patent for Statue of Liberty, 1879 • Tides {9.6 / 9.3	*happily*
19	Fr.	*In shallow waters, shrimps make fools of dragons.*	*huddled.*
20	Sa.	Record-breaking 95°F, Los Angeles, Calif., 1995 • {9.6 / 8.7	*Rain*
21	C	**1st S. in Lent** • Sunday of Orthodoxy • Tides {9.6 / 8.4	*on*
22	M.	Pres. George Washington born, 1732 • Tides {9.6 / 8.2	*frozen*
23	Tu.	☾ rides high • *The bitter heart eats its owner.* • Tides {9.7 / 8.3	*ponds*
24	W.	St. Matthias • Ember Day • 4.5 earthquake shook eastern Ontario and western Quebec, 2006	*is*
25	Th.	☾ at ☋ • First true aircraft carrier, USS *Ranger,* launched, 1933 • {10.4 / 9.2	*puddled,*
26	Fr.	Ember Day • ☌♂☾ • Buffalo Creek dam disaster, W.Va., 1972 • Tides {11.0 / 9.9	*ice-*
27	Sa.	Ember Day • ☾ at perig. • ☌☿♆ • Tides {11.4 / 10.6	*boats*
28	C	**2nd S. in Lent** • Full Snow ○ • ☌♃☉	*scuttled.*

Love seems the swiftest, but it is the slowest of all growths. No man or woman really knows what perfect love is until they have been married a quarter of a century. –Mark Twain

Farmer's Calendar

■ Every bird feeder is a stage on which a company of actors performs for the delight of an attentive audience. The show is not an extravaganza, not a parade of marvels. Its pleasures are to be found more in familiarity than in spectacle or surprise. The play is known, so are the players. We're not talking about Las Vegas here, or Broadway, but about a provincial theater, well loved but seldom flashy.

In my district, the theater of the birds is a repertory company, having a permanent cast of seven or eight. These are the chickadee, white-breasted nuthatch, slate-colored junco, tufted titmouse, blue jay, hairy woodpecker, downy woodpecker, and goldfinch. They make up the core members of the company: able, versatile, consistent. What they lack in glamour they more than pay off in reliability.

For the greater entertainment of patrons, our bird feeder also recruits each year an irregular cast of visiting performers who turn up unexpectedly in some seasons: the evening grosbeak, pine siskin, purple finch, and redpoll. These are the marquee names, the high-priced talent that a small house must stretch to afford. They work with the core company to provide that happy union of the familiar and the new that is central to the enjoyment of theater, and which the bird feeder's audience gets for the price of a bag of sunflower seed and six ounces of beef suet.

SKY WATCH ☆ *This is Saturn's month, as the Ringed World makes its closest approach to Earth this year on the night of the 21st. At magnitude 0.5, brighter than all but four of the night's stars, it nonetheless has a relatively dim opposition thanks to its nearly edgewise rings. It's the brightest star in the east, rising at sunset and out all night long. Mars, well up at dusk and still quite bright, again loses half of its light even as it continues to outshine every star except Sirius. Venus returns during the last week of the month, quite low in the western sky after sunset, joined by Mercury just below it. Spring arrives with the vernal equinox on March 20 at 1:32 P.M.*

◐	**Last Quarter**	7th day	10th hour	42nd minute
●	**New Moon**	15th day	17th hour	1st minute
◑	**First Quarter**	23rd day	7th hour	0 minute
○	**Full Moon**	29th day	22nd hour	25th minute

After 2:00 A.M. on March 14, Eastern Daylight Time is given.

Purchase these pages with times set to your zip code at MyLocalAlmanac.com.

Day of Year	Day of Month	Day of Week	☀ Rises h. m.	Rise Key	☀ Sets h. m.	Set Key	Length of Day h. m.	Sun Fast m.	Declination of Sun ° '	High Tide Times Boston		☾ Rises h. m.	Rise Key	☾ Sets h. m.	Set Key	☾ Place	☾ Age
60	1	M.	6:19	D	5:34	C	11 15	4	7 s.26	11½	11¾	7:13	E	6:26	C	LEO	16
61	2	Tu.	6:18	D	5:35	C	11 17	4	7 03	12¼	—	8:30	E	6:53	C	VIR	17
62	3	W.	6:16	D	5:36	C	11 20	4	6 40	12¾	1	9:45	E	7:22	B	VIR	18
63	4	Th.	6:14	D	5:37	C	11 23	4	6 17	1½	2	10:57	E	7:53	B	VIR	19
64	5	Fr.	6:13	D	5:38	C	11 25	4	5 54	2¼	2¾	—	—	8:29	B	LIB	20
65	6	Sa.	6:11	D	5:40	C	11 29	5	5 31	3	3¾	12:05	E	9:11	A	LIB	21
66	7	C	6:09	D	5:41	C	11 32	5	5 07	4	4¾	1:07	E	9:59	A	SCO	22
67	8	M.	6:08	D	5:42	C	11 34	5	4 44	5	5¾	2:01	E	10:54	B	OPH	23
68	9	Tu.	6:06	D	5:43	C	11 37	5	4 20	6	6¾	2:46	E	11:52	B	SAG	24
69	10	W.	6:04	C	5:44	C	11 40	6	3 57	7	7¾	3:24	E	12:53	B	SAG	25
70	11	Th.	6:03	C	5:45	C	11 42	6	3 33	8	8¾	3:55	E	1:54	B	CAP	26
71	12	Fr.	6:01	C	5:47	C	11 46	6	3 10	9	9½	4:22	E	2:55	C	CAP	27
72	13	Sa.	5:59	C	5:48	C	11 49	6	2 46	9¾	10	4:45	D	3:56	C	CAP	28
73	14	C	6:57	C	6:49	C	11 52	7	2 22	11¼	11¾	6:07	D	5:57	D	AQU	29
74	15	M.	6:56	C	6:50	C	11 54	7	1 59	12	—	6:28	C	6:58	D	PSC	0
75	16	Tu.	6:54	C	6:51	C	11 57	7	1 35	12¼	12½	6:49	C	8:00	E	PSC	1
76	17	W.	6:52	C	6:52	C	12 00	8	1 11	12¾	1¼	7:12	C	9:04	E	PSC	2
77	18	Th.	6:51	C	6:54	C	12 03	8	0 47	1½	1¾	7:38	B	10:09	E	PSC	3
78	19	Fr.	6:49	C	6:55	C	12 06	8	0 24	2	2½	8:08	B	11:16	E	ARI	4
79	20	Sa.	6:47	C	6:56	C	12 09	8	0 s.00	2¾	3¼	8:44	B	—	—	ARI	5
80	21	C	6:45	C	6:57	C	12 12	9	0 N.23	3¼	4	9:28	A	12:22	E	TAU	6
81	22	M.	6:44	C	6:58	C	12 14	9	0 46	4¼	4¾	10:22	B	1:25	E	TAU	7
82	23	Tu.	6:42	C	6:59	C	12 17	9	1 10	5	5¾	11:26	B	2:21	E	TAU	8
83	24	W.	6:40	C	7:01	C	12 21	10	1 34	6¼	7	12:37	B	3:10	E	GEM	9
84	25	Th.	6:38	C	7:02	C	12 24	10	1 57	7¼	8	1:53	C	3:51	E	GEM	10
85	26	Fr.	6:37	C	7:03	C	12 26	10	2 21	8¼	9	3:10	C	4:25	E	CAN	11
86	27	Sa.	6:35	C	7:04	D	12 29	11	2 44	9¼	10	4:28	D	4:56	D	LEO	12
87	28	C	6:33	C	7:05	D	12 32	11	3 08	10¼	10¾	5:45	D	5:23	D	SEX	13
88	29	M.	6:31	C	7:06	D	12 35	11	3 31	11¼	11½	7:01	E	5:50	C	VIR	14
89	30	Tu.	6:30	C	7:07	D	12 37	11	3 54	12	—	8:18	E	6:18	C	VIR	15
90	31	W.	6:28	C	7:08	D	12 40	12	4 N.18	12½	1	9:33	E	6:49	B	VIR	16

MARCH HATH 31 DAYS • 2010

Facing thy blasts is sport while it lasts
To those who're brave and true, March. –Marc Cook

Day of Month	Day of Week	Dates, Feasts, Fasts, Aspects, Tide Heights	Weather
1	M.	**St. David** • ☾ ON EQ. • Fatal avalanche hit trains in Wellington, Wash., 1910	*Lamb-y,*
2	Tu.	**St. Chad** • ☌♄☾ • *Don't stick your head into the lion's mouth.* • Tides {11.6 / —	*then*
3	W.	☌♀♅ • First annual meeting of General Wildlife Federation (later, NWF), 1937	*whammy!*
4	Th.	Blizzard struck Cape Cod, Mass., 1960 • Tides {11.4 / 10.5	*Get*
5	Fr.	**St. Piran** • Writer Benjamin Franklin Norris born, 1870 • Tides {11.0 / 9.8	*some*
6	Sa.	U.S. Football League began first season, 1983 • {10.5 / 9.1	*tickets*
7	C	**3rd S. in Lent** • ☾ RUNS LOW • ☌☿♃ • {9.9 / 8.5	*to*
8	M.	☌♇☾ • E. Horton patented fishing rod with telescoping metal tubes, 1887 • {9.4 / 8.1	*Miami!*
9	Tu.	Maria Monroe became first daughter of a president to marry in White House, 1820 • Tides {9.1 / 8.0	*Snow*
10	W.	☾ AT ☊ • *A lazy sheep thinks its wool is heavy.* • {9.0 / 8.1	*is*
11	Th.	♂ STAT. • First public game of basketball played, Springfield, Mass., 1892 • {9.1 / 8.4	*easing,*
12	Fr.	☾ AT APO. • "Superstorm" developed in eastern U.S., 1993	*but*
13	Sa.	☌♆☾ • Chicken nugget inventor Robert C. Baker died, 2006 • Tides {9.5 / 9.1	*we're*
14	C	**Daylight Saving Time begins, 2:00 A.M.** • ☌♃☾ • ☿ IN SUP. ☌ • {9.7 / 9.4	*still*
15	M.	Beware the ides of March. • **New** ● • ☾ ON EQ. • ☌☿♅ • {9.8 / —	*freezing.*
16	Tu.	☌☿☾ • ☌♅☾ • Physicist Georg Ohm born, 1789 • Tides {9.7 / 9.8	*It*
17	W.	**St. Patrick** • ☌♀☾ • ☌♅☉ • USS *Skate* first sub to surface at N. Pole, 1959	*may*
18	Th.	Daylilies return to Earth on space shuttle *Discovery,* 1989	*be*
19	Fr.	**St. Joseph** • Chipmunks emerge from hibernation now.	*spring*
20	Sa.	**Vernal Equinox** • Libby Riddles became first woman to win Iditarod race, 1985 • {10.1 / 9.1	*by*
21	C	**5th S. in Lent** • ♄ AT ☍ • Pocahontas buried in Gravesend, England, 1617	*the*
22	M.	☾ RIDES HIGH • Wampanoag chief Massasoit signed peace treaty with Pilgrims, 1621	*astronomer,*
23	Tu.	Deadly "Easter Tornado," Omaha, Nebr., 1913 • Tides {9.9 / 8.6	*but*
24	W.	☾ AT ☋ • Contract signed to build Euro Disneyland near Paris, 1987 • Tides {9.9 / 8.7	*not*
25	Th.	**Annunciation** • ☌♂☾ • Singer Aretha Franklin born, 1942 • {10.1 / 9.1	*by*
26	Fr.	*Friday night's dream, on Saturday told, is sure to come true be it never so old.* • Tides {10.4 / 9.7	*the*
27	Sa.	Regina made capital of N.W.T., 1883 • {10.7 / 10.4	*thermometer.*
28	C	**Palm Sunday** • ☾ ON EQ. • ☾ AT PERIG. • {11.1 / 11.1	*Mighty*
29	M.	**Full Worm** ○ • ☌♄☾ • Shiveluch volcano erupted, Kamchatka, Russia, 2007 • {11.3 / 11.5	*fine,*
30	Tu.	**First day of Passover** • *March, many weathers.* • {11.3 / —	*then*
31	W.	Chemist Robert Bunsen born, 1811 • Tides {11.7 / 11.1	*leonine!*

Farmer's Calendar

■ By the middle of this month, the morning Sun has some traction. As it mounts higher in the southern sky, it brings to the house some real warming at last. All are prepared to welcome it, but none more so than a very old cat who at this time begins to organize her life around the strengthening sunlight.

She starts her day at about 9:15 A.M., when the sun begins to come through the south-facing windows of the sitting room as a parallelogram of light lying on the window seat. It's a warm spot, and the cat curls up in it and goes to sleep. She's good there for a couple of hours, but by noon the Sun's apparent journey to the west has shifted its light to the east. Now the warm patch lies on the floor in the kitchen doorway. The cat wakes, stretches, and moves to the new location. By 2:00 P.M., she's in the kitchen itself, where the sun has advanced to prepare a toasty place on the floor under the long table. Her solar day is about over now, however: In midafternoon, the sun has left the kitchen windows. The cat takes up her default position under the woodstove.

This cat is a senior citizen. She's had her 20th birthday. Her days of exploring and hunting are done. She figures she's earned a rest. Even in retirement, however, she has her role to play. In her daily quest for warmth across 25 feet of floor, she serves as a kind of feline sundial.

THE FOURTH MONTH • 2010

SKY WATCH ☆ *April is a month of striking conjunctions. Mercury, joined by brilliant Venus, is at its best of the year, as both gain height in the western dusk 40 minutes after sunset, and stand together from the 1st to the 10th. On the 15th, the crescent Moon hovers very close to Mercury, 10 degrees high in the fading twilight. Mars again loses half of its brightness as it passes near the Beehive star cluster from the 16th–19th; use binoculars. The Moon moves on to meet the Orange Planet on the 21st, as Mercury fades after midmonth. Venus keeps improving, floating just to the left of the famous Pleiades "Seven Sisters" star cluster from the 23rd to the 26th. For early risers, Jupiter emerges in the east, just before dawn.*

◑	**Last Quarter**	6th day	5th hour	37th minute
●	**New Moon**	14th day	8th hour	29th minute
◐	**First Quarter**	21st day	14th hour	20th minute
○	**Full Moon**	28th day	8th hour	18th minute

All times are given in Eastern Daylight Time.

Purchase these pages with times set to your zip code at MyLocalAlmanac.com.

Day of Year	Day of Month	Day of Week	☼ Rises h. m.	Rise Key	☼ Sets h. m.	Set Key	Length of Day h.	m.	Sun Fast m.	Declination of Sun °	'	High Tide Times Boston		☾ Rises h. m.	Rise Key	☾ Sets h. m.	Set Key	☾ Place	☾ Age
91	1	Th.	6:26	C	**7:10**	D	12	44	12	4N.	41	1¼	**1¾**	**10:45**	E	7:24	B	LIB	17
92	2	Fr.	6:25	C	**7:11**	D	12	46	12	5	04	2	**2½**	**11:52**	E	8:04	B	LIB	18
93	3	Sa.	6:23	C	**7:12**	D	12	49	13	5	27	2¾	**3½**	—	–	8:51	B	SCO	19
94	4	**C**	6:21	C	**7:13**	D	12	52	13	5	50	3½	**4¼**	12:50	E	9:44	A	OPH	20
95	5	M.	6:19	C	**7:14**	D	12	55	13	6	13	4½	**5¼**	1:40	E	10:42	B	SAG	21
96	6	Tu.	6:18	C	**7:15**	D	12	57	13	6	35	5½	**6¼**	2:21	E	11:43	B	SAG	22
97	7	W.	6:16	B	**7:16**	D	13	00	14	6	58	6½	**7¼**	2:55	E	**12:45**	B	SAG	23
98	8	Th.	6:14	B	**7:17**	D	13	03	14	7	20	7½	**8¼**	3:24	E	**1:46**	C	CAP	24
99	9	Fr.	6:13	B	**7:19**	D	13	06	14	7	43	8½	**9**	3:48	D	**2:47**	C	CAP	25
100	10	Sa.	6:11	B	**7:20**	D	13	09	15	8	05	9¼	**9¾**	4:11	D	**3:47**	D	AQU	26
101	11	**C**	6:09	B	**7:21**	D	13	12	15	8	27	10	**10½**	4:32	D	**4:48**	D	PSC	27
102	12	M.	6:08	B	**7:22**	D	13	14	15	8	49	10¾	**11**	4:54	C	**5:50**	E	PSC	28
103	13	Tu.	6:06	B	**7:23**	D	13	17	15	9	11	11½	**11¾**	5:16	C	**6:53**	E	PSC	29
104	14	W.	6:04	B	**7:24**	D	13	20	16	9	32	**12**	—	5:41	B	**7:59**	E	PSC	0
105	15	Th.	6:03	B	**7:25**	D	13	22	16	9	54	12¼	**12¾**	6:10	B	**9:06**	E	ARI	1
106	16	Fr.	6:01	B	**7:26**	D	13	25	16	10	15	12¾	**1½**	6:45	B	**10:14**	E	ARI	2
107	17	Sa.	6:00	B	**7:28**	D	13	28	16	10	36	1½	**2¼**	7:27	B	**11:18**	E	TAU	3
108	18	**C**	5:58	B	**7:29**	D	13	31	16	10	57	2¼	**3**	8:19	B	—	–	TAU	4
109	19	M.	5:57	B	**7:30**	D	13	33	17	11	18	3	**3¾**	9:20	B	12:17	E	TAU	5
110	20	Tu.	5:55	B	**7:31**	D	13	36	17	11	39	4	**4¾**	10:28	B	1:07	E	GEM	6
111	21	W.	5:53	B	**7:32**	D	13	39	17	11	59	4¾	**5½**	11:41	B	1:50	E	GEM	7
112	22	Th.	5:52	B	**7:33**	D	13	41	17	12	19	6	**6¾**	**12:56**	C	2:25	E	CAN	8
113	23	Fr.	5:50	B	**7:34**	D	13	44	17	12	39	7	**7¾**	**2:10**	D	2:56	E	LEO	9
114	24	Sa.	5:49	B	**7:35**	D	13	46	18	12	59	8	**8¾**	**3:25**	D	3:24	D	SEX	10
115	25	**C**	5:47	B	**7:37**	D	13	50	18	13	18	9	**9½**	**4:39**	E	3:50	C	LEO	11
116	26	M.	5:46	B	**7:38**	D	13	52	18	13	38	10	**10½**	**5:54**	E	4:17	C	VIR	12
117	27	Tu.	5:45	B	**7:39**	E	13	54	18	13	57	11	**11¼**	**7:09**	E	4:46	B	VIR	13
118	28	W.	5:43	B	**7:40**	E	13	57	18	14	16	11¾	—	**8:22**	E	5:18	B	VIR	14
119	29	Th.	5:42	B	**7:41**	E	13	59	18	14	34	12	**12¾**	**9:32**	E	5:56	B	LIB	15
120	30	Fr.	5:40	B	**7:42**	E	14	02	19	14N.	53	12¾	**1½**	**10:35**	E	6:41	B	SCO	16

 To use this page, see p. 106; for Key Letters, see p. 234. ☞ **Bold = P.M.** ☞ Light = A.M.

April hath 30 days • 2010

Aprul's come back; the swellin' buds of oak
Dim the fur hillsides with a purplish smoke. –James Russell Lowell

Day of Month	Day of Week	Dates, Feasts, Fasts, Aspects, Tide Heights	Weather
1	Th.	**Maundy Thursday** • **All Fools'** • Satellite *Tiros I* launched, 1960 • {11.7 / 10.7	*Snow*
2	Fr.	**Good Friday** • 7.9 earthquake triggered tsunami, Hawaii, 1868 • Tides {11.4 / 10.2	*and*
3	Sa.	First national issue of *TV Guide,* 1953 • Tides {10.9 / 9.6	*showers*
4	C	**Easter** • ☾ RUNS LOW • *If the sun shines on Easter Day, it shines on Whitsunday likewise.*	*bring*
5	M.	**Easter Monday** • ☌♇☾ • Golfer Elsie McLean made hole-in-one, 2007	*glowers,*
6	Tu.	☾ AT ☊ • ♇ STAT. • Jimmy Dewar invented Twinkies, 1930 • {9.3 / 8.2	*not*
7	W.	John Wayne won Oscar for *True Grit,* 1970 • {8.9 / 8.2	*flowers.*
8	Th.	☾ AT APO. • ☿ GR. ELONG. (19° EAST) • First Lady Betty Ford born, 1918 • {8.8 / 8.3	*Bright*
9	Fr.	☌♆☾ • Jumbo the elephant arrived in U.S., 1882 • Tides {8.9 / 8.6	*but*
10	Sa.	*A promise is a cloud; fulfillment is rain.* • {9.0 / 9.0	*bracing:*
11	C	**2nd S. of Easter** • ☾ ON EQ. • ☌♃☾ • {9.2 / 9.4	*too*
12	M.	☌♅☾ • First U.S. championship billiards game, 1859 • Tides {9.4 / 9.7	*cool*
13	Tu.	Thomas Jefferson born, 1743 • Conservationist Archie "Grey Owl" Belaney died, 1938 • {9.5 / 10.1	*for*
14	W.	New ● • Judge ruled "aspirin" is generic trademark in U.S., 1921 • {9.6 / —	*the pool,*
15	Th.	☌☿☾ • First state entomologist position approved, N.Y., 1854 • {10.3 / 9.6	*just*
16	Fr.	☌♀☾ • Three tornadoes struck Nashville, Tenn., 1998	*right*
17	Sa.	Order of Canada, to honor outstanding contributions to society and country, instituted, 1967 • {10.6 / 9.4	*for*
18	C	**3rd S. of Easter** • ☾ RIDES HIGH • ☿ STAT.	*marathon*
19	M.	*When prosperity smiles, beware of its guiles.* • {10.5 / 9.1	*racing!*
20	Tu.	☾ AT ☋ • Preakness and Kentucky Derby winner Funny Cide born, 2000 • Tides {10.4 / 9.1	*Rain*
21	W.	Astronomer Peter Apianus died, 1552 • Tides {10.2 / 9.1	*fallin',*
22	Th.	☌♂☾ • Albert Einstein Memorial unveiled, Wash., D.C., 1979 • {10.1 / 9.4	*temperature*
23	Fr.	**St. George** • *Ranger 4* spacecraft launched, 1962 • Tides {10.1 / 9.8	*risin'—*
24	Sa.	☾ ON EQ. • ☾ AT PERIG. • Robert B. Thomas born, 1766 • {10.2 / 10.3	*could*
25	C	**4th S. of Easter** • ☌♄☾ • Tides {10.4 / 10.8	*that*
26	M.	**St. Mark**[T] • William Shakespeare baptized, 1564 • {10.5 / 11.3	*be*
27	Tu.	Soil Conservation Service created, 1935 • Tides {10.6 / 11.5	*spring*
28	W.	**Full Pink** ○ • ☿ IN INF. ☌ • *If the full Moon rise red, expect wind.* • {10.6 / —	*on*
29	Th.	Poplars leaf out about now. • Theta Xi, first professional fraternity founded, Troy, N.Y., 1864 • {11.6 / 10.4	*the*
30	Fr.	Railroad engineer Casey Jones died in train wreck, 1900 • Tides {11.5 / 10.1	*horizon?*

Silence is not only golden, it is seldom misquoted. –Bob Monkhouse

Farmer's Calendar

■ Some years ago, the scientific press reported on a dispute among astronomers about what makes a heavenly body count as a planet. The problem arose with the discovery in 1930 of Pluto, the ninth planet. Pluto has always been an anomaly among planets, an object so distant, so small, and with such a peculiar orbit that it strains the very concept of what a planet is. An international conference of astronomers, held in 2006 in Prague, went so far as to resolve to drop Pluto as a planet, reducing the planets to eight similar bodies. Scientific opponents of this step proposed instead to define a planet as a massive, spherical body orbiting a star. This formula retains Pluto's planethood. Trouble is, it would also oblige us to add to the list of planets, potentially, scores of obscure chunks of matter that also meet the more capacious definition. Planets would become common, mundane, like car washes, baseball caps, and cell phones. Do we want that?

You see where the problem lies: not with Pluto, but with the exigencies of definition. The planets were getting along well enough—until we tried to put them in order. Now we have an unseemly and undignified battle, more a political battle than a scientific one, in which the question seems almost to be Pluto's citizenship. It's a debate whose only winners will be the publishers of astronomy textbooks.

SKY WATCH ☆ *The Moon skims just above Jupiter, in Aquarius, on the morning of the 9th. Mars fades to where it's only a bit brighter than the blue star Regulus to its left, as it chugs into Leo at midmonth, visible in the evening sky. The Moon stands near Mars on the 19th. By contrast, Venus keeps a steady brightness for months as it slowly ascends higher each evening at dusk to stand above the crescent Moon on the 15th. A week later, on the 22nd, the Moon floats below Saturn. Interestingly, Mars and Saturn have precisely the same brightness all month long, fading together in lockstep in the adjoining constellations of Leo and Virgo.*

◗ **Last Quarter**	6th day	0 hour	15th minute
● **New Moon**	13th day	21st hour	4th minute
◐ **First Quarter**	20th day	19th hour	43rd minute
○ **Full Moon**	27th day	19th hour	7th minute

All times are given in Eastern Daylight Time.

Purchase these pages with times set to your zip code at MyLocalAlmanac.com.

Day of Year	Day of Month	Day of Week	☀ Rises h. m.	Rise Key	☀ Sets h. m.	Set Key	Length of Day h. m.	Sun Fast m.	Declination of Sun ° ′	High Tide Times Boston		☾ Rises h. m.	Rise Key	☾ Sets h. m.	Set Key	☾ Place	☾ Age
121	1	Sa.	5:39	B	7:43	E	14 04	19	15ɴ.11	1½	2¼	**11:30**	E	7:32	B	OPH	17
122	2	C	5:38	B	7:44	E	14 06	19	15 29	2¼	3	—		8:29	B	SAG	18
123	3	M.	5:36	B	7:46	E	14 10	19	15 47	3¼	3¾	12:15	B	9:30	B	SAG	19
124	4	Tu.	5:35	B	7:47	E	14 12	19	16 04	4	4¾	12:53	B	10:32	B	CAP	20
125	5	W.	5:34	B	7:48	E	14 14	19	16 21	4¾	5½	1:23	E	11:34	C	CAP	21
126	6	Th.	5:32	B	7:49	E	14 17	19	16 38	5¾	6½	1:50	E	**12:35**	C	AQU	22
127	7	Fr.	5:31	B	7:50	E	14 19	19	16 55	6¾	7¼	2:13	D	**1:36**	D	CAP	23
128	8	Sa.	5:30	B	7:51	E	14 21	19	17 11	7½	8¼	2:35	D	**2:36**	D	AQU	24
129	9	C	5:29	B	7:52	E	14 23	19	17 27	8½	9	2:56	C	**3:37**	E	PSC	25
130	10	M.	5:28	B	7:53	E	14 25	19	17 43	9¼	9¾	3:18	C	**4:40**	E	PSC	26
131	11	Tu.	5:27	B	7:54	E	14 27	19	17 58	10¼	10¼	3:42	B	**5:45**	E	PSC	27
132	12	W.	5:25	B	7:55	E	14 30	19	18 13	11	11	4:10	B	**6:52**	E	PSC	28
133	13	Th.	5:24	B	7:56	E	14 32	19	18 28	11½	11¾	4:43	B	**8:00**	E	ARI	0
134	14	Fr.	5:23	B	7:57	E	14 34	19	18 43	12¼	—	5:23	B	**9:07**	E	TAU	1
135	15	Sa.	5:22	A	7:58	E	14 36	19	18 57	12½	1	6:12	B	**10:09**	E	TAU	2
136	16	C	5:21	A	7:59	E	14 38	19	19 11	1¼	1¾	7:12	B	**11:03**	E	TAU	3
137	17	M.	5:20	A	8:00	E	14 40	19	19 24	2	2¾	8:19	B	**11:49**	E	GEM	4
138	18	Tu.	5:19	A	8:02	E	14 43	19	19 38	2¾	3½	9:32	B	—		GEM	5
139	19	W.	5:18	A	8:02	E	14 44	19	19 51	3¾	4½	10:47	C	**12:27**	E	CAN	6
140	20	Th.	5:18	A	8:03	E	14 45	19	20 03	4¾	5¼	**12:01**	C	**12:59**	E	LEO	7
141	21	Fr.	5:17	A	8:04	E	14 47	19	20 15	5¾	6¼	**1:14**	D	**1:27**	D	LEO	8
142	22	Sa.	5:16	A	8:05	E	14 49	19	20 27	6¾	7¼	**2:27**	E	**1:53**	C	LEO	9
143	23	C	5:15	A	8:06	E	14 51	19	20 39	7¾	8¼	**3:39**	E	**2:19**	C	VIR	10
144	24	M.	5:14	A	8:07	E	14 53	19	20 50	8¾	9¼	**4:52**	E	**2:47**	C	VIR	11
145	25	Tu.	5:14	A	8:08	E	14 54	19	21 01	9¾	10	**6:04**	E	**3:17**	B	VIR	12
146	26	W.	5:13	A	8:09	E	14 56	19	21 11	10¾	10¾	**7:14**	E	**3:52**	B	LIB	13
147	27	Th.	5:12	A	8:10	E	14 58	19	21 21	11½	11¾	**8:20**	E	**4:33**	B	LIB	14
148	28	Fr.	5:12	A	8:11	E	14 59	18	21 31	12¼	—	**9:18**	E	**5:21**	B	OPH	15
149	29	Sa.	5:11	A	8:12	E	15 01	18	21 40	12½	1	**10:08**	E	**6:16**	B	OPH	16
150	30	C	5:10	A	8:12	E	15 02	18	21 49	1¼	1¾	**10:49**	E	**7:16**	B	SAG	17
151	31	M.	5:10	A	8:13	E	15 03	18	21ɴ.58	2	2½	**11:22**	E	**8:18**	B	SAG	18

May hath 31 days • 2010

And rosy and white on the wanton breeze
The petals fall from the apple trees. –Francis William Bourdillon

Day of Month	Day of Week	Dates, Feasts, Fasts, Aspects, Tide Heights	Weather
1	Sa.	Sts. Philip & James • May Day • ☾ RUNS LOW • { 11.2 / 9.7	*Lightning*
2	C	5th S. of Easter • ☌♇☾ • Tides { 10.7 / 9.4	*storm*
3	M.	☾ AT ☊ • First broadcast of National Public Radio's *All Things Considered,* 1971 • { 10.2 / 9.0	*sounds*
4	Tu.	*Quiet rivers have flowery banks.* • Tides { 9.7 / 8.7	*thunderful;*
5	W.	Cinco de Mayo • Baseball pitcher Cy Young threw perfect game, 1904 • { 9.3 / 8.5	*these*
6	Th.	☾ AT APO. • Director Orson Welles born, 1915 • { 9.0 / 8.5	*days*
7	Fr.	☌♆☾ • 54°F, Sacramento, Calif, 1905 • Tides { 8.8 / 8.6	*are*
8	Sa.	St. Julian of Norwich • ☾ ON EQ. • Tides { 8.7 / 8.9	*warm*
9	C	Rogation S. • ☌♃☾ • ☌⛢☾ • Tides { 8.8 / 9.2	*and*
10	M.	☿ STAT. • First undersea voyage around world completed by sub USS *Triton,* 1960	*wonderful!*
11	Tu.	Cranberries in bud now. • Three • Tides { 9.1 / 10.0	*Sunshine*
12	W.	☌☿☾ • Manitoba's flag officially adopted, 1966 • Chilly • { 9.2 / 10.3	*flickers,*
13	Th.	Ascension • New ● • Saints • Tides { 9.4 / 10.6	*traffic*
14	Fr.	*The traveler with empty pockets may laugh in the bandit's face.* • Tides { 9.5 / —	*sloshes.*
15	Sa.	☾ RIDES HIGH • Astronomer Williamina Fleming born, 1857 • Tides { 10.9 / 9.6	*Grab*
16	C	1st S. af. Asc. • ☌♀☾ • Tides { 11.0 / 9.6	*your*
17	M.	☾ AT ☋ • *GoFast* became first amateur rocket to reach space, Nev., 2004 • { 11.1 / 9.6	*slickers*
18	Tu.	Major Arkansas River flood, Wichita, Kans., 1877	*and*
19	W.	St. Dunstan • Shavuot • Writer T. E. Lawrence (of Arabia) died, 1935	*galoshes.*
20	Th.	☾ AT PERIG. • ☌♂☾ • *The haddocks are good When dipped in May flood.*	*Mainers*
21	Fr.	Cyrus McCormick's reaper patented, 1834 • Tides { 10.3 / 10.0	*wear*
22	Sa.	☾ ON EQ. • Rep. Preston Brooks caned Sen. Charles Sumner in Senate, 1856 • { 10.1 / 10.3	*sweaters,*
23	C	Whit S. • Pentecost • ☌♄☾ • { 9.9 / 10.7	*while*
24	M.	Victoria Day (Canada) • Ohio Anti-Saloon League founded, Oberlin, Ohio, 1893	*Georgians*
25	Tu.	St. Bede • ☿ GR. ELONG. (25° WEST) • Tides { 9.8 / 11.2	*sweat:*
26	W.	Ember Day • Tornado left 155-mile trail, central Ill., 1917 • Tides { 9.8 / 11.2	*how*
27	Th.	Vesak • Full Flower ○ • Diplomat Henry Kissinger born, 1923 • { 9.8 / 11.2	*much*
28	Fr.	Ember Day • ☾ RUNS LOW • *Use makes mastery.* • Tides { 9.7 / —	*wetter*
29	Sa.	Ember Day • ☌♇☾ • Rhode Island became 13th state, 1790 • { 11.0 / 9.6	*can*
30	C	Trinity • Orthodox All Saints' • ☾ AT ☊ • Tides { 10.8 / 9.4	*it*
31	M.	Visit. of Mary • Memorial Day (observed) • ♄ STAT. • ♆ STAT.	*get?*

Farmer's Calendar

■ By tradition, we make New Year's Day the occasion of personal rededication. It's on the first day of the new calendar that we are supposed to take stock of ourselves and, in our New Year's resolutions, to pledge ourselves to improve our conduct of life. Unfortunately, though we may be quite sincere in our resolves, we know well that they will prove to be, for the most part, vain, empty, and of no force. Perhaps we'd have better luck if we shifted the date of our annual renewal of purpose to another season.

New Year's resolutions fail because they are ambitious and, especially, abstract. I resolve to get more exercise, to be more moderate, to be a more attentive spouse, and the like. Such grand moral undertakings are easy to make in January, an inactive time of year when energy and initiative are low and nothing much need be done about our good intentions. We might do better to make May Day resolutions, and to direct them to the specific, limited, and practical. I will fix the garden fence, jack up the corner of the shed, and burn the brush pile in the field. On May Day, these projects are present, visible, and doable. As the spring advances, the real need for the tasks at hand coincides with a season in which we have the opportunity and the ambition to accomplish them. We need no longer defeat ourselves by making in the deepest winter the covenants of spring.

SKY WATCH ☆ *Look for a striking, close meeting of orange Mars and Leo's blue star Regulus during the first 10 days of June. They're well matched in brightness but identifiable by the stark color contrast. A nice drama unfolds also in the hours before dawn: Jupiter, having crossed into Pisces a month ago, hovers below the Moon on the 6th and then passes very near blue-green Uranus from the 7th to the 11th. Binoculars easily show Uranus above Jupiter. Look for the crescent Moon below Venus on the 14th and use binoculars to see Venus within the lovely Beehive star cluster on the 19th and 20th. Summer begins with the solstice, on the 21st at 7:28 A.M.*

☽	Last Quarter	4th day	18th hour	13th minute
●	New Moon	12th day	7th hour	15th minute
☾	First Quarter	19th day	0 hour	29th minute
○	Full Moon	26th day	7th hour	30th minute

All times are given in Eastern Daylight Time.

Purchase these pages with times set to your zip code at MyLocalAlmanac.com.

Day of Year	Day of Month	Day of Week	☀ Rises h. m.	Rise Key	☀ Sets h. m.	Set Key	Length of Day h. m.	Sun Fast m.	Declination of Sun ° '	High Tide Times Boston		☽ Rises h. m.	Rise Key	☽ Sets h. m.	Set Key	☽ Place	☽ Age
152	1	Tu.	5:09	A	8:14	E	15 05	18	22N.06	2¾	3¼	**11:51**	E	9:21	B	CAP	19
153	2	W.	5:09	A	8:15	E	15 06	18	22 14	3½	4	—	–	10:23	C	CAP	20
154	3	Th.	5:09	A	8:16	E	15 07	17	22 21	4¼	5	12:15	D	11:24	C	CAP	21
155	4	Fr.	5:08	A	8:16	E	15 08	17	22 28	5	5¾	12:38	D	**12:24**	D	AQU	22
156	5	Sa.	5:08	A	8:17	E	15 09	17	22 35	6	6½	12:59	D	**1:24**	D	PSC	23
157	6	**C**	5:07	A	8:18	E	15 11	17	22 41	6¾	7¼	1:20	C	**2:25**	E	PSC	24
158	7	M.	5:07	A	8:18	E	15 11	17	22 47	7¾	8	1:43	C	**3:28**	E	PSC	25
159	8	Tu.	5:07	A	8:19	E	15 12	17	22 52	8½	9	2:09	B	**4:34**	E	PSC	26
160	9	W.	5:07	A	8:19	E	15 12	16	22 57	9½	9¾	2:39	B	**5:42**	E	ARI	27
161	10	Th.	5:07	A	8:20	E	15 13	16	23 02	10¼	10½	3:16	B	**6:50**	E	ARI	28
162	11	Fr.	5:06	A	8:21	E	15 15	16	23 06	11	11¼	4:01	B	**7:55**	E	TAU	29
163	12	Sa.	5:06	A	8:21	E	15 15	16	23 10	12	—	4:58	B	**8:54**	E	TAU	0
164	13	**C**	5:06	A	8:22	E	15 16	15	23 13	12	12¾	6:04	B	**9:44**	E	GEM	1
165	14	M.	5:06	A	8:22	E	15 16	15	23 16	12¾	1½	7:17	B	**10:26**	E	GEM	2
166	15	Tu.	5:06	A	8:22	E	15 16	15	23 19	1¾	2¼	8:34	C	**11:01**	E	CAN	3
167	16	W.	5:06	A	8:23	E	15 17	15	23 21	2½	3¼	9:50	C	**11:30**	D	CAN	4
168	17	Th.	5:06	A	8:23	E	15 17	15	23 23	3½	4	11:05	D	**11:57**	D	LEO	5
169	18	Fr.	5:06	A	8:23	E	15 17	15	23 24	4½	5	**12:18**	D	—	–	LEO	6
170	19	Sa.	5:07	A	8:24	E	15 17	14	23 25	5½	6	**1:30**	E	12:24	C	VIR	7
171	20	**C**	5:07	A	8:24	E	15 17	14	23 26	6½	7	**2:42**	E	12:50	C	VIR	8
172	21	M.	5:07	A	8:24	E	15 17	14	23 26	7½	8	**3:53**	E	1:19	B	VIR	9
173	22	Tu.	5:07	A	8:24	E	15 17	14	23 25	8½	8¾	**5:03**	E	1:51	B	LIB	10
174	23	W.	5:07	A	8:24	E	15 17	13	23 25	9½	9¾	**6:09**	E	2:30	B	LIB	11
175	24	Th.	5:08	A	8:25	E	15 17	13	23 24	10½	10½	**7:10**	E	3:14	B	SCO	12
176	25	Fr.	5:08	A	8:25	E	15 17	13	23 22	11¼	11½	**8:02**	E	4:06	B	OPH	13
177	26	Sa.	5:08	A	8:25	E	15 17	13	23 20	12	—	**8:46**	E	5:04	B	SAG	14
178	27	**C**	5:09	A	8:25	E	15 16	13	23 18	12¼	12¾	**9:22**	E	6:06	B	SAG	15
179	28	M.	5:09	A	8:25	E	15 16	12	23 15	12¾	1½	**9:52**	E	7:09	B	SAG	16
180	29	Tu.	5:10	A	8:25	E	15 15	12	23 12	1½	2¼	**10:18**	E	8:11	C	CAP	17
181	30	W.	5:10	A	8:25	E	15 15	12	23N.08	2¼	2¾	**10:41**	D	9:13	C	CAP	18

JUNE HATH 30 DAYS • 2010

We'll watch the Sun as his chariot rolls
Far down the horizon's rim. –Mary L. Wyatt

Day of Month	Day of Week	Dates, Feasts, Fasts, Aspects, Tide Heights	Weather
1	Tu.	Earthquake shook Plymouth, Mass., 1638 • { 10.1 / 9.0	*Golfers*
2	W.	First nighttime baseball game under electric lights, Fort Wayne, Ind., 1883 • { 9.8 / 8.9	*swelter,*
3	Th.	☾ at apo. • ☌♆☾ • Actress Frances Bay inducted into Canada's Walk of Fame, 2008	*then*
4	Fr.	*He that brings good news knocks hard.* • Tides { 9.1 / 8.9	*take*
5	Sa.	**St. Boniface** • ☾ on Eq. • Writer O. Henry died, 1910 • { 8.8 / 9.0	*shelter!*
6	**C**	**Corpus Christi** • D-Day, 1944 • ☌♃☾ • ☌♃⛢ • ☌⛢☾	*Blushing*
7	M.	Hudson Stuck's expedition reached summit of Mt. McKinley, Alaska, 1913 • Tides { 8.5 / 9.4	*brides*
8	Tu.	Transit of Venus occurred, first time in 121½ years, 2004	*and*
9	W.	Donald Duck debuted in cartoon film *The Wise Little Hen*, 1934 • Tides { 8.7 / 10.1	*lucky*
10	Th.	☌☿☾ • Canadian prime minister Sir Robert Laird Borden died, 1937 • { 8.9 / 10.5	*fellas*
11	Fr.	**St. Barnabas** • *On St. Barnabas Day The sun is here to stay.* • Tides { 9.2 / 10.9	*tie*
12	Sa.	New ● • ☾ rides high • President Reagan's "Tear Down This Wall" speech, Berlin, 1987	*the*
13	**C**	**3rd S. af. P.** • ☾ at ☋ • Musician Benny Goodman died, 1986	*knot*
14	M.	**St. Basil** • Discovery of the neutrino announced, 1956 • Tides { 11.4 / 9.9	*beneath*
15	Tu.	☾ at perig. • ☌♀☾ • Ark. became 25th state, 1836 • { 11.5 / 10.1	*umbrellas.*
16	W.	*A harvest of peace is produced from a seed of contentment.* • { 11.4 / 10.3	*Valedictorians*
17	Th.	☌♂☾ • 133°F, Santa Barbara, Calif., 1859 • { 11.1 / 10.4	*finish*
18	Fr.	☾ on Eq. • 63-lb. 8-oz. flathead catfish caught, James River, S.Dak., 2006 • { 10.7 / 10.5	*their*
19	Sa.	☌♄☾ • Slavery abolished in U.S. territories, 1862 • Tides { 10.3 / 10.6	*speeches,*
20	**C**	**4th S. af. P.** • Queen Victoria ascended British throne, 1837 • { 9.8 / 10.6	*doff*
21	M.	**Summer Solstice** • 25-foot-tall, 17½-ton ice pop melted, flooding Union Square, N.Y.C., 2005 • { 9.5 / 10.7	*their*
22	Tu.	**St. Alban** • *Love, cough, and a smoke can't well be hid.* • Tides { 9.3 / 10.7	*gowns,*
23	W.	William Penn purchased land from Delaware Indians, Shackamaxon, (Pa.), 1683 • Tides { 9.2 / 10.8	*and*
24	Th.	**Nativ. John the Baptist** • Midsummer Day • Tides { 9.2 / 10.7	*hit*
25	Fr.	☾ runs low • ♇ at ☍ • Gov. Winthrop of Mass. Bay Colony introduced fork to America, 1630	*the*
26	Sa.	**Full Strawberry** ○ • **Eclipse** ☾ • ☾ at ☊ • ☌♇☾	*beaches.*
27	**C**	**5th S. af. P.** • Kmart trademark registered, 1967 • { 10.6 / 9.2	*Thunder*
28	M.	**St. Irenaeus** • ☿ in sup. ☌ • Painter Sir Peter Paul Rubens born, 1577	*mutters,*
29	Tu.	**Sts. Peter & Paul** • *No root, no fruit.* • Tides { 10.3 / 9.2	*filling*
30	W.	☌♆☾ • Meat Inspection Act passed, 1906 • { 10.1 / 9.2	*gutters.*

A flower is an educated weed. –Luther Burbank

Farmer's Calendar

■ *June 1.* A vast flight of returning Canada geese must have arrived at the woodland pond at the top of our hill last night, for, walking there this morning, I could hear their cries from a quarter-mile off. I turned through the woods to welcome them. As I approached the pond, the geese were setting up an extraordinary clamor of honks, blats, groans, hoots, yodels, coughs, grunts, barks, and yawps. In the woods at the pond's edge, I peeped out, expecting from the volume and variety of their racket to find geese in company strength, at least.

Four birds. There were four of them. When I appeared, they fell silent and paddled sedately away. Prepared for 100 geese, I had been fooled into multiplying their number by 25. Not a bad trick. I was reminded of the maneuver in the spring of 1862 when the Confederate general Magruder, charged with defending the outskirts of Richmond against a Union army that greatly outnumbered his own, employed a similar ruse. Magruder marched his small force past a gap in the terrain through which the Union observers watched them. Day after day, he marched them—in a circle. Each of Magruder's men was counted by the opposition over and over again, convincing the northern general that the defending force was equal to his own. This caused him to hesitate, which led to a failed assault on the southern capital.

SKY WATCH ☆ *Earth reaches aphelion, its farthest point from the Sun, on the 6th. Venus finally budges in brightness, up from magnitude –3.9, where it's been stuck since January, to –4.0. Changes will now come more rapidly. Although Venus keeps widening its angular separation from the Sun, its orbit appears at an increasingly low slant on the western horizon. Result: The brilliant planet is lower at dusk than it was a month ago, as it passes Regulus on the 9th and 10th. Venus approaches Mars as Mars approaches Saturn. Low in the west an hour after sunset in the final days of July, Mars passes below Saturn and is the dimmer of the two.*

◑ **Last Quarter**	4th day	10th hour	35th minute
● **New Moon**	11th day	15th hour	40th minute
◐ **First Quarter**	18th day	6th hour	11th minute
○ **Full Moon**	25th day	21st hour	37th minute

All times are given in Eastern Daylight Time.

Purchase these pages with times set to your zip code at MyLocalAlmanac.com.

Day of Year	Day of Month	Day of Week	☼ Rises h. m.	Rise Key	☼ Sets h. m.	Set Key	Length of Day h.	m.	Sun Fast m.	Declination of Sun °	'	High Tide Times Boston		☾ Rises h. m.	Rise Key	☾ Sets h. m.	Set Key	☾ Place	☾ Age
182	1	Th.	5:11	A	**8:24**	E	15	13	12	23N.	04	3	**3½**	**11:02**	D	10:13	D	AQU	19
183	2	Fr.	5:11	A	**8:24**	E	15	13	12	23	00	3¾	**4¼**	**11:24**	C	11:12	D	PSC	20
184	3	Sa.	5:12	A	**8:24**	E	15	12	11	22	55	4½	**5**	**11:45**	C	**12:12**	E	PSC	21
185	4	**C**	5:12	A	**8:24**	E	15	12	11	22	50	5¼	**5¾**	—	–	**1:14**	E	PSC	22
186	5	M.	5:13	A	**8:23**	E	15	10	11	22	44	6	**6½**	12:09	B	**2:17**	E	PSC	23
187	6	Tu.	5:13	A	**8:23**	E	15	10	11	22	38	7	**7¼**	12:37	B	**3:23**	E	ARI	24
188	7	W.	5:14	A	**8:23**	E	15	09	11	22	32	8	**8¼**	1:09	B	**4:30**	E	ARI	25
189	8	Th.	5:15	A	**8:22**	E	15	07	11	22	25	8¾	**9**	1:50	B	**5:36**	E	TAU	26
190	9	Fr.	5:16	A	**8:22**	E	15	06	10	22	18	9¾	**10**	2:41	B	**6:38**	E	TAU	27
191	10	Sa.	5:16	A	**8:22**	E	15	06	10	22	10	10¾	**10¾**	3:42	B	**7:33**	E	TAU	28
192	11	**C**	5:17	A	**8:21**	E	15	04	10	22	03	11½	**11¾**	4:54	B	**8:20**	E	GEM	0
193	12	M.	5:18	A	**8:21**	E	15	03	10	21	54	**12¼**	—	6:11	B	**8:58**	E	GEM	1
194	13	Tu.	5:19	A	**8:20**	E	15	01	10	21	46	12½	**1¼**	7:30	C	**9:31**	E	CAN	2
195	14	W.	5:19	A	**8:19**	E	15	00	10	21	37	1½	**2**	8:48	D	**10:00**	D	LEO	3
196	15	Th.	5:20	A	**8:19**	E	14	59	10	21	27	2¼	**2¾**	10:04	D	**10:27**	C	SEX	4
197	16	Fr.	5:21	A	**8:18**	E	14	57	10	21	17	3¼	**3¾**	11:19	E	**10:54**	C	LEO	5
198	17	Sa.	5:22	A	**8:17**	E	14	55	10	21	07	4	**4¾**	**12:32**	E	**11:22**	B	VIR	6
199	18	**C**	5:23	A	**8:17**	E	14	54	10	20	57	5	**5½**	**1:45**	E	**11:54**	B	VIR	7
200	19	M.	5:24	A	**8:16**	E	14	52	9	20	46	6	**6½**	**2:55**	E	—	–	VIR	8
201	20	Tu.	5:24	A	**8:15**	E	14	51	9	20	35	7¼	**7½**	**4:02**	E	12:30	B	LIB	9
202	21	W.	5:25	A	**8:14**	E	14	49	9	20	23	8¼	**8½**	**5:04**	E	1:12	B	SCO	10
203	22	Th.	5:26	A	**8:13**	E	14	47	9	20	11	9¼	**9½**	**5:58**	E	2:01	B	OPH	11
204	23	Fr.	5:27	A	**8:13**	E	14	46	9	19	59	10¼	**10¼**	**6:44**	E	2:57	B	SAG	12
205	24	Sa.	5:28	A	**8:12**	E	14	44	9	19	46	11	**11**	**7:22**	E	3:57	B	SAG	13
206	25	**C**	5:29	A	**8:11**	E	14	42	9	19	34	11¾	**11¾**	**7:54**	E	4:59	B	SAG	14
207	26	M.	5:30	A	**8:10**	E	14	40	9	19	20	**12½**	—	**8:22**	E	6:01	C	CAP	15
208	27	Tu.	5:31	A	**8:09**	E	14	38	9	19	07	12½	**1**	**8:46**	D	7:03	C	AQU	16
209	28	W.	5:32	A	**8:08**	E	14	36	9	18	53	1¼	**1¾**	**9:07**	D	8:04	C	AQU	17
210	29	Th.	5:33	B	**8:07**	E	14	34	9	18	39	1¾	**2¼**	**9:29**	C	9:03	D	AQU	18
211	30	Fr.	5:34	B	**8:06**	E	14	32	9	18	24	2½	**3**	**9:50**	C	10:03	D	PSC	19
212	31	Sa.	5:35	B	**8:04**	E	14	29	9	18N.	10	3¼	**3½**	**10:13**	C	11:03	E	PSC	20

 To use this page, see p. 106; for Key Letters, see p. 234. ☞ **Bold = P.M.** ☞ Light = A.M.

JULY HATH 31 DAYS • 2010

O summer day, surpassing fair,
With hints of heaven in earth and air. –Eben Eugene Rexford

Day of Month	Day of Week	Dates, Feasts, Fasts, Aspects, Tide Heights	Weather
1	Th.	**Canada Day** • ☾ AT APO. • Sir John A. Macdonald became prime minister, Canada, 1867	*From*
2	Fr.	☾ ON EQ. • Lake Washington Floating Bridge dedicated, Seattle, Wash., 1940 • { 9.4 / 9.2	*twilight's*
3	Sa.	Dog Days begin. • ☌♃☾ • ☌♅☾ • Tides { 9.1 / 9.2	*gleams*
4	**C**	**6th S. af. P.** • **Independence Day** • Tides { 8.8 / 9.2	*to*
5	M.	♅ STAT. • Circus owner P. T. Barnum born, 1810 • { 8.5 / 9.4	*dawn's*
6	Tu.	⊕ AT APHELION • *Many drops make a shower.* • { 8.4 / 9.6	*early*
7	W.	Solar-powered aircraft *Solar Challenger* flew 163 miles in 5 hrs., 23 min., 1981 • Tides { 8.4 / 9.9	*light,*
8	Th.	Artist Tom Thomson last seen alive, Canoe Lake, Algonquin Park, Ont., 1917 • Tides { 8.5 / 10.2	*it*
9	Fr.	☾ RIDES HIGH • Jim Purol sat in 39,250 seats in 48 hours, setting world record, 2008 • { 8.8 / 10.7	*seems*
10	Sa.	Tornado outbreak in northeastern U.S., 1989 • { 9.2 / 11.2	*there's*
11	**C**	**New ●** • **Eclipse ☉** • ☾ AT ☋ • Tides { 9.6 / 11.5	*fireworks*
12	M.	☌☿☾ • Cornscateous air is everywhere. • { 10.0 / —	*every*
13	Tu.	☾ AT PERIG. • Current U.S. patent numbering system began, 1836 • { 11.8 / 10.4	*night!*
14	W.	**Bastille Day** • ☌♀☾ • Armadillos mate now. • { 11.8 / 10.8	*Picnics,*
15	Th.	**St. Swithin** • ☾ ON EQ. • Hail at least 3" around fell in SE Conn., 1799	*ball games,*
16	Fr.	☌♂☾ • ☌♄☾ • Black-eyed Susans in bloom now. • { 11.2 / 11.0	*concerts,*
17	Sa.	*As the wind blows you must set your sail.* • { 10.7 / 10.9	*parades*
18	**C**	**8th S. af. P.** • 16.91" rain in 24 hours, Aurora, Ill., 1996 • { 10.1 / 10.8	*drowned*
19	M.	N.Y.C. subway's first air-conditioned cars began service, 1967 • Tides { 9.5 / 10.6	*out*
20	Tu.	*Viking 1* lander touched down on Mars, 1976 • Tides { 9.1 / 10.4	*by*
21	W.	Film composer Jerry Goldsmith died, 2004 • { 8.8 / 10.3	*Nature's*
22	Th.	**St. Mary Magdalene** • ☾ RUNS LOW • Tides { 8.8 / 10.3	*cannonades!*
23	Fr.	☌♇☾ • ♃ STAT. • William Burt received patent for typographer, 1829 • { 8.8 / 10.3	*Now's*
24	Sa.	☾ AT ☊ • James MacGillivray published first tale of Paul Bunyan, Detroit, Mich., 1910	*perfect*
25	**C**	**9th S. af. P.** • **Full Buck ○** • Tides { 9.0 / 10.3	*weather*
26	M.	**St. James**[T] • 107°F, Salt Lake City, Utah, 1960 • Adult gypsy moths emerge. • { 9.1 / —	*for*
27	Tu.	*A proverb is the wisdom of many and the wit of one.* • Tides { 10.2 / 9.2	*vacations,*
28	W.	☾ AT APO. • ☌♆☾ • NFL added a fourth official, the field judge, 1929 • { 10.1 / 9.3	*safe*
29	Th.	**St. Martha** • ☾ ON EQ. • Annibale de Gasparis discovered asteroid 15 Eunomia, 1851	*from*
30	Fr.	☌♅☾ • Olympic Games of Los Angeles opened, 1932 • Tides { 9.7 / 9.4	*nightly*
31	Sa.	**St. Ignatius of Loyola** • ☌♃☾ • Tides { 9.4 / 9.4	*detonations!*

Farmer's Calendar

■ Overnight, it seems, legions of mushrooms spring up in the shadowy woods, and with them arrives their pale familiar, the spectral Indian pipe, the strangest flower that we have.

The Indian pipe *(Monotropa uniflora)* appears just after midsummer, growing out of the leaf mold under pines, maples, beeches, and other trees in the damp woods. It's also called the corpse plant for its color—a dead, almost translucent white, occasionally with flecks of black or gray. It has a single, five-petal flower and a single, 3- to 6-inch-tall stalk clasped by small, scaly leaves like the stalk of a ghostly asparagus. Sometimes the flower parts take on a tan or pink color, but there isn't a green cell in the plant, and this, with its habitat and way of growth, leads many to think that the Indian pipe is itself a kind of mushroom. In fact, it's a flowering plant related to the heath family and a true wildflower. But, rare among North American higher plants, it has no chlorophyll and so doesn't conduct photosynthesis. Rather, it takes nutriments from tapping the filamentous, rootlike mycelia of mushrooms and other fungi that, themselves, tap the roots of trees.

The Indian pipe may grow as a solitary plant or appear in colonies of six or eight, like the forest mushrooms it resembles. This uncanny flower furnishes another case of nature's inveterate habit of imitating itself.

THE EIGHTH MONTH • 2010

SKY WATCH ☆ *Mars skims below Saturn on the 1st. Venus passes below Saturn from the 6th to the 8th, then finally catches Mars from the 15th to the 22nd. All are now low in the southwest at nightfall. The trio form interesting triangles during the first half of the month, with the crescent Moon dangling below them on the 12th. Perfect moonless conditions prevail for the great Perseid meteor shower on the night of the 11th–12th. The action intensifies after midnight, with one meteor per minute, on average. Jupiter, at a dazzling magnitude –2.8, rises by 10:00 P.M. at midmonth and is nicely up at midnight, dominating the sky. Venus closely meets Virgo's blue star Spica on the 30th and 31st.*

◑	**Last Quarter**	3rd day	0 hour	59th minute
●	**New Moon**	9th day	23rd hour	8th minute
◐	**First Quarter**	16th day	14th hour	14th minute
○	**Full Moon**	24th day	13th hour	5th minute

All times are given in Eastern Daylight Time.

Purchase these pages with times set to your zip code at MyLocalAlmanac.com.

Day of Year	Day of Month	Day of Week	☼ Rises h. m.	Rise Key	☼ Sets h. m.	Set Key	Length of Day h.	Length of Day m.	Sun Fast m.	Declination of Sun °	Declination of Sun '	High Tide Times Boston		☾ Rises h. m.	Rise Key	☾ Sets h. m.	Set Key	☾ Place	☾ Age
213	1	**C**	5:36	B	**8:03**	E	14	27	9	17N.	54	3¾	**4¼**	**10:38**	B	**12:05**	E	PSC	21
214	2	M.	5:37	B	**8:02**	E	14	25	10	17	39	4¾	**5**	**11:08**	B	**1:08**	E	PSC	22
215	3	Tu.	5:38	B	**8:01**	E	14	23	10	17	23	5½	**5¾**	**11:44**	B	**2:13**	E	ARI	23
216	4	W.	5:39	B	**8:00**	E	14	21	10	17	08	6¼	**6¾**	—	—	**3:18**	E	ARI	24
217	5	Th.	5:40	B	**7:58**	E	14	18	10	16	51	7¼	**7½**	12:28	B	**4:21**	E	TAU	25
218	6	Fr.	5:41	B	**7:57**	E	14	16	10	16	35	8¼	**8½**	1:23	B	**5:19**	E	TAU	26
219	7	Sa.	5:42	B	**7:56**	E	14	14	10	16	18	9¼	**9½**	2:29	B	**6:09**	E	GEM	27
220	8	**C**	5:43	B	**7:55**	E	14	12	10	16	01	10¼	**10½**	3:43	B	**6:51**	E	GEM	28
221	9	M.	5:44	B	**7:53**	E	14	09	10	15	44	11	**11¼**	5:02	C	**7:27**	E	CAN	0
222	10	Tu.	5:45	B	**7:52**	E	14	07	10	15	26	**12**	—	6:22	C	**7:58**	D	LEO	1
223	11	W.	5:47	B	**7:51**	E	14	04	11	15	09	12¼	**12¾**	7:41	D	**8:27**	D	SEX	2
224	12	Th.	5:48	B	**7:49**	D	14	01	11	14	51	1	**1½**	8:59	E	**8:55**	C	LEO	3
225	13	Fr.	5:49	B	**7:48**	D	13	59	11	14	32	2	**2½**	10:15	E	**9:24**	C	VIR	4
226	14	Sa.	5:50	B	**7:46**	D	13	56	11	14	14	2¾	**3¼**	11:30	E	**9:55**	B	VIR	5
227	15	**C**	5:51	B	**7:45**	D	13	54	11	13	55	3¾	**4¼**	**12:44**	E	**10:31**	B	VIR	6
228	16	M.	5:52	B	**7:43**	D	13	51	12	13	36	4¾	**5**	**1:53**	E	**11:11**	B	LIB	7
229	17	Tu.	5:53	B	**7:42**	D	13	49	12	13	17	5¾	**6**	**2:57**	E	**11:59**	B	SCO	8
230	18	W.	5:54	B	**7:40**	D	13	46	12	12	58	6¾	**7¼**	**3:54**	E	—	—	OPH	9
231	19	Th.	5:55	B	**7:39**	D	13	44	12	12	38	8	**8¼**	**4:43**	E	12:52	B	OPH	10
232	20	Fr.	5:56	B	**7:37**	D	13	41	12	12	18	9	**9¼**	**5:23**	E	1:51	B	SAG	11
233	21	Sa.	5:57	B	**7:36**	D	13	39	13	11	58	9¾	**10**	**5:57**	E	2:52	B	SAG	12
234	22	**C**	5:58	B	**7:34**	D	13	36	13	11	38	10¾	**10¾**	**6:26**	E	3:54	B	CAP	13
235	23	M.	5:59	B	**7:33**	D	13	34	13	11	18	11¼	**11½**	**6:51**	D	4:55	C	AQU	14
236	24	Tu.	6:00	B	**7:31**	D	13	31	14	10	58	**12**	—	**7:13**	D	5:56	C	CAP	15
237	25	W.	6:01	B	**7:29**	D	13	28	14	10	37	12	**12½**	**7:35**	D	6:56	D	AQU	16
238	26	Th.	6:02	B	**7:28**	D	13	26	14	10	16	12¾	**1**	**7:56**	C	7:56	D	PSC	17
239	27	Fr.	6:03	B	**7:26**	D	13	23	14	9	55	1¼	**1¾**	**8:18**	C	8:55	E	PSC	18
240	28	Sa.	6:05	B	**7:25**	D	13	20	15	9	34	2	**2¼**	**8:42**	B	9:56	E	PSC	19
241	29	**C**	6:06	B	**7:23**	D	13	17	15	9	13	2¾	**3**	**9:10**	B	10:58	E	PSC	20
242	30	M.	6:07	B	**7:21**	D	13	14	15	8	51	3¼	**3½**	**9:43**	B	**12:02**	E	ARI	21
243	31	Tu.	6:08	B	**7:20**	D	13	12	16	8N.	30	4	**4¼**	**10:23**	B	**1:06**	E	ARI	22

 To use this page, see p. 106; for Key Letters, see p. 234. ☞ **Bold = P.M.** ☞ Light = A.M.

Subscribe today to the Premium Edition of *The Old Farmer's Almanac!*

☑ **YES!** Enter my subscription to *The Old Farmer's Almanac!* I'll pay just **$6.95** (plus $2.95 s/h) and receive my **FREE 2011 pocket calendar** plus all the benefits of the Almanac's Preferred Subscriber Program!*

_____
Name (please print above line)

_____
Address / Apt. no.

_____
City / State / Zip

Subscription begins with the 2011 edition. To start with the 2010 edition, check here ☐

Send no money, we'll bill you later!

FREE 2011 POCKET CALENDAR INCLUDED

*Preferred Subscriber Program Benefits:
Each year, your subscription will be renewed automatically unless you cancel service. You'll receive a reminder notice in July, followed by the Almanac delivered right to your doorstep and an invoice for the lowest rate then in effect. You can cancel at any time by calling: 1-800-ALMANAC (1-800-256-2622).   B99PA1

32 BONUS PAGES

SUBSCRIBE TODAY!
(see reverse for details)

Name: _____

Address: _____

_____

City/Town: _____ State: ____ Zip: ____

☛ *RUSH Order Enclosed!*

BUSINESS REPLY MAIL

FIRST-CLASS MAIL   PERMIT NO. 572   FLAGLER BEACH FL

POSTAGE WILL BE PAID BY ADDRESSEE

The Old Farmer's Almanac
Subscriptions

PO BOX 422453
PALM COAST, FL 32142-8287

Name: _____

Address: _____

_____

City/Town: _____ State: ____ Zip: ____

☛ *RUSH Order Enclosed!*

NO POSTAGE
NECESSARY
IF MAILED
IN THE
UNITED STATES

BUSINESS REPLY MAIL

FIRST-CLASS MAIL   PERMIT NO. 572   FLAGLER BEACH FL

POSTAGE WILL BE PAID BY ADDRESSEE

The Old Farmer's Almanac
Subscriptions

PO BOX 422453
PALM COAST, FL 32142-8287

AUGUST HATH 31 DAYS • 2010

The silent orchard aisles are sweet,
With smell of ripening fruit. –William Dean Howells

Day of Month	Day of Week	Dates, Feasts, Fasts, Aspects, Tide Heights	Weather
1	C	10th S. af. P. • Lammas Day • ☌♂♄ • { 9.1 9.4	*It's*
2	M.	Puppeteer Shari Lewis died, 1998 • Tides { 8.7 9.4	*steamy,*
3	Tu.	First okapi imported into U.S. went on display, Bronx Zoo, N.Y.C., 1937 • Tides { 8.5 9.5	*then*
4	W.	*Genius without education is like silver in the mine.*	*dreamy.*
5	Th.	☾ RIDES HIGH • 16" rain in 3 hours, Delaware Cty., Pa., 1843 • Tides { 8.3 9.9	*Gardeners*
6	Fr.	Transfiguration • ☿ GR. ELONG. (27° EAST) • Tides { 8.5 10.3	*can't*
7	Sa.	☾ AT ☋ • Record-breaking flight around world by single-engine plane completed, 1982	*give*
8	C	11th S. af. P. • Gray squirrels have second litters now. • Tides { 9.4 11.3	*away*
9	M.	New ● • ☌♀♄ • Webster-Ashburton Treaty signed, 1842 • { 10.0 11.7	*zucchini!*
10	Tu.	St. Lawrence • ☾ AT PERIG. • Dog got alimony, Edmonton, Alta., 2004	*Perseids*
11	W.	St. Clare • First day of Ramadan • Dog Days end. • ☌☿☾ • { 11.9 11.1	*plunge*
12	Th.	☾ ON EQ. • First successful communications satellite, *Echo I,* launched, 1960 • Tides { 11.9 11.4	*in*
13	Fr.	☌♀☾ • ☌♂☾ • ☌♄☾ • Nurse Florence Nightingale died, 1910	*fiery*
14	Sa.	Cristeta Comerford became White House executive chef, 2005 • Tides { 11.1 11.4	*filigree;*
15	C	Assumption • Discovery of 2nd planet orbiting a star in Big Dipper announced, 2001	*lightning*
16	M.	Delaware Memorial bridge opened, 1951 • { 9.8 10.7	*crashes,*
17	Tu.	Cat Nights commence. • *Better to ask twice than lose your way once.* • Tides { 9.2 10.3	*bashes—*
18	W.	☾ RUNS LOW • Ragweed in bloom. • Tides { 8.8 10.0	*what*
19	Th.	☌☿☾ • ☿ STAT. • ♀ GR. ELONG. (46° EAST) • Tides { 8.6 9.8	*a*
20	Fr.	☾ AT ☊ • ♆ AT ☍ • Project *Manhigh II* completed, 1957 • { 8.6 9.8	*jamboree!*
21	Sa.	Family claimed home invaded by goblin-like space creatures, Kelly, Ky., 1955 • Tides { 8.7 9.9	*Cold*
22	C	13th S. af. P. • Tornado, Middlesex County, Mass., 1851 • Tides { 8.9 10.0	*rain*
23	M.	☌♀♂ • *A lizard on a cushion will still seek leaves.* • Tides { 9.1 10.0	*ruins*
24	Tu.	St. Bartholomew • Full Sturgeon ○ • ☌♆☾ • Tides { 9.3 —	*our*
25	W.	☾ AT APO. • Theodore Roosevelt first U.S. president to descend in sub, 1905	*barbecues.*
26	Th.	☾ ON EQ. • 19th Amendment adopted, 1920 • { 10.0 9.6	*Crystal*
27	Fr.	☌♃☾ • ☌♅☾ • Hummingbirds migrate south. • Tides { 9.8 9.7	*nights*
28	Sa.	St. Augustine of Hippo • Prince Charles and Princess Diana divorced, 1996	*leave*
29	C	Senator Strom Thurmond finished record-setting 24-hour, 18-minute speech, 1957 • Tides { 9.3 9.7	*us*
30	M.	Vicki Keith first to swim across all five Great Lakes, 1988	*star-*
31	Tu.	*Nothing should be done in haste but gripping a flea.*	*bemused.*

Farmer's Calendar

■ Vegetable gardening, even on a small and casual scale, is an expression of the will to provide. The gardener wishes to do for himself, to supply some of his own basic needs, even if only to a very limited extent. This is an admirable ambition, to be sure, but the impulse to provide can be carried over the line.

In gardening, for me, this line has always lain somewhere near the border between growing fresh produce and preserving the harvest. In particular, my downfall has been green beans. Beans are easy to grow, and when they begin to produce, they arrive not in convenient increments but in a tidal wave. Fortunately, everybody on this place loves dilled beans, pickled with plenty of spices and garlic. The brining and canning of them, however, takes some doing. Too often, I fall behind the bean wave. Crisp, youthful, dilly beans are among the garden's treasures, but elderly dilly beans are not, and the difference between them is a day or two, no more. Get behind the wave, and you might as well use your beans for slingshot ammunition. You might, but I don't.

This is where the will to provide comes in. However old, however neglected my beans may be, I put them up anyway. I've dilled beans when the process was less akin to preserving than it was to embalming. A sane and commendable thrift has crossed into folly, and I have gone with it.

SEPTEMBER

THE NINTH MONTH • 2010

SKY WATCH ☆ *The month belongs to Jupiter. Not only is Saturn lost in solar glare and Mars now low and dim, but also Venus, despite brightening to a riveting magnitude −4.8 on the 30th, sets just an hour after sunset. By contrast, Jupiter rises at dusk, reaches opposition on the 21st, and shines at its brightest since 1963. At a magnitude −2.9, Jupiter dominates the sky all night long. Interestingly, Uranus comes to opposition on the 21st, too, so the two worlds stand side by side, especially midmonth. Jupiter's close visit makes this a good time to own a telescope. Fall begins with the equinox on the 22nd, at 11:09 P.M.; look for the full Harvest Moon on the 23rd.*

◑	Last Quarter	1st day	13th hour	22nd minute
●	New Moon	8th day	6th hour	30th minute
◐	First Quarter	15th day	1st hour	50th minute
○	Full Moon	23rd day	5th hour	17th minute
◑	Last Quarter	30th day	23rd hour	52nd minute

All times are given in Eastern Daylight Time.

Purchase these pages with times set to your zip code at MyLocalAlmanac.com.

Day of Year	Day of Month	Day of Week	Rises h. m.	Rise Key	Sets h. m.	Set Key	Length of Day h. m.	Sun Fast m.	Declination of Sun ° '	High Tide Times Boston		Rises h. m.	Rise Key	Sets h. m.	Set Key	Place	Age
244	1	W.	6:09	B	7:18	D	13 09	16	8 N.08	5	5¼	11:12	B	2:08	E	TAU	23
245	2	Th.	6:10	C	7:16	D	13 06	16	7 46	5¾	6	—		3:06	E	TAU	24
246	3	Fr.	6:11	C	7:14	D	13 03	17	7 24	6¾	7	12:11	B	3:58	E	TAU	25
247	4	Sa.	6:12	C	7:13	D	13 01	17	7 02	7¾	8¼	1:19	B	4:42	E	GEM	26
248	5	C	6:13	C	7:11	D	12 58	17	6 40	8¾	9¼	2:34	C	5:21	E	CAN	27
249	6	M.	6:14	C	7:09	D	12 55	18	6 17	9¾	10	3:52	C	5:54	E	CAN	28
250	7	Tu.	6:15	C	7:08	D	12 53	18	5 55	10¾	11	5:11	D	6:24	D	LEO	29
251	8	W.	6:16	C	7:06	D	12 50	18	5 32	11½	12	6:30	D	6:53	C	SEX	0
252	9	Th.	6:17	C	7:04	D	12 47	19	5 10	12¼	—	7:49	E	7:22	C	VIR	1
253	10	Fr.	6:18	C	7:02	D	12 44	19	4 47	12¾	1¼	9:07	E	7:53	B	VIR	2
254	11	Sa.	6:19	C	7:01	D	12 42	19	4 24	1¾	2	10:23	E	8:28	B	VIR	3
255	12	C	6:20	C	6:59	D	12 39	20	4 01	2½	2¾	11:37	E	9:08	B	LIB	4
256	13	M.	6:21	C	6:57	D	12 36	20	3 38	3½	3¾	12:46	E	9:54	B	LIB	5
257	14	Tu.	6:22	C	6:55	C	12 33	20	3 15	4½	4¾	1:47	E	10:47	B	OPH	6
258	15	W.	6:24	C	6:54	C	12 30	21	2 52	5½	5¾	2:39	E	11:44	B	OPH	7
259	16	Th.	6:25	C	6:52	C	12 27	21	2 29	6½	6¾	3:22	E	—		SAG	8
260	17	Fr.	6:26	C	6:50	C	12 24	21	2 06	7½	7¾	3:58	E	12:45	B	SAG	9
261	18	Sa.	6:27	C	6:48	C	12 21	22	1 43	8½	8¾	4:29	E	1:47	B	SAG	10
262	19	C	6:28	C	6:46	C	12 18	22	1 19	9¼	9½	4:55	E	2:48	C	CAP	11
263	20	M.	6:29	C	6:45	C	12 16	22	0 56	10	10¼	5:18	D	3:49	C	CAP	12
264	21	Tu.	6:30	C	6:43	C	12 13	23	0 33	10¾	11	5:40	D	4:49	D	AQU	13
265	22	W.	6:31	C	6:41	C	12 10	23	0 N.09	11½	11¾	6:02	C	5:49	D	PSC	14
266	23	Th.	6:32	C	6:39	C	12 07	23	0 S.13	12	—	6:24	C	6:48	E	PSC	15
267	24	Fr.	6:33	C	6:38	C	12 05	24	0 36	12¼	12½	6:48	C	7:49	E	PSC	16
268	25	Sa.	6:34	C	6:36	C	12 02	24	1 00	1	1	7:15	B	8:51	E	PSC	17
269	26	C	6:35	C	6:34	C	11 59	25	1 23	1½	1¾	7:46	B	9:54	E	ARI	18
270	27	M.	6:36	C	6:32	C	11 56	25	1 46	2¼	2¼	8:24	B	10:58	E	ARI	19
271	28	Tu.	6:37	C	6:31	C	11 54	25	2 10	3	3	9:09	B	12:00	E	TAU	20
272	29	W.	6:38	C	6:29	C	11 51	26	2 33	3¾	3¾	10:03	B	12:58	E	TAU	21
273	30	Th.	6:40	C	6:27	C	11 47	26	2 S.56	4½	4¾	11:06	B	1:51	E	TAU	22

SEPTEMBER HATH 30 DAYS • 2010

Here and yonder, high and low,
Goldenrod and sunflowers glow. –Robert Kelley Weeks

Day of Month	Day of Week	Dates, Feasts, Fasts, Aspects, Tide Heights	Weather
1	W.	Louis XIV, the Sun King, died, 1715 • Tides { 8.5 / 9.6	*Drizzle,*
2	Th.	☾ RIDES HIGH • Bobby Fischer/Boris Spassky chess rematch began, 1992 • { 8.4 / 9.7	*drizzle,*
3	Fr.	☾ AT ☋ • ☿ IN INF. ☌ • *September blow soft, Till the fruit's in the loft.* • { 8.4 / 10.0	*hair*
4	Sa.	"Crocodile Hunter" Steve Irwin died from a stingray barb wound, 2006 • Tides { 8.7 / 10.4	*will*
5	C	**15th S. af. P.** • B. Pasternak's *Doctor Zhivago* available in U.S., 1958	*frizzle*
6	M.	**Labor Day** • CBFT first Canadian TV station to go on air, 1952 • Tides { 9.9 / 11.3	*(if*
7	Tu.	☾ AT PERIG. • ☌☿☾ • Edith Eleanor McLean first baby placed in an incubator, 1888	*not*
8	W.	**New ●** • ☾ ON EQ. • Cranberry bog harvest begins, Cape Cod, Mass. • { 11.2 / 11.8	*hers,*
9	Th.	**St. Omer** • **Rosh Hashanah** • ☌♄☾ • Tides { 11.7 / —	*then*
10	Fr.	*That which will not be butter must be made into cheese.*	*surely*
11	Sa.	**Patriot Day** • ☌♀☾ • ☌♂☾ • ☿ STAT. • { 11.4 / 11.8	*his'll).*
12	C	**16th S. af. P.** • Winds 130 mph at Block Island, R.I., from hurricane Donna, 1960	*Sunny,*
13	M.	♇ STAT. • IBM introduced first computer with disk storage system, 1956 • { 10.2 / 11.0	*hot,*
14	Tu.	**Holy Cross** • ☾ RUNS LOW • World Series canceled due to strike, 1994 • { 9.6 / 10.5	*hang*
15	W.	Ember Day • ☌♇☾ • 27°F, Wilmington, Vt., 1983 • Tides { 9.0 / 10.0	*out*
16	Th.	☾ AT ☊ • Montreal Protocol (about ozone) signed by 24 countries, 1987 • Tides { 8.6 / 9.6	*the*
17	Fr.	Ember Day • Vice President Spiro T. Agnew died, 1996 • Tides { 8.5 / 9.4	*linen;*
18	Sa.	Ember Day • **Yom Kippur** • N.H. territory separated from Massachusetts, 1679 • { 8.5 / 9.5	*chilly*
19	C	**17th S. af. P.** • ☿ GR. ELONG. (18° WEST) • Tides { 8.8 / 9.5	*and*
20	M.	**St. Eustace** • ☌♆☾ • *Heavy September rains bring drought.* • { 9.0 / 9.7	*wet*
21	Tu.	**St. Matthew** • ☾ AT APO. • ♃ AT ☍ • ♅ AT ☍ • Tides { 9.3 / 9.7	*for*
22	W.	Harvest Home • **Autumnal Equinox** • ☾ ON EQ. • ☌♃♅ • { 9.6 / 9.8	*fall's*
23	Th.	**Sukkoth** • **Full Harvest** ○ • ☌♃☾ • ♀ GR. ILLUM. EXT.	*beginnin'.*
24	Fr.	Fire at U.S. Patent Office, Wash., D.C., 1877 • { 9.7 / 10.0	*Air's*
25	Sa.	*Be not afraid of going slowly; be afraid only of standing still.*	*crisp*
26	C	**18th S. af. P.** • Woodchucks hibernate now. • { 9.5 / 10.0	*as*
27	M.	**St. Vincent de Paul** • Breakthrough in deciphering Rosetta Stone announced, 1822 • { 9.2 / 10.0	*a*
28	Tu.	*Li'l Abner* cartoonist Al Capp born, 1909 • { 9.0 / 9.9	*McIntosh,*
29	W.	**St. Michael** • ☾ RIDES HIGH • ☌♀♂ • Tides { 8.8 / 9.9	*by*
30	Th.	**St. Sophia** • ☾ AT ☋ • ☌♄☉ • 108°F, Wichita Falls, Tex., 1977 • { 8.6 / 9.8	*gosh!*

We may achieve climate, but weather is thrust upon us. –O. Henry

Farmer's Calendar

■ A practical and authoritative book on the tools and tasks of cordwood-gathering asserts that "felling, splitting, cutting, and storing your firewood, you will cumulatively lift about 24 tons for each cord." Twenty-four tons, or 48,000 pounds: We're talking about a weight greater than that of a standard school bus with a full load of high school students. In contemplation, the statement is absurdly exaggerated.

When contemplation ends, however, and the work begins, the matter is otherwise. In my case, to transport my firewood, I use a small pickup truck. It's pretty maneuverable and, not without incurring a few scrapes and dents, can snake its way into the woods well enough, but I can't get it close to every tree that I cut. Therefore, I must move the cut wood to the truck. This I usually accomplish by tossing small chunks, say, halfway to the truck, then the rest of the way, then into the bed. Tossing the wood to a convenient spot is fun, kind of: a little like penny-pitching or lawn bowls. The job gets done, but every living piece of wood must be picked up, then picked up again, then again. And the unloading, splitting, and stacking have yet to begin. By season's end, skepticism has dissolved. I don't doubt even one of our author's 24 tons. Indeed, I feel as though I'd pushed that school bus along its route by myself, going uphill all the way.

CALENDAR

SKY WATCH ☆ *The show is over for Saturn, Mars, and Venus: All are lost in the Sun's glare, and just for good measure, Mercury's there, too. At a dazzling early-month magnitude of –4.7, Venus would be eye-catching if its orbit angled vertically above the sunset, as it does in the spring. As things now stand, however, it sets before twilight ends. Between 4:00 P.M. and 5:00 P.M. during the first week of the month, binocular-equipped observers taking care to block the Sun from direct view can see Venus's beautifully thin crescent exactly 30 degrees to the left of the Sun. Venus passes in front of the Sun at inferior conjunction on the 28th. Meanwhile, Jupiter remains superb as the brightest "star" in the heavens, out all night long.*

●	**New Moon**	7th day	14th hour	44th minute
◐	**First Quarter**	14th day	17th hour	27th minute
○	**Full Moon**	22nd day	21st hour	37th minute
◑	**Last Quarter**	30th day	8th hour	46th minute

All times are given in Eastern Daylight Time.

Purchase these pages with times set to your zip code at MyLocalAlmanac.com.

Day of Year	Day of Month	Day of Week	☼ Rises h. m.	Rise Key	☼ Sets h. m.	Set Key	Length of Day h. m.	Sun Fast m.	Declination of Sun ° '	High Tide Times Boston		☾ Rises h. m.	Rise Key	☾ Sets h. m.	Set Key	☾ Place	☾ Age
274	1	Fr.	6:41	C	**6:25**	C	11 44	26	3 s.20	5½	**5¾**	—	–	**2:36**	E	GEM	23
275	2	Sa.	6:42	C	**6:24**	C	11 42	26	3 43	6½	**6¾**	12:15	B	**3:16**	E	GEM	24
276	3	**C**	6:43	C	**6:22**	C	11 39	27	4 06	7½	**7¾**	1:29	C	**3:50**	E	CAN	25
277	4	M.	6:44	C	**6:20**	C	11 36	27	4 29	8½	**8¾**	2:45	C	**4:21**	D	LEO	26
278	5	Tu.	6:45	C	**6:18**	C	11 33	27	4 52	9½	**9¾**	4:02	D	**4:50**	D	SEX	27
279	6	W.	6:46	D	**6:17**	C	11 31	28	5 15	10¼	**10¾**	5:19	E	**5:18**	C	LEO	28
280	7	Th.	6:47	D	**6:15**	C	11 28	28	5 38	11	**11½**	6:37	E	**5:49**	C	VIR	0
281	8	Fr.	6:48	D	**6:13**	C	11 25	28	6 01	**12**	—	7:56	E	**6:22**	B	VIR	1
282	9	Sa.	6:50	D	**6:12**	C	11 22	29	6 24	12½	**12¾**	9:12	E	**7:01**	B	VIR	2
283	10	**C**	6:51	D	**6:10**	C	11 19	29	6 47	1¼	**1½**	10:26	E	**7:46**	B	LIB	3
284	11	M.	6:52	D	**6:08**	C	11 16	29	7 09	2¼	**2½**	11:32	E	**8:37**	B	SCO	4
285	12	Tu.	6:53	D	**6:07**	C	11 14	29	7 32	3	**3¼**	**12:30**	E	**9:34**	B	OPH	5
286	13	W.	6:54	D	**6:05**	B	11 11	30	7 54	4	**4¼**	**1:18**	E	**10:35**	B	SAG	6
287	14	Th.	6:55	D	**6:03**	B	11 08	30	8 17	5	**5¼**	**1:57**	E	**11:38**	B	SAG	7
288	15	Fr.	6:56	D	**6:02**	B	11 06	30	8 39	6	**6¼**	**2:30**	E	—	–	SAG	8
289	16	Sa.	6:58	D	**6:00**	B	11 02	30	9 01	7	**7¼**	**2:57**	E	12:40	C	CAP	9
290	17	**C**	6:59	D	**5:59**	B	11 00	30	9 23	7¾	**8**	**3:22**	D	1:41	C	AQU	10
291	18	M.	7:00	D	**5:57**	B	10 57	31	9 45	8¾	**9**	**3:44**	D	2:41	D	AQU	11
292	19	Tu.	7:01	D	**5:56**	B	10 55	31	10 06	9½	**9¾**	**4:06**	C	3:40	D	PSC	12
293	20	W.	7:02	D	**5:54**	B	10 52	31	10 28	10	**10½**	**4:28**	C	4:40	D	PSC	13
294	21	Th.	7:04	D	**5:53**	B	10 49	31	10 49	10¾	**11¼**	**4:52**	C	5:41	E	PSC	14
295	22	Fr.	7:05	D	**5:51**	B	10 46	31	11 11	11¼	**11¾**	**5:18**	B	6:42	E	PSC	15
296	23	Sa.	7:06	D	**5:50**	B	10 44	31	11 32	**12**	—	**5:48**	B	7:46	E	ARI	16
297	24	**C**	7:07	D	**5:48**	B	10 41	32	11 53	12½	**12½**	**6:24**	B	8:50	E	ARI	17
298	25	M.	7:08	D	**5:47**	B	10 39	32	12 13	1¼	**1¼**	**7:08**	B	9:53	E	TAU	18
299	26	Tu.	7:10	D	**5:45**	B	10 35	32	12 34	1¾	**2**	**8:00**	B	10:53	E	TAU	19
300	27	W.	7:11	D	**5:44**	B	10 33	32	12 54	2½	**2¾**	**9:00**	B	11:47	E	TAU	20
301	28	Th.	7:12	D	**5:42**	B	10 30	32	13 14	3¼	**3½**	**10:06**	B	**12:34**	E	GEM	21
302	29	Fr.	7:13	D	**5:41**	B	10 28	32	13 34	4¼	**4¼**	**11:17**	C	**1:15**	E	GEM	22
303	30	Sa.	7:14	D	**5:40**	B	10 26	32	13 54	5¼	**5¼**	—	–	**1:50**	E	CAN	23
304	31	**C**	7:16	D	**5:38**	B	10 22	32	14 s.13	6	**6½**	12:30	C	**2:20**	D	CAN	24

 To use this page, see p. 106; for Key Letters, see p. 234. ☞ **Bold = P.M.** ☞ Light = A.M.

OCTOBER

OCTOBER HATH 31 DAYS • 2010

At midnight hour, as shines the Moon,
A sheet of silver spreads below. –James Gates Percival

Day of Month	Day of Week	Dates, Feasts, Fasts, Aspects, Tide Heights	Weather
1	Fr.	St. Gregory • Walt Disney World opened, Orlando, Fla., 1971 • Tides { 8.6 / 9.9	*A*
2	Sa.	*Alfred Hitchcock Presents* debuted on TV, 1955	*cloudburst*
3	C	19th S. af. P. • *Habits are cobwebs at first; cables at last.* • Tides { 9.2 / 10.3	*or*
4	M.	St. Francis of Assisi • Pres. Rutherford B. Hayes born, 1822 • Tides { 9.8 / 10.7	*two*
5	Tu.	☽ ON EQ. • 116°F, Sentinel, Ariz., 1917 • Tides { 10.5 / 11.0	*won't*
6	W.	☽ AT PERIG. • Greater Winnipeg Floodway (Duff's Ditch) completed, Man., 1969 • { 11.1 / 11.2	*spoil*
7	Th.	New ● • ☌☿☽ • ☌♄☽ • ♀ STAT. • Tides { 11.7 / 11.3	*the*
8	Fr.	☌☿♄ • Tom Ridge became first director of Office of Homeland Security, 2001 • { 12.0 / —	*view;*
9	Sa.	☌♀☽ • ☌♂☽ • 7.7 earthquake, Kodiak Island, Alaska, 1900 • { 11.2 / 12.0	*sunlight*
10	C	20th S. af. P. • *Soyuz 25* mission scrapped after docking troubles, 1977	*ignites*
11	M.	Columbus Day • Thanksgiving Day (Canada) • Tides { 10.4 / 11.4	*maples,*
12	Tu.	☽ RUNS LOW • 19th Summer Olympic Games began, Mexico City, Mex., 1968 • { 9.9 / 10.8	*birches,*
13	W.	☽ AT ☊ • ☌♇☽ • Stock market's Friday the 13th mini-crash, 1989 • { 9.3 / 10.2	*sumacs,*
14	Th.	Officials confirmed invasive snakehead fish found in Chicago's Burnham Harbor, Lake Mich., 2004 • { 8.9 / 9.7	*too.*
15	Fr.	*Though a tree grow ever so high, the falling leaves return to the root.* • Tides { 8.6 / 9.3	*Rain*
16	Sa.	☿ IN SUP. ☌ • First Quebec vs. Ontario football game, 1875 • Tides { 8.5 / 9.1	*can't*
17	C	21st S. af. P. • ☌♆☽ • Tides { 8.6 / 9.1	*extinguish*
18	M.	St. Luke • ☽ AT APO. • St. Luke's little summer. • { 8.9 / 9.1	*the*
19	Tu.	☽ ON EQ. • Victoria Cross recipient Leo Clarke died, 1916	*vast*
20	W.	☌♃☽ • ☌♅☽ • Snowstorm in Sheridan, Wyo., 1958	*conflagration,*
21	Th.	Timber rattlesnakes move to winter dens. • { 9.8 / 9.4	*and*
22	Fr.	Full Hunter's ○ • Chester Carlson produced first xerographic copy, 1938 • { 10.0 / 9.4	*snow*
23	Sa.	*There are three things extremely hard: steel, a diamond, and to know one's self.* • { 10.2 / —	*only*
24	C	22nd S. af. P. • ☌☿♀ • Tides { 9.4 / 10.3	*quickens*
25	M.	Leslie L. Curtis first to be granted U.S. patent for air brush device, 1881 • Tides { 9.3 / 10.4	*the*
26	Tu.	☽ RIDES HIGH • Little brown bats hibernate now. • { 9.2 / 10.4	*heart's*
27	W.	☽ AT ☋ • Last performance by opera singer Beverly Sills, 1980 • { 9.0 / 10.3	*palpitation.*
28	Th.	Sts. Simon & Jude • ♀ IN INF. ☌ • Tides { 8.9 / 10.2	*Cool*
29	Fr.	First peacetime draft in U.S. history, 1940 • Tides { 8.9 / 10.1	*nights,*
30	Sa.	*Keep conscience clear, then never fear.*	*jack-o-lantern*
31	C	All Hallows' Eve • Mt. Rushmore completed, near Keystone, S.Dak., 1941 • { 9.2 / 10.0	*lights.*

Farmer's Calendar

■ After all the leaves are down, after the first frosts have come, after the fallacious reprieve of Indian summer, but before the snow begins to fly in earnest, there arrives a segment of the year that has no name, but that might be called Inside-Out Time.

Inside-Out Time—it may last for a few days, or it may take up the latter half of this month and beyond—is a perverse little subseason in which the normal order of daily living is reversed. I start the day in a cold house: The floors are cold, the walls are cold. I pile on sweaters. I make a fire in the woodstove. But on going outdoors, I find a summer day, or close to it. The air is mild, the sun is warm. Off come the sweaters, out goes the stove. At midday, however, the house still feels as cold as it did at seven o'clock, and it continues to feel cold through the afternoon, even as the outdoor temperature remains almost like summer. Cold within, warm without: This is not how things were supposed to work; this is not why we live in houses.

The ambiguous temperatures of Inside-Out Time are more than frustrating. They also require nice economic calculations, especially in periods, such as last year, when heating oil costs the same as Grade A maple syrup and firewood, like chainsaw Chippendale. Should you warm the house or simply leave it, to live outdoors with the squirrels and the deer until winter comes?

THE ELEVENTH MONTH • 2010

SKY WATCH ☆ *During the first six hours after sunset, Jupiter, having retrograded to the Aquarius–Pisces border, remains brilliant and dominant in the south even as it fades ever so slightly to magnitude –2.6. The Moon floats to the right of Jupiter on the 15th. In the predawn insomniac hours, Saturn and Venus speedily return, with Venus rivetingly brilliant as it explosively brightens from magnitude –4.1 to –4.9. At midmonth, 40 minutes before sunrise, UFO-like Venus stands 15 degrees high, with Virgo's blue star Spica just above it and Saturn higher still. The group's brightness range is enormous. While the Ringed Planet barely exceeds Spica's so-so magnitude 1, Venus is 250 times more brilliant than the other two.*

● **New Moon**	6th day	0 hour	52nd minute
◐ **First Quarter**	13th day	11th hour	39th minute
○ **Full Moon**	21st day	12th hour	27th minute
◑ **Last Quarter**	28th day	15th hour	36th minute

After 2:00 A.M. on November 7, Eastern Standard Time is given.

Purchase these pages with times set to your zip code at MyLocalAlmanac.com.

Day of Year	Day of Month	Day of Week	☼ Rises h. m.	Rise Key	☼ Sets h. m.	Set Key	Length of Day h.	Length of Day m.	Sun Fast m.	Declination of Sun °	Declination of Sun '	High Tide Times Boston		☾ Rises h. m.	Rise Key	☾ Sets h. m.	Set Key	☾ Place	☾ Age
305	1	M.	7:17	D	**5:37**	B	10	20	32	14 s.	32	7	**7½**	1:43	D	**2:49**	D	LEO	25
306	2	Tu.	7:18	D	**5:36**	B	10	18	32	14	51	8	**8½**	2:58	D	**3:17**	C	LEO	26
307	3	W.	7:19	D	**5:35**	B	10	16	32	15	10	9	**9½**	4:13	E	**3:45**	C	VIR	27
308	4	Th.	7:21	E	**5:33**	B	10	12	32	15	29	10	**10½**	5:29	E	**4:17**	B	VIR	28
309	5	Fr.	7:22	E	**5:32**	B	10	10	32	15	47	10¾	**11¼**	6:45	E	**4:52**	B	VIR	29
310	6	Sa.	7:23	E	**5:31**	B	10	08	32	16	05	11½	—	8:00	E	**5:34**	B	LIB	0
311	7	**C**	6:24	E	**4:30**	B	10	06	32	16	23	12¼	11¼	8:11	E	**5:23**	B	LIB	1
312	8	M.	6:26	E	**4:29**	B	10	03	32	16	40	12	**12¼**	9:14	E	**6:19**	B	OPH	2
313	9	Tu.	6:27	E	**4:28**	B	10	01	32	16	57	12¾	**1**	10:08	E	**7:20**	B	OPH	3
314	10	W.	6:28	E	**4:27**	B	9	59	32	17	14	1¾	**1¾**	10:52	E	**8:24**	B	SAG	4
315	11	Th.	6:29	E	**4:26**	B	9	57	32	17	31	2½	**2¾**	11:28	E	**9:27**	B	SAG	5
316	12	Fr.	6:31	E	**4:25**	B	9	54	32	17	47	3½	**3½**	11:58	E	**10:30**	C	CAP	6
317	13	Sa.	6:32	E	**4:24**	B	9	52	31	18	03	4¼	**4½**	**12:24**	D	**11:30**	C	AQU	7
318	14	**C**	6:33	E	**4:23**	B	9	50	31	18	19	5¼	**5½**	**12:47**	D	—	–	CAP	8
319	15	M.	6:34	E	**4:22**	B	9	48	31	18	34	6	**6¼**	**1:09**	C	12:30	D	AQU	9
320	16	Tu.	6:36	E	**4:21**	B	9	45	31	18	49	7	**7¼**	**1:31**	C	1:29	D	PSC	10
321	17	W.	6:37	E	**4:20**	B	9	43	31	19	04	7¾	**8**	**1:54**	C	2:29	E	PSC	11
322	18	Th.	6:38	E	**4:19**	B	9	41	31	19	18	8½	**9**	**2:19**	B	3:30	E	PSC	12
323	19	Fr.	6:39	E	**4:19**	B	9	40	30	19	32	9	**9¾**	**2:48**	B	4:33	E	PSC	13
324	20	Sa.	6:41	E	**4:18**	B	9	37	30	19	46	9¾	**10¼**	**3:22**	B	5:37	E	ARI	14
325	21	**C**	6:42	E	**4:17**	A	9	35	30	19	59	10½	**11**	**4:04**	B	6:42	E	ARI	15
326	22	M.	6:43	E	**4:16**	A	9	33	30	20	12	11	**11¾**	**4:54**	B	7:44	E	TAU	16
327	23	Tu.	6:44	E	**4:16**	A	9	32	29	20	25	11¾	—	**5:53**	B	8:41	E	TAU	17
328	24	W.	6:45	E	**4:15**	A	9	30	29	20	37	12½	**12½**	**6:58**	B	9:32	E	GEM	18
329	25	Th.	6:46	E	**4:15**	A	9	29	29	20	49	1¼	**1¼**	**8:09**	C	10:15	E	GEM	19
330	26	Fr.	6:48	E	**4:14**	A	9	26	28	21	00	2	**2¼**	**9:21**	C	10:51	E	CAN	20
331	27	Sa.	6:49	E	**4:14**	A	9	25	28	21	11	3	**3**	**10:34**	D	11:23	D	CAN	21
332	28	**C**	6:50	E	**4:13**	A	9	23	28	21	22	3¾	**4**	**11:46**	D	11:52	D	LEO	22
333	29	M.	6:51	E	**4:13**	A	9	22	27	21	32	4¾	**5**	—	–	**12:19**	D	SEX	23
334	30	Tu.	6:52	E	**4:12**	A	9	20	27	21 s.	42	5¾	**6¼**	12:59	E	**12:46**	C	VIR	24

 To use this page, see p. 106; for Key Letters, see p. 234. ☞ **Bold** = P.M. ☞ Light = A.M.

NOVEMBER HATH 30 DAYS • 2010

The autumn is old,
The sere leaves are flying. –Thomas Hood

Day of Month	Day of Week	Dates, Feasts, Fasts, Aspects, Tide Heights	Weather
1	M.	**All Saints'** • Michelangelo's fresco on Sistine Chapel ceiling unveiled, 1512 • { 9.7 10.1	*Skim*
2	Tu.	**All Souls'** • **Election Day** • ☾ ON EQ. • Tides { 10.2 10.3	*ice*
3	W.	☾ AT PERIG. • Mary Jacobs granted patent for first modern bra, 1914 • { 10.8 10.4	*cracking,*
4	Th.	☌♄☾ • (Royal) Montreal Golf Club, oldest in North America, founded, 1873 • { 11.4 10.6	*snow*
5	Fr.	☌♀☾ • *Keep your shop and your shop will keep you.* • Tides { 11.7 10.6	*for*
6	Sa.	Sadie Hawkins Day • **New ●** • Tides { 11.9 —	*tracking.*
7	C	**Daylight Saving Time ends, 2:00 A.M.** • ☌☿☾ • ☌♂☾ • ♆ STAT.	*Sodden:*
8	M.	☾ RUNS LOW • Black bears head to winter dens now. • Tides { 10.3 11.5	*Snow's*
9	Tu.	☾ AT ☊ • ☌♇☾ • Worst day of lethal Great Lakes storm, 1913 • { 9.9 11.1	*gone*
10	W.	Continental Marines (now U.S. Marine Corps) established, 1755	*but*
11	Th.	**St. Martin of Tours** • **Veterans Day** • Tides { 9.2 10.0	*not*
12	Fr.	Indian Summer • Lobsters move to offshore waters. • Tides { 8.9 9.5	*forgotten.*
13	Sa.	Ground-breaking ceremony for Martin Luther King Jr. Memorial, Wash., D.C., 2006 • { 8.7 9.1	*Glory*
14	C	**25th S. af. P.** • ☌♆☾ • Actress Veronica Lake born, 1919	*days*
15	M.	☾ ON EQ. • ☾ AT APO. • Crab apples are ripe now. • { 8.7 8.7	*for*
16	Tu.	☌♃☾ • ☌⛢☾ • ♀ STAT. • The Philadephia Orchestra debuted, 1900	*football*
17	W.	**St. Hugh of Lincoln** • First U.S. postage stamp with American eagle issued, 1851 • { 9.2 8.7	*stars,*
18	Th.	Botanist Asa Gray born, 1810 • Desoto car discontinued, 1960 • Tides { 9.5 8.8	*heavy*
19	Fr.	♃ STAT. • *Old friends, old wine, and old gold are best.*	*snow*
20	Sa.	☌☿♂ • Skunks hibernate now. • Tides { 10.1 9.1	*buries*
21	C	**26th S. af. P.** • **Full Beaver ○** • Tides { 10.4 9.2	*our*
22	M.	☾ RIDES HIGH • Santa Ana winds in parts of southern Calif. made airborne rubble a hazard, 1957	*cars.*
23	Tu.	**St. Clement** • U.S. president Franklin Pierce born, 1804 • Tides { 10.7 —	*Thanks*
24	W.	☾ AT ☋ • *The belly carries the legs and not the legs the belly.* • Tides { 9.3 10.8	*for*
25	Th.	**Thanksgiving Day** • National Independent Party organized, 1874 • Tides { 9.3 10.7	*turkey,*
26	Fr.	France's first satellite, *Astérix 1,* launched 1961 • { 9.3 10.6	*bless*
27	Sa.	0.5" snow began falling in northern Fla., 1912 • Tides { 9.4 10.3	*the*
28	C	**1st S. of Advent** • Basketball inventor James Naismith died, 1939	*sage:*
29	M.	☾ ON EQ. • Richard Byrd's expedition first to fly over South Pole, 1929 • Tides { 9.8 9.9	*ice*
30	Tu.	**St. Andrew** • ☾ AT PERIG. • Deadly tornado, Simsboro, La., 1996 • { 10.1 9.7	*age!*

I never think of the future—it comes soon enough. –Albert Einstein

Farmer's Calendar

■ The thing to remember about weather signs in nature is that they are highly reliable. In fact, many are never wrong. Consider the celebrated woolly bear caterpillar, larva of the Isabella tiger moth *(Pyrrharctia isabella).* It's a plump, 2-inch worm covered in soft bristles—black at the creature's ends and in its middle the color of a red fox. Everybody knows that the ratio of black bristles to rust on the woolly bear foretells the coming winter: More black bristles mean a hard winter; more rust, a mild one.

Or maybe it's the other way around. It scarcely matters. This is because woolly bears have been predicting the weather for a long time, and they know how to cover themselves. Some years ago, for example, we had an unusual spate of woolly bears in this neighborhood. They appeared late in the fall, after the frosts had set in, and they appeared in numbers. In a half-hour's walk, you'd see hundreds of woolly bears creeping across the road. On examination, they showed a great variety of color proportions, from nearly all-black to rust with the least dip of black at the ends. Evidently, then, there could be no kind of winter that some of them would not accurately predict.

The benefit for the would-be weather-wise is obvious. If you distrust the augury of a given woolly bear, then you simply ignore that caterpillar, take a step, and believe another.

DECEMBER

THE TWELFTH MONTH • 2010

SKY WATCH ☆ *Dazzling in the east during the 2½ hours before dawn, Venus attains its greatest brilliancy during the first week of this month, at a shadow-casting magnitude –4.9. This is its best month as a morning star. Venus floats just to the left of the crescent Moon on the mornings of the 2nd and the 31st. Mercury appears far below and to the left of Venus on the 30th and 31st. Brilliant Jupiter is prominent in the first 5 hours after dusk, setting at around midnight. The Geminid meteors should perform well after nightfall on the 13th. An exceptional total eclipse of the Moon is visible throughout North America early on the 21st. The partial eclipse begins at 1:32* A.M.*, with totality starting at 2:40* A.M. *Winter arrives the same day, with the solstice at 6:38* P.M.

●	**New Moon**	5th day	12th hour	36th minute
◐	**First Quarter**	13th day	8th hour	59th minute
○	**Full Moon**	21st day	3rd hour	13th minute
◑	**Last Quarter**	27th day	23rd hour	18th minute

All times are given in Eastern Standard Time.

Purchase these pages with times set to your zip code at MyLocalAlmanac.com.

Day of Year	Day of Month	Day of Week	☼ Rises h. m.	Rise Key	☼ Sets h. m.	Set Key	Length of Day h.	m.	Sun Fast m.	Declination of Sun °	'	High Tide Times Boston		☾ Rises h. m.	Rise Key	☾ Sets h. m.	Set Key	☾ Place	☾ Age
335	1	W.	6:53	E	**4:12**	A	9	19	27	21s.	51	6¾	**7¼**	2:12	E	**1:15**	C	VIR	25
336	2	Th.	6:54	E	**4:12**	A	9	18	26	22	00	7¾	**8¼**	3:25	E	**1:48**	B	VIR	26
337	3	Fr.	6:55	E	**4:12**	A	9	17	26	22	08	8½	**9¼**	4:39	E	**2:26**	B	VIR	27
338	4	Sa.	6:56	E	**4:11**	A	9	15	26	22	17	9½	**10**	5:51	E	**3:11**	B	LIB	28
339	5	**C**	6:57	E	**4:11**	A	9	14	25	22	24	10¼	**11**	6:57	E	**4:04**	B	SCO	0
340	6	M.	6:58	E	**4:11**	A	9	13	25	22	32	11	**11¾**	7:55	E	**5:03**	B	OPH	1
341	7	Tu.	6:59	E	**4:11**	A	9	12	24	22	38	11¾	—	8:44	E	**6:06**	B	SAG	2
342	8	W.	7:00	E	**4:11**	A	9	11	24	22	45	12½	**12½**	9:24	E	**7:11**	B	SAG	3
343	9	Th.	7:01	E	**4:11**	A	9	10	23	22	51	1¼	**1½**	9:57	E	**8:15**	C	SAG	4
344	10	Fr.	7:02	E	**4:11**	A	9	09	23	22	56	2	**2¼**	10:24	E	**9:17**	C	AQU	5
345	11	Sa.	7:03	E	**4:11**	A	9	08	22	23	01	2¾	**3**	10:49	D	**10:18**	D	CAP	6
346	12	**C**	7:04	E	**4:11**	A	9	07	22	23	06	3½	**3¾**	11:11	D	**11:17**	D	AQU	7
347	13	M.	7:04	E	**4:11**	A	9	07	22	23	10	4½	**4¾**	11:33	C	—	–	PSC	8
348	14	Tu.	7:05	E	**4:12**	A	9	07	21	23	13	5¼	**5½**	11:56	C	12:16	D	PSC	9
349	15	W.	7:06	E	**4:12**	A	9	06	21	23	17	6	**6½**	**12:20**	C	1:16	E	PSC	10
350	16	Th.	7:07	E	**4:12**	A	9	05	20	23	19	6¾	**7½**	**12:46**	B	2:18	E	PSC	11
351	17	Fr.	7:07	E	**4:12**	A	9	05	20	23	21	7¾	**8¼**	**1:18**	B	3:21	E	ARI	12
352	18	Sa.	7:08	E	**4:13**	A	9	05	19	23	23	8½	**9**	**1:56**	B	4:26	E	ARI	13
353	19	**C**	7:08	E	**4:13**	A	9	05	19	23	25	9¼	**9¾**	**2:43**	B	5:29	E	TAU	14
354	20	M.	7:09	E	**4:14**	A	9	05	18	23	25	10	**10¾**	**3:39**	B	6:30	E	TAU	15
355	21	Tu.	7:10	E	**4:14**	A	9	04	18	23	26	10¾	**11½**	**4:44**	B	7:24	E	TAU	16
356	22	W.	7:10	E	**4:15**	A	9	05	17	23	26	11½	—	**5:55**	B	8:11	E	GEM	17
357	23	Th.	7:10	E	**4:15**	A	9	05	17	23	25	12¼	**12¼**	**7:09**	C	8:51	E	GEM	18
358	24	Fr.	7:11	E	**4:16**	A	9	05	16	23	24	1	**1**	**8:23**	C	9:25	E	CAN	19
359	25	Sa.	7:11	E	**4:16**	A	9	05	16	23	23	1¾	**2**	**9:37**	D	9:55	D	LEO	20
360	26	**C**	7:12	E	**4:17**	A	9	05	15	23	21	2½	**2¾**	**10:50**	D	10:23	D	SEX	21
361	27	M.	7:12	E	**4:18**	A	9	06	15	23	18	3½	**3¾**	—	–	10:50	C	LEO	22
362	28	Tu.	7:12	E	**4:18**	A	9	06	14	23	15	4¼	**4¾**	12:02	E	11:19	C	VIR	23
363	29	W.	7:12	E	**4:19**	A	9	07	14	23	12	5¼	**5¾**	1:15	E	11:49	B	VIR	24
364	30	Th.	7:13	E	**4:20**	A	9	07	13	23	08	6¼	**7**	2:27	E	**12:25**	B	VIR	25
365	31	Fr.	7:13	E	**4:21**	A	9	08	13	23s.	04	7¼	**8**	3:38	E	**1:06**	B	LIB	26

 To use this page, see p. 106; for Key Letters, see p. 234. ☞ **Bold = P.M.** ☞ Light = A.M.

DECEMBER HATH 31 DAYS • 2010

So timely you came, and well you chose,
You came when most needed, my winter rose. –Alfred Austin

Day of Month	Day of Week	Dates, Feasts, Fasts, Aspects, Tide Heights	Weather
1	W.	☌♄☾ • ☿ GR. ELONG. (21° EAST) • First 12 nations signed Antarctic Treaty, 1959 • {10.5 / 9.7	Mild
2	Th.	St. Viviana • First day of Chanukah • ☌♀☾ • {10.9 / 9.7	relief,
3	Fr.	Quebec Bridge opened to rail traffic, Quebec City, 1917 • Tides {11.2 / 9.8	briefly—
4	Sa.	♀ GR. ILLUM. EXT. • Actress Deanna Durbin born, 1921 • Tides {11.4 / 9.8	cold
5	**C**	**2nd S. of Advent** • New ● • ☾ RUNS LOW • ☌☿♇	and
6	M.	St. Nicholas • ☾ AT ☊ • ☌♂☾ • ♅ STAT. • {11.3 / 9.7	snowy,
7	Tu.	St. Ambrose • Nat'l Pearl Harbor Remembrance Day • ☌☿☾ • ☌♇☾	chiefly.
8	W.	Islamic New Year • Astronaut Robert Lawrence killed during training exercise, 1967 • {9.6 / 10.8	Breath
9	Th.	*Visits should be short, like a winter's day.* • Tides {9.4 / 10.4	makes
10	Fr.	St. Eulalia • ☿ STAT. • Winterberry fruits especially showy now. • {9.1 / 9.9	vapors
11	Sa.	☌♆☾ • One of earliest recorded sightings of northern lights in North America, 1719 • {9.0 / 9.4	as
12	**C**	**3rd S. of Advent** • 20.4" snow covered Newark, N.J., 1960 • Tides {8.8 / 9.0	we
13	M.	St. Lucia • ☾ ON EQ. • ☾ AT APO. • ☌☿♂ • ☌♃☾ • {8.8 / 8.6	wield
14	Tu.	Halcyon Days begin. • ☌☿♇ • ☌♅☾ • Tides {8.8 / 8.3	ice
15	W.	Ember Day • *Moderate measures succeed best.* • Tides {8.9 / 8.2	scrapers.
16	Th.	Colonists dumped British tea in harbor to protest taxation without representation, Boston, 1773 • {9.1 / 8.2	It's
17	Fr.	Ember Day • Beware the Pogonip. • Tides {9.4 / 8.3	so wet
18	Sa.	Ember Day • *Gifts burst rocks.* • Wind rolled snow into balls, Howe, Ind., 1933 • Tides {9.7 / 8.5	we
19	**C**	**4th S. of Advent** • ☿ IN INF. ☌ • Tides {10.0 / 8.8	look
20	M.	☾ RIDES HIGH • S.C. seceded from Union, 1860 • Tides {10.5 / 9.0	amphibian;
21	Tu.	St. Thomas • Winter Solstice • Full Cold ○ • Eclipse ☾ • ☾ AT ☋	
22	W.	*In youth, we believe many things that are not true; in old age, we doubt many truths.* • {11.1 / —	Christmas
23	Th.	Marjorie Child Husted, Betty Crocker creator, died, 1986	Day
24	Fr.	*Stille Nacht (Silent Night)* first performed, Oberndorf, Austria, 1818 • Tides {9.8 / 11.1	will
25	Sa.	**Christmas** • ☾ AT PERIG. • *Santa Maria* abandoned near Hispaniola, 1492	feel
26	**C**	Boxing Day (Canada) • First day of Kwanzaa • ☾ ON EQ. • ☌♇☉	Caribbean!
27	M.	St. John • Poet Charles Olson born, 1910 • {10.2 / 10.1	Freezin's
28	Tu.	Holy Innocents • ☌♄☾ • Iowa became 29th state, 1846 • {10.3 / 9.6	greetings,
29	W.	St. Stephen[T] • Patriots' Randy Moss set NFL record with season's 23rd TD catch, 2007	everyone!
30	Th.	☿ STAT. • *A red Sun has water in his eye.* • {10.4 / 9.1	Welcome to
31	Fr.	St. Sylvester • ☌♀☾ • Tides {10.5 / 9.1	two-oh-one-one!

Farmer's Calendar

■ Thirty-one days hath December, as the world knows. In northern New England, this may strike us as a pitiful understatement. This long month can pack a lot into its days. Perhaps nature has given us December as a preview of the winter it inaugurates.

Every part of winter's repertoire is apt to be on offer this month. Hereabouts, the first days of December are really autumn days: There's seldom much snowfall and almost never any lasting snow cover. The days are short, but the sun is often warm, the temperature mild. The oaks and beeches may still bear most of their brown leaves.

By midmonth, things look different. The first snows have come and often, unfortunately, the first ice storms. Pleasant, semiautumnal days are over. The low Sun seems hardly to have risen properly before it's passing behind the western hills, setting in a brief, cold, rosy dusk that is beautiful in its way but that nobody would doubt belonged to winter. The hardwoods are mostly bare.

Then, by month's end, the world is frigid and, often, white. The snow shovel is in use. Daylight dwindles to a mere spark. But now, the solstice has passed. The days are growing longer. In the grand celestial mechanism, spring is inexorably advancing. December's characteristic synopsis of the months to come is complete. By Christmas, we've had a whole winter in a single month.

Glossary of Almanac Oddities

■ Many readers have expressed puzzlement over the rather obscure notations that appear on our **Right-Hand Calendar Pages, 111–137.** These "oddities" have long been fixtures in the Almanac, and we are pleased to provide some definitions. (Once explained, they may not seem so odd after all!)

–Beth Krommes

Ember Days: The four periods formerly observed by the Roman Catholic and Anglican churches for prayer, fasting, and the ordination of clergy are called Ember Days. Specifically, these are the Wednesdays, Fridays, and Saturdays that follow in succession following (1) the First Sunday in Lent; (2) Whitsunday–Pentecost; (3) the Feast of the Holy Cross, September 14; and (4) the Feast of St. Lucia, December 13. The word *ember* is perhaps a corruption of the Latin *quatuor tempora,* "four times."

Folklore has it that the weather on each of the three days foretells the weather for the next three months; that is, for September's Ember Days, Wednesday forecasts the weather for October, Friday for November, and Saturday for December.

Distaff Day (January 7): This was the first day after Epiphany (January 6), when women were expected to return to their spinning following the Christmas holiday. A distaff is the staff that women used for holding the flax or wool in spinning. (Hence the term "distaff" refers to women's work or the maternal side of the family.)

Plough Monday (January): Traditionally, the first Monday after Epiphany was called Plough Monday because it was the day that men returned to their plough, or daily work, following the Christmas holiday. (Every few years, Plough Monday and Distaff Day fall on the same day.) It was customary at this time for farm laborers to draw a plough through the village, soliciting money for a "plough light," which was kept burning in the parish church all year. One proverb notes that

> *"Yule is come and Yule is gone,*
> *and we have feasted well;*
> *so Jack must to his flail again*
> *and Jenny to her wheel."*

Three Chilly Saints (May): Mamertus, Pancras, and Gervais were three early Christian saints. Because their feast days, on May 11, 12, and 13, respectively, are traditionally cold, they have come to be known as the Three Chilly Saints. An old French saying translates to: "St. Mamertus, St. Pancras, and St. Gervais do not pass without a frost."

Midsummer Day (June 24): To the farmer, this day is the midpoint of the growing season, halfway between planting and harvest. (Midsummer Eve is an occasion for festivity and celebrates fertility.) The Anglican church considered it a "Quarter Day," one of the four major

C
A
L
E
N
D
A
R

divisions of the liturgical year. It also marks the feast day of St. John the Baptist.

Cornscateous Air (July): First used by early almanac makers, this term signifies warm, damp air. Though it signals ideal climatic conditions for growing corn, it poses a danger to those affected by asthma and other respiratory problems.

Dog Days (July 3–August 11): These are the hottest and most unhealthy days of the year. Also known as Canicular Days, their name derives from the Dog Star, Sirius. The traditional 40-day period of Dog Days coincides with the heliacal (at sunrise) rising of Sirius.

Lammas Day (August 1): Derived from the Old English *hlaf maesse,* meaning "loaf mass," Lammas Day marked the beginning of the harvest. Traditionally, loaves of bread were baked from the first-ripened grain and brought to the churches to be consecrated. Eventually, "loaf mass" became "Lammas." In Scotland, Lammastide fairs became famous as the time when trial marriages could be made. These marriages could end after a year with no strings attached.

Cat Nights Begin (August 17): This term harks back to the days when people believed in witches. An Irish legend says that a witch could turn into a cat and regain herself eight times, but on the ninth time, August 17, she couldn't change back, hence the saying: "A cat has nine lives." Because August is a "yowly" time for cats, this may have initially prompted the speculation about witches on the prowl.

Harvest Home (September): In Europe and Britain, the conclusion of the harvest each autumn was once marked by festivals of fun, feasting, and thanksgiving known as "Harvest Home." It was also a time to hold elections, pay workers, and collect rents. These festivals usually took place around the autumnal equinox. Certain groups in this country, particularly the Pennsylvania Dutch, have kept the tradition alive.

St. Luke's Little Summer (October): A spell of warm weather that occurs about the time of the saint's feast day, October 18, this period is sometimes referred to as Indian summer.

Indian Summer (November): A period of warm weather following a cold spell or a hard frost, Indian summer can occur between St. Martin's Day (November 11) and November 20. Although there are differing dates for its occurrence, for more than 200 years the Almanac has adhered to the saying "If All Saints' brings out winter, St. Martin's brings out Indian summer." Some say that the term comes from the early Native Americans, who believed that the condition was caused by a warm wind sent from the court of their southwestern god, Cautantowwit.

Halcyon Days (December): About two weeks of calm weather often follow the blustery winds of autumn's end. Ancient Greeks and Romans believed these occurred around the time of the winter solstice, when the halcyon, or kingfisher, was brooding. In a nest floating on the sea, the bird was said to have charmed the wind and waves so that the waters were especially calm during this period.

Beware the Pogonip (December): The word *pogonip* is a meteorological term used to describe an uncommon occurrence—frozen fog. The word was coined by Native Americans to describe the frozen fogs of fine ice needles that occur in the mountain valleys of the western United States and Canada. According to their tradition, breathing the fog is injurious to the lungs. □□

Long-Term Care Coverage

Who needs it; How to find the right policy

Americans are living longer than ever and are now facing the important decision of whether to purchase long-term care insurance. Most people buy this coverage to help protect assets, preserve independence and provide quality care. A growing number of younger people are buying it to help their aging parents.

In general, long-term care protection makes the most sense for people with a net worth of $100,000 to $2 million. Those with less will likely exhaust their assets and qualify for Medicaid; those with more can generally fund their own care if they choose to do so.

With over 100 policies on the market, it pays to comparison shop. In fact, the cost of similar coverage from different companies varies by 50 percent or more.

According to *Money Magazine* editor, Jean Chatzky, "Your best bet is to get quotes from at least three companies." In addition, you should consider a policy with at least a three-year term—the average time people need care.

Look for a <u>daily benefit</u> that would cover the average daily nursing-facility cost in your area. The national average is $213 per day, or over $77,745 per year.**

Look for an <u>elimination period</u> (the time before your benefits begin) of 90 days. Remember, this is "catastrophic" coverage. Most people who need the insurance can afford the cost of care for three months, and this approach lowers your cost — in some cases, by as much as 30% per year. Equally important, inquire about <u>inflation protection</u> and insist on insurers rated "A" or better by A.M. Best and "strong" by Standard & Poor's.

If you'd like to receive three quotes with just one call, **Long-Term Care Quote** will provide them— free of charge. The company— recommended in *Consumers Digest, The Wall Street Journal, Kiplinger's, Money Magazine* and on NBC— will ask for basic information on your age, health and location, then shop up to 8 top-rated carriers on your behalf. You'll get details and quotes on up to three high-quality, low-cost policies selected— and a free copy of *The Consumer's Guide to Long-Term Care Insurance*.

To request your ***complimentary*** policy comparisons and personalized quotes, call toll-free **1-800-587-3279 ext 2010** or visit **www.LTCQ.net**.

70%
of Americans
65 or older
are expected to need
long-term care
during their lifetime.*

40%
needing care today
are between
18 and 64.[†]

This advertisement is not intended to solicit insurance business in Texas.

*San Diego Daily Transcript, *Living long has its benefits, and its costs*, Sept. 26, 2003; [†]*Who Buys Long-Term Care Insurance*, Health Insurance Association of America and Lifeplans, Inc., 2005. **MetLife Mature Market Institute, *The MetLife Market Survey of Nursing Home & Home Care Costs*, 10/08. Long-Term Care Quote, a subsidiary of Longevity LTC, Inc., is located at 1580 N. Fiesta Blvd., Ste. 103, Gilbert, AZ 85233. Longevity LTC, Inc. is licensed to sell insurance in all 50 states and the District of Columbia. LA# 425558, MA# 1844089, UT# 260353. Longevity does business under the name Longevity LTC Insurance Services, Inc. in CA, CA# 0F82027.

Holidays and Observances

For Movable Religious Observances, see page 109.
Federal holidays listed in bold.

Jan. 1	New Year's Day
Jan. 18	**Martin Luther King Jr.'s Birthday** (observed)
Jan. 19	Robert E. Lee Day (Fla., Ky., La., S.C.)
Feb. 2	Groundhog Day
Feb. 12	Abraham Lincoln's Birthday
Feb. 14	Valentine's Day
Feb. 15	**George Washington's Birthday** (observed) Susan B. Anthony's Birthday (Fla., Wis.) National Flag of Canada Day
Feb. 16	Mardi Gras (Baldwin & Mobile counties, Ala.; La.)
Mar. 2	Texas Independence Day Town Meeting Day (Vt.)
Mar. 15	Andrew Jackson Day (Tenn.)
Mar. 17	St. Patrick's Day Evacuation Day (Suffolk Co., Mass.)
Mar. 29	Seward's Day (Alaska)
Apr. 2	Pascua Florida Day
Apr. 19	Patriots Day (Maine, Mass.)
Apr. 21	San Jacinto Day (Tex.)
Apr. 22	Earth Day
Apr. 30	National Arbor Day
May 5	Cinco de Mayo
May 8	Truman Day (Mo.)
May 9	Mother's Day
May 15	Armed Forces Day
May 22	National Maritime Day
May 24	Victoria Day (Canada)
May 31	**Memorial Day** (observed)
June 5	World Environment Day
June 11	King Kamehameha I Day (Hawaii)
June 14	Flag Day
June 17	Bunker Hill Day (Suffolk Co., Mass.)
June 19	Emancipation Day (Tex.)
June 20	Father's Day West Virginia Day
July 1	Canada Day
July 4	**Independence Day**
July 24	Pioneer Day (Utah)
Aug. 2	Colorado Day Civic Holiday (Canada)
Aug. 16	Bennington Battle Day (Vt.)
Aug. 19	National Aviation Day
Aug. 26	Women's Equality Day
Sept. 6	**Labor Day**
Sept. 9	Admission Day (Calif.)
Sept. 11	Patriot Day
Sept. 12	Grandparents Day
Sept. 17	Constitution Day
Sept. 21	International Day of Peace
Oct. 4	Child Health Day
Oct. 9	Leif Eriksson Day
Oct. 11	**Columbus Day** (observed) Native Americans' Day (S.Dak.) Thanksgiving Day (Canada)
Oct. 18	Alaska Day
Oct. 24	United Nations Day
Oct. 29	Nevada Day
Oct. 31	Halloween
Nov. 2	Election Day
Nov. 4	Will Rogers Day (Okla.)
Nov. 11	**Veterans Day** Remembrance Day (Canada)
Nov. 19	Discovery Day (Puerto Rico)
Nov. 25	**Thanksgiving Day**
Nov. 26	Acadian Day (La.)
Dec. 7	National Pearl Harbor Remembrance Day
Dec. 15	Bill of Rights Day
Dec. 17	Wright Brothers Day
Dec. 25	**Christmas Day**
Dec. 26	Boxing Day (Canada) First day of Kwanzaa

CALENDAR

Love calendar lore? Find more at Almanac.com.

2009

January
S	M	T	W	T	F	S
				1	2	3
4	5	6	7	8	9	10
11	12	13	14	15	16	17
18	19	20	21	22	23	24
25	26	27	28	29	30	31

February
S	M	T	W	T	F	S
1	2	3	4	5	6	7
8	9	10	11	12	13	14
15	16	17	18	19	20	21
22	23	24	25	26	27	28

March
S	M	T	W	T	F	S
1	2	3	4	5	6	7
8	9	10	11	12	13	14
15	16	17	18	19	20	21
22	23	24	25	26	27	28
29	30	31				

April
S	M	T	W	T	F	S
			1	2	3	4
5	6	7	8	9	10	11
12	13	14	15	16	17	18
19	20	21	22	23	24	25
26	27	28	29	30		

May
S	M	T	W	T	F	S
					1	2
3	4	5	6	7	8	9
10	11	12	13	14	15	16
17	18	19	20	21	22	23
24	25	26	27	28	29	30
31						

June
S	M	T	W	T	F	S
	1	2	3	4	5	6
7	8	9	10	11	12	13
14	15	16	17	18	19	20
21	22	23	24	25	26	27
28	29	30				

July
S	M	T	W	T	F	S
			1	2	3	4
5	6	7	8	9	10	11
12	13	14	15	16	17	18
19	20	21	22	23	24	25
26	27	28	29	30	31	

August
S	M	T	W	T	F	S
						1
2	3	4	5	6	7	8
9	10	11	12	13	14	15
16	17	18	19	20	21	22
23	24	25	26	27	28	29
30	31					

September
S	M	T	W	T	F	S
		1	2	3	4	5
6	7	8	9	10	11	12
13	14	15	16	17	18	19
20	21	22	23	24	25	26
27	28	29	30			

October
S	M	T	W	T	F	S
				1	2	3
4	5	6	7	8	9	10
11	12	13	14	15	16	17
18	19	20	21	22	23	24
25	26	27	28	29	30	31

November
S	M	T	W	T	F	S
1	2	3	4	5	6	7
8	9	10	11	12	13	14
15	16	17	18	19	20	21
22	23	24	25	26	27	28
29	30					

December
S	M	T	W	T	F	S
		1	2	3	4	5
6	7	8	9	10	11	12
13	14	15	16	17	18	19
20	21	22	23	24	25	26
27	28	29	30	31		

2010

January
S	M	T	W	T	F	S
					1	2
3	4	5	6	7	8	9
10	11	12	13	14	15	16
17	18	19	20	21	22	23
24	25	26	27	28	29	30
31						

February
S	M	T	W	T	F	S
	1	2	3	4	5	6
7	8	9	10	11	12	13
14	15	16	17	18	19	20
21	22	23	24	25	26	27
28						

March
S	M	T	W	T	F	S
	1	2	3	4	5	6
7	8	9	10	11	12	13
14	15	16	17	18	19	20
21	22	23	24	25	26	27
28	29	30	31			

April
S	M	T	W	T	F	S
				1	2	3
4	5	6	7	8	9	10
11	12	13	14	15	16	17
18	19	20	21	22	23	24
25	26	27	28	29	30	

May
S	M	T	W	T	F	S
						1
2	3	4	5	6	7	8
9	10	11	12	13	14	15
16	17	18	19	20	21	22
23	24	25	26	27	28	29
30	31					

June
S	M	T	W	T	F	S
		1	2	3	4	5
6	7	8	9	10	11	12
13	14	15	16	17	18	19
20	21	22	23	24	25	26
27	28	29	30			

July
S	M	T	W	T	F	S
				1	2	3
4	5	6	7	8	9	10
11	12	13	14	15	16	17
18	19	20	21	22	23	24
25	26	27	28	29	30	31

August
S	M	T	W	T	F	S
1	2	3	4	5	6	7
8	9	10	11	12	13	14
15	16	17	18	19	20	21
22	23	24	25	26	27	28
29	30	31				

September
S	M	T	W	T	F	S
			1	2	3	4
5	6	7	8	9	10	11
12	13	14	15	16	17	18
19	20	21	22	23	24	25
26	27	28	29	30		

October
S	M	T	W	T	F	S
					1	2
3	4	5	6	7	8	9
10	11	12	13	14	15	16
17	18	19	20	21	22	23
24	25	26	27	28	29	30
31						

November
S	M	T	W	T	F	S
	1	2	3	4	5	6
7	8	9	10	11	12	13
14	15	16	17	18	19	20
21	22	23	24	25	26	27
28	29	30				

December
S	M	T	W	T	F	S
			1	2	3	4
5	6	7	8	9	10	11
12	13	14	15	16	17	18
19	20	21	22	23	24	25
26	27	28	29	30	31	

2011

January
S	M	T	W	T	F	S
						1
2	3	4	5	6	7	8
9	10	11	12	13	14	15
16	17	18	19	20	21	22
23	24	25	26	27	28	29
30	31					

February
S	M	T	W	T	F	S
		1	2	3	4	5
6	7	8	9	10	11	12
13	14	15	16	17	18	19
20	21	22	23	24	25	26
27	28					

March
S	M	T	W	T	F	S
		1	2	3	4	5
6	7	8	9	10	11	12
13	14	15	16	17	18	19
20	21	22	23	24	25	26
27	28	29	30	31		

April
S	M	T	W	T	F	S
					1	2
3	4	5	6	7	8	9
10	11	12	13	14	15	16
17	18	19	20	21	22	23
24	25	26	27	28	29	30

May
S	M	T	W	T	F	S
1	2	3	4	5	6	7
8	9	10	11	12	13	14
15	16	17	18	19	20	21
22	23	24	25	26	27	28
29	30	31				

June
S	M	T	W	T	F	S
			1	2	3	4
5	6	7	8	9	10	11
12	13	14	15	16	17	18
19	20	21	22	23	24	25
26	27	28	29	30		

July
S	M	T	W	T	F	S
					1	2
3	4	5	6	7	8	9
10	11	12	13	14	15	16
17	18	19	20	21	22	23
24	25	26	27	28	29	30
31						

August
S	M	T	W	T	F	S
	1	2	3	4	5	6
7	8	9	10	11	12	13
14	15	16	17	18	19	20
21	22	23	24	25	26	27
28	29	30	31			

September
S	M	T	W	T	F	S
				1	2	3
4	5	6	7	8	9	10
11	12	13	14	15	16	17
18	19	20	21	22	23	24
25	26	27	28	29	30	

October
S	M	T	W	T	F	S
						1
2	3	4	5	6	7	8
9	10	11	12	13	14	15
16	17	18	19	20	21	22
23	24	25	26	27	28	29
30	31					

November
S	M	T	W	T	F	S
		1	2	3	4	5
6	7	8	9	10	11	12
13	14	15	16	17	18	19
20	21	22	23	24	25	26
27	28	29	30			

December
S	M	T	W	T	F	S
				1	2	3
4	5	6	7	8	9	10
11	12	13	14	15	16	17
18	19	20	21	22	23	24
25	26	27	28	29	30	31

Best Fishing Days and Times

The best times to fish are when the fish are naturally most active. The Sun, Moon, tides, and weather all influence fish activity. For example, fish tend to feed more at sunrise and sunset. During a full Moon, tides are higher than average and fish tend to feed more. However, most of us go fishing when we can get the time off, not because it is the best time. But there *are* best times, according to fishing lore:

The Best Fishing Days for 2010, when the Moon is between new and full:

January 15–30

February 13–28

March 15–29

April 14–28

May 13–27

June 12–26

July 11–25

August 9–24

September 8–23

October 7–22

November 6–21

December 5–21

■ One hour before and one hour after high tides, and one hour before and one hour after low tides. (The times of high tides for Boston are given on pages 110–136; also see pages 239–240. Inland, the times for high tides correspond with the times when the Moon is due south. Low tides are halfway between high tides.)

■ During the "morning rise" (after sunup for a spell) and the "evening rise" (just before sundown and the hour or so after).

■ When the barometer is steady or on the rise. (But even during stormy periods, the fish aren't going to give up feeding. The smart fisherman will find just the right bait.)

■ When there is a hatch of flies—caddis flies or mayflies, commonly. (The fisherman will have to match *his* fly with the hatching flies or go fishless.)

■ When the breeze is from a westerly quarter rather than from the north or east.

■ When the water is still or rippled, rather than during a wind.

How to Estimate the Weight of a Fish

Measure the fish from the tip of its nose to the tip of its tail. Then measure its girth at the thickest portion of its midsection.

The weight of a fat-bodied fish (bass, salmon) = (length x girth x girth)/800

The weight of a slender fish (trout, northern pike) = (length x girth x girth)/900

Example: If a fish is 20 inches long and has a 12-inch girth, its estimated weight is (20 x 12 x 12)/900 = 2,880/900 = 3.2 pounds

salmon

trout

catfish

New lure's catch rate may be too high for some tournaments.

Out-fishes other bait 19 to 4 in one contest.

Uses aerospace technology to mimic a real fish.

Swims with its tail.

New lure swims like a real fish--nearly triples catch in Florida contest.

ORLANDO, FL– A small company in Connecticut has developed a new lure that mimics the motion of a real fish so realistically eight professionals couldn't tell the difference between it and a live shad when it "swam" toward them on retrieval. The design eliminates wobbling, angled swim-

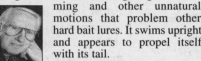

by Charlie Allen

ming and other unnatural motions that problem other hard bait lures. It swims upright and appears to propel itself with its tail.

Curiously, the company may have designed it too well. Tournament fishermen who have used it said it's possible officials will not allow it in contests where live bait is prohibited. They claim it swims more realistically than anything they have ever seen. If so, that would hurt the company's promotional efforts. Winning tournaments is an important part of marketing a new lure.

Fish would probably prefer to see it

Inventor Scott Wilson lands a 10-pounder.

restricted. I watched eight veteran fishermen test the new lure (called The KickTail®) on a lake outside Orlando FL for about four hours. Four used the KickTail and four used a combination of their favorite lures and shiners (live bait). The four using the KickTail caught 41 fish versus 14 for the other four. In one boat the KickTail won 19 to 4. The KickTail also caught bigger fish, which suggests it triggers larger, less aggressive fish to strike.

The KickTail's magic comes from a patented technology that breaks the tail

into five segments. As water rushes by on retrieval, a little-known principle called aeronautical flutter causes the tail to wag left and right, as if the lure were propelling itself with its tail. Unlike other hard baits, the head remains stationary—only the tail wags. A company spokesman told me this.

"Marine biologists will tell you that the more a lure swims like a real fish, the more fish it will catch. Well, the only live thing the KickTail doesn't do is breathe. It's always swimming wild and free. Fish can't stand it. We've seen fish that have just eaten go for the KickTail. It's like having another potato chip."

Whether you fish for fun or profit, if you want a near 3 to 1 advantage, I would order now before the KickTail becomes known. The company even guarantees a refund, if you don't catch more fish and return the lures within 30 days. There are three versions: a floater, a diver and a "dying shad" with a weed guard. Each lure costs $9.95 and you must order at least two. There is also a "Super 10-Pack" with additional colors for only $79.95, a savings of almost $20.00. S/h is only $7.00 no matter how many you order.

To order call **1-800-873-4415** or click **www.ngcsports.com/gear** anytime or day or send a check or M.O. (or cc number and exp. date) to NGC Sports **(Dept. KT-1551)**, 60 Church Street, Yalesville, CT 06492. CT add sales tax. The KickTail is four inches long and works in salt and fresh water.

KTS-8 © NGC Worldwide, Inc. 2010 **Dept. KT-1551**

Let's All Cheer for FATHERS

William Jackson Smart of Spokane, Washington, was such a great dad that he inspired his daughter, Sonora Smart Dodd, to create a holiday honoring fathers. Smart, a farmer and Civil War veteran, raised Sonora and her five younger brothers by himself after his wife, Ellen, died giving birth to their youngest child in 1898. While attending a Mother's Day church service in 1909, Sonora,

Here's your responsibility,

The greatest mortal ever had—

Just to be worthy, friend, to be

Some youngster's dad.

–Douglas Malloch,
American poet (1877–1938)

then 27, came up with the idea.

Sonora's efforts to honor fathers met with resistance at first. One group of Spokane conventioneers preferred a National Fishing Day to Father's Day. But Sonora, as charming as she was stubborn, within a few months had convinced the Spokane Ministerial Association and the YMCA to set aside a Sunday in June to celebrate fathers. She proposed June 5, her

It's the 100th anniversary of their day

by Aurelia C. Scott

Sonora Smart Dodd

father's birthday, but the ministers chose the third Sunday in June so that they would have more time after Mother's Day (the second Sunday in May) to prepare their sermons.

So it was that on June 19, 1910, Sonora rode in a horse-drawn carriage to deliver presents to handicapped fathers, boys from the YMCA decorated their lapels with fresh-cut roses (red for living fathers, white for the deceased), and the city's ministers devoted their homilies to fatherhood.

The widely publicized events struck a chord. In 1916, President Woodrow Wilson and his family personally observed the day. Eight years later, President Calvin Coolidge signed a resolution in favor of Father's Day "to establish more intimate relations between fathers and their children and to impress upon fathers the full measure of their obligations." In 1966, President Lyndon Johnson signed an executive order that the holiday be celebrated on the third Sunday in June. Under President Richard Nixon, in 1972, Congress passed an act officially making Father's Day a national holiday. (Six years later, Sonora died at age 96.)

Different DAYS *for* Different DADS

North America is not the only place where Father's Day is celebrated.

■ In traditionally Catholic countries such as **Spain** and **Portugal,** Father's Day is observed on March 19, the Feast of St. Joseph.

■ **Taiwanese** celebrate Father's Day on August 8, the eighth day of the eighth month, because the Mandarin Chinese word for eight sounds like the word for "Papa."

■ In **Thailand,** Father's Day occurs on the king's birthday, which for current King Bhumibol Adulyadej is December 5.

□ □

Aurelia C. Scott
writes from Portland,
Maine. She is the author
of *Otherwise Normal
People* (Algonquin
Books, 2007).

147

by Alice Cary

–illustrated by John Manders

SIMPLE SOLUTIONS for

TOSS A COIN

EVER SINCE THERE HAVE BEEN COINS, PEOPLE HAVE BEEN
flipping them. Whether it's deciding who goes first or something
more monumental, Heads or Tails is often the first—or last—resort.
Coin tosses are popular because they're fair, right?

ndecisive Times

Think again.

The question has been studied for years. While South African
mathematician John Kerrich was interned by the Germans during World War II, he passed the time by tossing a coin 10,000
times and recording the results.

More recently, the issue was tackled by Persi Diaconis, a professor of statistics and mathematics at Stanford University. He
commissioned a team of Harvard University technicians to
build a mechanical coin tosser to launch a coin into a cup
in the same way every time. Using this gadget, he found
that a coin lands the same side up every time. It's physics,
Diaconis reasoned: The same force applied to the same
spot on a coin produces the same result. The professor was
then able to teach himself to flip a coin with his thumb the
same way every time.

However, people don't usually flip coins in the same exact way time after time. That's where the "randomness" of
coin tosses comes into play—people flip with different
speeds, spins, forces, and angles. To learn more about
these tosses and landings, Diaconis teamed up with Susan Holmes, an associate professor of statistics, and
Richard Montgomery, a mathematics professor
renowned for his "Falling Cat Theorem"—which ex-
plains how falling cats always land on their feet.

They found that in addition to tumbling from side to
side, coins also wobble, or rotate on an axis like a pizza
being tossed. Sometimes coins appear to have flipped but
never actually do. The researchers attached a long ribbon to
a coin and observed that four times out of 100, the ribbon, and
therefore the coin, never turned.

continued

The team concluded that a tossed coin is slightly (51 percent) more likely to land with the same side up as when it was flipped. In other words, start with heads up, end with heads up.

A coin toss has altered the course of human events more times than we will ever know, but these occasions live in infamy:

■ **In 1845, two New Englanders helped** found a city in Oregon, but they couldn't agree on what to call it. Asa Lovejoy, from Massachusetts, proposed "Boston." Francis Pettygrove, from Maine, wanted to use the name of his hometown. In the end, they flipped a coin, which became known as the "Portland Penny." Guess who won!

■ **On December 14, 1903, Wilbur Wright** won a coin toss with his brother, Orville, but lost a place in history. Wilbur got to try out their latest glider for the first time at Kitty Hawk. It didn't fly. Three days later, Orville became the first person in the world to make a powered flight in a machine heavier than air.

■ **When the Detroit Lions** played the Pittsburgh Steelers on Thanksgiving Day in 1998, NFL referee Phil Luckett officiated the toss to see which team would get the ball to start the overtime period.

Luckett asked Pittsburgh captain Jerome Bettis to make a call while the coin was in the air. TV viewers were dumb-struck when they heard Bettis say "tails" and then Luckett announce that "heads" had been the call. The coin had landed tails up, supposedly giving Detroit the ball.

It turned out that Luckett had heard Bettis say, "Heads-tails." Bettis had changed his mind while the coin was in the air. Luckett stuck with Bettis's first choice, as NFL rules at the time dictated. Since then, the rules have been changed and calls are made before the coin is tossed.

Throw Rock, Paper, Scissors

IT'S CALLED "CHING, CHONG, CHA" in South Africa and "Pierre, Papier, Ciseaux" in France. This hand game is

used around the world. It's such an effective tool that there's an official society devoted to it, as well as televised, international tournaments with big money prizes. It's been around for centuries, perhaps originating in Japan. There

eople often use it to see who gets the last eat on a bus.

Experts advise players to be unpredictable. Beginners, for instance, often throw rock when they're losing. Men tend to throw rock as an opening move; omen often throw scissors.

Don't think for an instant that all of his is merely child's play.

In 2005, a Japanese corporation was elling its $20 million art collection. When its president could not decide whether Christie's or Sotheby's should ell the art—he deemed both auction ouses equally good—he ordered them o settle the matter with a round of Rock, 'aper, Scissors.

One Christie's official consulted his 1-year-old twins, playground experts at the game. The girls advised starting with scissors, and the auction house took their advice.

On the chosen day, representatives from the two houses sat at a conference table, where they each wrote down their choice. Sotheby's chose paper, so Christie's won the deal.

■ **During the summer of 2006, Florida** federal judge Gregory Presnell grew weary of arguments about where a deposition should be held. The bickering attorneys, after all, had offices in the same building. Finally, to settle the matter, Judge Presnell ordered a Rock, Paper, Scissors showdown to be held on the steps of the federal courthouse. □□

Alice Cary writes about popular culture for *The Old Farmer's Almanac.*

10 CURIOUS FACTS ABOUT MARK TWAIN

by Alice Cary

amuel Langhorn Clemens, aka Mar Twain, provided u with endless enter tainment throug numerous novel nonfiction books, short stories, and essays—a despite having ended formal schooling after th fifth grade. On the 100th anniversary of his death here is his life, abbreviated.

1 **Baby Clemens** arrived prematurely in a two-room shack in Florida, Missouri, on November 30, 1835. He was a frail infant and sickly child, prompting his mother to admit, "When I first saw him, I could see no promise in him."

Mark Twain's mother Jane Lampton Clemen

2 **The Clemens family had 19 cats at on** time during Twain's childhood. Over th years, he gave his cats inventive name such as Bambino, Famine, Pestilence, Satar Sin, Sour Mash, and Stray Kit.

3 **Sam Clemens** tried out several pseudonyms, including Rambler, W. Epaminondas Adrastus Blab, and Josh, before settling on Mark Twain (the phrase used by Mississippi River steamboat crews when measuring water depth).

Samuel Langhorne Clemens at age 15

4 **In 1874, the author** spotted one of the first typewriters, a Remington, in a Boston store window. Although it could type only capital letters and he had to operate the carriage return with a foot pedal, he bought it for $125. Twain also claimed to be the first person in New England to have had a telephone for private use.

5 **This literary giant** stood 5 feet 8½ inches tall and was so well known that he once received a letter addressed "Mark Twain, God Knows Where."

6 **In 1905, he spent the** first of two summers in Dublin, New Hampshire. There he wrote (but never

Mark Twain and friend in Dublin, New Hampshire

–The Mark Twain Memorial/Yankee Archives

finished) a book called *Three Thousand Years Among the Microbes*. To keep him company,

–The Granger Collection, New York

he rented three kittens from a local farm. While lecturing at the Dublin Lake Club, he noticed that an audience member was knitting a pair of socks while he spoke. Infuriated, Twain declared that he had never played second fiddle to a sock and left the room. The following year, he returned to the Lake Club and spoke for over 2 hours on various topics. He received a standing ovation.

7 **Twain made headlines in** 1907 by walking from his London hotel to a public bath across the street attired in his blue bathrobe and slippers. Back in America, he often wore scarlet socks and all-white suits, which he called his "don'tcareadam suits."

Mark Twain enjoys playing the piano for his daughter Clara (at left) and a family friend.

-The Granger Collection, New York

Test Your Knowledge of Mark Twain

Mark Twain designed a game. Patented in 1895 and called "Memory-Builder—A Game for Acquiring and Retaining All Sorts of Facts and Dates," it focused on European royalty. Play a similar game, based on Twain's life, at http://etext.virginia.edu/railton/timeline.

8 **Twain loved to write in bed,** and reporters chatted with him there more than once. He said, "I have never taken any exercise, except sleeping and resting, and I never intend to take any."

9 **He once observed: "When I** was younger, I could remember anything, whether it happened or not; but my faculties are decaying now and soon I shall be so that I can not remember any but the things that never happened. It is sad to go to pieces like this, but we all have to do it."

10 **He was born and died when** a comet passed, once noting: "I came in with Halley's Comet in 1835. It is coming again next year [1910], and I expect to go out with it. It will be the greatest disappointment of my life if I don't." He got his wish. He died on April 21, 1910, just two days after Halley's Comet had reached its point closest to the Sun. *(continued)*

Black Listed Cancer Treatment Could Save Your Life

As unbelievable as it seems the key to stopping many cancers has been around for over 30 years. Yet it has been banned. Blocked. And kept out of your medicine cabinet by the very agency designed to protect your health—the FDA.

In 1966, the senior oncologist at a prominent New York hospital rocked the medical world when he developed a serum that **"shrank cancer tumors!"** 90 minutes later they were gone... Headlines hit every major paper around the world. Time and again this life saving treatment worked miracles, but the FDA ignored the research and hope he brought and shut him down.

You read that right. He was not only shut down—but also forced out of the country where others benefited from his discovery. How many other treatments have they been allowed to hide?

Decades ago, European research scientist Dr. Johanna Budwig, a six-time Nobel Award nominee, discovered a totally natural formula that not only protects against the development of cancer, but has helped people all over the world diagnosed with incurable cancer—now lead normal lives.

After 30 years of study, Dr. Budwig discovered that the blood of seriously ill cancer patients was deficient in certain substances and nutrients. Yet, healthy blood always contained these ingredients. It was the lack of these nutrients that allowed cancer cells to grow wild and out of control.

It has been shown that by simply eating a combination of two natural and delicious foods (found on page 134) not only can cancer be prevented—but in some cases it was actually healed! "Symptoms of cancer, liver dysfunction, and diabetes were completely alleviated." Remarkably, what Dr. Budwig discovered was a totally natural way for eradicating cancer.

However, when she went to publish these results so that everyone could benefit—**she was blocked by manufacturers with heavy financial stakes!** For over 10 years now her methods have proved effective—yet she is denied publication—blocked by the giants who don't want you to read her words.

What's more, the world is full of expert minds like Dr. Budwig who have pursued cancer remedies and come up with remarkable natural formulas and diets that work for hundreds and thousands of patients. *How to Fight Cancer & Win* author William Fischer has studied these methods and revealed their secrets for you—so that you or someone you love may be spared the horrors of conventional cancer treatments.

As early as 1947, Virginia Livingston, M.D., isolated a cancer-causing microbe. She noted that every cancer sample analyzed contained it.

This microbe—a bacteria that is actually in each of us from birth to death—multiplies and promotes cancer when the immune system is weakened by disease, stress, or poor nutrition. Worst of all, the microbes secrete a special hormone protector that short-circuits our body's immune system—allowing the microbes to grow undetected for years. No wonder so many patients are riddled with cancer by the time it is detected. But there is hope even for them...

Throughout the pages of *How to Fight Cancer & Win* you'll meet real people who were diagnosed with cancer—suffered through harsh conventional treatments—turned their backs on so called modern medicine—only to be miraculously healed by natural means! Here is just a sampling of what others have to say about the book.

"We purchased *How to Fight Cancer & Win*, and immediately my husband started following the recommended diet for his just diagnosed colon cancer. He refused the surgery that our doctors advised. Since following the regime recommended in the book he has had no problems at all, cancer-wise. If not cured, we believe the cancer has to be in remission." —*Thelma B.*

"As a cancer patient who has been battling lymphatic cancer on and off for almost three years now, I was very pleased to stumble across *How to Fight Cancer & Win*. The book was inspiring, well-written and packed with useful information for any cancer patient looking to maximize his or her chances for recovery." —*Romany S.*

"I've been incorporating Dr. Budwig's natural remedy into my diet and have told others about it. Your book is very informative and has information I've never heard about before. Thanks for the wonderful information." —*Molly G.*

Claim your book today and you will be one of the lucky few who no longer have to wait for cures that get pushed "underground" by big business and money hungry giants.

To get your copy of *How to Fight Cancer & Win* go to www.agorahealthbooks.com or call **1-888-884-7598 and ask for code P6K92** to order by credit card. Or write "Fight Cancer—Dept. P6K92" on a plain piece of paper with your name, address, phone number (in case we have a question about your order) and mail it with a check for $19.95 plus $5.00 shipping to: **Agora Health Books, Dept. P6K92, P.O. Box 925, Frederick, MD 21705-9838**

If you are not completely satisfied, return the book within one year for a complete and total refund—no questions asked. This will probably be the most important information you and your loved ones receive—so order today!

ID#P6K92

LOVED AND LOST

Mark Twain fell head over heels in love with Olivia ("Livy") Langdon in 1868. He proposed to her after knowing her for only a few days. At her insistence, they waited and married in 1870.

Their first child, Langdon, was born prematurely and died 19 months later. Susy died of meningitis at age 24. Jean died after suffering an epileptic seizure while bathing at age 29. Clara survived—and she and her father did not always get along.

Olivia Clemens with her daughters Susy, Jean, and Clara

—The Mark Twain Memorial/Yankee Archives

Book Marks

- The Concord [Massachusetts] Public Library banned *The Adventures of Huckleberry Finn* in March 1885, judging it to be coarse, crude, and inelegant.

- *Pudd'nhead Wilson* (1894) was the first detective story in which fingerprints were used to solve a crime.

- Twain claimed that the most difficult writing that he had ever done was *The Personal Recollections of Joan of Arc* (1896). He said that he had researched the book for 12 years and written it in two.

- President Franklin D. Roosevelt got the name for his economic reform from *A Connecticut Yankee in King Arthur's Court* (1889). According to the Yankee, when only six people out of a thousand have any voice in government, the 994 dupes need a "new deal." □□

How to Keep
MORE
MONEY
in Your Pocket

That man is the richest whose pleasures are the cheapest.

–Henry David Thoreau,
American writer (1817–62)

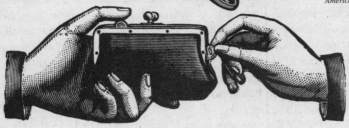

Have a spa day at home. Here are two facials that smooth wrinkles:

■ Whip the white of an egg until it's stiff and rub it over your face and neck. Allow it to dry. Then rinse away with warm water.

■ Mix cornstarch and evaporated milk together to make a thick paste. Apply it to your face and allow it to dry. Then rinse away with cold water.

To wipe up spills, use rags made from old clothing instead of using paper towels. Wash the rags as needed.

Fill a plastic bag with dryer lint and use it as padding for a package.

Instead of letting the cold water that precedes hot water out of the faucet run down the drain, capture it in a pot or kettle for later use.

Reuse dishpan or bathtub water on garden beds. Leave the dishpan under the faucet to catch water whenever you rinse your hands or sponge off a countertop.

158

Making a cake? Use the oven's heat to bake potatoes or other foods at the same time. When you turn off the oven, leave the door ajar to dissipate the heat into the room.

Out of croutons for the salad or soup? Popcorn is a good substitute.

Wash glass jars and plastic food containers and reuse to store leftovers, lunches, and so forth instead of buying containers, bags, and wrap.

Bring your own shopping bag(s) to the store. (If you are a clever seamstress, make colorful sacks from scraps of fabric.) Some grocery stores give you a 5-cent credit for each one of your own that you use.

Reduce the wear on your socks by "switching feet" when you wear them for a second consecutive time.

Periodically remove and dust the light bulbs in your home. They will be up to 40 percent more efficient.

Use vegetable scraps (broccoli stalks, celery greens, cauliflower centers, and the like) to make vegetable stock for soups. Freeze the stock until you are ready to use it.

(continued)

Unravel an outgrown wool sweater (or one purchased at a thrift shop) and use the yarn to make something else— mittens, a scarf, or another sweater.

Remove the covers (or fronts) of old greeting cards, cut them into fanciful shapes, and use them as gift tags.

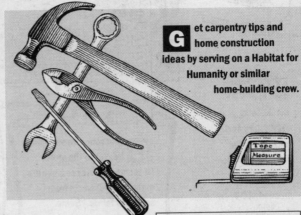

Get carpentry tips and home construction ideas by serving on a Habitat for Humanity or similar home-building crew.

Go to schools where students provide services with teachers' supervision: Get haircuts at beauty schools, dental work at dental schools, meals at cooking schools.

Volunteer at theaters and cultural organizations to save on ticket and membership fees.

Acquire basic foreign language skills by helping a foreign student learn English.

Celebrate birthdays at places that offer free meals, tickets, or other perks to the honoree.

HOW DO *YOU* PINCH PENNIES?

What's your best easy, unusual, or wacky money-saving tip? Share it at **Almanac.com /SavingMoney**.

BETTER THAN
Barebones
Cooking

THE NEXT TIME YOU VISIT YOUR FARMERS'
MARKET, LOOK PAST THE RIB EYE STEAKS
AND THE LAMB CHOPS, MEET YOUR FARMER
EYE-TO-EYE, AND SAY, "GOT ANY BONES?"

by Shannon Hayes

–illustrated by Renée Quintal Daily

The world's greatest cuisines have been founded on the prudent use of the 20 percent of the animal that is frequently discarded—the bones. Incorporating bones into your cooking improves the flavor of soups, stews, and braised dishes while at the same time offering health benefits.

Nearly anything you can find in your kitchen can be added to a broth or stock to enrich its flavor and nutritional value. The five basic ingredients are bones, vegetables, herbs, water, and acid (vinegar or wine).

THE BONES

A pure beef or chicken stock is lovely, but good stocks result from mixing species.

Toss into your pot that leftover bone from Monday night's rib eye steak or the remains from Sunday's leg of lamb. If you're buying bones, remember that knucklebones and oxtails are a great source of gelatin. Neck, rib, and other meaty bones add color and flavor. Marrow bones, cross sections from the legs, add flavor and minerals.

THE VEGETABLES

U se fresh veggies but also broccoli that is about to flower; carrots gone floppy; peppers, tomatoes, and onions growing soft on the kitchen counter; and any leftover cooked vegetables.

THE HERBS

M ake a bouquet garni by tying fresh herbs together with a piece of kitchen string before

adding them to the stockpot. If using dried herbs, make a sachet of cheesecloth so that they are easily removed.

THE ACID

U se vinegar or wine, to taste —as little as a tablespoon of vinegar or as much as a few cups of wine. The acid draws minerals out of the bones and improves the flavor.

THE SIMMER

T he longer you simmer a stock, the better. Twelve hours is sufficient, but 72 hours is better. (The stockpot can simmer all day, be turned off at bedtime, and then be turned on again the next morning.) If the liquid level gets below the top of the bones, add more water.

THE ETERNAL
Kettle

Long ago in France, cooks had the eternal kettle, a large pot that never left the fire. If a piece of meat was removed, a new piece was added. Whenever stock was removed, water was added, resulting in a steady supply of delicious stock and a ready pot for quickly boiling meats.

Basic Meat Stock

4 pounds bones (beef, lamb, pork, and/or poultry)

2 large carrots, cut into large chunks

3 ribs celery, cut into large chunks

2 onions, peeled and quartered

7 quarts water

3 to 4 sprigs fresh thyme, or 1 teaspoon dried

3 to 4 sprigs oregano, or 1 teaspoon dried

3 cloves garlic, unpeeled and crushed

1 tomato, coarsely chopped

2 teaspoons salt

2 tablespoons vinegar, or 1 to 2 cups wine

P reheat the oven to 450°F. Place the bones and the vegetables in a large roasting pan and roast for 40 minutes, or until the bones have thoroughly browned. Periodically turn them over, basting with any accumulated fat drippings. Pour the bones and vegetables into a very large stockpot.

Set the pan, with drippings, on the stovetop, and pour in 2 cups of water. Over medium heat, bring the water to a simmer. Scrape up the browned bits and add the water and bits to the stockpot. Add the remaining ingredients. Rest the stock for 30 minutes to 1 hour.

Bring the stock to a boil slowly, skimming off any scum that rises to the surface. Reduce the heat to low and simmer the stock for 12 hours, minimum, remembering to keep a sufficient fluid level.

Remove and discard all of the bones, vegetables, and herbs. Cool the stock to room temperature and refrigerate. Once cold, it should be firm, like gelatin. If it does not congeal, it's still okay—this means simply that its richness is less than ideal. Skim off any fat before using. Use the stock immediately or pack it into freezer containers and freeze. **Makes 4 to 5 quarts.**

(continued)

WHAT'S COOKING?

Stock **is made by simmering bones (or shells) and vegetables in water.**

Broth **is made by simmering meat or fish and vegetables in water.**

Goulash

1 cup flour
2 tablespoons coarse salt
1 tablespoon ground black pepper
2 tablespoons sweet paprika, divided
3 pounds beef stew meat, oxtails, bone-in
  shanks, or short ribs
4 tablespoons butter, lard, or a combination
  of the two, plus more if necessary
6 onions, sliced thin
1 tablespoon Hungarian paprika
1 quart stock or broth (any kind)
2 tablespoons orange zest (optional)
½ cup white wine
2 cups sour cream

egg noodles
butter (optional)
2 teaspoons caraway seeds

C ombine the flour, salt, pepper, and 1 tablespoon of sweet paprika. Dredge the meat in the mixture, then sauté in the butter over medium heat in a nonreactive Dutch oven until browned, working in batches if necessary. Use more butter or lard if your pan becomes dry.

Return all of the beef back to the pan, then add the onions. Stir in the Hungarian paprika, remaining sweet paprika, stock, orange zest, and wine. Simmer over low heat, stirring constantly and incorporating any browned bits into the sauce. Cover and simmer over low heat for 2 to 3 hours, or until the meat is fork-tender. Check occasionally for liquid, adding more white wine, water, or stock, if necessary. When the meat is cooked, stir in the sour cream and heat through, but do not boil. Prepare the noodles according to the package directions. Serve the goulash over buttered noodles and sprinkle with caraway seeds. **Makes 6 to 8 servings.**

(See page 168 for the slow cooker version.)

(continued)

Diabetes Healing Secret

Here's important news for anyone with diabetes. A remarkable book is now available that reveals medically tested principles that can help normalize blood sugar naturally ...and greatly improve the complications associated with diabetes. People report **better vision, more energy, faster healing, regained feeling in their feet**, as well as a reduction of various risk factors associated with other diseases.

It's called *"How to Reverse Diabetes"* and it was researched, developed and written by a leading nutrition specialist. It shows you exactly how nature can activate your body's built-in healers once you start eating the right combination of foods. It can work for both Type I and Type II diabetes and people report it has helped reduce their insulin resistance. It can give diabetics control of their lives and a feeling of satisfaction that comes from having normal blood sugar profiles.

The results speak for themselves. *"How to Reverse Diabetes"* is based on research that many doctors may not be aware of yet. It tells you which delicious foods to eat and which to avoid. It also warns you of the potential danger of certain so-called "diabetes" diets. Diabetics are calling this program "very outstanding"..."a tremendous help"... and saying it made "a difference in my life." *"How to Reverse Diabetes"* is based on documented scientific principles that can help:

- **Eliminate ketones and give you more abundant energy**
- **Make blood sugar levels go from High Risk to Normal**
- **Stimulate scratches and scrapes to heal faster**
- **Improve eyesight**
- **Improve your balance**
- **Help numb feet regain a level of feeling**
- **Reverse neuropathy and resultant heel ulcers**

Improvement may be seen in other areas as well, such as **lower blood pressure, lower cholesterol** and **reduced triglyceride levels**. There may also be a reduction of other risk factors associated with: **heart attacks, stroke, retinopathy, kidney damage**.

What's more, it may help improve **short term memory** and make you feel **more alert** and **no longer chronically tired**. Improvements of **double vision** or *diplopia* may also be experienced.

If you or someone you know have diabetes, this could be the most important book you'll ever read. As part of a special introductory offer, right now you can order a special press run of *"How to Reverse Diabetes"* for only $12.95 plus $2.00 shipping. It comes with a 90 day money back guarantee. If you are not 100% satisfied, simply return it for a full refund...no questions asked.

Order an extra copy for family or friend and SAVE. You can order 2 for only $20 total.

HERE'S HOW TO ORDER:

Simply PRINT your name and address and the words "Reverse Diabetes" on a piece of paper and mail it along with a check or money order to: Diabetes Health Publishers, Dept. HD304, P.O. Box 8347, Canton, OH 44711. VISA or MasterCard send card number and expiration date. Act now. Orders are fulfilled on a first come, first served basis.

©2010 Diabetes Health

SLOW COOKER GOULASH: Dredge the meat and sauté (in a skillet) as described on page 166. Put the onions into a large slow cooker and layer the browned meat on top. Combine the stock and wine in a shallow saucepan. Simmer over medium heat until reduced by half. Pour the liquid into the slow cooker, and add the remaining ingredients, except the sour cream and noodle fixings. Cook on low for 4 to 6 hours, until the beef is fork-tender. Stir in the sour cream and heat through (do not allow to boil). **Serve as noted on page 166.**

Curried Lamb

3 to 4 pounds lamb shanks and/or meaty neck bones
salt and ground black pepper, to taste
¼ cup olive oil, lard, or butter
1 large onion, chopped
3 to 4 cloves garlic, minced
1 tablespoon grated fresh ginger
2 teaspoons cumin
1 teaspoon freshly ground cardamom
2 cinnamon sticks
4 whole cloves
½ teaspoon cayenne pepper, or to taste
1 teaspoon turmeric
1 can (6 ounces) tomato paste
1 cup stock or broth (any kind)
1 large or 2 small boiling potatoes, cut into bite-size chunks
½ cup fresh cilantro (optional)

couscous or rice

S prinkle the lamb with salt and pepper. Heat the oil in a large, deep skillet over medium heat, add lamb, and

HOT LINK
For more recipes using stock or broth, go to **Almanac.com/Cooking.**

brown on all sides. Remove the meat to a dish.

Add the chopped onion to the skillet and sauté until translucent. Stir in the garlic and cook for 1 minute. Add the ginger, cumin, cardamom, cinnamon sticks, cloves, cayenne pepper, and turmeric. Mix thoroughly. Stir in the tomato paste and stock. Return the meat to the skillet and mix to coat.

Reduce the heat to low, cover, and simmer until the meat is tender, 45 minutes to 1 hour. Add the potatoes, cover, and cook 30 minutes longer, or until they are tender.

In the meantime, prepare the couscous or rice according to the package directions. Add the cilantro to the skillet, stir, and simmer, uncovered, for 10 minutes. Remove the cinnamon sticks and serve over couscous or rice. **Makes 3 to 4 servings.**

□□

Shannon Hayes is the host of www.grassfedcooking.com, as well as the author of *The Grassfed Gourmet Cookbook* (Eating Fresh Publications, 2004), from which these recipes have been adapted, and *The Farmer and the Grill* (Left to Write Press, 2008). She works with her family on Sap Bush Hollow Farm in upstate New York.

Winners in the 2009 Buttermilk Recipe Contest

Shrimp and Corn Soup

- 2 tablespoons butter
- 1 cup chopped onion
- 2 tablespoons all-purpose flour
- 3 cups chicken broth
- 1 cup fresh corn kernels, cut off the cob or thawed frozen corn
- 1 pound raw shrimp, peeled and cut into ½-inch pieces
- 1 cup buttermilk
- ½ teaspoon seafood seasoning (such as Old Bay)
- ½ cup chopped fresh parsley

Heat the butter in a medium saucepan over medium-high heat. Add the onion and cook for 5 to 7 minutes, or until tender. Stir in the flour and cook for 1 minute. Gradually whisk in the broth and bring to a boil, whisking constantly. Reduce the heat to medium-low, add the corn, and simmer for 5 minutes. Add the shrimp, stir, and cook until the shrimp turn pink, about 2 minutes. Stir in the buttermilk and the seafood seasoning. Remove from the heat, cover, and let stand for 4 minutes. Stir in the parsley and serve. **Makes 4 servings.**

–Beverly O'Ferrall, Linkwood, Maryland

Crispy-Coated Catfish in Creamy Buttermilk Sauce

- 4 fresh farm-raised catfish fillets (6 ounces each)
- 2 cups buttermilk
- 2 tablespoons minced fresh dill
- 1 teaspoon garlic salt
- ¼ teaspoon fresh ground pepper
- 2 cups uncooked traditional Cream of Wheat (not instant)
- ¼ cup olive oil or butter, divided

Rinse and pat the fish dry. Put the buttermilk, dill, garlic salt, and pepper in a large, shallow dish and mix well. Soak the fish in the buttermilk mixture for 10 minutes, turning frequently. Reserve 1 cup of the buttermilk marinade for the sauce. Put the Cream of Wheat in a separate, shallow dish. Warm the oven to 200°F. Heat a large, nonstick skillet over medium-high heat. Add two tablespoons of the oil. Dredge each fillet in the Cream of Wheat. Cook two fillets in the skillet, 2 to 3 minutes on each side, or until light golden and crisp. Drain on paper towels, then transfer to an ovenproof plate and keep in the oven until ready to serve. Repeat with the remaining fillets.

SAUCE:

1 cup buttermilk marinade
2 tablespoons butter
2 tablespoons fresh lemon juice
dill, sprigs or minced fresh, for garnish (optional)

■ Put the reserved marinade and butter in a small saucepan. Bring to a gentle boil over medium-high heat, whisking until the butter melts. Whisk in the lemon juice. Arrange each fillet in a shallow bowl and surround with ¼ cup of the sauce. Garnish with dill, if desired. **Makes 4 servings.**

–*Linda Morten, Somerville, Texas*

Meat Loaf With Buttermilk

1 pound ground beef
½ pound ground pork
1 cup buttermilk
1 tablespoon Worcestershire sauce
¼ teaspoon dried sage
½ teaspoon salt
½ teaspoon dry mustard
¼ teaspoon fresh ground pepper
2 cloves garlic, minced
½ cup dry bread crumbs
½ cup steak sauce
1 teaspoon finely chopped fresh rosemary
rosemary sprigs, for garnish (optional)

Preheat the oven to 350°F. Combine the first ten ingredients in a large bowl and mix well. Put the mixture into an ungreased loaf pan. Spread steak sauce over the top of the loaf and sprinkle with chopped rosemary. Bake uncovered for 1 to 1¼ hours, or until no pink remains in the center. (If using a meat thermometer, the internal temperature should be 160°F.) Pour off any liquid. Garnish with rosemary, if desired. **Makes 6 servings.**

–*Susan Scarborough, Fernandina Beach, Florida*

*Thank you to everyone who submitted buttermilk recipes. We received hundreds, and they all are "winners." Two runners-up—*Roasted Butternut Squash Soup *by Lauren Rooney of Harrisburg, Pennsylvania, and* Crispy Buttermilk Chicken Tenders With Tangy Buttermilk Sauce *by Jane Estrin of Jacksonville, Florida—are now available online at Almanac.com/Cooking. Enjoy!* □□

ANNOUNCING THE 2010 RECIPE CONTEST

Pumpkin

Send us your favorite recipe using pumpkin. It must be yours, original, and unpublished. Amateur cooks only, please. See page 223 for contest rules.

Table of Measures

APOTHECARIES'
1 scruple = 20 grains
1 dram = 3 scruples
1 ounce = 8 drams
1 pound = 12 ounces

AVOIRDUPOIS
1 ounce = 16 drams
1 pound = 16 ounces
1 hundredweight = 100 pounds
1 ton = 2,000 pounds
1 long ton = 2,240 pounds

LIQUID
4 gills = 1 pint
63 gallons = 1 hogshead
2 hogsheads = 1 pipe or butt
2 pipes = 1 tun

DRY
2 pints = 1 quart
4 quarts = 1 gallon
2 gallons = 1 peck
4 pecks = 1 bushel

LINEAR
1 hand = 4 inches
1 link = 7.92 inches

1 span = 9 inches
1 foot = 12 inches
1 yard = 3 feet
1 rod = 5$\frac{1}{2}$ yards
1 mile = 320 rods = 1,760 yards =
    5,280 feet
1 Int. nautical mile =
    6,076.1155 feet
1 knot = 1 nautical mile per
    hour
1 fathom = 2 yards = 6 feet
1 furlong = $\frac{1}{8}$ mile = 660 feet =
    220 yards
1 league = 3 miles = 24 furlongs
1 chain = 100 links = 22 yards

SQUARE
1 square foot = 144 square
    inches
1 square yard = 9 square feet
1 square rod = 30$\frac{1}{4}$ square
    yards = 272$\frac{1}{4}$ square feet
1 acre = 160 square rods =
    43,560 square feet
1 square mile = 640 acres =
    102,400 square rods
1 square rod = 625 square links

1 square chain = 16 square rods
1 acre = 10 square chains

CUBIC
1 cubic foot = 1,728 cubic
    inches
1 cubic yard = 27 cubic feet
1 cord = 128 cubic feet
1 U.S. liquid gallon = 4 quarts =
    231 cubic inches
1 imperial gallon = 1.20 U.S.
    gallons = 0.16 cubic foot
1 board foot = 144 cubic inches

KITCHEN
3 teaspoons = 1 tablespoon
16 tablespoons = 1 cup
1 cup = 8 ounces
2 cups = 1 pint
2 pints = 1 quart
4 quarts = 1 gallon

**TO CONVERT CELSIUS AND
FAHRENHEIT:**

$°C = (°F - 32)/1.8$
$°F = (°C \times 1.8) + 32$

Metric Conversions

LINEAR
1 inch = 2.54 centimeters
1 centimeter = 0.39 inch
1 meter = 39.37 inches
1 yard = 0.914 meter
1 mile = 1.61 kilometers
1 kilometer = 0.62 mile

SQUARE
1 square inch = 6.45 square
    centimeters
1 square yard = 0.84 square
    meter

1 square mile = 2.59 square
    kilometers
1 square kilometer = 0.386
    square mile
1 acre = 0.40 hectare
1 hectare = 2.47 acres

CUBIC
1 cubic yard = 0.76 cubic meter
1 cubic meter = 1.31 cubic yards

HOUSEHOLD
$\frac{1}{2}$ teaspoon = 2 mL
1 teaspoon = 5 mL
1 tablespoon = 15 mL

$\frac{1}{4}$ cup = 60 mL
$\frac{1}{3}$ cup = 75 mL
$\frac{1}{2}$ cup = 125 mL
$\frac{2}{3}$ cup = 150 mL
$\frac{3}{4}$ cup = 175 mL
1 cup = 250 mL

1 liter = 1.057 U.S. liquid quarts
1 U.S. liquid quart = 0.946 liter
1 U.S. liquid gallon = 3.78 liters
1 gram = 0.035 ounce
1 ounce = 28.349 grams
1 kilogram = 2.2 pounds
1 pound = 0.45 kilogram

2010   THE OLD FARMER'S ALMANAC   173

• The Old (and New) Farmer's •

ESSENTIAL

MANURE MANUAL

Manure, manure, sir, is the thing!
–*The Old Farmer's Almanac*, 1818

BY ROBIN
SWEETSER

–Kim Kurki

The value of manure in a garden is inestimable. Whether grown as a "green" cover crop or collected from farm animals, it improves the fertility, structure, and water-holding capacity of soil and reduces—or even eliminates—the need for fertilizer. In the tradition of this Almanac through the centuries, we offer a primer on manures and their applications.

GREEN MANURE

The planting of cover crops is becoming an established practice among the best farmers.

–The Old Farmer's Almanac, 1916

■ "Green manure" is the product of a variety of fast-growing ground cover crops that provide alternatives to animal manure. Growing green manure is an age-old technique—and a little goes a long way: When turned into soil, cover crops can add the equivalent of 9 to 13 tons of fresh manure per acre, according to researchers at the Woods End Agricultural Institute in Mt. Vernon, Maine. The most common cover crops are legumes and grasses; brassicas are another option.

MANEUVER YOUR MANURE

The words "maneuver" and "manure" both come from the Latin *manuoperare,* "to work by hand." In Middle English, both words referred to working with the hands or cultivating the earth, alluding to the labor involved in handling dung.

–Ed Young/Corbis

continued

In northern areas, cover crops are usually planted in late summer or early fall, after most vegetables have been harvested. In the South, they can be planted anytime there is a bare spot in the garden. No matter where you live or the size of your garden, you can grow cover crops.

Land laid down with clover is better than money in the bank.

–*The Old Farmer's Almanac*, 1883

Legumes thrive and maximize their ability to store, or fix, nitrogen if they are inoculated with beneficial bacteria called rhizobia (of the genus *Rhizobium*). Purchase seeds described as "rhizo-coated" or inoculate the seeds yourself: Shake dampened seeds in a container containing the powdered inoculant until they are covered or, if you are

GETTING TO THE ROOTS

The taproots of some cover crops penetrate and loosen compacted subsoil, or hardpan, creating channels that allow oxygen and water to penetrate the soil long after the roots have decomposed. Because of this, these crops have been called "biological plows."

GREEN MANURE CROP	ROOT DEPTH
Hairy vetch, white clover	1 to 3 feet
Black medic; common vetch; mustard; Canola, or rape	3 to 5 feet
Lupine, radish, red clover, turnip	5 to 7 feet

–adapted from the National Sustainable Agriculture Information Service

planting by hand, sprinkle a small amount of inoculant into the seed hole, set the seed, and cover it with soil immediately. Heat and sunshine will kill the beneficial bacteria. Each legume requires specific bacteria, so buy the correct match.

For fixing nitrogen, the best legumes are alfalfa, cowpeas, and hairy vetch. Other legumes are clovers, field peas, fava beans, lupine, trefoil, lespedeza, peas, snap beans, soybeans, and woolly pod vetch. Some of these crops, such as the beans and peas, give twice: They produce a harvest before being turned into the soil. (Peas, rotated every year, help to spread nitrogen in a small garden.)

Winter rye is a good crop to sow on poor land to plough in the next spring after it begins to head.

–The Old Farmer's Almanac, 1903

Green grasses and grains are fast-growing crops that can be planted in season. Buckwheat may be the best all-around choice: It will smother weeds, convert insoluble phosphorus to a form that crops can absorb, and reach blossoming size in 30 days (when it is ready to incorporate into the soil). Even northern gardeners can get two crops in one season. Other fast-growing grasses are annual ryegrass, barley, bromegrass, millet, oats, Sudan grass or sorghum, wheat, and winter rye.

We are in a great grass age. Two-thirds of all active U.S. farms are now planted to grass crops.

–The Old Farmer's Almanac, 1958

Canola, kale, mustard, and tyfon (a Chinese cabbage/turnip cross), members of the brassica family, also make good green manure. These fast-growing, cool-season crops can be planted in spring or fall. Their massive root systems extend deep into the subsoil, and their decayed remains amend it.

Buckwheat has many qualities that recommend it highly, including filling the soil with vegetable matter.

–The Old Farmer's Almanac, 1842

–Keystone/Hulton Archive/Getty Images

continued

> **Enriching the farm enriches the farmer, and the foundation of it all is manure. . . . There must be manure of some kind, or the crop will rarely pay the labor.**
>
> *–The Old Farmer's Almanac, 1859*

Incorporate them into the soil earlier in season for nitrogen, later for organic matter.

Can't choose? Plant a legume and a grass together: Vetch and rye or peas and oats are common choices. Plus, a mix provides food and habitat, attracting a wide range of beneficial insects. Consider your planting time, purpose, soil type, and climate. To learn suggestions for your region, go to Almanac.com/CoverCrops or ask your local extension service for recommendations.

Knowing when to plant green manure can be as important as growing crops. During the growing season, plant dwarf white clover or vetch between rows of anything to add nitrogen to the soil. To suppress weeds, underplant green manure grass around a main crop (for example, seed buckwheat around established squash plants). Cut it in 4 to 6 weeks and use the clippings as mulch.

In northern areas in autumn, after harvest but before the snow (or in spring—but delay planting), prepare the garden for a cover crop. Clear away any debris and weeds. Rake the bed smooth. Add any soil amendments. Broadcast the cover crop seed by hand, rake it in, and tamp down the soil with a roller or the back of the rake. If no rain is expected, water.

GET THEE TO A BEACH

Plowed directly into the land or composted, [seaweed] makes excellent plant food and improves the physical character of the soil. It can also be used for top dressing.

–The Old Farmer's Almanac, 1911

GOOD, BETTER, BEST

The benefits of digging in green manure vary with the crop's maturity.

- A young crop decomposes quickly and releases minerals immediately, yet provides little organic matter. Allow about 2 weeks before planting.

- A midseason crop is harder to dig in, decomposes more slowly, and provides organic matter; however, its nutrients may be temporarily unavailable due to soil microbes that are digesting it. Once the microbes die, the nutrients become available to plantings that follow. Allow at least 4 weeks before planting.

- A mature crop decomposes and releases nutrients slowly, but provides the most organic matter. Allow 6 to 8 weeks before planting.

REMOVING THE COVER

Cover crops that are allowed to go to seed will reseed themselves and become a nuisance. In the old days, gardeners were encouraged to till and dig the soil (remember double digging?). The prevailing wisdom is to avoid disturbing soil layers. Choose your method:

The man who, in his enthusiasm for deep ploughing, buried his fertile soil under several inches of stiff clay which the plow brought up, was not improving his chances for a large crop that season.

–The Old Farmer's Almanac, 1908

- Mow or chop down cover crops or cut them with a string trimmer. Then, dig them into the topsoil with a shovel, garden fork, or rear-tine rototiller.

- Pull up cover crops by hand and use them as mulch. Kill tough plants (rye and vetch) by cutting them off at the crown. Then, lay them over the roots. Eventually, they will decompose, roots and all, and return their nutrients to the soil.

> By taking care to manure highly, the farmer will find that he has larger and better crops and his fields are richer.
>
> –*The New England Farmer,* 1849

TAKE HEED . . .

After cutting, some cover crops (such as Sudan grass, winter barley, and winter rye) exude compounds that indiscriminately prevent seeds from germinating: They can affect vegetables (beets, carrots, chard, lettuce, radishes, spinach) as well as weeds. To avoid crop failure, use transplants with two to four leaves and follow green manure (for example, winter rye) with late-season crops such as corn or squash, after the manure's growth-suppressing toxins have dissipated.

ANIMAL MANURE

- "The good farmer not only saves all of his manure, but he increases it with large quantities of mud, muck, peat, loam, sand, clay, sods, and so forth. All of these, composted with animal manures, are excellent. The mud, clay, and muck improve the texture of light soils; sand and loam are improvers of heavy soils. These and

> It should be a main business to make all the manure possible.
>
> –*The Old Farmer's Almanac,* 1818

various other substances, such as sawdust, leaves, refuse hay, straw, and other litter, absorb liquid manure and save solid manure from being wasted by mixing with it, which moderates fermentation and causes gases to be absorbed, making the substances themselves into good manure." These principles, from *The New England Farmer* (J. Nourse, 1849), still apply today. As all-around fertilizer, barnyard or stable manure—often available free from farmers and stables, if you haul it away—is a good source of organic matter and nutrients. Never use it fresh, when it is too "hot," or raw, and could burn plants. Use only aged or composted animal manure.

> **Dung of animals that chew the cud, being more thoroughly putrefied than that of others, is fit to be mixed with the soil without being collected into a dunghill.**
> –*The Old Farmer's Almanac*, 1811

> **Above all are animals valuable to the farmer, because they convert the coarse products of the farm into manure.**
> –*Facts for Farmers*, 1865

Horse manure ferments easily, but in the process it loses much of its nitrogen in the form of ammonia. To slow fermentation, keep the pile wet or mix it with aged cow or hog manure. To kill any weed seeds, hot, or active, compost it before using. (Learn more about composting at Almanac.com/Composting.)

Cow manure contains more water than horse manure and has the lowest value as plant food and fertilizer.

Hog manure ferments slowly, and, because it comes from a diet that tends to be richer than that of horses and cows, it is of similarly high value.

Sheep manure is drier and richer than any other except that of poultry. Sheep chew their cud so finely that there are no weed seeds being inadvertently applied to the garden bed.

Poultry manure, the richest of the barnyard, is high in nitrogen and ferments easily. Always compost it before using.

continued

WHEN TO SPREAD WHAT

You can carry much more dung on a sled in February than you can on a cart in April, with less damage to your ground.

–The Old Farmer's Almanac, 1793

IN . . .	USE MANURE FROM . . .	ON . . .
early spring	cows, horses	flower gardens
spring	poultry	vegetable and flower gardens
spring and summer (when crops are up)	sheep	vegetables (as top dressing)
spring and fall	cows, hogs, horses, poultry	vegetable gardens
early fall or not at all	cows, horses	acid-loving plants (as top dressing)
fall	cows, horses	potato or root crop beds

If we can obtain valuable manure for nothing but the labor, it is better than putting our hands into our pockets, and paying six or eight dollars an acre for artificial manure.

–The New England Farmer, 1849

-Nick Yapp/Hulton Archive/Getty Images

ELEPHANTS ON PARADE?

When the circus comes to town, bring your wheelbarrow. Pachyderm poop can be as useful as any other. (The elephants must be American born. There are no federal restrictions on domestic elephant waste; that of imported animals must be burned or buried.)

WHEN OUTHOUSES WERE COMMON, SO WAS PRIVY SOIL

Four loads of earth, mixed with one load of privy soil, will be equal to five loads of barnyard dung. Let it lie for several months and occasionally turn it over with a shovel, and it will be of use as manure.

–The Old Farmer's Almanac, 1806

Note: *Human waste, as well as that of dogs and cats, is not recommended as manure or fertilizer today.*

FOR STARTERS, THE HOT BED

Similar in concept to a cold frame, a hot bed draws bottom heat from fermenting animal manure in addition to top-down warmth from the Sun. (A cold frame is heated by only the Sun.) Want to try it?

- Build a frame of brick or wood, with a bottom.
- Fork a generous load of manure into it.
- Cover the manure with a thick layer of loam.
- Plant seeds or seedlings and cover, as needed, with an old window or see-through glass or plastic.

The most sophisticated hot beds had removable panels to allow for the addition of fresh dung. In the old days, Parisian market gardeners grew carrots using this method.

The best manure for an orchard is two parts dung and one part coal soot spread all over the ground.
—The Old Farmer's Almanac, 1819

Dung your corn ground with rich, rotten manure; if it be raw, spread it and plow it in.
—The Old Farmer's Almanac, 1804

The quantity of manure may be increased by mixing other substances with the urine of animals.
—The Old Farmer's Almanac, 1819

MANURE TEA

There are many methods for making manure tea. Try this one:

- Fill a large trash can two-thirds full of water. Add two large buckets of manure. (If you prefer, put it into a permeable bag, such as one made from burlap, plastic, or mesh.) Let it steep until it appears murky (1 to 2 weeks). Dilute the "tea" until it resembles kitchen tea. Ladle the liquid around vegetables or flowers.

☐☐

Robin Sweetser, who gardens in New Hampshire, contributed the green manure portion of this article. The remainder was prepared by Almanac editors.

Gestation and Mating Tables

	Proper Age for First Mating	Period of Fertility (yrs.)	Number of Females for One Male	Period of Gestation (days) AVERAGE	RANGE
Ewe	90 lbs. or 1 yr.	6		147 / 151[1]	142–154
Ram	12–14 mos., well matured	7	50–75[2] / 35–40[3]		
Mare	3 yrs.	10–12		336	310–370
Stallion	3 yrs.	12–15	40–45[4] / Record 252[5]		
Cow	15–18 mos.[6]	10–14		283	279–290[7] 262–300[8]
Bull	1 yr., well matured	10–12	50[4] / Thousands[5]		
Sow	5–6 mos. or 250 lbs.	6		115	110–120
Boar	250–300 lbs.	6	50[2] / 35–40[3]		
Doe goat	10 mos. or 85–90 lbs.	6		150	145–155
Buck goat	Well matured	5	30		
Bitch	16–18 mos.	8		63	58–67
Male dog	12–16 mos.	8	8–10		
Queen cat	12 mos.	6		63	60–68
Tom cat	12 mos.	6	6–8		
Doe rabbit	6 mos.	5–6		31	30–32
Buck rabbit	6 mos.	5–6	30		

[1]For fine wool breeds. [2]Hand-mated. [3]Pasture. [4]Natural. [5]Artificial. [6]Holstein and beef: 750 lbs.; Jersey: 500 lbs. [7]Beef; 8–10 days shorter for Angus. [8]Dairy.

Incubation Period of Poultry (days)
Chicken 21
Duck. 26–32
Goose. 30–34
Guinea 26–28

Average Life Span of Animals in Captivity (years)
Cat (domestic) 14
Chicken (domestic) 8
Dog (domestic) 13
Duck (domestic) 10
Goat (domestic) 14
Goose (domestic) 20
Horse 22
Rabbit (domestic) 6

	Estral/Estrous Cycle (including heat period) AVERAGE	RANGE	Length of Estrus (heat) AVERAGE	RANGE	Usual Time of Ovulation	When Cycle Recurs If Not Bred
Mare	21 days	10–37 days	5–6 days	2–11 days	24–48 hours before end of estrus	21 days
Sow	21 days	18–24 days	2–3 days	1–5 days	30–36 hours after start of estrus	21 days
Ewe	16½ days	14–19 days	30 hours	24–32 hours	12–24 hours before end of estrus	16½ days
Goat	21 days	18–24 days	2–3 days	1–4 days	Near end of estrus	21 days
Cow	21 days	18–24 days	18 hours	10–24 hours	10–12 hours after end of estrus	21 days
Bitch	24 days	16–30 days	7 days	5–9 days	1–3 days after first acceptance	Pseudo-pregnancy
Cat		15–21 days	3–4 days, if mated	9–10 days, in absence of male	24–56 hours after coitus	Pseudo-pregnancy

Pain Relief Discovery:

Special $\overset{relief}{\wedge}$ cream for arthritis

(SPECIAL) A special cream has been developed that relieves arthritis pain in minutes, even chronic arthritis pain – deep in the joints. The product, which is called **PAIN BUST-R II®**, is one of the fastest acting therapeutic formulas ever developed in the fight against arthritis pain. Immediately upon application, it goes to work by penetrating deep to the areas most affected – the joints themselves, bringing fast relief where relief is needed most. Men and woman who have suffered arthritis pain for years are reporting incredible results with this product. Even a single application seems to work remarkably well in relieving pain and bringing comfort to cramped, knotted joints.

PAIN BUST-R II was researched and formulated to be absorbed directly into the joints and muscles – where the pain originates. Long-time arthritis sufferers will be glad to know that this formula will help put an end to agonizing days and sleepless nights. It is highly recommended by users who have resumed daily activities and are enjoying life again.

Read what our users have to say:
"I use **PAIN BUST-R II** because I suffer from tension in my back and shoulders. I can't praise your product enough. I've used other ointments but they don't seem to work as fast nor last as long. Thank you. Thank you…Thank you!" *C.K.F.*

"Last night when I went to sleep, I rubbed some **PAIN BUST-R II** on my sore, aching knee. 15 minutes later, I fell sound asleep and woke 8 hours later with absolutely no pain. I wish I knew about **PAIN BUST-R II** long ago." *B.M.S.*

NO-RISK FREE TRIAL
We Trust You – Send No Money!

TO ORDER: Just write "**PAIN BUST-R II®**" on a sheet of paper and send it along with your name, address and the number of tubes you wish to order. We will promptly ship you 1 large tube for **$9.90**, 2 large tubes for **$16.80** (Saves $3.00) or 3 large tubes for only **$21.90** (Saves $7.80). Prices include all shipping and handling. We will enclose an invoice and if for any reason you don't agree that **PAIN BUST-R II** relieves pain more effectively than anything you've tried, simply mark "cancel" on the invoice and there will be no charge to you. You don't even have to bother returning the merchandise. Act quickly – this offer may not be repeated. **CALL NOW! TOLL FREE 1-877-212-2272 and ask for offer OFA-10** or write today to: CCA Industries, Inc., Dept OFA-10, 200 Murray Hill Parkway, E. Rutherford, NJ 07073

©2009 CCA Industries, Inc

Great Moments

in the History of

LAUGHTER

by Jeff Baker

illustrated by Eldon Doty

LAUGHIN ZONE

Laugh and the World Laughs With You . . .

Laugh at your friends if your friends are sore, / So much the better, you may laugh the more.

–Alexander Pope, English poet (1688–1744)

Roman philosopher Democritus (460–370 B.C.) earned great respect for determining that all matter in the universe is made up of atoms, but his neighbors found him strange because he laughed. At everything.

Concerned, they called in Hippocrates. He found Democritus unkempt, dissecting animal spleens in order to study their bile, and laughing all the while. The pair began discussing the absurdities of human nature, and, before long, each agreed that life is laughable.

Hippocrates assured the townspeople that Democritus was not deranged; indeed, he believed that Democritus's measured view of the world proved his sanity. Ever after, Democritus was known as "the laughing philosopher."

(continued)

187

Sometimes the Goat Gets You

'Tis a good thing to laugh at any rate; and if a straw can tickle a man, it is an instrument of happiness.

–John Dryden, English poet (1631–1700)

The Moravian Brethren, a sect of Anabaptists that originated in 15th-century Bohemia, believed in nonviolence toward miscreants, no matter how devilish the deeds. These pacifists reserved a fate worse than death for the most serious offenders: tickling, which can be tortuous when prolonged.

The brothers liberally coated a victim's feet with salt and then brought in one or more goats for a salty snack of . . . sole food. The condemned did not die directly from the tickling but most likely expired from cardiac arrest or brain hemorrhage brought on by the squirming, struggling, heavy breathing, and laughing that the tickling had induced.

If You're Happy and You Know It . . . Don't Show It

Beware you don't laugh, for then you show all your faults.

–Ralph Waldo Emerson, American poet (1803–82)

Philip Dormer Stanhope (1694–1773),
English statesman and author of *Letters to His Son,* a book of advice and commentary upon the morality of the day, advised that when amused, a gentleman should show the ultimate in restraint: "A man of parts and fashion is . . . only seen to smile but never heard to laugh. Frequent and loud laughter is the characteristic of folly and ill manners."

N₂O Pain, N₂O Gain

N_2O Pain, N_2O Gain

Laugh and be well.

–Matthew Green, English poet (1696–1737)

Although chemist Joseph Priestley (1733–1804) in 1772 became the first person to isolate and study nitrous oxide (N_2O), or laughing gas, a practical scientific use for it would not come along until the second half of the 19th century. In the interim, it remained a sort of recreational drug, taken for its euphoric, giddy, and relaxing effects. Robert Southey and Samuel Taylor Coleridge waxed poetic about the colorless, sweet-smelling gas. Chemistry and medical students were known to hold "laughing gas parties."

Self-proclaimed "professors" traveled the countryside, purportedly lecturing on chemistry and conducting demonstrations, inviting attendees to partake. Among these teachers was Samuel Colt (aka "Dr. Coult"), later famous for his revolvers, and P. T. Barnum, who opened a laughing gas show at his American Museum in New York in 1844.

In December of that year, while attending an "exhilarating gas" show, dentist Horace Wells observed that a gas-intoxicated man didn't flinch when he stumbled and cut his leg. Recognizing the gas's potential as an anesthetic, Wells convinced a group of physicians to observe a demonstration at which he would have one of his own wisdom teeth extracted while under the effect of the gas.

The operation went off without a scream, and one of the mainstays of dental anesthetics was born.

Monkey See, Monkey Do—Not

Laffing iz the sensation ov pheeling good all over and showing it principally in one spot.

–Josh Billings, American humorist (1818–85)

English biologist Charles Darwin (1809–82) published *The Expression of the Emotions in Man and Animals* in 1872. This work contained at least one notable observation: "If a young chimpanzee be tickled—the armpits are particularly sensitive to tickling, as in the case of our children—a more decided chuckling or laughing sound is uttered; though the laughter is somewhat noiseless."

Play It Again (and Again)

Can you withhold your laughter, my friends?

–Horace, Roman poet and satirist (65–8 B.C.)

One of the recording industry's first hits was "The Laughing Record." Released in 1922 by Okeh Records, the recording contained a trumpet solo and the guffawing of a fictional German tavern-keeper and his wife.

This inspired a field of imitators, including Jelly Roll Morton, who released "Hyena Stomp" in 1927; Louis Armstrong, who made "Laughin' Louie" in 1933; and Sidney Bechet and his band, who released "Laughing in Rhythm" in 1941, with Bechet imitating the sounds of laughter on his saxophone.

The song that most closely follows the form of the Okeh record is Spike Jones's "The Flight of the Bumblebee" (also known as "the Jones laughing record"), popular in the late 1940s. On it, a trombonist's solo is interrupted by outbursts of laughter by professional laughers.

"The Laughing Record" is often cited

If a young chimpanzee be tickled, a decided chuckling or laughing sound is uttered.

as the first successful novelty record, and it remains one of the most popular niche recordings of all time.

Cue the Laughter

Where is the laughter that shook the rafter?
Where is the rafter, by the way?
–Thomas Bailey Aldrich, American author (1836–1907)

The TV situation comedy *The Hank McCune Show,* first broadcast in September 1950, was distinctive for the first-ever use of a laugh track, an edited audio tape of people laughing. The show lasted only three months but the sound effect lived on, despite the skeptical review of its debut in *Variety:* "There are chuckles and yocks dubbed in. Whether this induces a jovial mood in home viewers is still to be determined, but the practice may have unlimited possibilities."

Today, laugh tracks are created by secretive "laugh men" with a keyboard and a foot pedal or digital technology (few will discuss or even acknowledge their work), although industry legend has it that tracks from 1950s TV classics *I Love Lucy* and *The Red Skelton Show* are still in use.

Readers may have gotten the best guffaw: In 1999, *TIME* magazine included the laugh track in its list of The 100 Worst Ideas of the Century.

The Last Laugh

He laughs best who laughs last.
–proverb

In March 1975, a 50-year-old bricklayer was at home in Norfolk, England, watching a television comedy called *The Goodies,* during which a kilted Scotsman used his bagpipe to defend himself against attack from a black pudding (blood sausage). The man found the scene so hilarious that he laughed uncontrollably and hard—and did not stop. His laughing fit lasted for 25 minutes, after which time, according to his wife, he gave a final "tremendous belly laugh, slumped on the settee, and died."

A Healthy Laugh

Laughter's never an end, it's a by-product.
–Maxwell Struthers Burt, American poet and rancher (1882–1954)

If you pass a public park, don't be surprised to see a group of people laughing in unison. It may be a meeting of members of Laughing Clubs International. The organization was founded by Madan Kataria, M.D., who in the early 1990s ran a private medical practice in Bombay, India. Kataria became fascinated with scientific evidence indicating that laughter is beneficial to mental and physical health. He and his wife, Madhuri, a yoga teacher, began integrating yoga breathing, stretching, clapping, and exercises to create what they called Laughter Yoga.

The first group met in the couple's home and exchanged jokes to induce laughter. Quickly, Kataria realized that humor was not necessary. After a warm-up of "ho-ho, ha-ha" in unison, the group engaged in laughter exercises for 30 to 45 minutes. Soon, they were laughing freely and uncontrollably, spurred on by the laughter of the other attendees, and Laughter Yoga took off. ☐☐

Jeff Baker learned to read by studying the cue cards on TV's *Laugh-In* in the early 1970s. His work has appeared in *The New York Times Magazine, The Oxford American,* and other publications.

WRINKLES, PRUNE LIPS, SKIN DISCOLORATION?

My dear mother's face was covered with wrinkles, she had severe prune lips, crows feet and dark discolorations that were getting worse. Tears would come to her eyes when she spoke of the old days when her face glowed with perfection. She was so embarrassed by her appearance, she had nearly given up hope when we discovered a cream, **NEW FACE WRINKLE AND DISCOLARATION™ and the New Face Plan.**

In just a few weeks, we could see a remarkable transformation in the appearance of her skin. My mother's wrinkles began disappearing, her facial muscles tightened up and she no longer had severe drooping jowls. The discoloration had faded; and she looked like a million dollars without those horrible deep-seated prune lips. **Today mother looks years younger. She is getting honest compliments for the first time in years on how great she looks.** She swears by the cream and plan and recommends it to everyone. Best of all—mother loves the way she looks and she saved money because she decided not to have plastic surgery! It's 100% guaranteed to work for you or your money back — nobody can beat that! **To order NEW FACE™ which includes two jars (a day cream and a night cream) send $16.95 plus $4.00 shipping and processing to: Total Research, Inc., Dept. FA-2010NF, Box 637, Taylor, MI 48180** The FAR, BEST DEAL is **New Face FULL KIT Special™**. The kit includes day cream, night cream, and a 10-Minute Face Lift™ gel. When used as directed, this dynamic combination helps protect and rejuvenate your skin. And there is a substantial savings if you order the kit. **Send Only $26.95 plus $4.00 S&H.** **It is simply the best.** Order now and see for yourself!

PSORIASIS
Finally An Answer!

If you suffer from Psoriasis like I do, you should know about a wonderful new cream that is guaranteed to work better than anything you have ever used before!

My name is Tom Randles and I have suffered with Psoriasis for more than 20 years, and found very little relief with other products. **Then I discovered the gentle, rub-on Burdock Folate Lotion™.** Before I knew it my Psoriasis disappeared. All my scaly, itchy skin disappeared; in its place was new natural skin -- soft and normal looking. The redness and irritation was gone and I never felt better. I swear by it and highly recommend it to anyone with Psoriasis, eczema, contact allergies or other skin disorders. **It works very fast, almost overnight, and provides long lasting, soothing relief.** Stop suffering! Order **Burdock Folate Lotion™** right now. It is guaranteed to work for you, or you will get every penny of your money back.

Send $16.95 plus $4.00 S&H (total of $20.95) for 4 ounce bottle; or better yet save nearly $9.00 by sending $26.95 plus $4.00 S&H (total of $30.95) for an 8 ounce bottle to: **TOTAL RESEARCH, INC., DEPT FA-2010PC, BOX 637, TAYLOR, MI 48180**

ALSO **Burdock Folate Shampoo™** (for scalp trouble) ONLY $15.95 plus $4.00 S&H

THE

RIGHT WAY --

TO DO THINGS

The ADVICE PARADOX

TAKE IT . . .

Fifteenth-century Dutch scholar Desiderius Erasmus claimed that "no gift is more precious than good advice."

⟢ OR ⟣

LEAVE IT . . .

Nineteenth-century parodist Horace Smith counseled, "Good advice is one of those injuries which a good man ought, if possible, to forgive, but at all events to forget at once."

COMPILED BY ANN THURLOW

Advice abounds. You can not visit a Web site, turn on a radio or TV, open a book (including this one), or even phone a friend without getting some kind of advice, tip, or suggestion. But who has the best advice? What's the "right" way to do something?

With that in mind, we asked readers of the Almanac's electronic newsletter and visitors to Almanac.com to tell us how they do several common tasks. Then we asked "experts" how to do these things.

What follows, for each of six simple undertakings, is a sampling of our readers' suggestions (which are sometimes contradictory!) and then the advice of an "expert."

We drew two conclusions from this exercise: There is no single "right" way to do most things—and you can never have too much advice.

One gives nothing so liberally as advice.

–François VI, duc de La Rochefoucauld, French writer (1613–80)

WHAT'S THE RIGHT WAY TO SHOVEL SNOW?

- **Don't shovel snow, scoop it.**

- **Shovel a straight line down the middle of the drive.** Then "push/shovel" to the side as you work your way perpendicular to your original path.

- **Carve square blocks if it's light.** Otherwise, angle-push one side, then the other, working from the top down in 4- to 6-inch cuts.

- **After 25 swipes, sip a toddy, take a breath, then do another 25.** After 100 swipes, go inside and call your son to come over for dinner. While he's there, hand him a shovel.

THE EXPERT SAYS

☞ **Stand with your feet about hip-width apart for balance and keep the shovel close to your body. Bend from the knees (not the back) and tighten your stomach muscles as you lift the snow.**

–FarmGate, an e-magazine in eastern Ontario, where the snowfall is 7½ feet per year, on average

WHAT'S THE RIGHT WAY TO HARD-BOIL AN EGG?

- **Don't use fresh eggs.**

- **Add a dash of vinegar to the pot.**

- **Don't continuously boil the water.** If you turn off the heat, the yolks will remain completely yellow.

- **Break off the head of a wooden kitchen match** and throw the "stick" portion into the water.

- **Slip a wooden spoon into the water** so that the eggs don't bump into each other as they boil.

CONTINUED

■ **Put a dozen eggs into a slow cooker,** add water to cover the eggs, and put the cooker on high for 90 minutes.

■ **Use a pushpin to prick a hole in the "blunt" end of the shell before boiling.** The shell will better separate from the egg afterward.

EXPERT SAYS

THE ☞ Cook eggs in water that is 1 inch over the eggs. Let the water come to a boil. Put the lid on the pot when the water is boiling. Move the pot onto a cold burner. Set the timer for 18 minutes for extra-large eggs, 15 minutes for large, or 12 minutes for medium.

–American Egg Board

WHAT'S THE RIGHT WAY TO

WASH WINDOWS?

■ **Wash the inside using up-and-down strokes** and the outside using side-to-side strokes.

■ **Always wash on a cloudy day.**

■ **Start from the top on a sunny day;** do the inside, then the outside.

■ **Dry with black-and-white newspapers.**

■ **Use coffee filters.**

■ **Use cloth diapers.**

EXPERT SAYS

THE ☞ Use 1 tablespoon of vinegar to a bucket of warm water to get marks, insects, or stains from glass. Wait for a cloudy day to wash normally "sunny" windows. Otherwise, the sun will cause the glass to dry too quickly, leaving unsightly streaks.

–adapted from *Great Uses for Vinegar* (George Hughes, 2005) by "TipKing"

WHAT'S THE RIGHT WAY TO
PACK FOR
PLANE TRAVEL?

■ **Pack a heavy, protective layer first,** such as jeans. Then pack a layer of delicate fabrics followed by a layer of sweaters, pants, and shirts. Finish with another protective layer of jeans or a coat.

■ **Fold in the sleeves** of shirts and fold pants/skirts in half, then roll them tightly.

■ **Pack by outfits:** Put a shirt, pants, socks, and underwear all together.

■ **Fold knit tops and sweaters and place in 2-gallon zipper-lock plastic bags.** Close the bag at least three-quarters of the way and then tightly roll the bag from the bottom up to press out all the air.

■ **Roll your clothes and mail them to your destination.**

THE EXPERT SAYS

☞ Put socks and underwear in plastic bags, then put these inside your shoes or boots. Put shoes in old clean socks before putting them into your luggage (the socks keep everything from smelling like feet). Make sure that toiletries are not full and try to squeeze the air out of them before you close them, so that they won't explode from the pressure in the airplane. —Erin Lundrigan, flight attendant

WHAT'S THE RIGHT WAY TO MOW THE LAWN?

■ **In the spring and fall, mow two times a week**—not too short—and let the clippings fall to mulch.

■ **Mow in a pattern like a Zamboni driver** would to scrape an ice surface.

■ **Always mow in a pattern**—diagonal, street-to-house straight lines, side-to-side straight lines, opposite diagonal, and, if it has been more than 4 days, mow round and round. Mark on the calendar in which direction you go.

■ **Change the mowing pattern each time,** using up to three variations.

THE EXPERT SAYS

☞ Start by mowing around the edge of the lawn. If you are using a wheeled rotary mower, don't let the wheels fall off the lawn edge, as the blades will gouge a ring out of the surface. Working from the left-hand side, mow up and down the lawn until you reach the far side. On each turn, line up the mower so that each strip slightly overlaps the last.

–Royal Horticultural Society, London, England

If you would like to participate in future Almanac reader surveys, please go to Almanac.com /Newsletters and sign up for our free electronic newsletter.

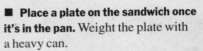

WHAT'S THE RIGHT WAY TO MAKE A GRILLED CHEESE SANDWICH?

■ **Use shredded cheese.**

■ **Shmoosh down the bread** so that it gets flat.

■ **Spread mayonnaise** on the outside of one of the bread slices.

■ **Place a plate on the sandwich once it's in the pan.** Weight the plate with a heavy can.

■ **Use white bread,** American cheese, and real butter.

■ **Use a clothes iron.** Remember to keep the iron moving.

THE EXPERT SAYS

☞ Slice a tomato and a couple of cloves of garlic. With a plate underneath, place the garlic slices on the tomato slices, sprinkle with fresh thyme, and drizzle with olive oil. Marinate for about an hour. Butter one side of two thick slices of sourdough bread. On the dry sides of the bread, layer a slice of cheddar cheese and a portion of the marinated tomatoes and garlic. Put the two pieces of bread together and grill each buttered side on medium heat until golden.

–Surf Lodge, Gabriola Island, British Columbia

□ □

Ann Thurlow writes from Charlottetown, Prince Edward Island, and, as her friends will attest, is very free with advice.

The MAN WHO SHOT EVERYONE IN TOWN

No one paid much attention to this eccentric, small-town photographer—until collectors paid millions for his images.

by *Jeff Baker*

With remarkable technical skill, Mike Disfarmer (above) photographed hundreds of Heber Springs residents.

Between 1915 and 1959, any resident of Heber Springs, Arkansas, who wanted to have his or her picture made had only one place to go: a damp, sparsely furnished studio on Main Street that was operated by a sullen man named Mike Disfarmer. Over the years, Disfarmer photographed hundreds of the town's residents: mothers proudly holding their babies, farm families on their Saturday visits to town, newly engaged couples, hunters alongside their prize hounds, children in their Sunday best, and men in uniform about to be shipped off to war.

For 50 cents, the subjects received four prints and the unsettling experience of posing for Disfarmer, who didn't even so much as greet his customers and would disappear under the black drape behind the camera for minutes at a time, emerging only to bark orders about where to stand.

Disfarmer's sometimes grumpy personality was only one reason that he was an outsider in the tight-knit community of 3,800. He was a reclusive bachelor who lived in a spare room at his studio and an agnostic among churchgoing Baptists and Methodists. Born in Indiana, he also was possibly this Confederate town's only son of a Union soldier. The closest he had to a friend was a man with whom he played country music, but even this acquaintance reported that Disfarmer "didn't say much that was personal."

There are always two people in every picture: the photographer and the viewer.

–Ansel Adams,
American photographer
(1902–84)

man and "dis" meant "not," and that he was neither a Meyer nor a farmer.

By the 1950s, Disfarmer's health and productivity had declined; he reportedly drank heavily and subsisted almost entirely on chocolate ice cream. After he died in 1959, it was two days before anyone thought to wonder where he was.

Mike Disfarmer might have faded

What little Disfarmer did reveal about himself sounded like an Ozarks tall tale. Although he had a large family nearby, Disfarmer insisted that he wasn't related to them; instead, he claimed, as a baby he'd been picked up by a tornado from his real family's residence and deposited at the home of the Meyer family, who had raised him. In 1939, he made the break official, legally changing his surname of Meyer to Disfarmer, with the explanation that "Meier" meant "farmer" in Ger-

from memory, and his photographs might have remained mounted in family albums, if not for a fortuitous discovery. Upon Disfarmer's death, a local man bought the contents of the studio from a bank for five dollars. Amidst the old furniture and camera equipment he found 4,200 glass-plate negatives. He wasn't sure what to do with them, so they sat in his garage until 1973, when the publisher of the local newspaper announced that he was interested in seeing old pictures from the town's

Mike Disfarmer's greatest contribution may lie in what his photographs captured: unassuming people from a simpler time.

past. The publisher, a photographer himself, recognized that Disfarmer's portraits were of more than local importance and sent a sampling to the editor of *Modern Photography* magazine. She was so impressed that she arranged for the publication of a book featuring 180 of the images in 1976 and a concurrent showing at New York City's prestigious International Center of Photography.

Raves from the art world were immediate. Part of the appeal was due to Disfarmer's apparently innate technical skill. His studio featured a skylight to make use of natural light, he printed on high-quality paper, he used sensitive glass-plate negatives decades after other photographers had switched to film, and he was talented at arranging groups of people.

Interest in Disfarmer's work remained steady in the ensuing years, but a significant resurgence came in 2004, when a collector came across 50 previously unseen prints (originals, developed by Disfarmer). He bought them all and eventually scouted out and acquired more than 3,000 others, at a reported cost of $2 million. Coincidentally, an art gallery owner was also buying Disfarmer prints, and the two quests culminated in separate exhibitions that opened at the same time in New York City.

Mike Disfarmer's greatest contribution, however, perhaps lies in what his photographs captured: unassuming people from a simpler time that was fast disappearing. □□

Learn how to store photographs safely at Almanac.com/StorePhotos.

Frosts and Growing Seasons

■ Dates given are normal averages for a light freeze; local weather and topography may cause considerable variations. The possibility of frost occurring after the spring dates and before the fall dates is 50 percent. The classification of freeze temperatures is usually based on their effect on plants. **Light freeze:** 29° to 32°F—tender plants killed. **Moderate freeze:** 25° to 28°F—widely destructive effect on most vegetation. **Severe freeze:** 24°F and colder—heavy damage to most plants. *–courtesy of National Climatic Data Center*

State	City	Growing Season (days)	Last Spring Frost	First Fall Frost	State	City	Growing Season (days)	Last Spring Frost	First Fall Frost
AK	Juneau	148	May 8	Oct. 4	ND	Bismarck	129	May 14	Sept. 21
AL	Mobile	273	Feb. 28	Nov. 29	NE	Blair	167	Apr. 25	Oct. 10
AR	Pine Bluff	240	Mar. 16	Nov. 12	NE	North Platt	137	May 9	Sept. 24
AZ	Phoenix	*	*	*	NH	Concord	124	May 20	Sept. 21
AZ	Tucson	324	Jan.19	Dec. 18	NJ	Newark	217	Apr. 3	Nov. 7
CA	Eureka	323	Jan. 27	Dec. 16	NM	Carlsbad	215	Mar. 31	Nov. 2
CA	Sacramento	296	Feb. 10	Dec. 4	NM	Los Alamos	149	May 11	Oct. 8
CA	San Francisco	*	*	*	NV	Las Vegas	283	Feb. 16	Nov. 27
CO	Denver	157	Apr. 30	Oct. 4	NY	Albany	153	May 2	Oct. 3
CT	Hartford	166	Apr. 26	Oct. 9	NY	Syracuse	168	Apr. 28	Oct. 13
DE	Wilmington	202	Apr. 10	Oct. 30	OH	Akron	192	Apr. 18	Oct. 28
FL	Miami	*	*	*	OH	Cincinnati	192	Apr. 13	Oct. 23
FL	Tallahassee	239	Mar. 22	Nov. 17	OK	Lawton	223	Mar. 29	Nov. 7
GA	Athens	227	Mar. 24	Nov. 7	OK	Tulsa	225	Mar. 27	Nov. 7
GA	Savannah	268	Mar. 1	Nov. 25	OR	Pendleton	187	Apr. 13	Oct. 18
IA	Atlantic	148	May 2	Sept. 28	OR	Portland	236	Mar. 23	Nov. 15
IA	Cedar Rapids	163	Apr. 25	Oct. 6	PA	Franklin	164	May 6	Oct. 17
ID	Boise	147	May 10	Oct. 6	PA	Williamsport	168	Apr. 30	Oct. 15
IL	Chicago	187	Apr. 20	Oct. 24	RI	Kingston	147	May 8	Oct. 3
IL	Springfield	182	Apr. 13	Oct. 13	SC	Charleston	260	Mar. 9	Nov. 25
IN	Indianapolis	181	Apr. 17	Oct. 16	SC	Columbia	214	Apr. 1	Nov. 1
IN	South Bend	175	Apr. 26	Oct. 19	SD	Rapid City	140	May 9	Sept. 27
KS	Topeka	174	Apr. 19	Oct. 11	TN	Memphis	235	Mar. 22	Nov. 13
KY	Lexington	192	Apr. 15	Oct. 25	TN	Nashville	204	Apr. 6	Oct. 28
LA	Monroe	256	Mar. 3	Nov. 15	TX	Amarillo	185	Apr. 18	Oct. 20
LA	New Orleans	300	Feb. 12	Dec. 11	TX	Denton	243	Mar. 18	Nov. 16
MA	Worcester	170	Apr. 26	Oct. 14	TX	San Antonio	270	Feb. 28	Nov. 25
MD	Baltimore	200	Apr. 11	Oct. 29	UT	Cedar City	133	May 21	Oct. 1
ME	Portland	156	May 2	Oct. 6	UT	Spanish Fork	167	May 1	Oct. 16
MI	Lansing	145	May 10	Oct. 3	VA	Norfolk	247	Mar. 20	Nov. 23
MI	Marquette	154	May 11	Oct. 13	VA	Richmond	206	Apr. 6	Oct. 30
MN	Duluth	124	May 21	Sept. 23	VT	Burlington	147	May 8	Oct. 3
MN	Willmar	154	Apr. 30	Oct. 1	WA	Seattle	251	Mar. 10	Nov. 17
MO	Jefferson City	188	Apr. 13	Oct. 18	WA	Spokane	153	May 2	Oct. 3
MS	Columbia	248	Mar. 13	Nov. 16	WI	Green Bay	150	May 6	Oct. 4
MS	Vicksburg	240	Mar. 20	Nov. 16	WI	Sparta	133	May 13	Sept. 24
MT	Fort Peck	141	May 8	Sept. 26	WV	Parkersburg	183	Apr. 21	Oct. 22
MT	Helena	121	May 19	Sept. 18	WY	Casper	120	May 22	Sept. 19
NC	Fayetteville	222	Mar. 28	Nov. 5					

Frosts do not occur every year.

How We Predict the Weather

We derive our weather forecasts from a secret formula that was devised by the founder of this Almanac, Robert B. Thomas, in 1792. Thomas believed that weather on Earth was influenced by sunspots, which are magnetic storms on the surface of the Sun.

Over the years, we have refined and enhanced that formula with state-of-the-art technology and modern scientific calculations. We employ three scientific disciplines to make our long-range predictions: solar science, the study of solar activity; climatology, the study of weather patterns; and meteorology, the study of the atmosphere. We predict weather trends and events by comparing solar patterns and historical weather conditions with current solar activity.

Our forecasts emphasize temperature and precipitation deviations from averages, or normals. These are based on 30-year statistical averages prepared by government meteorological agencies and updated every 10 years. (See "What Is 'Normal' Weather?," page 68.) The most recent tabulations span the period from 1971 through 2000.

We believe that nothing in the universe happens haphazardly, that there is a cause-and-effect pattern to all phenomena. However, although neither we nor any other forecasters have yet gained sufficient insight into the mysteries of the universe to predict the weather with *total* accuracy, our results are almost always *very* close to our traditional claim of 80 percent.

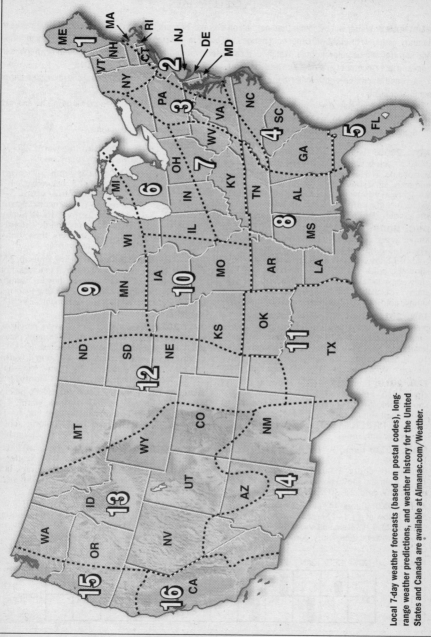

WEATHER

Local 7-day weather forecasts (based on postal codes), long-range weather predictions, and weather history for the United States and Canada are available at Almanac.com/Weather.

Northeast

SUMMARY: Winter will be colder than normal, on average, primarily due to persistent cold temperatures in January, with only brief thaws. Other cold periods will occur in mid-December and mid-February. Precipitation and snowfall will be below normal. Watch for a snowstorm around Thanksgiving, with other snowy periods in mid- and late December and mid- and late January.

April and May will be slightly cooler than normal, with below-normal precipitation continuing and raising concern of summer drought.

Summer will be cooler than normal, with slightly below normal rainfall. The hottest periods will be in early and mid-June, late July, and early to mid-August.

September and October will be slightly drier than normal, with near-normal temperatures.

NOV. 2009: Temp. 37° (1° below avg.); precip. 3" (0.5" below avg.). 1–4 Sunny, then showers, seasonable. 5–8 Snow, then sunny, cold. 9–17 Rain and snow, then sunny, cold. 18–20 Showers, mild. 21–25 Heavy snow northeast, showers south and west; turning cold. 26–28 Rain and snow, cold. 29–30 Flurries, cold.

DEC. 2009: Temp. 28.5° (2.5° above avg.); precip. 2" (1" below avg.). 1–4 Rain and snow showers, cold. 5–7 Showers, mild. 8–14 Snow showers, cold. 15–19 Snow, then showers, warm. 20–23 Snow, then sunny, seasonable. 24–27 Snow, then sunny, cold. 28–31 Sunny, seasonable.

JAN. 2010: Temp. 16° (4° below avg.); precip. 2" (1" below avg.). 1–4 Rain to snow, then sunny, seasonable. 5–10 Snow showers, then sunny, bitter cold. 11–15 Snow showers, then sunny, mild. 16–24 Snowstorm, then sunny, cold. 25–28 Snow showers, very cold. 29–31 Snow, then rain, mild.

FEB. 2010: Temp. 24.5° (3.5° above avg.); precip. 2" (0.5" below avg.). 1–6 Periods of rain and snow, mild. 7–10 Sunny; cold, then mild. 11–13 Snow, then sunny, very cold. 14–17 Snow showers, cold. 18–21 Rain and snow, then sunny, cold. 22–28 Showers, mild.

MAR. 2010: Temp. 29° (4° below avg.); precip. 1" (2" below avg.). 1–2 Sunny, mild. 3–9 Snow, then sunny, chilly. 10–16 Snow showers, cold. 17–21 Rain and snow showers, chilly. 22–26 Snow, then sunny, cold. 27–30 Sunny. 31 Rain and snow.

APR. 2010: Temp. 44° (1° below avg.); precip. 2" (1" below avg.). 1–4 Snow showers, then sunny, seasonable. 5–13 Rain and snow, then sunny, cool. 14–18 Showers, then sunny, cool. 19–26 Showers,

then sunny, turning warm. 27–30 Showers, then sunny, cool.

MAY 2010: Temp. 56° (avg.); precip. 2" (1.5" below avg.). 1–4 Scattered t-storms, warm. 5–7 Sunny. 8–10 Showers, warm. 11–15 Rainy periods. 16–18 Sunny, cool. 19–21 Rain, cool north; t-storms, hot south. 22–28 Showers, then sunny, cool. 29–31 T-storms, warm.

JUNE 2010: Temp. 65° (avg.); precip. 2.5" (1" below avg.). 1–3 Scattered t-storms, hot. 4–7 Rain, cool. 8–16 Scattered showers, turning warm. 17–19 Sunny, cool. 20–22 A few t-storms, hot. 23–27 Scattered t-storms, seasonable. 28–30 T-storms, cool.

JULY 2010: Temp. 68° (2° below avg.); precip. 3" (1" below avg.). 1–3 T-storms. 4–6 Sunny, pleasant. 7–9 T-storms, then sunny, pleasant. 10–15 T-storms, then sunny, cool. 16–18 Sunny, warm. 19–22 T-storms, cool. 23–25 Sunny, pleasant. 26–28 Showers, then sunny. 29–31 T-storms, hot.

AUG. 2010: Temp. 66° (1° below avg.); precip. 5.5" (1.5" above avg.). 1–3 T-storms, warm. 4–5 Sunny, cool. 6–9 T-storms, then sunny, hot. 10–14 T-storms, then sunny, cool. 15–20 T-storms, cool. 21–25 Heavy rain, chilly. 26–31 Sunny, seasonable.

SEPT. 2010: Temp. 59° (avg.); precip. 3" (0.5" below avg.). 1–3 Showers, warm. 4–10 Scattered showers, cool. 11–16 Showers, then sunny, hot. 17–21 Rain, then sunny, chilly. 22–26 Rainy periods, cool. 27–30 Sunny, crisp.

OCT. 2010: Temp. 48° (avg.); precip. 3" (0.5" below avg.). 1–8 Rainy periods. 9–14 Sunny, turning warm. 15–19 Rain, then sunny. 20–26 Rain and snow showers, cold. 27–31 Sunny, cool.

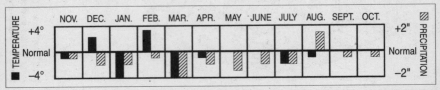

Atlantic Corridor

SUMMARY: Winter will be colder than normal, on average, especially north of the Chesapeake Bay. The coldest periods will occur in early to mid- and late January and mid-February. While precipitation will be below normal, slightly above-normal snowfall will occur in many parts of the region. Watch for snow around Thanksgiving, with other snowy periods in mid-January and mid- and late February.

April and May will be warmer and drier than normal, with water reservoirs running low.

Summer will be cooler and drier than normal, with a drought possible despite heavy rain in early June from a tropical storm. The hottest periods will be in mid-June, mid-July, and early to mid-August.

September and October will continue drier than normal, with near-normal temperatures.

NOV. 2009: Temp. 47.5° (2° below avg. north, 3° above south); precip. 3" (0.5" below avg.). 1–2 Sunny. 3–4 Windy, drizzle north; sunny, warm south. 5–6 Sunny, warm. 7–10 Showers, then sunny, mild. 11–17 Rain, then sunny, cold; hard freeze. 18–22 Rainy periods, mild. 23–25 Sunny, cold. 26–30 Rain to snow.

DEC. 2009: Temp. 39° (1° above avg.); precip. 2.5" (0.5" below avg.). 1–3 Snow north, rain south, then sunny, cold. 4–7 Rain, mild. 8–9 Sunny, cold. 10–16 Rain and snow, then sunny, cold. 17–20 Heavy rain, warm. 21–24 Sunny, mild. 25–31 Rain and snow, then sunny, seasonable.

JAN. 2010: Temp. 29° (4° below avg.); precip. 2.5" (1" below avg.). 1–7 Rain to snow, then sunny, cold. 8–12 Snowstorm, then sunny, cold. 13–20 Sunny, then rain and snow, seasonable. 21–24 Snow, then sunny, cold. 25–29 Snow showers, then sunny, very cold. 30–31 Heavy rain, warm.

FEB. 2010: Temp. 34° (1° above avg.); precip. 3.5" (0.5" above avg.). 1–5 Showers, warm. 6–10 Rain to snow, then sunny, seasonable. 11–14 Snow showers, then sunny, very cold. 15–18 Snow, then rain, milder. 19–24 Sunny; cold, then mild. 25–28 Snow, then heavy rain, seasonable.

MAR. 2010: Temp. 39° (2° below avg.); precip. 2" (2" below avg.). 1–6 Rain and snow showers, then sunny, cool. 7–9 Rain and snow showers, cool. 10–18 Rain and snow, unseasonably cold. 19–21 Rain, then sunny, cool. 22–25 Snow north, rain south, then sunny, cool. 26–29 Rain and snow, then sunny, cool. 30–31 Showers, cool.

APR. 2010: Temp. 52° (avg.); precip. 2.5" (1" below avg.). 1–3 Showers, then sunny. 4–6 Rain cool north; t-storms, warm south. 7–11 Sunny, then rain, seasonable. 12–14 Sunny. 15–20 Rainy periods, cool. 21–24 Sunny, turning warm. 25–27 Showers, then sunny, warm. 28–30 T-storms, turning cool.

MAY 2010: Temp. 62° (2° above avg.); precip. 2.5" (1.5" below avg.). 1–3 Sunny, hot. 4–8 T-storms, then sunny, cooler. 9–17 A few t-storms. 18–19 Sunny, hot. 20–24 T-storms, then sunny, cool. 25–27 Showers, cool. 28–31 Sunny, hot.

JUNE 2010: Temp. 70° (1° below avg.); precip. 2.5" (1" below avg.). 1–4 T-storms, hot. 5–9 Heavy rain, cool. 10–14 Sunny, warm. 15–16 Sunny, hot. 17–20 T-storms, then sunny, cool. 21–23 T-storms, hot. 24–30 Scattered t-storms, seasonable.

JULY 2010: Temp. 74° (2° below avg.); precip. 3" (1" below avg.). 1–7 T-storms, then sunny. 8–17 T-storms, then sunny, turning hot. 18–24 T-storms, then sunny, cool. 25–31 Showers, then sunny, warm.

AUG. 2010: Temp. 72° (2° below avg.); precip. 2.5" (1.5" below avg.). 1–5 T-storms, then sunny. 6–10 T-storms, then sunny, hot. 11–13 T-storms. 14–15 Rain, cool. 16–19 Showers. 20–24 T-storms, then sunny, cool. 25–31 Rain, then sunny, cool.

SEPT. 2010: Temp. 66.5° (2° below avg. north, 1° above south); precip. 2.5" (1" below avg.). 1–3 Sunny, hot. 4–8 T-storms, then sunny, cooler. 9–16 T-storms, then sunny, warm. 17–23 T-storms, then sunny, cool. 24–29 Rain, then sunny, chilly. 30 Rain.

OCT. 2010: Temp. 56° (avg.); precip. 1.5" (2" below avg.). 1–4 Rain, then sunny. 5–8 Rain, then sunny, warm. 9–10 Showers, cool. 11–14 Sunny, warm. 15–23 Showers, then sunny, cool. 24–29 Showers, then sunny, cool. 30–31 Rain, warm.

WEATHER

Boston
Hartford
New York
Philadelphia
Baltimore
Atlantic City
Washington
Richmond

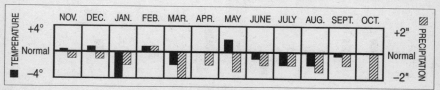

Appalachians

SUMMARY: Winter will be slightly colder and drier than normal, with below-normal snowfall. The coldest periods will occur in early to mid-January and mid-February. The snowiest periods will be around Thanksgiving, in late December, mid- to late January, early and mid-February, and early March.

April and May will be much warmer and slightly drier than normal, despite a cool and wet start to April.

Summer will be slightly cooler and drier than normal, with the hottest periods in mid-June, mid-July, and early to mid-August.

September and October will be warmer and drier than normal.

NOV. 2009: Temp. 45° (2.5° above avg.); precip. 3.5" (avg.). 1–5 Sunny, warm. 6–11 Scattered showers, mild. 12–16 Rain, then sunny, cold. 17–21 Heavy rain, then sunny, mild. 22–24 Snow showers, then sunny, cold. 25–30 Rain and snow, then sunny, cold.

DEC. 2009: Temp. 36.5° (2.5° above avg.); precip. 3" (avg.). 1–2 Flurries, cold. 3–4 Rain, mild. 5–14 Snow showers, cold. 15–19 Heavy rain, turning warm. 20–24 Flurries, seasonable. 25–30 Snow, then sunny, seasonable. 31 Rain, mild.

JAN. 2010: Temp. 25.5° (2.5° below avg.); precip. 3.5" (0.5" above avg.). 1–3 Rain to snow, turning cold. 4–5 Sunny, seasonable. 6–11 Snow showers, very cold. 12–16 Rain and snow arriving, turning milder. 17–20 Rain and snow showers, seasonable. 21–22 Sunny, cold. 23–28 Snow, then sunny, cold. 29–31 Heavy rain, mild.

FEB. 2010: Temp. 29° (1° above avg.); precip. 2.5" (avg.). 1–5 Scattered showers, mild. 6–8 Snow, then sunny, cold. 9–10 Sunny, mild. 11–16 Snow, then sunny, cold. 17–20 Ice and rain, then sunny, cold. 21–23 Sunny, mild. 24–28 Rain to snow, then sunny, seasonable.

MAR. 2010: Temp. 34.5° (4.5° below avg.); precip. 2" (1" below avg.). 1–5 Snow, then sunny, cold. 6–13 Periods of rain and snow, chilly. 14–15 Sunny, cold. 16–19 Rain, cool. 20–26 Rain and snow showers, chilly. 27–29 Sunny, cool. 30–31 T-storms, turning warm.

APR. 2010: Temp. 52° (2° above avg.); precip. 3" (0.5" below avg.). 1–3 Showers, then sunny, seasonable. 4–12 Rainy periods, cool. 13–16 Sunny, warm. 17–22 Rain, then sunny, seasonable. 23–27 Scattered t-storms, very warm. 28–30 T-storms;

seasonable north, very warm south.

MAY 2010: Temp. 64° (4° above avg.); precip. 2.5" (1.5" below avg.). 1–3 Sunny, very warm. 4–7 T-storms, then sunny, seasonable. 8–14 Scattered t-storms, warm. 15–20 Sunny, then t-storms, very warm. 21–23 Sunny, cool. 24–28 T-storms, then sunny, cool. 29–31 Sunny, hot.

JUNE 2010: Temp. 68° (avg.); precip. 2" (2" below avg.). 1–4 Scattered t-storms, very warm. 5–7 Sunny, cool. 8–11 Rain, then sunny, cool. 12–16 Sunny, then t-storms, hot. 17–21 Sunny; cool, then hot. 22–25 T-storms, then sunny, cool. 26–30 T-storms, seasonable.

JULY 2010: Temp. 72° (1° below avg.); precip. 3.5" (avg.). 1–6 T-storms, then sunny, warm. 7–14 T-storms, then sunny, cool. 15–18 Sunny, hot. 19–23 T-storms, then sunny, cooler. 24–28 T-storms, then sunny, cool. 29–31 T-storms, warm.

AUG. 2010: Temp. 71° (avg.); precip. 3" (1" above avg. north, 2" below south). 1–4 T-storms, then sunny, seasonable. 5–9 T-storms, then sunny, hot. 10–15 Scattered t-storms, turning cooler. 16–19 Sunny, then t-storms, warm. 20–23 Sunny, cool. 24–31 T-storms, then sunny, cool.

SEPT. 2010: Temp. 66° (2° above avg.); precip. 2.5" (1" below avg.). 1–3 Sunny, very warm. 4–5 Rain, cool. 6–8 Sunny, warm. 9–15 Scattered t-storms, very warm. 16–22 T-storms, then sunny, cool. 23–28 Rain, then sunny, chilly. 29–30 Rain, cool.

OCT. 2010: Temp. 53° (avg.); precip. 2" (1" below avg.). 1–5 Showers, then sunny, seasonable. 6–13 Rain, then sunny, warm. 14–19 Rain, then sunny, cool. 20–22 Snow showers north, sunny south; cold. 23–29 Showers, then sunny, seasonable. 30–31 Rain, mild.

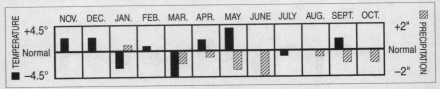

Southeast

SUMMARY: Winter will be colder than normal, on average, primarily due to a cool March. The coldest periods will occur in early to mid-December, early to mid-January, and early to mid-February. Precipitation will be above normal near the South Carolina coast, below normal west of Raleigh, and near normal elsewhere. Expect above-normal snowfall in much of the region, with the greatest threats for snow in mid-January and mid-February.

April and May will be much warmer and drier than normal.

Summer will be cooler and slightly rainier than normal, with the hottest temperatures in early to mid-August and other hot periods in mid-July and late August.

September and October will be slightly cooler and drier than normal.

NOV. 2009: Temp. 57° (2° above avg.); precip. 4.5" (avg. north, 3" above south). 1–10 Showers, then sunny, very warm. 11–15 Rain, then sunny, cold. 16–18 Heavy rain, seasonable. 19–22 Sunny, mild. 23–25 Rain and snow, then sunny, cold. 26–28 Rain, mild. 29–30 Sunny, cool.

DEC. 2009: Temp. 50° (2° above avg.); precip. 2.5" (1" below avg.). 1–4 Sunny; cool, then warmer. 5–9 Rain, then sunny, cold. 10–13 Rain, chilly. 14–16 Sprinkles, turning mild. 17–19 Heavy rain, warm. 20–22 Sunny, cool. 23–26 Scattered showers, warm. 27–31 Sunny, seasonable.

JAN. 2010: Temp. 44.5° (1.5° below avg.); precip. 3" (1.5" below avg.). 1–3 Showers, warm. 4–7 Sunny, seasonable. 8–12 Rain and snow, then sunny, cold. 13–17 Sunny, then rain, warmer. 18–22 Showers, then sunny, cold. 23–29 Snow north, rain south, then sunny, cold. 30–31 Heavy rain, warm.

FEB. 2010: Temp. 46.5° (0.5° above avg. east, 1" below west). 1–4 Sunny, warm. 5–8 T-storms, then sunny, cold. 9–11 Showers, seasonable. 12–15 Sunny, chilly. 16–21 Rain and snow, then sunny, chilly. 22–24 Heavy rain, seasonable. 25–28 Snow showers, then sunny, cold.

MAR. 2010: Temp. 51.5° (3.5° below avg.); precip. 5" (0.5" above avg.). 1–5 Sunny, then rain, chilly. 6–9 Sunny, seasonable. 10–11 Severe t-storms. 12–15 Rain, then sunny, chilly. 16–19 Rain, turning warmer. 20–23 Scattered showers, warm. 24–28 Showers, cool. 29–31 Sunny, warm.

APR. 2010: Temp. 66.5° (3.5° above avg.); pre-cip. 1" (2" below avg.). 1–4 Sunny, warm. 5–11 T-storms, then sunny, seasonable. 12–16 T-storms, then sunny, warm. 17–22 Scattered showers, turning cool. 23–30 Sunny, very warm.

MAY 2010: Temp. 74° (3° above avg.); precip. 2.5" (1" below avg.). 1–5 Scattered t-storms, warm. 6–10 Sunny, seasonable. 11–13 Scattered t-storms, very warm. 14–19 Sunny, warm. 20–26 Heavy t-storms, then sunny, pleasant. 27–31 Scattered t-storms, cool.

JUNE 2010: Temp. 74.5° (2.5° below avg.); precip. 8.5" (4" above avg.). 1–5 T-storms P.M., warm. 6–12 Heavy t-storms, then sunny, cool. 13–16 Sunny, warm. 17–20 T-storms, cool. 21–30 Scattered t-storms, seasonable.

JULY 2010: Temp. 79° (2° below avg.); precip. 5" (avg.). 1–12 Scattered t-storms, seasonable. 13–16 Sunny, cool. 17–21 T-storms, seasonable. 22–27 Sunny, cool. 28–31 T-storms, seasonable.

AUG. 2010: Temp. 79° (avg.); precip. 3" (2" below avg.). 1–7 Scattered t-storms, seasonable. 8–10 Sunny, hot. 11–19 Scattered t-storms, hot. 20–24 T-storms, then sunny, cool. 25–28 T-storms, then sunny, warm. 29–31 Sunny, warm.

SEPT. 2010: Temp. 75° (1° above avg.); precip. 3.5" (1" below avg.). 1–6 Scattered t-storms, warm. 7–14 Sunny, very warm. 15–19 T-storms, then sunny, cool. 20–25 T-storms, turning warm. 26–28 Sunny, chilly. 29–30 Rain, warmer.

OCT. 2010: Temp. 63.5° (0.5° below avg.); precip. 1" (2" below avg.). 1–6 Sunny, seasonable. 7–10 Sunny, warm. 11–15 Showers, warm. 16–23 Sunny, cold. 24–31 Sunny, mild.

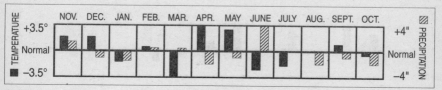

Florida

SUMMARY: Winter will be warmer than normal, on average, with the coldest temperatures occurring in mid-January. Rainfall will be above normal, with the best chance for any snow in the north around Christmas.

April and May will be warmer and much drier than normal.

Summer will be cooler and rainier than normal, with the hottest periods in early to mid- and mid- to late August. Watch for a major hurricane in late August or early September.

September and October will be slightly cooler and much rainier than normal.

NOV. 2009: Temp. 71° (2° above avg.); precip. 4" (1.5" above avg.). 1–5 Sunny, seasonable. 6–12 Showers, then sunny, warm. 13–21 Scattered t-storms, warm. 22–25 T-storms, then sunny, chilly. 26–28 T-storms, warm. 29–30 Sunny, cool.

DEC. 2009: Temp. 66° (3° above avg.); precip. 1.5" (1" below avg.). 1–5 Sunny, warm. 6–8 Showers, cool. 9–11 Sunny, warm. 12–14 Scattered t-storms, warm. 15–19 Sunny; cool, then warm. 20–24 Showers, then sunny, warm. 25–31 Scattered t-storms, seasonable.

JAN. 2010: Temp. 60.5° (0.5° below avg.); precip. 2" (0.5" below avg.). 1–3 Sunny, warm. 4–7 Scattered showers, seasonable. 8–13 T-storms, then sunny, cold. 14–17 Scattered showers, warm. 18–22 T-storms, then sunny, cool. 23–31 Scattered showers, turning warm.

FEB. 2010: Temp. 63.5° (2.5° above avg.); precip. 4.5" (2" above avg.). 1–6 Sunny, warm. 7–9 Scattered showers, warm. 10–13 Sunny, seasonable. 14–21 Heavy rain, then sunny, chilly. 22–25 T-storms, warm. 26–28 Sunny, cool.

MAR. 2010: Temp. 68.5° (1.5° above avg.); precip. 2.5" (0.5" below avg.). 1–4 Sunny, cool. 5–11 Scattered t-storms, turning warm. 12–21 T-storms, then sunny, warm. 22–31 T-storms, then sunny, seasonable.

APR. 2010: Temp. 74° (3° above avg.); precip. 0.5" (2" below avg.). 1–9 Sunny, very warm. 10–20 Scattered t-storms, warm. 21–26 Sunny, cool. 27–30 Scattered t-storms, warm.

MAY 2010: Temp. 78° (1° above avg.); precip. 1"

(3" below avg.). 1–4 Sunny, seasonable. 5–17 Scattered t-storms, then sunny, seasonable. 18–22 Scattered t-storms, warm. 23–31 Scattered t-storms, seasonable.

JUNE 2010: Temp. 80° (1° below avg.); precip. 6.5" (avg.). 1–5 T-storms, cool. 6–10 Scattered t-storms, warm. 11–14 Sunny north, t-storms south; cool. 15–22 Scattered t-storms, seasonable. 23–25 Sunny, warm. 26–30 T-storms, seasonable.

JULY 2010: Temp. 80.5° (1.5° below avg.). precip. 11.5" (5" above avg.). 1–16 Above-normal t-storm activity, below-normal temperatures. 17–24 T-storms, slightly cooler then normal. 25–31 Scattered t-storms, seasonable.

AUG. 2010: Temp. 81° (avg.); precip. 5.5" (2" below avg.). 1–6 Scattered t-storms, seasonable. 7–14 Scattered t-storms, hot. 15–20 Sunny, seasonable. 21–26 Scattered t-storms, hot. 27–30 Scattered t-storms, cooler. 31 Possible hurricane.

SEPT. 2010: Temp. 80° (avg.); precip. 10" (3" above avg.). 1–2 Possible hurricane. 3–5 Sunny, seasonable. 6–10 Scattered t-storms, cool. 11–16 Scattered t-storms, warm. 17–23 Heavy t-storms, seasonable. 24–27 Sunny, warm. 28–30 T-storms, warm.

OCT. 2010: Temp. 74° (1° below avg.); precip. 9" (5" above avg.). 1–5 Sunny, warm. 6–10 Heavy t-storms, then sunny, seasonable. 11–15 Scattered t-storms, seasonable. 16–22 Sunny, cool. 23–27 Heavy rain, then sunny, seasonable. 28–31 Scattered showers, seasonable.

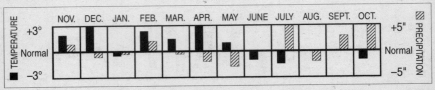

Lower Lakes

SUMMARY: Winter will be about a degree colder than normal, on average, despite a number of mild periods. The coldest periods will occur in the second week of December, early to mid-January, mid- to late January, and mid-February. Precipitation and snowfall will be below normal in the east and above normal in the west. Watch for a snowstorm around Thanksgiving, with other snowy periods in early and late December, late January, mid-February, and mid-March.

April and May will be warmer and drier than normal, with an early-season hot spell in mid-May.

Summer will be cooler than normal, with slightly below normal rainfall. The hottest periods will be in mid- to late June and mid- and late July.

September and October will be warmer than normal, with below-normal rainfall in the east and above-normal rainfall in the west.

NOV. 2009: Temp. 39° (1° below avg.); precip. 3" (1" below avg. east, 0.5" above west). 1–6 Sunny, warm. 7–11 T-storms, then sunny, cool. 12–17 Rain to snow, then sunny, cold. 18–21 Rainy periods. 22–25 Snow, cold. 26–30 Rain to snow, then snow showers, cold.

DEC. 2009: Temp. 32° (3° above avg.); precip. 3" (1" below avg. east, 0.5" above west). 1–2 Snow, cold. 3–6 Rain, mild. 7–13 Lake snows, cold. 14–17 Sunny, then rain, warm. 18–21 Rain and snow showers, seasonable. 22–24 Rain, mild. 25–30 Snowstorm, then sunny, mild. 31 Rain, mild.

JAN. 2010: Temp. 22° (2° below avg.); precip. 2.5" (avg.). 1–2 Rain, mild. 3–5 Snow showers. 6–12 Lake snows, very cold. 13–18 Snow to rain, mild. 19–23 Lake snows, very cold. 24–28 Snowstorm, bitter cold. 29–31 Sunny, then rain, mild.

FEB. 2010: Temp. 27° (3° above avg.); precip. 3" (1" above avg.). 1–5 Rainy periods, mild. 6–10 Sunny. 11–16 Snowstorm, then lake snows, cold. 17–20 Snowstorm, cold. 21–24 Sunny east, rain west; turning mild. 25–28 Rain east; snow west.

MAR. 2010: Temp. 27° (7° above avg.); precip. 2" (1" below avg.). 1–9 Snow showers, cold. 10–14 Snowstorm, then snow showers, cold. 15–22 Heavy snow, then snow showers, cold. 23–26 Rain and snow, cold. 27–31 Sunny, then rain, turning warm.

APR. 2010: Temp. 48.5° (1° below avg. east, 4.5° above west); precip. 3" (0.5" below avg.). 1–3 Sunny east, showers west; mild. 4–6 T-storms, then sunny, cool. 7–9 Showers, then sunny, cool. 10–12 Rain and snow, cool. 13–15 Showers. 16–21 Rain, then sunny, cool. 22–26 Sunny, very warm. 27–30 T-storms, then sunny, warm.

MAY 2010: Temp. 61° (3° above avg.); precip. 2" (1.5" below avg.). 1–2 Sunny, very warm. 3–7 T-storms, then sunny. 8–11 Scattered t-storms, warm. 12–14 Sunny; cool, then warm. 15–18 Scattered t-storms, hot. 19–23 T-storms, then sunny, cool. 24–28 Showers, then sunny, cool. 29–31 T-storms, warm.

JUNE 2010: Temp. 66° (1° below avg.); precip. 2" (1.5" below avg.). 1–8 T-storms, then sunny, cool. 9–12 Showers, then sunny, seasonable. 13–16 Scattered t-storms, very warm. 17–20 Sunny, pleasant. 21–24 T-storms, hot, then sunny, cool. 25–28 T-storms, then sunny. 29–30 T-storms, cool.

JULY 2010: Temp. 69.5° (2.5° below avg.); precip. 3" (0.5" below avg.). 1–5 T-storms, then sunny, cool. 6–8 T-storms, then sunny. 9–14 T-storms, then sunny, cool. 15–17 T-storms, hot. 18–28 Scattered t-storms, cool. 29–31 T-storms P.M., hot.

AUG. 2010: Temp. 69° (1° below avg.); precip. 5" (1" above avg.). 1–5 T-storms, then sunny, cool. 6–8 T-storms, then sunny, hot. 9–17 T-storms, then sunny, cool. 18–20 T-storms, warm. 21–22 Sunny. 23–27 Rain, then sunny, cool. 28–31 Rain, warm.

SEPT. 2010: Temp. 64° (1° above avg.); precip. 3.5" (2" below avg. east, 2" above west). 1–5 T-storms, then sunny, cool. 6–9 Rain. 10–13 Sunny, warm. 14–20 T-storms, then sunny, cool. 21–24 Showers, warm. 25–30 Sunny, then rain, cool.

OCT. 2010: Temp. 54° (avg. east, 3.5° above west); precip. 2.5" (avg.). 1–5 Showers, cool. 6–11 Sunny, turning warm. 12–14 Showers, warm. 15–18 Rain, then sunny, chilly. 19–22 Rain and snow showers, then sunny, cold. 23–30 Sunny, mild. 31 Rain.

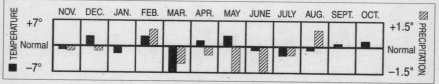

Ohio Valley

SUMMARY: Winter will bring rapid changes in the weather, from mild to very cold and back to mild again. Temperatures will be slightly below normal, on average, while precipitation will be above normal, with near-normal snowfall. The coldest periods will occur in the second week of December, early to mid-January, mid- to late January, mid- and late February, and early March. The snowiest periods will occur in late January, mid-February, and early March.

April and May will be much warmer and drier than normal—great weather for outdoor activities, but raising concern about summer drought.

Summer will be cooler than normal, with the hottest periods in mid- and late July and early to mid-August. Rainfall will be below normal, with the greatest threat of drought in the east.

September and October will be slightly cooler than normal. Tropical moisture in the first part of September will bring above-normal rainfall.

NOV. 2009: Temp. 45.5° (0.5° above avg.); precip. 4.5" (1" above avg.). 1–6 Sunny, warm. 7–11 Rain, then sunny, cool. 12–17 Rain to snow, then sunny, cold. 18–21 Rain, mild. 22–25 Rain and snow, cold. 26–27 Heavy rain, mild. 28–30 Snow showers, cold.

DEC. 2009: Temp. 39° (4° above avg.); precip. 4.5" (1.5" above avg.). 1–2 Snow showers, cold. 3–5 Heavy rain, warm. 6–13 Snow showers, cold. 14–20 Showers, warm. 21–24 Sunny, mild. 25–28 Rain, then sunny, seasonable. 29–31 Rain, mild.

JAN. 2010: Temp. 29° (2° below avg.); precip. 3" (avg.). 1–5 Rain to snow, then sunny, seasonable. 6–12 Snow showers, very cold. 13–18 Rainy periods, mild. 19–24 Snow showers, cold. 25–28 Snow then flurries, cold. 29–31 Sunny, then rain, mild.

FEB. 2010: Temp. 34° (2° above avg.); precip. 4.5" (1.5" above avg.). 1–4 Heavy rain, warm. 5–7 Flurries, cold. 8–10 Sunny, mild. 11–16 Snowy periods, cold. 17–19 Rain to snow. 20–23 Sunny, mild. 24–28 Rain to snow, then snow showers, cold.

MAR. 2010: Temp. 38° (6° below avg.); precip. 3" (1" below avg.). 1–4 Snowy periods, cold. 5–8 Snow showers, cold. 9–10 Rain, mild. 11–14 Snowy periods, cold. 15–19 Rain and wet snow, chilly. 20–24 Showers, then sunny, chilly. 25–31 Rainy periods; cool, then mild.

APR. 2010: Temp. 57° (3° above avg.); precip. 2.5" (1" below avg.). 1–5 Scattered t-storms, warm. 6–9 Sunny, cool. 10–16 Scattered showers, turning warm. 17–22 Sunny, cool. 23–27 Sunny, warm. 28–30 Scattered t-storms, warm.

MAY 2010: Temp. 67° (4° above avg.); precip. 2.5" (2" below avg.). 1–3 T-storms, warm. 4–7 Sunny. 8–14 T-storms, then sunny, warm. 15–20 Scattered t-storms, warm. 21–24 Sunny, cool. 25–29 T-storms, then sunny. 30–31 T-storms, warm.

JUNE 2010: Temp. 71.5° (0.5° below avg.); precip.1.5" (2.5" below avg.). 1–4 Sunny, warm. 5–8 T-storms, then sunny, cool. 9–13 T-storms, then sunny, pleasant. 14–18 T-storms, then sunny, seasonable. 19–21 Sunny, warm. 22–27 T-storms, then sunny, seasonable. 28–30 T-storms, warm.

JULY 2010: Temp. 73.5° (2.5° below avg.); precip. 4" (1.5" below avg. east, 1" above west.). 1–6 T-storms, then sunny, warm. 7–11 Scattered t-storms, seasonable. 12–14 Sunny, cool. 15–17 Sunny, hot. 18–24 T-storms, then sunny, cool. 25–28 A few t-storms, cool. 29–31 Sunny, hot.

AUG. 2010: Temp. 73° (1° below avg.); precip. 4.5" (1" above avg.). 1–2 T-storms, warm. 3–11 Sunny, turning hot. 12–19 Scattered t-storms, seasonable. 20–23 T-storms, then sunny, cool. 24–27 Rain, then sunny, cool. 28–31 Scattered showers, seasonable.

SEPT. 2010: Temp. 66.5° (0.5° below avg.); precip. 4" (1" above avg.). 1–3 Sunny, warm. 4–9 T-storms, seasonable. 10–14 Sunny, warm. 15–21 T-storms, then sunny, chilly. 22–29 T-storms, then sunny, chilly. 30 Rain.

OCT. 2010: Temp. 55.5° (0.5° below avg.); precip. 2.5" (avg.). 1–6 Showers, then sunny, cool. 7–12 Rain, then sunny, warm. 13–20 T-storms, then sunny, chilly. 21–29 Rain and snow showers, then sunny, warm. 30–31 Showers, warm.

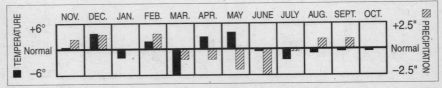

Deep South

SUMMARY: Winter temperatures will be near or slightly colder than normal, on average, in the north, but about a degree above normal in the south. The coldest periods will occur in early to mid-January, mid- to late January, and in early and mid-February. Precipitation and snowfall will be near normal, with the snowiest periods in mid-December, late January, and mid- and late February.

April and May will be about 3 degrees warmer than normal, with below-normal rainfall.

Summer will be slightly warmer than normal in the north, with below-normal temperatures in the south. The hottest periods will occur in late June, mid-July, and mid-August. Below-normal rainfall will bring drought conditions to portions of the region.

September and October will be slightly warmer than normal. Watch for hurricanes in early and mid- to late September, with below-normal rainfall in October.

NOV. 2009: Temp. 55° (0.5° above avg.); precip. 5" (avg.). 1–4 Sunny, warm. 5–9 Scattered t-storms, warm. 10–15 T-storms, then sunny, cold. 16–19 Rain, then sunny, seasonable. 20–24 T-storms, then sunny, cold. 25–30 Rain, then sunny, cold.

DEC. 2009: Temp. 51.5° (4.5° above avg.); precip. 4" (1" below avg.). 1–2 Sunny, cool. 3–9 Heavy rain, then sunny, cool. 10–13 Snow north, rain south; chilly. 14–16 Sunny, warm. 17–21 Rain, then sunny, seasonable. 22–26 Scattered t-storms, warm. 27–31 Sunny; cool, then warm.

JAN. 2010: Temp. 45° (1° above avg.); precip. 5" (avg.). 1–6 Heavy rain, then sunny. 7–12 Rain, then sunny, cold. 13–16 Showers, mild. 17–22 T-storms, then sunny, cold. 23–29 Snow north, rain south, then sunny, cold. 30–31 Rain, mild.

FEB. 2010: Temp. 45.5° (0.5° below avg.); precip. 6" (1" above avg.). 1–8 Rain, then sunny, cold. 9–13 Rain, then sunny, seasonable. 14–19 Periods of snow north, rain south, then sunny, cold. 20–22 T-storms, warm. 23–28 Periods of snow north, rain south, then sunny, cold.

MAR. 2010: Temp. 53° (6° below avg. north, avg. south); precip. 6" (avg.). 1–3 Sunny, chilly. 4–9 Rain, then sunny, turning warmer. 10–15 Rain, then sunny, cold. 16–20 Rain, then sunny, chilly. 21–25 Rain, then sunny, seasonable. 26–31 Scattered t-storms, warm.

APR. 2010: Temp. 66.5° (3.5° above avg.); precip. 2.5" (2" below avg.). 1–4 Scattered t-storms, warm. 5–6 Sunny, warm. 7–10 T-storms, then sunny, cool. 11–16 T-storms, then sunny, very warm. 17–20 T-storms, warm. 21–30 Sunny; cool, then hot.

MAY 2010: Temp. 74° (5° above avg. north, 1° above south); precip. 4" (1" below avg.). 1–6 Scattered t-storms, warm. 7–9 Sunny, warm. 10–20 Scattered t-storms, very warm. 21–26 Sunny, seasonable. 27–31 Scattered t-storms, warm.

JUNE 2010: Temp. 77.5° (0.5° below avg.); precip. 3" (2" below avg.). 1–9 Scattered t-storms. 10–14 Sunny, mild. 15–21 Sunny north, scattered t-storms south. 22–30 Scattered t-storms, warm.

JULY 2010: Temp. 81.5° (0.5° below avg.); precip. 4" (1" below avg.). 1–9 A few t-storms. 10–20 Scattered t-storms, hot. 21–24 Sunny, cool north; t-storms south. 25–31 Scattered t-storms, warm.

AUG. 2010: Temp. 80° (2° above avg. north, 4° below south); precip. 4.5" (avg.). 1–5 Sunny, pleasant north; t-storms south. 6–12 Sunny, hot north; t-storms south. 13–21 Scattered t-storms, warm. 22–28 Scattered showers, cool. 29–31 Sunny, warm.

SEPT. 2010: Temp. 76° (avg.); precip. 7.5" (3" above avg.). 1–2 Sunny, warm. 3–6 Possible hurricane. 7–14 Scattered t-storms, very warm. 15–20 T-storms, then sunny, cool. 21–24 Possible hurricane. 25–30 Sunny, then t-storms, cool.

OCT. 2010: Temp. 65.5° (0.5° above avg.); precip. 0.5" (2.5" below avg.). 1–6 Sunny, pleasant. 7–11 Sunny, warm. 12–26 T-storms, then sunny, cool. 27–31 Scattered t-storms, warm.

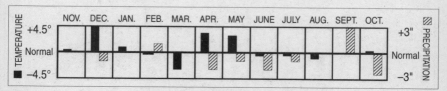

Upper Midwest

SUMMARY: Winter will be much colder than normal, with temperatures 3 degrees below normal, on average, in the east and 6 degrees below in the west. The coldest periods will occur in mid-December, early and mid- to late January, and early and mid- to late February. Precipitation and snowfall will be below normal in the east and above normal in the west. The snowiest periods will occur in mid- to late November, mid-December, early January, mid- to late February, and early to mid- and mid- to late March.

April and May will be warmer than normal in the east but cooler in the west. Precipitation will be above normal, with widespread snow in mid-April.

Summer will be cooler than normal, with below-normal rainfall in the east and near-normal rainfall in the west. The hottest periods will occur in mid-July and early August.

September and October will be slightly cooler than normal, with near-normal precipitation.

NOV. 2009: Temp. 25.5° (1° below avg. east, 4° below west); precip. 1.5" (0.5" below avg.). 1–2 Sunny, warm. 3–8 Rainy periods, warm. 9–15 Flurries, cold. 16–20 Rain to snow, seasonable. 21–30 Snow showers, very cold.

DEC. 2009: Temp. 13.5° (3° above avg. east, 4° below west); precip. 1" (avg.). 1–7 Rain and snow, then sunny, cold. 8–13 Snow showers, cold. 14–20 Snowy periods, cold. 21–23 Snow, then sunny, mild. 24–27 Snow showers, seasonable. 28–31 Sunny, mild.

JAN. 2010: Temp. 2.5° (6.5° below avg.); precip. 0.5" (0.5" below avg.). 1–7 Snow, then sunny, very cold. 8–15 Snow showers, then sunny, seasonable. 16–23 Snow showers, then sunny, very cold. 24–28 Snow, then sunny, cold. 29–31 Flurries, mild.

FEB. 2010: Temp. 9° (0.5° above avg. east, 5° below west); precip. 2" (1" above avg.). 1–5 Snowy periods, cold. 6–9 Snow showers, cold. 10–13 Flurries, mild. 14–21 Sunny; cold, then mild. 22–24 Snowstorm, then sunny, mild. 25–28 Flurries, mild.

MAR. 2010: Temp. 16° (11° below avg. east, 1° above west); precip. 1" (2" below avg. east, 1" above west). 1–8 Snow showers, cold. 9–19 Snowstorm, then sunny, cold. 20–23 Snowstorm, then sunny, cold. 24–31 Occasional rain and snow, milder.

APR. 2010: Temp. 42° (1° above avg.); precip. 2" (avg.). 1–2 Sunny, seasonable. 3–6 Rain, then sunny, cool. 7–10 Periods of rain and snow, cool. 11–13 Sunny, cool. 14–17 Rain, then sunny, cool. 18–21 Snow, then sunny, cool. 22–24 Sunny, warm. 25–30 T-storms, warm.

MAY 2010: Temp. 55° (3° above avg. east, 3° below west); precip. 5" (2" above avg.). 1–6 T-storms, then sunny, warm. 7–12 T-storms, then sunny, cool. 13–17 A few t-storms, seasonable. 18–23 Rain, then sunny, chilly. 24–26 T-storms, cool. 27–31 Scattered t-storms, warm.

JUNE 2010: Temp. 63° (1° below avg.); precip. 3" (1" below avg.). 1–4 Sunny, cool. 5–8 T-storms, then sunny, cool. 9–12 Sunny, warm. 13–15 Scattered t-storms. 16–18 Sunny, cool. 19–23 T-storms, then sunny, cool. 24–30 T-storms, cool.

JULY 2010: Temp. 67° (2° below avg. east, 2" above west); precip. 4" (0.5" below avg. east, 2" above west). 1–3 T-storms, then sunny, cool. 4–12 Scattered t-storms, then sunny, seasonable. 13–15 Sunny east, t-storms west; hot. 16–21 T-storms, then sunny, cool. 22–28 T-storms, cool east; sunny west. 29–31 T-storms, cool.

AUG. 2010: Temp. 65° (2° below avg.); precip. 2.5" (1" below avg. east; cool east, hot west. 5–7 Sunny, hot. 8–12 T-storms, then sunny, cool. 13–22 T-storms, then sunny, cool. 23–27 T-storms, then sunny. 28–31 T-storms, cool.

SEPT. 2010: Temp. 52° (6° below avg.); precip. 4.5" (1.5" above avg.). 1–3 Sunny, cool. 4–15 Rainy episodes, cool. 16–20 Rain and snow showers, cool. 21–28 Rain, then sunny, cool. 29–30 Rain, mild.

OCT. 2010: Temp. 50° (4° above avg.); precip. 1" (1.5" below avg.). 1–6 Rain, then sunny, cool. 7–9 Rain then sunny, warm. 10–12 T-storms, warm. 13–19 Sunny, seasonable. 20–27 Showers east, sunny west; warm. 28–31 Sunny, mild.

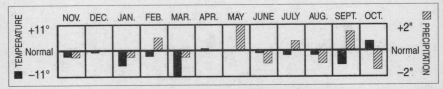

Heartland

SUMMARY: Winter will be colder than normal, on average, primarily due to persistent cold from mid-February through mid-March. The coldest periods will occur in early to mid-December, mid- to late January, and the latter half of February. Precipitation will be near or slightly above normal, with above-normal snowfall from Des Moines northeastward and below-normal snowfall elsewhere. The biggest snowstorms will occur in mid-December and early to mid-January.

April and May will be much warmer than normal, with below-normal precipitation, especially in the south.

Summer will be cooler and rainier than normal, despite hot spells in early, mid-, and late July and early and mid-August.

September and October will be warmer than normal. Rainfall will be above normal in the north and below normal in the south.

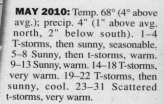

NOV. 2009: Temp. 41° (1° below avg.); precip. 2.5" (avg.). 1–6 Sunny, warm. 7–10 T-storms, turning cooler. 11–15 Rain to snow, then sunny, cold. 16–18 Sunny, warm. 19–21 Showers, seasonable. 22–26 Snowy periods, cold. 27–30 Sunny, cold.

DEC. 2009: Temp. 34° (4° above avg.); precip. 1" (0.5" below avg.). 1–5 Sunny, then rain, mild. 6–11 Sunny, turning very cold. 12–16 Snow and ice, then sunny, mild. 17–20 Rain to snow, then sunny, seasonable. 21–26 Showers, mild. 27–31 Sunny, mild.

JAN. 2010: Temp. 25.5° (0.5° below avg.); precip. 1" (avg.). 1–3 T-storms, then sunny, cold. 4–5 Sunny, mild. 6–10 Snowstorm, then sunny, cold. 11–18 Sunny, then rain, turning mild. 19–28 Rain to snow, then sunny, very cold. 29–31 Rain arriving, mild.

FEB. 2010: Temp. 26° (3° below avg.); precip. 2.5" (1" above avg.). 1–2 Rain, mild. 3–7 Rain to snow, then sunny, cold. 8–12 Snow showers, then sunny, mild. 13–19 Rain to snow, then sunny, cold. 20–28 Rain to snow, then sunny, cold.

MAR. 2010: Temp. 35° (8° below avg.); precip. 3" (0.5" above avg.). 1–5 Sunny, cold. 6–9 Rain and snow, chilly. 10–18 Snow showers, cold. 19–25 Sunny, turning warm. 26–31 T-storms, warm.

APR. 2010: Temp. 59.5° (5.5° above avg.); precip. 1.5" (2" below avg.). 1–4 Rain north; sunny, warm south. 5–7 Sunny, then rain, seasonable. 8–15 Sunny; cool, then very warm. 16–21 T-storms, then sunny, cool. 22–27 Sunny, very warm. 28–30 Scattered t-storms, very warm.

MAY 2010: Temp. 68° (4° above avg.); precip. 4" (1" above avg. north, 2" below south). 1–4 T-storms, then sunny, seasonable. 5–8 Sunny, then t-storms, warm. 9–13 Sunny, warm. 14–18 T-storms, very warm. 19–22 T-storms, then sunny, cool. 23–31 Scattered t-storms, very warm.

JUNE 2010: Temp. 72.5° (0.5° below avg.); precip. 4.5" (avg.). 1–5 Scattered t-storms, warm. 6–12 Sunny, cool. 13–17 T-storms, then sunny, seasonable. 18–22 Scattered t-storms, warm. 23–30 Scattered t-storms, warm and humid.

JULY 2010: Temp. 77° (1° below avg.); precip. 4.5" (0.5" above avg.). 1–2 Sunny, warm. 3–10 Scattered t-storms, hot. 11–13 T-storms, cool. 14–17 Sunny, hot. 18–25 Scattered t-storms, cool. 26–29 Sunny, hot. 30–31 T-storms.

AUG. 2010: Temp. 75° (1° above avg.); precip. 4.5" (1" above avg.). 1–7 Sunny; cool, then hot. 8–13 T-storms, seasonable. 14–17 Showers, cool. 18–19 Sunny, hot. 20–26 T-storms, then sunny, cool. 27–31 T-storms, warm.

SEPT. 2010: Temp. 66.5° (0.5° below avg.); precip. 4.5" (3" above avg. north, 1" below south). 1–4 Sunny, cool. 5–14 Scattered t-storms; cool north, hot south. 15–19 Sunny, cool. 20–22 Showers, warm. 23–28 T-storms, then sunny, cool. 29–30 Showers, seasonable.

OCT. 2010: Temp. 59° (3° above avg.); precip. 1" (2" below avg.). 1–3 Sunny; cool north, warm south. 4–6 Showers, cool. 7–12 Scattered t-storms, warm. 13–18 T-storms, then sunny, cool. 19–27 Sunny, warm. 28–31 T-storms, warm.

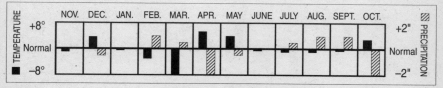

Texas–Oklahoma

SUMMARY: Winter will be colder than normal, on average, from the Metroplex north and westward, with near-normal temperatures elsewhere. The coldest periods will occur in the second week of December, early to mid-January, and early to mid-February. Precipitation and snowfall will be near or slightly below normal. The most significant snow and ice will occur in mid-December, early January, and early and mid-February.

April and May will be warmer then normal, with near-normal rainfall.

Summer will be hotter and drier than normal, with the hottest periods from late June through the first half of July and in early to mid-August. The likelihood of a major hurricane is below normal.

September and October will bring near-normal temperatures, on average, with slightly below normal rainfall.

NOV. 2009: Temp. 56° (2° below avg. north, 2° above south); precip. 2.5" (0.5" below avg.). 1–4 Sunny, warm. 5–7 Scattered t-storms, warm. 8–10 Rain, warm. 11–16 T-storms, then sunny, cold. 17–21 Sunny, cool north; rainy periods, mild south. 22–24 Sunny, cool. 25–30 Rain, then sunny, cold.

DEC. 2009: Temp. 52° (4° above avg.); precip. 2.5" (avg.). 1–5 Rain, then sunny, mild. 6–8 Showers, then sunny, cold. 9–13 Rain and snow, then sunny, cold. 14–18 Rain, then sunny, mild. 19–20 Showers, then colder. 21–25 Sunny, then rain, warm. 26–28 Rain, then colder. 29–31 Sunny, warm.

JAN. 2010: Temp. 47° (1° above avg.); precip. 2" (avg.). 1–5 Snow north, rain south; then sunny, cool. 6–7 Showers, mild. 8–11 Sunny, cold. 12–15 Rain, mild. 16–21 Sunny, seasonable. 22–26 Showers, then sunny, cool. 27–31 Rain, turning warmer.

FEB. 2010: Temp. 44° (4° below avg.); precip. 3" (1" above avg.). 1–4 T-storms, mild. 5–10 Snow north, rain south; cold. 11–13 Sunny, warm. 14–17 Rain to snow north, showers south; cold. 18–20 Sunny, mild. 21–28 T-storms, then sunny, cold.

MAR. 2010: Temp. 55° (3° below avg.); precip. 1.5" (1" below avg.). 1–3 Sunny, seasonable. 4–9 Rainy periods; cold, then mild. 10–14 Sunny, cold. 15–20 Rain and snow showers, then sunny, cold north; rainy periods, mild, then cool south. 21–26 Showers north, rainy periods south; turning warmer. 27–31 Scattered t-storms, warm.

APR. 2010: Temp. 70° (4° above avg.); precip. 1.5" (1.5" below avg.). 1–7 Scattered t-storms, warm. 8–11 Sunny, seasonable. 12–16 Sunny, warm

Oklahoma City ◉
Dallas ◉
Houston ◉
San Antonio ◉

north; clouds, seasonable south. 17–23 T-storms, then sunny, cool. 24–26 Sunny. 27–30 A few showers, warm.

MAY 2010: Temp. 74° (1° above avg.); precip. 6.5" (1.5" above avg.). 1–5 Scattered t-storms, warm. 6–8 T-storms, seasonable. 9–12 Scattered t-storms north, heavy t-storms south. 13–18 Scattered t-storms, warm. 19–23 T-storms, then sunny, warm. 24–31 Scattered t-storms, warm.

JUNE 2010: Temp. 81.5° (1.5° above avg.); precip. 2" (2" below avg.). 1–4 Sunny, warm. 5–11 Scattered t-storms, cool north; sunny, warm south. 12–16 Sunny, warm north; humid, showers south. 17–21 Scattered t-storms, warm. 22–25 Sunny, hot north; humid, scattered t-storms south. 26–30 Scattered t-storms, hot.

JULY 2010: Temp. 84° (1° above avg.); precip. 2" (1" below avg.). 1–6 Scattered t-storms, hot. 7–14 Sunny, hot. 15–20 Scattered t-storms; hot north, seasonable south. 21–31 Scattered t-storms, cooler.

AUG. 2010: Temp. 82° (avg.); precip. 1" (1.5" below avg.). 1–8 Scattered t-storms. 9–14 Isolated t-storms, hot. 15–20 A few t-storms, humid. 21–23 Scattered t-storms. 24–26 Sunny, cool north; t-storms south. 27–31 A few t-storms, warm, humid.

SEPT. 2010: Temp. 75° (1° below avg.); precip. 4" (0.5" above avg.). 1–4 Sunny. 5–8 Sunny, hot. 9–14 Frequent t-storms; cool north, humid south. 15–20 T-storms then sunny north; rain and t-storms south, cooler. 21–30 Showers, then sunny, cool.

OCT. 2010: Temp. 68° (1° above avg.); precip. 3" (1" below avg.). 1–2 Sunny, warm. 3–6 T-storms, then sunny, cooler. 7–12 Showers, warm. 13–25 Sunny; cool, then warmer. 26–31 Rain and t-storms.

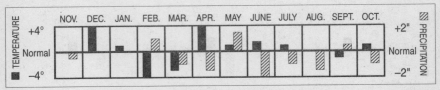

High Plains

SUMMARY: Winter will be much colder than normal in the north, with near-normal temperatures in the south. The coldest periods will occur in early to mid-December, early and late January, early and mid-February, and early March. Precipitation will be near or slightly below normal, with above-normal snowfall in the north and below-normal snowfall in the south. The snowiest periods will occur in mid-November, mid- and late January, mid-February, and early and mid-March.

April and May will be slightly warmer than normal, with near-normal precipitation.

Summer will be cooler and rainier than normal, despite hot weather in mid-July and early August.

September and October will bring near-normal precipitation. Temperatures will be below normal, on average, in the north and above normal in the south.

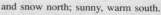

NOV. 2009: Temp. 33° (7° below avg. north, 1° above south); precip. 1" (avg.). 1–3 Sunny, warm. 4–6 Showers, cooler. 7–13 Periods of rain and snow, cold. 14–17 Sunny, mild. 18–21 Snow, cold north; sunny, mild south. 22–27 Snowy periods, cold. 28–30 Sunny, milder.

DEC. 2009: Temp. 25.5° (9° below avg. north, 6° above south); precip. 0.5" (avg.). 1–3 Sunny, north; showers south. 4–7 Snow showers, then sunny, cold. 8–11 Snow showers, then sunny, very cold. 12–14 Sunny, mild. 15–19 Rain to snow, then sunny, cold. 20–24 Snow showers north and west; sunny, mild southeast. 25–30 Sunny, mild. 31 Snow north, showers south.

JAN. 2010: Temp. 28° (3° above avg.); precip. 0.8" (0.3" above avg.). 1–3 Snow showers, cold. 4–13 Snow then sunny, turning mild. 14–21 Snow, then sunny, cold. 22–27 Snowstorm, then sunny, cold. 28–30 Sunny, mild. 31 Snow showers, cold.

FEB. 2010: Temp. 22° (5° below avg.); precip. 0.5" (avg.). 1–6 Snow, then sunny, cold. 7–9 Snow, then sunny, cold. 10–12 Sunny, mild. 13–17 Snowstorm, then sunny, very cold. 18–20 Sunny, warm. 21–25 Snow, then sunny, cold. 26–28 Flurries, seasonable.

MAR. 2010: Temp. 29.5° (13° below avg. north, 4° below south); precip. 0.5" (0.5" below avg.). 1–6 Snow showers, cold. 7–13 Snow, then sunny, very cold. 14–18 Snow, then sunny, cold. 19–24 Snow, then sunny, mild. 25–31 Rain and snow, cool.

APR. 2010: Temp. 51° (3° above avg.); precip. 1" (1" below avg.). 1–4 Rain to snow, then sunny, cool. 5–8 Showers, seasonable. 9–11 Rain and snow, cool north; sunny, warm south. 12–15 T-storms north; sunny, warm south. 16–20 Showers, then sunny, cool. 21–24 Sunny, warm. 25–30 Rain

and snow north; sunny, warm south.

MAY 2010: Temp. 57° (1° below avg.); precip. 3.5" (1" above avg.). 1–4 Rain to snow north, t-storms south, then sunny, cool. 5–12 T-storms, then sunny, warm. 13–21 Rainy periods, cool. 22–27 Scattered showers, warm. 28–31 T-storms, then sunny, cool.

JUNE 2010: Temp. 65° (2° below avg.); precip. 4" (1" above avg.). 1–4 Sunny, warm north; t-storms south. 5–10 T-storms, cool. 11–20 Scattered t-storms, warm. 21–24 Showers, cool north; sunny, warm south. 25–30 Scattered t-storms, warm.

JULY 2010: Temp. 73° (1° above avg.); precip. 3" (1" above avg.). 1–5 Scattered t-storms, cool. 6–9 Sunny, warm. 10–15 Scattered t-storms, hot. 16–20 A few t-storms. 21–26 T-storms, then sunny, cool. 27–31 Scattered t-storms.

AUG. 2010: Temp. 69° (2° below avg.); precip. 1.5" (0.5" below avg.). 1–5 Sunny, hot. 6–15 Scattered t-storms, cool. 16–22 Showers, cool north; sunny, hot south. 23–26 T-storms, then sunny, cool. 27–31 Showers, cool north; sunny, hot south.

SEPT. 2010: Temp. 55.5° (9° below avg. north, 2° below south); precip. 2" (0.5" above avg.). 1–4 Showers, cool north; sunny, warm south. 5–7 Rain, turning cool. 8–10 Snow north, rain south; turning cold. 11–12 Sunny, cool. 13–16 Rain and snow, cold. 17–18 Sunny, cool. 19–23 Rain to snow, then sunny, cool. 24–30 Sunny, turning mild.

OCT. 2010: Temp. 55° (6° above avg.); precip. 0.5" (0.5" below avg.). 1–8 Sunny, warm, then cool. 9–14 Showers, then sunny. 15–31 Sunny, warm.

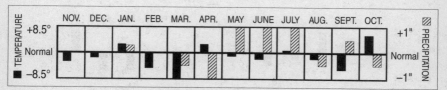

Intermountain

SUMMARY: Winter temperatures will be above normal, with the coldest periods in early to mid-December and early February. Precipitation will be above normal, with below-normal snowfall from Reno to Salt Lake City and above-normal snowfall in most other areas. The snowiest periods will occur in early and mid-November, mid- and late December, and mid- and late January.

April and May will be slightly warmer and wetter than normal.

Summer will be cooler and slightly rainier than normal, although there will be hot weather in early July and early August.

September and October will be slightly warmer and drier than normal.

NOV. 2009: Temp. 38° (1° below avg.); precip. 2" (0.5" above avg.). 1–2 Rain, mild. 3–14 Snowstorm, then sunny, cold. 15–18 Snow to rain, then sunny, mild. 19–22 Snow, then sunny, mild. 23–26 Rainy periods, mild. 27–30 Rain and snow showers, seasonable.

DEC. 2009: Temp. 34° (3° above avg.); precip. 3.5" (2" above avg.). 1–4 Periods of rain and snow, seasonable. 5–6 Sunny, cool. 7–10 Snow, then sunny, cold. 11–14 Snowstorm, then sunny, mild. 15–19 Snow, turning cold northwest; rainy periods, mild elsewhere. 20–24 Snow, seasonable. 25–29 Snowstorm, then sunny, mild. 30–31 Snow.

JAN. 2010: Temp. 34° (4° above avg.); precip. 2" (0.5" above avg.). 1–6 Snow showers, then sunny. 7–8 Sunny, mild. 9–12 Snow showers north; sunny, mild south. 13–18 Snowy periods, seasonable. 19–26 Rain, then sunny, mild. 27–29 Rain and snow showers, seasonable. 30–31 Snow, colder.

FEB. 2010: Temp. 32° (1° below avg.); precip. 0.5" (1" below avg.). 1–3 Sunny north, snow south; cold. 4–8 Snow showers, cold. 9–13 Sunny, mild. 14–17 Snow showers, seasonable. 18–22 Showers, then flurries, colder. 23–25 Sunny, cold. 26–28 Flurries, seasonable.

MAR. 2010: Temp. 40° (2° below avg.); precip. 1.5" (avg.). 1–3 Sunny, seasonable. 4–13 Rain and snow, then sunny, cold. 14–21 Snowy periods, cold. 22–24 Sunny, mild. 25–28 Rain and snow, cool. 29–31 Rain and snow showers, cool.

APR. 2010: Temp. 50° (1° above avg.); precip. 2" (1" above avg.). 1–7 Rain and snow, then sunny, cool. 8–15 Showers, then sunny, warm. 16–20 Sunny, warm north; rain south. 21–23 Sunny, warm. 24–27 Showers, cool. 28–30 Rain and snow.

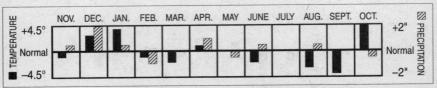

MAY 2010: Temp. 55° (avg.); precip. 0.5" (0.5" below avg.). 1–4 Rain, then sunny, seasonable. 5–7 Sunny, warm north; rain south. 8–13 Showers, cool north; sunny, warm south. 14–18 Rain, chilly. 19–28 Sunny, turning warmer. 29–31 Showers, seasonable.

JUNE 2010: Temp. 64° (2° below avg.); precip. 1" (0.5" above avg.). 1–4 Sunny, warm north; showers, cool south. 5–14 Rain, then sunny, cool. 15–21 Rain, then sunny, cool. 22–30 Isolated t-storms, warm.

JULY 2010: Temp. 73° (avg.); precip. 0.5" (avg.). 1–5 Scattered t-storms, seasonable. 6–8 Sunny, hot. 9–15 T-storms, then sunny, cool. 16–22 Scattered t-storms, warm. 23–25 Sunny, hot north; t-storms south. 26–28 Scattered showers, seasonable. 29–31 Sunny, hot.

AUG. 2010: Temp. 69° (3° below avg.); precip. 1.5" (0.5" above avg.). 1–3 Sunny, hot. 4–6 T-storms, then sunny, cool. 7–10 Scattered t-storms, seasonable. 11–16 T-storms, cool. 17–21 Sunny; cool north, warm south. 22–31 Sunny north, t-storms south; cool.

SEPT. 2010: Temp. 58° (4° below avg.); precip. 1" (avg.). 1–4 Scattered showers, cool. 5–8 Showers, cool north; sunny, warm south. 9–12 Sunny north, rain to snow south; cold. 13–19 Sunny, turning warm. 20–26 Showers, then sunny, seasonable. 27–30 Showers north, sunny south; warm.

OCT. 2010: Temp. 55.5° (4.5° above avg.); precip. 0.5" (0.5" below avg.). 1–4 Sunny, warm. 5–7 Showers, then sunny, seasonable. 8–10 Rain and snow showers. 11–26 Sunny, mild. 27–31 Showers north, sunny south; mild.

Desert Southwest

SUMMARY: Winter will be colder than normal, on average, especially in the west, with the coldest periods in early to mid-December, mid-January, and early to mid-February. Precipitation and snowfall will be near normal, with the snowiest periods in mid-December, early January, and mid-February.

April and May will be cooler than normal, with above-normal rainfall in the west.

Summer will be cooler and drier than normal, with the hottest temperatures in early and late July and early August. September and October will be cooler and drier than normal.

NOV. 2009: Temp. 52.5° (avg. east, 5° below west); precip. 0.5" (avg.). 1–7 Showers, then sunny, cold. 8–17 Rain and snow, then sunny, chilly. 18–24 Sunny, warmer. 25–30 Scattered t-storms, then sunny, cool.

DEC. 2009: Temp. 46° (1° above avg. east, 3° below west); precip. 0.5" (avg.). 1–5 Sunny, cool. 6–9 Sunny, cold. 10–13 Rain and snow, then sunny, seasonable. 14–16 Sunny, warm. 17–20 Showers east, sunny west; warm. 21–23 Sunny, warm east; showers, then cool west. 24–27 Showers, then sunny, cool. 28–31 Rain arriving; mild east, cool west.

JAN. 2010: Temp. 49.5° (2.5° above avg.); precip. 0.5" (avg.). 1–4 Rain and snow, then sunny, cool. 5–11 Sunny, warm. 12–16 Rain, then sunny, mild. 17–21 Rain and snow showers, then sunny, cold. 22–29 Sunny, warm. 30–31 Rain, cool.

FEB. 2010: Temp. 44° (6° below avg.); precip. 0.2" (0.3" below east, 0.3" below west); chilly. 4–9 Snow showers east, sunny west; cold. 10–15 Sunny, turning warm. 16–19 Snow east, sunny west; cool. 20–28 Rain and snow showers, then sunny, cold.

MAR. 2010: Temp. 54.5° (avg. east, 5° below west); precip. 1.2" (avg. east, 1.4" above west). 1–2 Sunny, cool. 3–7 T-storms, then sunny, cool. 8–14 Showers, then sunny, cool. 15–18 Scattered showers, warm. 19–24 Sunny, seasonable. 25–31 Rainy periods, cool.

APR. 2010: Temp. 63.5° (2° above avg. east, 3° below west); precip. 1" (avg. east, 1" above west). 1–5 Sunny, seasonable east; rainy, cool west. 6–16 Sunny, turning warm. 17–21 Scattered t-storms, then sunny, cool. 22–24 Sunny, warm.

25–30 Scattered t-storms, then sunny, cool.

MAY 2010: Temp. 69° (4° below avg.); precip. 0.5" (0.4" below avg. east, 0.4" above west). 1–4 Sunny, cool. 5–9 Scattered showers, cool. 10–13 Scattered showers east, sunny west; warm. 14–20 T-storms, then sunny, cool. 21–26 Scattered t-storms, then sunny, cool. 27–31 Sunny, warmer.

JUNE 2010: Temp. 78° (5° below avg.); precip. 0.7" (0.2" above avg.). 1–4 Scattered t-storms, cool. 5–8 Sunny, warm. 9–14 Scattered t-storms, cool. 15–20 T-storms, then sunny, cool. 21–26 Scattered t-storms, seasonable east; sunny, hot west. 27–30 Scattered t-storms, humid.

JULY 2010: Temp. 86.5° (0.5° below avg.); precip. 1" (0.5" below avg.). 1–9 Scattered t-storms, hot, humid. 10–17 A few t-storms, cool. 18–23 Scattered t-storms, seasonable. 24–29 Scattered t-storms, cool east; sunny, seasonable west. 30–31 Sunny, hot.

AUG. 2010: Temp. 84.5° (0.5° below avg.); precip. 1" (0.5" below avg.). 1–2 Sunny, hot. 3–9 Scattered t-storms, seasonable. 10–12 Scattered t-storms, cool. 13–16 Scattered t-storms east, sunny west; cool. 17–21 Sunny, warm. 22–31 Scattered t-storms, seasonable.

SEPT. 2010: Temp. 74° (4° below avg.); precip. 0.7" (0.3" below avg.). 1–4 Scattered t-storms east, sunny west; cool. 5–9 Sunny, warm. 10–15 T-storms, then sunny, very cool. 16–19 Sunny, warm. 20–26 Scattered t-storms, then sunny, cool. 27–30 Sunny, warm.

OCT. 2010: Temp. 68° (1° above avg.); precip. 0.7" (0.3" below avg.). 1–7 Sunny, warm. 8–12 T-storms, then sunny, cool. 13–27 Sunny, warm. 28–31 Scattered t-storms, warm.

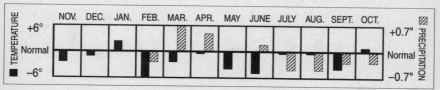

Pacific Northwest

SUMMARY: Winter temperatures and precipitation will be near normal, on average, with above-normal snowfall. The coldest periods will occur in early to mid- and late December, mid-January, and early to mid-February, with the snowiest periods in mid-December, early January, and mid-February.

April and May will be warmer than normal, with near-normal rainfall in Washington and drier-than-normal conditions elsewhere.

Summer will be drier than normal, with below-normal temperatures, on average, in Washington and above-normal temperatures in California and Oregon. The hottest periods will occur in late June and mid-July.

September and October will be warmer and drier than normal.

NOV. 2009: Temp. 46.5° (0.5° below avg.); precip. 7.5" (1" above avg.). 1–5 Stormy, heavy rain, cool. 6–14 Wet snow, then sunny, cold. 15–18 Heavy rain, mild. 19–21 Rain and snow, cold. 22–24 Heavy rain, mild. 25–30 Mist and showers, seasonable.

DEC. 2009: Temp. 41° (1° below avg.); precip. 10" (1" above avg. north, 6" above south). 1–5 Rainy periods, mild. 6–10 Rain to snow, then sunny, very cold. 11–16 Snowstorm, then flooding rain, mild. 17–20 Rain, seasonable. 21–27 Periods of rain and snow, cold. 28–31 Rain and snow showers, cool.

JAN. 2010: Temp. 44° (2° above avg.); precip. 7" (1" above avg.). 1–4 Rain, then sunny, cool. 5–12 Misty, seasonable. 13–15 Rain, mild. 16–19 Heavy rain, seasonable. 20–23 Rain and t-storms, windy, mild. 24–26 Sunny, cold. 27–31 Rainy intervals, mild.

FEB. 2010: Temp. 46° (2° above avg.); precip. 2" (3" below avg.). 1–8 Periods of rain and drizzle, seasonable. 9–12 Partly sunny, mild. 13–15 Showers, cool. 16–18 Sprinkles, mild. 19–21 Heavy rain, seasonable. 22–28 Sunny, warm.

MAR. 2010: Temp. 47° (avg.); precip. 1" (3" below avg.). 1–3 Sunny, warm. 4–8 A few showers, seasonable. 9–12 Sunny, cool. 13–17 Showers, then sunny, cool. 18–20 Wet snow to rain, cool. 21–24 Showers, mild. 25–28 Showers, then cool. 29–31 Showers, cool.

APR. 2010: Temp. 50.5° (1° below avg. north, 2° above south); precip. 3" (1" above avg. north, 1" below south). 1–5 Rain, then sunny, pleasant. 6–10 Showers, seasonable. 11–13 Heavy rain,

mild. 14–17 Showers, seasonable. 18–20 Sunny, warm. 21–30 Showers, then sunny, cool.

MAY 2010: Temp. 55° (2° below avg. north, 2° above south); precip. 1" (1" below avg.). 1–5 Sunny, turning warm. 6–11 Showers, cool. 12–17 Rain, then sunny, cool. 18–21 Sunny, warm. 22–24 Showers, cool. 25–31 Sunny, warm.

JUNE 2010: Temp. 61° (1° above avg.); precip. 1" (0.5" below avg.). 1–7 Scattered showers, cool. 8–16 Sunny, seasonable. 17–20 Scattered showers, cool. 21–30 Sunny, hot.

JULY 2010: Temp. 64.5° (1° below avg. north, 2° above south); precip. 0.2" (0.3" below avg.). 1–5 Scattered t-storms, cool. 6–10 Sunny, warm. 11–14 Scattered t-storms, cool. 15–17 Sunny, hot. 18–20 Scattered showers, seasonable. 21–24 Sunny, hot. 25–31 Showers, then sunny, seasonable.

AUG. 2010: Temp. 64.5° (2° below avg. north, 1° above south); precip. 0.3" (0.7" below avg.). 1–5 Rainy periods, seasonable. 6–10 Sunny, warm. 11–13 T-storms, cool. 14–22 Scattered showers, cool. 23–28 Sunny; warm, then cool. 29–31 Sunny, seasonable.

SEPT. 2010: Temp. 60° (1° below avg.); precip. 1" (0.5" below avg.). 1–8 Scattered showers, cool. 9–14 Sunny, cool. 15–18 Sunny, then showers, warm. 19–22 Scattered showers, cool. 23–25 Sunny, warm. 26–30 Rain, mild.

OCT. 2010: Temp. 57° (3° above avg.); precip. 2.5" (0.5" below avg.). 1–4 Sunny, seasonable. 5–7 Rain, wind, mild. 8–11 Rain, cool. 12–19 Showers, then sunny, warm. 20–26 Rainy periods, mild. 27–28 Heavy rain. 29–31 Showers.

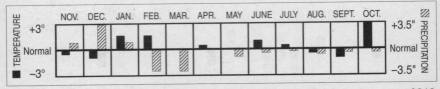

Pacific Southwest

SUMMARY: Winter temperatures will be near normal in the north, on average, with above-normal rainfall. In the south, temperatures and rainfall will be below average. The stormiest periods will occur in early November, mid- and late December, and late January. Expect the coldest periods to occur in early and late December, early January, and early February.

April and May will be cooler and rainier than normal.

Summer will be slightly cooler and rainier than normal, with the hottest periods in early and late July, early August, and late September.

September and October will be warmer and drier than normal.

W E A T H E R

NOV. 2009: Temp. 56° (2° below avg.); precip. 1.7" (0.5" above avg. north, 0.1" below south). 1–5 Stormy, heavy rain and t-storms. 6–8 Sunny, cool. 9–10 Sunny north, rain south; cool. 11–13 Sunny, cool. 14–16 Showers, then cloudy north, sunny south; cool. 17–19 Light rain, cool. 20–23 Sunny, turning warm. 24–27 Showers, seasonable. 28–30 Low clouds, cool.

DEC. 2009: Temp. 54° (4° above avg. north, 2° below south); precip. 4" (4" above avg. north, avg. south). 1–4 Showers north, sunny south; seasonable. 5–6 Sunny, cool. 7–10 Showers north, sunny south; cool. 11–20 Showers and t-storms, heavy north; mild. 21–26 Rain north, a few sprinkles south; cool. 27–31 Rain and t-storms, mild north; some sun, then showers, cool south.

JAN. 2010: Temp. 53° (avg.); precip. 1" (2" below avg.). 1–3 Sunny, cool. 4–8 Scattered showers. 9–11 Sunny, warm. 12–15 Showers, seasonable. 16–22 T-storms, then sunny, seasonable. 23–27 Some sun, sprinkles, cool. 28–31 T-storms.

FEB. 2010: Temp. 54° (1° below avg.); precip. 0.5" (2.5" below avg.). 1–5 Sunny, cool. 6–7 Showers north, sunny south; cool. 8–12 Sunny; cool, then warm. 13–18 Sunny. 19–23 Showers, then sunny. 24–28 T-storms, mild, then cool.

MAR. 2010: Temp. 56° (1° below avg.); precip. 3" (1" above avg.). 1–2 Sunny. 3–10 T-storms, then sunny, cool. 11–15 Sunny, warm. 16–22 Showers, cool. 23–31 Stormy, rain and t-storms, cool.

APR. 2010: Temp. 59° (1° below avg.); precip. 3" (2" above avg.). 1–4 Heavy rain and t-storms, then sunny, cool. 5–13 Rainy periods, seasonable north; sunny intervals, turning warmer south. 14–23 Sunny; cool coast, hot inland. 24–30 Sunny, cool.

MAY 2010: Temp. 63° (1° below avg.); precip. 0.4" (0.2" below avg. north, avg. south). 1–5 Morning coastal clouds, otherwise sunny, cool. 6–12 Clouds and fog, cool coast; sunny, warm inland. 13–19 Scattered showers, then sunny, cool. 20–23 Morning clouds, cool coast; sunny, warm inland. 24–27 Clouds, a few sprinkles, cool. 28–31 Coastal clouds, sunny inland.

JUNE 2010: Temp. 66° (2° below avg.); precip. 0.1" (avg.). 1–2 Scattered showers, cool. 3–7 Morning fog, afternoon sun; cool. 8–10 Sprinkles southwest, sunny elsewhere; cool. 11–13 Sunny. 14–19 Low clouds, morning drizzle, cool coast; sunny, turning cool inland. 20–21 Sunny, cool. 22–30 Morning clouds, afternoon sun, cool coast; sunny, turning hot inland.

JULY 2010: Temp. 70° (1° below avg.); precip. 0" (avg.). 1–4 Sunny, cool. 5–10 Morning clouds coast; hot inland. 11–16 Sunny. 17–21 Scattered showers, then sunny, cool. 22–31 Morning sun, cool coast; sunny, hot inland.

AUG. 2010: Temp. 72° (avg.); precip. 0.2" (0.1" above avg.). 1–3 Sunny, hot. 4–8 Scattered t-storms, then sunny, hot. 9–18 Morning coastal clouds, sunny inland; cool. 19–22 Sunny, warm. 23–31 Scattered showers, then sunny, cool.

SEPT. 2010: Temp. 68° (2° below avg.); precip. 0.2" (avg.). 1–8 Sunny, cool. 9–13 Showers, then sunny, cool. 14–18 Low clouds and fog coast, sunny inland. 19–22 Scattered showers, then sunny, cool. 23–25 Sunny, hot. 26–30 Sunny; cool, then warm.

OCT. 2010: Temp. 67.5° (2.5° above avg.); precip. 0" (0.5" below avg.). 1–6 Sunny. 7–10 Scattered t-storms, then sunny, cool. 11–12 Sprinkles north, sunny south. 13–18 Sunny, Santa Ana wind; hot coast, warm inland. 19–23 Sunny, warm. 24–30 Sunny, seasonable. 31 T-storms north, sunny south.

Map labels: San Francisco, Fresno, Los Angeles, San Diego

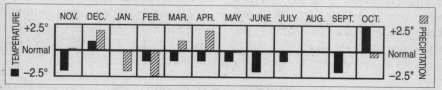

Winners in the 2009 Essay Contest

My Pet's
Best
Trick Ever

FIRST PRIZE

Our black lab, Bart, was 110 pounds of agreeable pal. He would follow the kids everywhere—especially my daughter, Wendy.

In the winter, Bart and Wendy would routinely ride together on a red plastic flying saucer, gliding down the hill that was our front yard. At the bottom, Bart would grab one of the canvas handles in his mouth and drag the saucer back up the hill.

The winter when Bart was 6 years old and Wendy was 14, they had been sliding as usual. One day, while Wendy was in school, I happened to look out the front room window. I saw that lovable mountain of a dog all alone sliding down the hill on the flying saucer. At the bottom, he grabbed the canvas handle, dragged the saucer to the top, and then went down again—four times in all. We knew that we had an unusual dog, but this sealed the deal.

–Jane Ferber, Zephyrhills, Florida

SECOND PRIZE

At 10 years old, I should have been in school. That's where my mother thought I was when she heard the first faint call for her: "Mama!"

She ignored it, but the call quickly became more insistent: "Mama, Mama!" She rushed to the living room of our old farmhouse, but when she looked around, I was nowhere to be seen. She tried the kitchen, tried my attic bedroom.

"Mama, help!" She ran to the back door. I was not in the yard.

Again she heard the call for help, and, to her ear, the voice was muffled, as if from behind a piece of furniture. Back to the living room she ran to look behind the couch and the big old oil stove.

Still puzzled, she stepped onto the front porch, leaving the door open behind her. "Mama! HELP!" came from the living room.

When she stepped back inside, the call came again—this time softly, without urgency. "Mama, help," said Turkey, the family parrot. Then he added his hearty "HA-HA-HA!" to the joke, having accomplished what he'd wanted all along: to have some company while his young best friend (me) was in class. Turkey was quite the humorist.

–Petrina Vecchio, Ashford, Washington

THIRD PRIZE

My German shepherd, Duchess, was quick when it came to learning new tricks. One day, I taught her to grab things when I made the motion of pinching my thumb and index finger together. My son was sitting in the den watching TV. I motioned the dog with my thumb and finger and whispered, "Robert." Duchess ran into the den, grabbed my son's pant leg, and pulled him off the chair. We all laughed.

It got even more hysterical when my friend Joan came to the house. My husband and I were standing in the kitchen and I said to Joan, "I taught the dog a new trick. Would you like to see it?" She nodded, and again I motioned the dog with my fingers and said, "Daddy." Duchess ran around the table, grabbed my husband by the seat of his pants, and pulled. With that, the top button of his pants popped open and the pants started to fall. I yelled for the dog to stop, as my husband ducked behind the table, trying to pull up and close his pants.

My friend laughed uncontrollably and then ran home to get her husband so that he could see Duchess's new trick, too.

–Ede Adams, Berkshire, New York

□□

ANNOUNCING THE 2010 ESSAY CONTEST TOPIC

The Kindest Thing Anyone Ever Did for Me

In 200 words or less, please tell us about an act of kindness that you experienced.

ESSAY AND RECIPE CONTEST RULES

Cash prizes (first, $250; second, $150; third, $100) will be awarded for the best essay on the subject "The Kindest Thing Anyone Ever Did for Me" and for the best recipe using pumpkin (see page 171). All entries become the property of Yankee Publishing, which reserves all rights to the material. The deadline for entries is Friday, January 29, 2010. Label "Essay Contest" or "Recipe Contest" and send to The Old Farmer's Almanac, P.O. Box 520, Dublin, NH, 03444; essaycontest@yankeepub.com; or recipecontest@yankeepub.com. Include your name, mailing address, and e-mail address. Winners will be announced in *The 2011 Old Farmer's Almanac* and on Almanac.com/Contests.

When All Else Fails, Try a Mad Stone

. . . if you can get one

In the summer of 1875, on the central Texas frontier, Sarah Hall was confronted by a polecat that had wandered in through a door she had left open. It bit her seven times, on the hand, arm, and face. Her family, responding to her screams, found Sarah holding the polecat by the scruff of its neck. In the ensuing turmoil, she dropped the beast and it made a hasty escape into the surrounding brush. Sarah's family rushed her to a neighbor who practiced folk medicine. Sarah begged to have gunpowder put on the wounds and touched off, a remedy that she hoped would protect her from hydrophobia (rabies), but

by Martha Deeringer

–illustration, David Austin Clar

the neighbor refused, preferring to treat the bites with turpentine, salt, and an egg yolk.

A few days later, Sarah's wounds became inflamed and began to ache. Her family sent her brother to borrow a "mad stone" (sometimes called a "bezoar stone") from a distant neighbor. The small, dark stone was soaked in warm, sweet milk and then dried off and applied to the wound. It stuck. Several hours later, when the stone had absorbed all of the poison that it could hold, it dropped off. The poison was removed from the stone by soaking it in sweet milk again. Green bubbles of noxious material leached from the stone into the milk. When the bubbling stopped, the stone was dried off and used again. Three continuous days of treatment detoxified all seven of Sarah's bites. A cure was confirmed when the stone ceased to stick to any of the wounds.

Mad stones, so called because of their frequent use in the treatment of bites from mad dogs, have been used for centuries:

- Ancient Chinese called mad stones "serpent stones" and used them to remove the poison from snakebites.

- Aristocratic Europeans in the 1600s used bezoar stones to remove poisons that they suspected were added to their wine. A submerged stone would supposedly render the wine safe to drink.

- Europeans also found mad stones inside toad skulls. (Shakespeare mentions the use of one in *As You Like It:* "Sweet are the uses of adversity, which, like the toad, ugly and venomous, wears yet a precious jewel in its head.")

—The Granger Collection, New York

The efficacy of mad stones has long been in dispute. In the *Journal of the American Medical Association* in 1900, Dr. Charles W. Dulles wrote of two sorts of mad stones: a porous form of calcareous rock and a concretion, or bezoar. He noted: "Serious writers usually treat the mad stone as having no specific virtue, but serving [only] as a means to calm the apprehensions of those who have been bitten by rabid animals."

(continued)

This bezoar stone from a steer measures 1.8 inches in diameter.

In a 1949 issue of *Dixie Roto Magazine*, Dr. Joseph Brierre of Vacherie, Louisiana, offered a differing opinion: "There is nothing supernatural about the mad stone. . . . It[s osmotic properties] will cause certain fluids to pass from one thing to another. It has a pull like a leech and will stay on the wound until the poison is gone, sometimes 24 to 36 hours. Then it falls off."

Mad stones are found in the stomach or intestines of cud-chewing animals, but not every animal carries a stone in its innards. Some mad stones are considered more valuable than others. A mad stone taken from a white deer is believed to be more potent than a stone retrieved from a brown deer.

Strict rules apply to the use of mad stones. They can never be bought or sold; to do so would negate their powers. (Families that own mad stones treasure them, passing them down from one generation to the next.) There can be no money charged for use of a mad stone, and for best results, the patient should travel to the home of the stone's owner (although, as Sarah's case proved, there are exceptions).

Please Pass the Stone

The challenge is getting hold of a mad stone. If you have experience with mad stones, please share your story or your stone at Almanac.com /MadStone.

☐ ☐

Magazine writer **Martha Deeringer** of McGregor, Texas, is thankful that she has never needed a mad stone.

MADDENING
Mind-Manglers

Test Your Bird Brain

Answers appear on page 241.

For each entry, name the bird described and the state(s) it represents.

1. Also known as the Virginia nightingale, this bird favors parklike urban settings. (7 states; name 2)

2. This game bird is smaller than a pigeon.

3. This member of the titmouse family has a black cap, gray beak, and gray wings. (2 states)

4. This bird forages in flocks in the winter and likes insects. Adults have thin beaks. (2 states)

5. Known for its short life span, this bird reportedly eats more ants than any other American bird.

6. This bird, about 6½ inches long, has a pointed bill, black head, and orange underparts. Its first name is that of a U.S. city and British lord.

7. This bird, also known as the nene, numbered only about 30 in 1952. Since then, its population has increased.

8. This chickenlike bird is called *Lagopus lagopus* in scientific circles.

9. This member of the thrush family is territorial and likes open grasslands. (2 states)

10. This long-billed bird has an underlying throat pouch. In 1970, it was declared an endangered species. Its population had recovered by 1985, and it was removed from the list.

11. This common bird came to the aid of Mormon settlers by helping to rid their crops of grasshhoppers.

12. This bird has a white stripe above each eye and lives in an arid climate, yet it rarely drinks water.

13. This reddish-brown chicken lays up to 300 eggs a year.

14. This fierce protector swoops down to attack dogs or cats that it fears might endanger its home and young. It is known for its song and has been

mentioned in music, poetry, and literature. (5 states; name 2)

15. This large, strong bird, more common in Canada than in the United States, makes a haunting sound.

16. Able to attain speeds of up to 17 mph, this bird catches and eats rattlesnakes.

17. This member of the sparrow family likes to nest on the ground in a grassy area. Males are black with a white wing patch.

18. Known for its loud song, this bird sometimes eats small lizards and often makes domed nests.

19. This bird's females prepare nests with inner walls of mud and can have three successful broods in a season. (3 states; name 2)

20. This prairie lover is about 9 inches long and has a black V on its chest. Its melodic song distinguishes it from other birds in its species. (6 states; name 2)

21. This game bird was a political symbol in early American politics.

22. Also known as a wild canary, this bird is very fond of thistles, eating the seeds and using the down in its nest. (3 states; name 2)

23. This reclusive bird, related to the mockingbird, prefers thickets and heavy brush.

24. This lover of woodlands and boggy forests is more often heard than seen, hence its name.

25. This bird dwells in coniferous forests. Adult males have raspberry-color heads, necks, and upper parts.

26. This native Asian game bird has delicious meat.

27. This relative of the kingbird has a long black tail and black wings, likes open shrubby areas, and often builds its nest in utility poles.

28. This bird can be up to 20 inches long and dives into soft snow to spend winter nights.

–D. Schipp, Nevada, Missouri

☐☐

Secrets of the Zodiac

Ancient astrologers believed that each astrological sign influenced a specific part of the
body. The first sign of the zodiac--Aries--was
attributed to the head, with the rest of the
signs moving down the body, ending with
Pisces at the feet.

♈ Aries, head...... **ARI** *Mar. 21–Apr. 20*
♉ Taurus, neck .... **TAU** *Apr. 21–May 20*
♊ Gemini, arms ... **GEM** *May 21–June 20*
♋ Cancer, breast ... **CAN** *June 21–July 22*
♌ Leo, heart....... **LEO** *July 23–Aug. 22*
♍ Virgo, belly ..... **VIR** *Aug. 23–Sept. 22*
♎ Libra, reins...... **LIB** *Sept. 23–Oct. 22*
♏ Scorpio, secrets .. **SCO** *Oct. 23–Nov. 22*
♐ Sagittarius, thighs. **SAG** *Nov. 23–Dec. 21*
♑ Capricorn, knees. **CAP** *Dec. 22–Jan. 19*
♒ Aquarius, legs... **AQU** *Jan. 20–Feb. 19*
♓ Pisces, feet ..... **PSC** *Feb. 20–Mar. 20*

Astrology vs. Astronomy

■ **Astrology** is a tool we use to plan events according to the placements of the Sun, the Moon,
and the planets in the 12 signs of the zodiac. In
astrology, the planetary movements do not
cause events; rather, they explain the path, or
"flow," that events tend to follow. **Astronomy** is
the study of the actual placement of the known
planets and constellations. *(The placement of
the planets in the signs of the zodiac is not the
same astrologically and astronomically.)* The
Moon's astrological place is given on **page 230**;
its astronomical place is given in the **Left-Hand
Calendar Pages, 110–136.**

The dates in the **Best Days table, page 231,** are
based on the astrological passage of the Moon.
However, consider all indicators before making
any major decisions.

When Mercury Is Retrograde

■ Sometimes the other planets appear to be
traveling backward through the zodiac; this is an
illusion. We call this illusion *retrograde motion.*

Mercury's retrograde periods can cause our
plans to go awry. However, this is an excellent
time to reflect on the past. Intuition is high during these periods, and coincidences can be extraordinary.

When Mercury is retrograde, remain flexible,
allow extra time for travel, and avoid signing
contracts. Review projects and plans at these
times, but wait until Mercury is direct again to
make any final decisions.

In 2010, Mercury will be retrograde from
January 1–15, April 18–May 11, August 20–
September 12, and December 10–30.

–Celeste Longacre

Gardening by the Moon's Sign

Use the chart on the next page to find the best
dates for the following garden tasks:

■ **Plant, transplant, and graft:** Cancer, Scorpio,
or Pisces. Taurus, Virgo, and Capricorn are
good second choices.

■ **Build/fix fences or garden beds:** Capricorn.

■ **Control insect pests, plow, and weed:** Aries,
Gemini, Leo, Sagittarius, or Aquarius.

■ **Prune:** Aries, Leo, or Sagittarius. During a
waxing Moon, pruning encourages growth;
during a waning Moon, it discourages growth.

■ **Clean out the garden shed:** Virgo.

(continued)

Secrets of the Zodiac (continued)

Setting Eggs by the Moon's Sign

■ Chicks take about 21 days to hatch. Those born under a waxing Moon, in the fruitful signs of Cancer, Scorpio, and Pisces, are healthier and mature faster. To ensure that chicks are born during these times, determine the best days to "set eggs" (to place eggs in an incubator or under a hen). To calculate, find the three fruitful birth signs on the chart below. **Use the Left-Hand Calendar Pages, 110–136,** to find the dates of the new and full Moons.

Using only the fruitful dates between the new and full Moons, count back 21 days to find the best days to set eggs.

E X A M P L E :

The Moon is new on June 12 and full on June 26. Between these dates, on June 13 and 14, the Moon is in the sign of Cancer. To have chicks born on June 13, count back 21 days; set eggs on May 23.

The Moon's Astrological Place, 2009–10													
	Nov.	Dec.	Jan.	Feb.	Mar.	Apr.	May	June	July	Aug.	Sept.	Oct.	Nov.	Dec.
1	ARI	GEM	CAN	VIR	VIR	SCO	SAG	AQU	PSC	ARI	GEM	CAN	VIR	LIB
2	TAU	GEM	LEO	LIB	LIB	SAG	CAP	AQU	PSC	TAU	GEM	CAN	VIR	SCO
3	TAU	CAN	LEO	LIB	LIB	SAG	CAP	PSC	ARI	TAU	CAN	LEO	LIB	SCO
4	GEM	CAN	VIR	SCO	SCO	SAG	CAP	PSC	ARI	GEM	CAN	LEO	LIB	SCO
5	GEM	CAN	VIR	SCO	SCO	CAP	AQU	PSC	ARI	GEM	LEO	VIR	SCO	SAG
6	CAN	LEO	LIB	SCO	SAG	CAP	AQU	ARI	TAU	GEM	LEO	VIR	SCO	SAG
7	CAN	LEO	LIB	SAG	SAG	AQU	PSC	ARI	TAU	CAN	VIR	LIB	SAG	CAP
8	LEO	VIR	SCO	SAG	CAP	AQU	PSC	TAU	GEM	CAN	VIR	LIB	SAG	CAP
9	LEO	VIR	SCO	CAP	CAP	AQU	PSC	TAU	GEM	CAN	LEO	LIB	SCO	CAP	AQU
10	VIR	LIB	SCO	CAP	CAP	PSC	ARI	TAU	CAN	VIR	SCO	SAG	CAP	AQU
11	VIR	LIB	SAG	CAP	AQU	PSC	ARI	GEM	CAN	VIR	SCO	SAG	CAP	AQU
12	VIR	SCO	SAG	AQU	AQU	ARI	TAU	GEM	LEO	VIR	SCO	SAG	AQU	PSC
13	LIB	SCO	CAP	AQU	AQU	ARI	TAU	CAN	LEO	LIB	SAG	CAP	AQU	PSC
14	LIB	SAG	CAP	PSC	PSC	ARI	GEM	CAN	VIR	LIB	SAG	CAP	PSC	ARI
15	SCO	SAG	AQU	PSC	PSC	TAU	GEM	LEO	VIR	SCO	SAG	AQU	PSC	ARI
16	SCO	SAG	AQU	PSC	ARI	TAU	GEM	LEO	LIB	SCO	CAP	AQU	PSC	ARI
17	SAG	CAP	AQU	ARI	ARI	GEM	CAN	VIR	LIB	SAG	CAP	AQU	ARI	TAU
18	SAG	CAP	PSC	ARI	TAU	GEM	CAN	VIR	LIB	SAG	CAP	AQU	PSC	ARI	TAU
19	CAP	AQU	PSC	TAU	TAU	CAN	LEO	LIB	SCO	CAP	AQU	PSC	TAU	GEM
20	CAP	AQU	PSC	TAU	TAU	CAN	LEO	LIB	SCO	CAP	AQU	ARI	TAU	GEM
21	CAP	AQU	ARI	TAU	GEM	LEO	VIR	SCO	SAG	CAP	PSC	ARI	TAU	CAN
22	AQU	PSC	ARI	GEM	GEM	LEO	VIR	SCO	SAG	AQU	PSC	ARI	GEM	CAN
23	AQU	PSC	TAU	GEM	CAN	LEO	LIB	SCO	CAP	AQU	ARI	TAU	GEM	LEO
24	PSC	ARI	TAU	CAN	CAN	VIR	LIB	SAG	CAP	PSC	ARI	TAU	CAN	LEO
25	PSC	ARI	GEM	CAN	LEO	VIR	SCO	SAG	CAP	PSC	ARI	GEM	CAN	VIR
26	PSC	ARI	GEM	LEO	LEO	LIB	SCO	CAP	AQU	PSC	TAU	GEM	LEO	VIR
27	ARI	TAU	CAN	LEO	VIR	LIB	SAG	CAP	AQU	ARI	TAU	GEM	LEO	VIR
28	ARI	TAU	CAN	VIR	VIR	SCO	SAG	AQU	PSC	ARI	GEM	CAN	VIR	LIB
29	TAU	GEM	LEO	—	LIB	SCO	SAG	AQU	PSC	TAU	GEM	CAN	VIR	LIB
30	TAU	GEM	LEO	—	LIB	SAG	CAP	AQU	PSC	TAU	CAN	LEO	LIB	SCO
31	—	CAN	VIR	—	SCO	—	CAP	—	ARI	TAU	—	LEO	—	SCO

Best Days for 2010

This chart is based on the Moon's sign and shows the best days each month for certain activities.

—Celeste Longacre

	JAN.	FEB.	MAR.	APR.	MAY	JUNE	JULY	AUG.	SEPT.	OCT.	NOV.	DEC.
Quit smoking	4, 8	1, 5	4, 9	1, 10	7, 12	4, 9	1, 6, 28	2, 25, 30	3, 26	5, 23	5, 28	3, 26, 30
Begin diet to lose weight	4, 8	1, 5	4, 9	1, 10	7, 12	4, 9	1, 6, 28	2, 25, 30	3, 26	5, 23	5, 28	3, 26, 30
Begin diet to gain weight	18, 23	15, 20, 28	19, 23, 27	15, 24	21, 25	17, 21	15, 19	11, 15	11, 21	9, 18	14, 19	12, 17
Cut hair to discourage growth	6, 7	2, 3	2, 3	10, 11	7, 8	4, 5	6, 7, 29, 30	2, 3, 30, 31	5, 6, 26, 27	7, 30, 31	3, 4, 26, 27	1, 28, 29
Cut hair to encourage growth	18, 19, 23, 24	19, 20, 26, 27	19, 20, 25, 26	15, 16, 26, 27	19, 20, 23, 24	15, 16, 19, 20	12, 13, 17, 18	13, 14	9, 10, 21, 22	3, 4, 30, 31	14, 15, 19, 20	12, 13, 17, 18
Have dental care	4, 5, 31	1, 28	1, 27, 28	24, 25	21, 22	17, 18	14, 15	11, 12	7, 8	5, 6	1, 2, 28, 29	26, 27
Start projects	16, 17	15, 16	16, 17	15, 16	15, 16	13, 14	12, 13	11, 12	9, 10	8, 9	7, 8	6, 7
End projects	13, 14	12, 13	13, 14	12, 13	12, 13	10, 11	9, 10	8, 9	6, 7	5, 6	4, 5	3, 4
Go camping	11, 12	7, 8	6, 7	3, 4, 30	1, 27, 28	24, 25	21, 22	17, 18	13, 14, 15	11, 12	7, 8	5, 6
Plant aboveground crops	19, 20, 27, 28	15, 16, 24, 25	23, 24	19, 20	17, 18, 25, 26	13, 14, 22, 23	19, 20	15, 16	11, 12, 21, 22	9, 10, 18, 19	15, 16	12, 13
Plant belowground crops	1, 8, 9	5, 6	4, 5, 31	1, 10, 11	7, 8	4, 5	1, 2, 10, 28, 29	7, 8, 25, 26	3, 4	1, 2, 28, 29	5, 24, 25	2, 3, 30, 31
Destroy pests and weeds	21, 22	17, 18	16, 17	13, 14	10, 11	6, 7	4, 5, 31	1, 27, 28	24, 25	20, 21, 22	17, 18	14, 15
Graft or pollinate	1, 27, 28	24, 25	23, 24	19, 20	17, 18	13, 14	10, 11	7, 8	3, 4, 30	1, 2, 28, 29	24, 25	21, 22
Prune to encourage growth	21, 22	17, 18	17, 25, 26	21, 22	19, 20	15, 16	12, 13, 21, 22	17, 18	14, 15	11, 12	7, 8, 17, 18	14, 15
Prune to discourage growth	2, 3	7, 8	6, 7	3, 4	10, 11	6, 7	4, 5, 31	1, 27, 28	5, 6, 24	3, 4, 30, 31	26, 27	23, 24
Harvest above-ground crops	23, 24	19, 20	19, 20, 27	15, 16, 24, 25	21, 22	17, 18	14, 15	11, 12	16, 17	13, 14	10, 11, 19, 20	7, 8
Harvest below-ground crops	3, 4, 13, 14	1, 9, 10	1, 9, 10	5, 6	2, 3, 4, 30, 31	9, 10, 27	6, 7	2, 3, 30, 31	7, 26, 27	5, 6	1, 2, 28, 29	25, 26
Can, pickle, or make sauerkraut	1, 8, 9	5, 6	4, 5, 14, 31	1, 10, 11	7, 8	4, 5	1, 2, 10, 28, 29	7, 8, 25, 26	3, 4	1, 2, 28, 29	5, 24, 25	2, 3, 30, 31
Cut hay	21, 22	17, 18	16, 17	13, 14	10, 11	6, 7	4, 5, 31	1, 27, 28	24, 25	20, 21, 22	17, 18	14, 15
Begin logging	13, 14	9, 10, 11	9, 10	5, 6	2, 3, 4, 30, 31	26, 27	23, 24	20, 21	16, 17	13, 14	10, 11	7, 8
Set posts or pour concrete	13, 14	9, 10, 11	9, 10	5, 6	2, 3, 4, 30, 31	26, 27	23, 24	20, 21	16, 17	13, 14	10, 11	7, 8
Breed animals	8, 9	5, 6	4, 5, 31	1, 28, 29	25, 26	21, 22	19, 20	15, 16	11, 12	9, 10	5, 6	2, 3, 30, 31
Wean animals or children	4, 8	1, 5	4, 9	1, 10	7, 12	4, 9	1, 6, 28	2, 25, 30	3, 26	5, 23	5, 28	3, 26, 30
Castrate animals	16, 17	12, 13	11, 12, 13	8, 9	5, 6	1, 2, 29, 30	26, 27	22, 23	18, 19, 20	16, 17	12, 13	9, 10
Slaughter livestock	8, 9	5, 6	4, 5, 31	1, 28, 29	25, 26	21, 22	19, 20	15, 16	11, 12	9, 10	5, 6	2, 3, 30, 31

Planting by the Moon's Phase

This age-old practice suggests that the Moon in its cycles affects plant growth.

■ Plant flowers and vegetables that bear crops above ground during the light, or waxing, of the Moon: from the day the Moon is new to the day it is full.

■ Plant flowering bulbs and vegetables that bear crops below ground during the dark, or waning, of the Moon: from the day after it is full to the day before it is new again.

The Moon Favorable columns *(right)* give the best planting days based on the Moon's phases for 2010. (See the **Left-Hand Calendar Pages, 110–136,** for the exact days of the new and full Moons.) The Planting Dates columns give the safe periods for planting in areas that receive frost. See **Frosts and Growing Seasons, page 203,** for first/last frost dates and the average length of the growing season in your area.

■ Aboveground crops are marked *.

■ (E) means early; (L) means late.

■ Map shades correspond to shades of date columns.

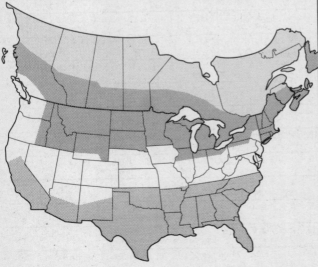

* Barley	
* Beans	(E)
	(L)
Beets	(E)
	(L)
* Broccoli plants	(E)
	(L)
* Brussels sprouts	
* Cabbage plants	
Carrots	(E)
	(L)
* Cauliflower plants	(E)
	(L)
* Celery plants	(E)
	(L)
* Collards	(E)
	(L)
* Corn, sweet	(E)
	(L)
* Cucumbers	
* Eggplant plants	
* Endive	(E)
	(L)
* Kale	(E)
	(L)
Leek plants	
* Lettuce	
* Muskmelons	
* Okra	
Onion sets	
* Parsley	
Parsnips	
* Peas	(E)
	(L)
* Pepper plants	
Potatoes	
* Pumpkins	
Radishes	(E)
	(L)
* Spinach	(E)
	(L)
* Squashes	
Sweet potatoes	
* Swiss chard	
* Tomato plants	
Turnips	(E)
	(L)
* Watermelons	
* Wheat, spring	
* Wheat, winter	

232

-3/7	2/15-28	3/15-4/7	3/15-29	5/15-6/21	5/15-27, 6/12-21	6/1-30	6/12-26
-4/7	3/15-29	4/15-30	4/15-28	5/7-6/21	5/13-27, 6/12-21	5/30-6/15	6/12-15
31	8/9-24	7/1-21	7/11-21	6/15-7/15	6/15-26, 7/11-15	—	
28	2/7-12	3/15-4/3	3/30-4/3	5/1-15	5/1-12	5/25-6/10	5/28-6/10
30	9/1-7, 9/24-30	8/15-31	8/25-31	7/15-8/15	7/26-8/8	6/15-7/8	6/27-7/8
-3/15	2/15-28, 3/15	3/7-31	3/15-29	5/15-31	5/15-27	6/1-25	6/12-25
30	9/8-23	8/1-20	8/9-20	6/15-7/7	6/15-26	—	—
-3/20	2/13-28, 3/15-20	3/7-4/15	3/15-29, 4/14-15	5/15-31	5/15-27	6/1-25	6/12-25
-3/20	2/13-28, 3/15-20	3/7-4/15	3/15-29, 4/14-15	5/15-31	5/15-27	6/1-25	6/12-25
-3/7	3/1-7	3/7-31	3/7-14, 3/30-31	5/15-31	5/28-31	5/25-6/10	5/28-6/10
9/7	8/1-8, 8/25-9/7	7/7-31	7/7-10, 7/26-31	6/15-7/21	6/27-7/10	6/15-7/8	6/27-7/8
-3/7	2/15-28	3/15-4/7	3/15-29	5/15-31	5/15-27	6/1-25	6/12-25
31	8/9-24	7/1-8/7	7/11-25	6/15-7/21	6/15-27, 7/11-21	—	—
-28	3/7-31	3/7-31	3/15-29	5/15-6/30	5/15-27, 6/12-26	6/1-30	6/12-26
-30	9/15-23	8/15-9/7	8/15-24	7/15-8/15	7/15-25, 8/9-15	—	—
-3/20	2/13-28, 3/15-20	3/7-4/7	3/15-29	5/15-31	5/15-27	6/1-25	6/12-25
30	9/8-23	8/15-31	8/15-24	7/1-8/7	7/11-25	—	—
-31	3/15-29	4/1-17	4/14-17	5/10-6/15	5/13-27, 6/12-15	5/30-6/20	6/12-20
31	8/9-24	7/7-21	7/11-21	6/15-30	6/15-26	—	—
4/15	3/15-29, 4/14-15	4/7-5/15	4/14-28, 5/13-15	5/7-6/20	5/13-27, 6/12-20	5/30-6/15	6/12-15
4/15	3/15-29, 4/14-15	4/7-5/15	4/14-28, 5/13-15	6/1-30	6/12-26	6/15-30	6/15-26
-3/20	2/15-28, 3/15-20	4/7-5/15	4/14-28, 5/13-15	5/15-31	5/15-27	6/1-25	6/12-25
-9/7	8/15-24	7/15-8/15	7/15-25, 8/9-15	6/7-30	6/12-26	—	—
-30	9/8-23	8/15-31	8/15-24	7/1-8/7	7/11-25	6/25-7/15	6/25-26, 7/11-15
-4/15	3/1-14, 3/30-4/13	3/7-4/7	3/7-14, 3/30-4/7	5/15-31	5/28-31	6/1-25	6/1-11
-3/7	2/15-28	3/1-31	3/15-29	5/15-6/30	5/15-27, 6/12-26	6/1-30	6/12-26
-4/7	3/15-29	4/15-5/7	4/15-28	5/15-6/30	5/15-27, 6/12-26	6/1-30	6/12-26
-6/1	4/15-28, 5/13-27	5/25-6/15	5/25-27, 6/12-15	6/15-7/10	6/15-26	6/25-7/7	6/25-26
28	2/1-12	3/1-31	3/1-14, 3/30-31	5/15-6/7	5/28-6/7	6/1-25	6/1-11
-3/15	2/20-28, 3/15	3/1-31	3/15-29	5/15-31	5/15-27	6/1-15	6/12-15
-2/4	1/31-2/4	3/7-31	3/7-14, 3/30-31	4/1-30	4/1-13, 4/29-30	5/10-31	5/10-12, 5/28-31
-2/7	1/15-30	3/7-31	3/15-29	4/15-5/7	4/15-28	5/15-31	5/15-27
-30	9/15-23	8/7-31	8/9-24	7/15-31	7/15-25	7/10-25	7/11-25
-20	3/15-20	4/1-30	4/14-28	5/15-6/30	5/15-27, 6/12-26	6/1-30	6/12-26
-28	2/10-12	4/1-30	4/1-13, 4/29-30	5/1-31	5/1-12, 5/28-31	6/1-25	6/1-11
-20	3/15-20	4/23-5/15	4/23-28, 5/13-15	5/15-31	5/15-27	6/1-30	6/12-26
-3/1	1/31-2/12, 3/1	3/7-31	3/7-14, 3/30-31	4/15-30	4/29-30	5/15-6/5	5/28-6/5
-21	10/1-6	9/7-30	9/7, 9/24-30	8/15-31	8/25-31	7/10-31	7/10, 7/26-31
-3/15	2/13-28, 3/15	3/15-4/20	3/15-29, 4/14-20	5/15-31	5/15-27	6/1-25	6/12-25
-21	10/7-21	8/1-9/15	8/9-24, 9/8-15	7/17-9/7	7/17-25, 8/9-24	7/20-8/5	7/20-25
-4/15	3/15-29, 4/14-15	4/15-30	4/15-28	5/15-6/15	5/15-27, 6/12-15	6/1-30	6/12-26
-4/6	3/30-4/6	4/21-5/9	4/29-5/9	5/15-6/15	5/28-6/11	6/1-30	6/1-11, 6/27-30
-3/15	2/13-28, 3/15	3/15-4/15	3/15-29, 4/14-15	5/1-31	5/13-27	5/15-31	5/15-27
-20	3/15-20	4/7-30	4/14-28	5/15-31	5/15-27	6/1-15	6/12-15
-2/15	1/31-2/12	3/15-31	3/30-31	4/7-30	4/7-13, 4/29-30	5/10-31	5/10-12, 5/28-31
-10/15	9/1-7, 9/24-10/6	8/1-20	8/1-8	7/1-8/15	7/1-10, 7/26-8/8	—	—
-4/7	3/15-29	4/15-5/7	4/15-28	5/15-6/30	5/15-27, 6/12-26	6/1-30	6/12-26
-28	2/15-28	3/1-20	3/15-20	4/7-30	4/14-28	5/15-6/10	5/15-27
5-12/7	10/15-22, 11/6-21, 12/5-7	9/15-10/20	9/15-23, 10/7-20	8/11-9/15	8/11-24, 9/8-15	8/5-30	8/9-24

Time Corrections

■ Astronomical data for Boston is given on **pages 90, 94–95,** and **110–136.** Use the Key Letter shown to the right of each time on those pages with this table to find the number of minutes that you must add to or subtract from Boston time to get the correct time for your city. (Because of complex calculations for different locales, times are approximate.) For more information on the use of Key Letters and this table, **see How to Use This Almanac, page 106.**

CONFUSED? Purchase astronomical times calculated for your zip code and presented like a Left-Hand Calendar page at **MyLocalAlmanac.com.**

TIME ZONES: Codes represent *standard time.* Atlantic is −1, Eastern is 0, Central is 1, Mountain is 2, Pacific is 3, Alaska is 4, and Hawaii-Aleutian is 5.

State	City	North Latitude °	′	West Longitude °	′	Time Zone Code	A (min.)	B (min.)	C (min.)	D (min.)	E (min.)
AK	Anchorage	61	10	149	59	4	−46	+27	+71	+122	+171
AK	Cordova	60	33	145	45	4	−55	+13	+55	+103	+149
AK	Fairbanks	64	48	147	51	4	−127	+2	+61	+131	+205
AK	Juneau	58	18	134	25	4	−76	−23	+10	+49	+86
AK	Ketchikan	55	21	131	39	4	−62	−25	0	+29	+56
AK	Kodiak	57	47	152	24	4	0	+49	+82	+120	+154
AL	Birmingham	33	31	86	49	1	+30	+15	+3	−10	−20
AL	Decatur	34	36	86	59	1	+27	+14	+4	−7	−17
AL	Mobile	30	42	88	3	1	+42	+23	+8	−8	−22
AL	Montgomery	32	23	86	19	1	+31	+14	+1	−13	−25
AR	Fort Smith	35	23	94	25	1	+55	+43	+33	+22	+14
AR	Little Rock	34	45	92	17	1	+48	+35	+25	+13	+4
AR	Texarkana	33	26	94	3	1	+59	+44	+32	+18	+8
AZ	Flagstaff	35	12	111	39	2	+64	+52	+42	+31	+22
AZ	Phoenix	33	27	112	4	2	+71	+56	+44	+30	+20
AZ	Tucson	32	13	110	58	2	+70	+53	+40	+24	+12
AZ	Yuma	32	43	114	37	2	+83	+67	+54	+40	+28
CA	Bakersfield	35	23	119	1	3	+33	+21	+12	+1	−7
CA	Barstow	34	54	117	1	3	+27	+14	+4	−7	−16
CA	Fresno	36	44	119	47	3	+32	+22	+15	+6	0
CA	Los Angeles–Pasadena– Santa Monica	34	3	118	14	3	+34	+20	+9	−3	−13
CA	Palm Springs	33	49	116	32	3	+28	+13	+1	−12	−22
CA	Redding	40	35	122	24	3	+31	+27	+25	+22	+19
CA	Sacramento	38	35	121	30	3	+34	+27	+21	+15	+10
CA	San Diego	32	43	117	9	3	+33	+17	+4	−9	−21
CA	San Francisco–Oakland– San Jose	37	47	122	25	3	+40	+31	+25	+18	+12
CO	Craig	40	31	107	33	2	+32	+28	+25	+22	+20
CO	Denver–Boulder	39	44	104	59	2	+24	+19	+15	+11	+7
CO	Grand Junction	39	4	108	33	2	+40	+34	+29	+24	+20
CO	Pueblo	38	16	104	37	2	+27	+20	+14	+7	+2
CO	Trinidad	37	10	104	31	2	+30	+21	+13	+5	0
CT	Bridgeport	41	11	73	11	0	+12	+10	+8	+6	+4
CT	Hartford–New Britain	41	46	72	41	0	+8	+7	+6	+5	+4
CT	New Haven	41	18	72	56	0	+11	+8	+7	+5	+4
CT	New London	41	22	72	6	0	+7	+5	+4	+2	+1
CT	Norwalk–Stamford	41	7	73	22	0	+13	+10	+9	+7	+5
CT	Waterbury–Meriden	41	33	73	3	0	+10	+9	+7	+6	+5
DC	Washington	38	54	77	1	0	+35	+28	+23	+18	+13
DE	Wilmington	39	45	75	33	0	+26	+21	+18	+13	+10

Get local rise, set, and tide times at Almanac.com.

State	City	North Latitude °	North Latitude ′	West Longitude °	West Longitude ′	Time Zone Code	A (min.)	B (min.)	C (min.)	D (min.)	E (min.)
FL	Fort Myers	26	38	81	52	0	+87	+63	+44	+21	+4
FL	Jacksonville	30	20	81	40	0	+77	+58	+43	+25	+11
FL	Miami	25	47	80	12	0	+88	+57	+37	+14	−3
FL	Orlando	28	32	81	22	0	+80	+59	+42	+22	+6
FL	Pensacola	30	25	87	13	1	+39	+20	+5	−12	−26
FL	St. Petersburg	27	46	82	39	0	+87	+65	+47	+26	+10
FL	Tallahassee	30	27	84	17	0	+87	+68	+53	+35	+22
FL	Tampa	27	57	82	27	0	+86	+64	+46	+25	+9
FL	West Palm Beach	26	43	80	3	0	+79	+55	+36	+14	−2
GA	Atlanta	33	45	84	24	0	+79	+65	+53	+40	+30
GA	Augusta	33	28	81	58	0	+70	+55	+44	+30	+19
GA	Macon	32	50	83	38	0	+79	+63	+50	+36	+24
GA	Savannah	32	5	81	6	0	+70	+54	+40	+25	+13
HI	Hilo	19	44	155	5	5	+94	+62	+37	+7	−15
HI	Honolulu	21	18	157	52	5	+102	+72	+48	+19	−1
HI	Lanai City	20	50	156	55	5	+99	+69	+44	+15	−6
HI	Lihue	21	59	159	23	5	+107	+77	+54	+26	+5
IA	Davenport	41	32	90	35	1	+20	+19	+17	+16	+15
IA	Des Moines	41	35	93	37	1	+32	+31	+30	+28	+27
IA	Dubuque	42	30	90	41	1	+17	+18	+18	+18	+18
IA	Waterloo	42	30	92	20	1	+24	+24	+24	+25	+25
ID	Boise	43	37	116	12	2	+55	+58	+60	+62	+64
ID	Lewiston	46	25	117	1	3	−12	−3	+2	+10	+17
ID	Pocatello	42	52	112	27	2	+43	+44	+45	+46	+46
IL	Cairo	37	0	89	11	1	+29	+20	+12	+4	−2
IL	Chicago–Oak Park	41	52	87	38	1	+7	+6	+6	+5	+4
IL	Danville	40	8	87	37	1	+13	+9	+6	+2	0
IL	Decatur	39	51	88	57	1	+19	+15	+11	+7	+4
IL	Peoria	40	42	89	36	1	+19	+16	+14	+11	+9
IL	Springfield	39	48	89	39	1	+22	+18	+14	+10	+6
IN	Fort Wayne	41	4	85	9	0	+60	+58	+56	+54	+52
IN	Gary	41	36	87	20	1	+7	+6	+4	+3	+2
IN	Indianapolis	39	46	86	10	0	+69	+64	+60	+56	+52
IN	Muncie	40	12	85	23	0	+64	+60	+57	+53	+50
IN	South Bend	41	41	86	15	0	+62	+61	+60	+59	+58
IN	Terre Haute	39	28	87	24	0	+74	+69	+65	+60	+56
KS	Fort Scott	37	50	94	42	1	+49	+41	+34	+27	+21
KS	Liberal	37	3	100	55	1	+76	+66	+59	+51	+44
KS	Oakley	39	8	100	51	1	+69	+63	+59	+53	+49
KS	Salina	38	50	97	37	1	+57	+51	+46	+40	+35
KS	Topeka	39	3	95	40	1	+49	+43	+38	+32	+28
KS	Wichita	37	42	97	20	1	+60	+51	+45	+37	+31
KY	Lexington–Frankfort	38	3	84	30	0	+67	+59	+53	+46	+41
KY	Louisville	38	15	85	46	0	+72	+64	+58	+52	+46
LA	Alexandria	31	18	92	27	1	+58	+40	+26	+9	−3
LA	Baton Rouge	30	27	91	11	1	+55	+36	+21	+3	−10
LA	Lake Charles	30	14	93	13	1	+64	+44	+29	+11	−2
LA	Monroe	32	30	92	7	1	+53	+37	+24	+9	−1
LA	New Orleans	29	57	90	4	1	+52	+32	+16	−1	−15
LA	Shreveport	32	31	93	45	1	+60	+44	+31	+16	+4
MA	Brockton	42	5	71	1	0	0	0	0	0	−1
MA	Fall River–New Bedford	41	42	71	9	0	+2	+1	0	0	−1
MA	Lawrence–Lowell	42	42	71	10	0	0	0	0	0	+1
MA	Pittsfield	42	27	73	15	0	+8	+8	+8	+8	+8
MA	Springfield–Holyoke	42	6	72	36	0	+6	+6	+6	+5	+5
MA	Worcester	42	16	71	48	0	+3	+2	+2	+2	+2

Time Corrections

State	City	North Latitude °	North Latitude '	West Longitude °	West Longitude '	Time Zone Code	A (min.)	B (min.)	C (min.)	D (min.)	E (min.)
MD	Baltimore	39	17	76	37	0	+32	+26	+22	+17	+13
MD	Hagerstown	39	39	77	43	0	+35	+30	+26	+22	+18
MD	Salisbury	38	22	75	36	0	+31	+23	+18	+11	+6
ME	Augusta	44	19	69	46	0	−12	−8	−5	−1	0
ME	Bangor	44	48	68	46	0	−18	−13	−9	−5	−1
ME	Eastport	44	54	67	0	0	−26	−20	−16	−11	−8
ME	Ellsworth	44	33	68	25	0	−18	−14	−10	−6	−3
ME	Portland	43	40	70	15	0	−8	−5	−3	−1	0
ME	Presque Isle	46	41	68	1	0	−29	−19	−12	−4	+2
MI	Cheboygan	45	39	84	29	0	+40	+47	+53	+59	+64
MI	Detroit–Dearborn	42	20	83	3	0	+47	+47	+47	+47	+47
MI	Flint	43	1	83	41	0	+47	+49	+50	+51	+52
MI	Ironwood	46	27	90	9	1	0	+9	+15	+23	+29
MI	Jackson	42	15	84	24	0	+53	+53	+53	+52	+52
MI	Kalamazoo	42	17	85	35	0	+58	+57	+57	+57	+57
MI	Lansing	42	44	84	33	0	+52	+53	+53	+54	+54
MI	St. Joseph	42	5	86	26	0	+61	+61	+60	+60	+59
MI	Traverse City	44	46	85	38	0	+49	+54	+57	+62	+65
MN	Albert Lea	43	39	93	22	1	+24	+26	+28	+31	+33
MN	Bemidji	47	28	94	53	1	+14	+26	+34	+44	+52
MN	Duluth	46	47	92	6	1	+6	+16	+23	+31	+38
MN	Minneapolis–St. Paul	44	59	93	16	1	+18	+24	+28	+33	+37
MN	Ortonville	45	19	96	27	1	+30	+36	+40	+46	+51
MO	Jefferson City	38	34	92	10	1	+36	+29	+24	+18	+13
MO	Joplin	37	6	94	30	1	+50	+41	+33	+25	+18
MO	Kansas City	39	1	94	20	1	+44	+37	+33	+27	+23
MO	Poplar Bluff	36	46	90	24	1	+35	+25	+17	+8	+1
MO	St. Joseph	39	46	94	50	1	+43	+38	+35	+30	+27
MO	St. Louis	38	37	90	12	1	+28	+21	+16	+10	+5
MO	Springfield	37	13	93	18	1	+45	+36	+29	+20	+14
MS	Biloxi	30	24	88	53	1	+46	+27	+11	−5	−19
MS	Jackson	32	18	90	11	1	+46	+30	+17	+1	−10
MS	Meridian	32	22	88	42	1	+40	+24	+11	−4	−15
MS	Tupelo	34	16	88	34	1	+35	+21	+10	−2	−11
MT	Billings	45	47	108	30	2	+16	+23	+29	+35	+40
MT	Butte	46	1	112	32	2	+31	+39	+45	+52	+57
MT	Glasgow	48	12	106	38	2	−1	+11	+21	+32	+42
MT	Great Falls	47	30	111	17	2	+20	+31	+39	+49	+58
MT	Helena	46	36	112	2	2	+27	+36	+43	+51	+57
MT	Miles City	46	25	105	51	2	+3	+11	+18	+26	+32
NC	Asheville	35	36	82	33	0	+67	+55	+46	+35	+27
NC	Charlotte	35	14	80	51	0	+61	+49	+39	+28	+19
NC	Durham	36	0	78	55	0	+51	+40	+31	+21	+13
NC	Greensboro	36	4	79	47	0	+54	+43	+35	+25	+17
NC	Raleigh	35	47	78	38	0	+51	+39	+30	+20	+12
NC	Wilmington	34	14	77	55	0	+52	+38	+27	+15	+5
ND	Bismarck	46	48	100	47	1	+41	+50	+58	+66	+73
ND	Fargo	46	53	96	47	1	+24	+34	+42	+50	+57
ND	Grand Forks	47	55	97	3	1	+21	+33	+43	+53	+62
ND	Minot	48	14	101	18	1	+36	+50	+59	+71	+81
ND	Williston	48	9	103	37	1	+46	+59	+69	+80	+90
NE	Grand Island	40	55	98	21	1	+53	+51	+49	+46	+44
NE	Lincoln	40	49	96	41	1	+47	+44	+42	+39	+37
NE	North Platte	41	8	100	46	1	+62	+60	+58	+56	+54
NE	Omaha	41	16	95	56	1	+43	+40	+39	+37	+36
NH	Berlin	44	28	71	11	0	−7	−3	0	+3	+7
NH	Keene	42	56	72	17	0	+2	+3	+4	+5	+6

State	City	North Latitude °	North Latitude '	West Longitude °	West Longitude '	Time Zone Code	A (min.)	B (min.)	C (min.)	D (min.)	E (min.)
NH	Manchester–Concord	42	59	71	28	0	0	0	+1	+2	+3
NH	Portsmouth	43	5	70	45	0	−4	−2	−1	0	0
NJ	Atlantic City	39	22	74	26	0	+23	+17	+13	+8	+4
NJ	Camden	39	57	75	7	0	+24	+19	+16	+12	+9
NJ	Cape May	38	56	74	56	0	+26	+20	+15	+9	+5
NJ	Newark–East Orange	40	44	74	10	0	+17	+14	+12	+9	+7
NJ	Paterson	40	55	74	10	0	+17	+14	+12	+9	+7
NJ	Trenton	40	13	74	46	0	+21	+17	+14	+11	+8
NM	Albuquerque	35	5	106	39	2	+45	+32	+22	+11	+2
NM	Gallup	35	32	108	45	2	+52	+40	+31	+20	+11
NM	Las Cruces	32	19	106	47	2	+53	+36	+23	+8	−3
NM	Roswell	33	24	104	32	2	+41	+26	+14	0	−10
NM	Santa Fe	35	41	105	56	2	+40	+28	+19	+9	0
NV	Carson City–Reno	39	10	119	46	3	+25	+19	+14	+9	+5
NV	Elko	40	50	115	46	3	+3	0	−1	−3	−5
NV	Las Vegas	36	10	115	9	3	+16	+4	−3	−13	−20
NY	Albany	42	39	73	45	0	+9	+10	+10	+11	+11
NY	Binghamton	42	6	75	55	0	+20	+19	+19	+18	+18
NY	Buffalo	42	53	78	52	0	+29	+30	+30	+31	+32
NY	New York	40	45	74	0	0	+17	+14	+11	+9	+6
NY	Ogdensburg	44	42	75	30	0	+8	+13	+17	+21	+25
NY	Syracuse	43	3	76	9	0	+17	+19	+20	+21	+22
OH	Akron	41	5	81	31	0	+46	+43	+41	+39	+37
OH	Canton	40	48	81	23	0	+46	+43	+41	+38	+36
OH	Cincinnati–Hamilton	39	6	84	31	0	+64	+58	+53	+48	+44
OH	Cleveland–Lakewood	41	30	81	42	0	+45	+43	+42	+40	+39
OH	Columbus	39	57	83	1	0	+55	+51	+47	+43	+40
OH	Dayton	39	45	84	10	0	+61	+56	+52	+48	+44
OH	Toledo	41	39	83	33	0	+52	+50	+49	+48	+47
OH	Youngstown	41	6	80	39	0	+42	+40	+38	+36	+34
OK	Oklahoma City	35	28	97	31	1	+67	+55	+46	+35	+26
OK	Tulsa	36	9	95	60	1	+59	+48	+40	+30	+22
OR	Eugene	44	3	123	6	3	+21	+24	+27	+30	+33
OR	Pendleton	45	40	118	47	3	−1	+4	+10	+16	+21
OR	Portland	45	31	122	41	3	+14	+20	+25	+31	+36
OR	Salem	44	57	123	1	3	+17	+23	+27	+31	+35
PA	Allentown–Bethlehem	40	36	75	28	0	+23	+20	+17	+14	+12
PA	Erie	42	7	80	5	0	+36	+36	+35	+35	+35
PA	Harrisburg	40	16	76	53	0	+30	+26	+23	+19	+16
PA	Lancaster	40	2	76	18	0	+28	+24	+20	+17	+13
PA	Philadelphia–Chester	39	57	75	9	0	+24	+19	+16	+12	+9
PA	Pittsburgh–McKeesport	40	26	80	0	0	+42	+38	+35	+32	+29
PA	Reading	40	20	75	56	0	+26	+22	+19	+16	+13
PA	Scranton–Wilkes-Barre	41	25	75	40	0	+21	+19	+18	+16	+15
PA	York	39	58	76	43	0	+30	+26	+22	+18	+15
RI	Providence	41	50	71	25	0	+3	+2	+1	0	0
SC	Charleston	32	47	79	56	0	+64	+48	+36	+21	+10
SC	Columbia	34	0	81	2	0	+65	+51	+40	+27	+17
SC	Spartanburg	34	56	81	57	0	+66	+53	+43	+32	+23
SD	Aberdeen	45	28	98	29	1	+37	+44	+49	+54	+59
SD	Pierre	44	22	100	21	1	+49	+53	+56	+60	+63
SD	Rapid City	44	5	103	14	2	+2	+5	+8	+11	+13
SD	Sioux Falls	43	33	96	44	1	+38	+40	+42	+44	+46
TN	Chattanooga	35	3	85	19	0	+79	+67	+57	+45	+36
TN	Knoxville	35	58	83	55	0	+71	+60	+51	+41	+33
TN	Memphis	35	9	90	3	1	+38	+26	+16	+5	−3
TN	Nashville	36	10	86	47	1	+22	+11	+3	−6	−14

Time Corrections

State/ Province	City	North Latitude °	'	West Longitude °	'	Time Zone Code	A (min.)	B (min.)	C (min.)	D (min.)	E (min.)
TX	Amarillo	35	12	101	50	1	+85	+73	+63	+52	+43
TX	Austin	30	16	97	45	1	+82	+62	+47	+29	+15
TX	Beaumont	30	5	94	6	1	+67	+48	+32	+14	0
TX	Brownsville	25	54	97	30	1	+91	+66	+46	+23	+5
TX	Corpus Christi	27	48	97	24	1	+86	+64	+46	+25	+9
TX	Dallas–Fort Worth	32	47	96	48	1	+71	+55	+43	+28	+17
TX	El Paso	31	45	106	29	2	+53	+35	+22	+6	−6
TX	Galveston	29	18	94	48	1	+72	+52	+35	+16	+1
TX	Houston	29	45	95	22	1	+73	+53	+37	+19	+5
TX	McAllen	26	12	98	14	1	+93	+69	+49	+26	+9
TX	San Antonio	29	25	98	30	1	+87	+66	+50	+31	+16
UT	Kanab	37	3	112	32	2	+62	+53	+46	+37	+30
UT	Moab	38	35	109	33	2	+46	+39	+33	+27	+22
UT	Ogden	41	13	111	58	2	+47	+45	+43	+41	+40
UT	Salt Lake City	40	45	111	53	2	+48	+45	+43	+40	+38
UT	Vernal	40	27	109	32	2	+40	+36	+33	+30	+28
VA	Charlottesville	38	2	78	30	0	+43	+35	+29	+22	+17
VA	Danville	36	36	79	23	0	+51	+41	+33	+24	+17
VA	Norfolk	36	51	76	17	0	+38	+28	+21	+12	+5
VA	Richmond	37	32	77	26	0	+41	+32	+25	+17	+11
VA	Roanoke	37	16	79	57	0	+51	+42	+35	+27	+21
VA	Winchester	39	11	78	10	0	+38	+33	+28	+23	+19
VT	Brattleboro	42	51	72	34	0	+4	+5	+5	+6	+7
VT	Burlington	44	29	73	13	0	0	+4	+8	+12	+15
VT	Rutland	43	37	72	58	0	+2	+5	+7	+9	+11
VT	St. Johnsbury	44	25	72	1	0	−4	0	+3	+7	+10
WA	Bellingham	48	45	122	29	3	0	+13	+24	+37	+47
WA	Seattle–Tacoma–Olympia	47	37	122	20	3	+3	+15	+24	+34	+42
WA	Spokane	47	40	117	24	3	−16	−4	+4	+14	+23
WA	Walla Walla	46	4	118	20	3	−5	+2	+8	+15	+21
WI	Eau Claire	44	49	91	30	1	+12	+17	+21	+25	+29
WI	Green Bay	44	31	88	0	1	0	+3	+7	+11	+14
WI	La Crosse	43	48	91	15	1	+15	+18	+20	+22	+25
WI	Madison	43	4	89	23	1	+10	+11	+12	+14	+15
WI	Milwaukee	43	2	87	54	1	+4	+6	+7	+8	+9
WI	Oshkosh	44	1	88	33	1	+3	+6	+9	+12	+15
WI	Wausau	44	58	89	38	1	+4	+9	+13	+18	+22
WV	Charleston	38	21	81	38	0	+55	+48	+42	+35	+30
WV	Parkersburg	39	16	81	34	0	+52	+46	+42	+36	+32
WY	Casper	42	51	106	19	2	+19	+19	+20	+21	+22
WY	Cheyenne	41	8	104	49	2	+19	+16	+14	+12	+11
WY	Sheridan	44	48	106	58	2	+14	+19	+23	+27	+31
CANADA											
AB	Calgary	51	5	114	5	2	+13	+35	+50	+68	+84
AB	Edmonton	53	34	113	25	2	−3	+26	+47	+72	+93
BC	Vancouver	49	13	123	6	3	0	+15	+26	+40	+52
MB	Winnipeg	49	53	97	10	1	+12	+30	+43	+58	+71
NB	Saint John	45	16	66	3	−1	+28	+34	+39	+44	+49
NS	Halifax	44	38	63	35	−1	+21	+26	+29	+33	+37
NS	Sydney	46	10	60	10	−1	+1	+9	+15	+23	+28
ON	Ottawa	45	25	75	43	0	+6	+13	+18	+23	+28
ON	Peterborough	44	18	78	19	0	+21	+25	+28	+32	+35
ON	Thunder Bay	48	27	89	12	0	+47	+61	+71	+83	+93
ON	Toronto	43	39	79	23	0	+28	+30	+32	+35	+37
QC	Montreal	45	28	73	39	0	−1	+4	+9	+15	+20
SK	Saskatoon	52	10	106	40	1	+37	+63	+80	+101	+119

Get local rise, set, and tide times at Almanac.com.

Tide Corrections

■ Many factors affect the times and heights of the tides: the coastal configuration, the time of the Moon's southing (crossing the meridian), and the Moon's phase. The High Tide column on the **Left-Hand Calendar Pages, 110–136,** lists the times of high tide at Commonwealth Pier in Boston Harbor. The heights of some of these tides, reckoned from Mean Lower Low Water, are given on the **Right-Hand Calendar Pages, 111–137.** Use the table below to calculate the approximate times and heights of high tide at the places shown. Apply the time difference to the times of high tide at Boston and the height difference to the heights at Boston.

EXAMPLE:

The conversion of the times and heights of the tides at Boston to those at Cape Fear, North Carolina, is given below:

High tide at Boston	11:45 A.M.
Correction for Cape Fear	−3 55
High tide at Cape Fear	7:50 A.M.
Tide height at Boston	11.6 ft.
Correction for Cape Fear	−5.0 ft.
Tide height at Cape Fear	6.6 ft.

Estimations derived from this table are *not* meant to be used for navigation. *The Old Farmer's Almanac* accepts no responsibility for errors or any consequences ensuing from the use of this table.

Coastal Site Difference:	Time (h. m.)	Height (ft.)
Canada		
Alberton, PE	*−5 45	−7.5
Charlottetown, PE	*−0 45	−3.5
Halifax, NS.	−3 23	−4.5
North Sydney, NS.	−3 15	−6.5
Saint John, NB	+0 30	+15.0
St. John's, NL.	−4 00	−6.5
Yarmouth, NS.	−0 40	+3.0
Maine		
Bar Harbor	−0 34	+0.9
Belfast	−0 20	+0.4
Boothbay Harbor	−0 18	−0.8
Chebeague Island......	−0 16	−0.6
Eastport..............	−0 28	+8.4
Kennebunkport........	+0 04	−1.0
Machias	−0 28	+2.8
Monhegan Island	−0 25	−0.8
Old Orchard	0 00	−0.8
Portland.............	−0 12	−0.6
Rockland.............	−0 28	+0.1
Stonington...........	−0 30	+0.1
York................	−0 09	−1.0
New Hampshire		
Hampton	+0 02	−1.3
Portsmouth	+0 11	−1.5
Rye Beach...........	−0 09	−0.9
Massachusetts		
Annisquam	−0 02	−1.1
Beverly Farms	0 00	−0.5
Boston..............	0 00	0.0

Coastal Site Difference:	Time (h. m.)	Height (ft.)
Cape Cod Canal		
East Entrance........	−0 01	−0.8
West Entrance	−2 16	−5.9
Chatham Outer Coast...	+0 30	−2.8
Inside	+1 54	**0.4
Cohasset............	+0 02	−0.07
Cotuit Highlands	+1 15	**0.3
Dennis Port..........	+1 01	**0.4
Duxbury–Gurnet Point...	+0 02	−0.3
Fall River	−3 03	−5.0
Gloucester...........	−0 03	−0.8
Hingham	+0 07	0.0
Hull	+0 03	−0.2
Hyannis Port.........	+1 01	**0.3
Magnolia–Manchester...	−0 02	−0.7
Marblehead..........	−0 02	−0.4
Marion	−3 22	−5.4
Monument Beach......	−3 08	−5.4
Nahant..............	−0 01	−0.5
Nantasket	+0 04	−0.1
Nantucket	+0 56	**0.3
Nauset Beach	+0 30	**0.6
New Bedford	−3 24	−5.7
Newburyport	+0 19	−1.8
Oak Bluffs	+0 30	**0.2
Onset–R.R. Bridge.....	−2 16	−5.9
Plymouth............	+0 05	0.0
Provincetown	+0 14	−0.4
Revere Beach	−0 01	−0.3
Rockport............	−0 08	−1.0
Salem	0 00	−0.5
Scituate.............	−0 05	−0.7

Tide Corrections

Coastal Site	Difference: Time (h. m.)	Height (ft.)
Wareham	−3 09	−5.3
Wellfleet	+0 12	+0.5
West Falmouth	−3 10	−5.4
Westport Harbor	−3 22	−6.4
Woods Hole		
Little Harbor........	−2 50	**0.2
Oceanographic		
Institute	−3 07	**0.2
Rhode Island		
Bristol	−3 24	−5.3
Narragansett Pier......	−3 42	−6.2
Newport............	−3 34	−5.9
Point Judith	−3 41	−6.3
Providence..........	−3 20	−4.8
Sakonnet	−3 44	−5.6
Watch Hill	−2 50	−6.8
Connecticut		
Bridgeport	+0 01	−2.6
Madison	−0 22	−2.3
New Haven	−0 11	−3.2
New London	−1 54	−6.7
Norwalk............	+0 01	−2.2
Old Lyme		
Highway Bridge	−0 30	−6.2
Stamford	+0 01	−2.2
Stonington	−2 27	−6.6
New York		
Coney Island	−3 33	−4.9
Fire Island Light	−2 43	**0.1
Long Beach	−3 11	−5.7
Montauk Harbor	−2 19	−7.4
New York City–Battery ..	−2 43	−5.0
Oyster Bay..........	+0 04	−1.8
Port Chester.........	−0 09	−2.2
Port Washington	−0 01	−2.1
Sag Harbor..........	−0 55	−6.8
Southampton		
Shinnecock Inlet.....	−4 20	**0.2
Willets Point	0 00	−2.3
New Jersey		
Asbury Park.........	−4 04	−5.3
Atlantic City	−3 56	−5.5
Bay Head–Sea Girt	−4 04	−5.3
Beach Haven	−1 43	**0.24
Cape May...........	−3 28	−5.3
Ocean City..........	−3 06	−5.9
Sandy Hook.........	−3 30	−5.0
Seaside Park	−4 03	−5.4
Pennsylvania		
Philadelphia.........	+2 40	−3.5
Delaware		
Cape Henlopen	−2 48	−5.3

Coastal Site	Difference: Time (h. m.)	Height (ft.)
Rehoboth Beach	−3 37	−5.7
Wilmington	+1 56	−3.8
Maryland		
Annapolis	+6 23	−8.5
Baltimore...........	+7 59	−8.3
Cambridge..........	+5 05	−7.8
Havre de Grace	+11 21	−7.7
Point No Point.......	+2 28	−8.1
Prince Frederick		
Plum Point	+4 25	−8.5
Virginia		
Cape Charles	−2 20	−7.0
Hampton Roads.......	−2 02	−6.9
Norfolk	−2 06	−6.6
Virginia Beach........	−4 00	−6.0
Yorktown	−2 13	−7.0
North Carolina		
Cape Fear...........	−3 55	−5.0
Cape Lookout	−4 28	−5.7
Currituck	−4 10	−5.8
Hatteras		
Inlet.............	−4 03	−7.4
Kitty Hawk	−4 14	−6.2
Ocean	−4 26	−6.0
South Carolina		
Charleston	−3 22	−4.3
Georgetown..........	−1 48	**0.36
Hilton Head.........	−3 22	−2.9
Myrtle Beach........	−3 49	−4.4
St. Helena		
Harbor Entrance.....	−3 15	−3.4
Georgia		
Jekyll Island	−3 46	−2.9
St. Simon's Island	−2 50	−2.9
Savannah Beach		
River Entrance	−3 14	−5.5
Tybee Light.........	−3 22	−2.7
Florida		
Cape Canaveral	−3 59	−6.0
Daytona Beach	−3 28	−5.3
Fort Lauderdale	−2 50	−7.2
Fort Pierce Inlet.......	−3 32	−6.9
Jacksonville		
Railroad Bridge	−6 55	**0.1
Miami Harbor Entrance..	−3 18	−7.0
St. Augustine	−2 55	−4.9

Varies widely; accurate within only 1½ hours. Consult local tide tables for precise times and heights.

**Where the difference in the Height column is so marked, the height at Boston should be multiplied by this ratio.*

Tidal Glossary

Apogean Tide: A monthly tide of decreased range that occurs when the Moon is at apogee (farthest from Earth).

Diurnal Tide: A tide with one high water and one low water in a tidal day of approximately 24 hours.

Mean Lower Low Water: The arithmetic mean of the lesser of a daily pair of low waters, observed over a specific 19-year cycle called the National Tidal Datum Epoch.

Neap Tide: A tide of decreased range that occurs twice a month, when the Moon is in quadrature (during its first and last quarters, when the Sun and the Moon are at right angles to each other relative to Earth).

Perigean Tide: A monthly tide of increased range that occurs when the Moon is at perigee (closest to Earth).

Semidiurnal Tide: A tide with one high water and one low water every half day. East Coast tides, for example, are semidiurnal, with two highs and two lows during a tidal day of approximately 24 hours.

Spring Tide: A tide of increased range that occurs at times of syzygy each month. Named not for the season of spring but from the German *springen* ("to leap up"), a spring tide also brings a lower low water.

Syzygy: The nearly straight-line configuration that occurs twice a month, when the Sun and the Moon are in conjunction (on the same side of Earth, at the new Moon) and when they are in opposition (on opposite sides of Earth, at the full Moon). In both cases, the gravitational effects of the Sun and the Moon reinforce each other, and tidal range is increased.

Vanishing Tide: A mixed tide of considerable inequality in the two highs and two lows, so that the lower high (or higher low) may appear to vanish. ☐☐

Answers to
Maddening Mind-Manglers

FROM PAGE 227

1. Northern cardinal; Illinois, Indiana, Kentucky, North Carolina, Ohio, Virginia, West Virginia
2. California valley quail; California
3. Black-capped chickadee; Maine, Massachusetts
4. Mountain bluebird; Idaho, Nevada
5. Yellowhammer; Alabama
6. Baltimore oriole; Maryland
7. Hawaiian goose; Hawaii
8. Willow ptarmigan; Alaska
9. Eastern bluebird; Missouri, New York
10. Brown pelican; Louisiana
11. California gull; Utah
12. Cactus wren; Arizona
13. Rhode Island Red; Rhode Island
14. Northern mockingbird; Arkansas, Florida, Mississippi, Tennessee, Texas
15. Common loon; Minnesota
16. Roadrunner; New Mexico
17. Lark bunting; Colorado
18. Carolina wren; South Carolina
19. American robin; Connecticut, Michigan, Wisconsin
20. Western meadowlark; Kansas, Montana, Nebraska, North Dakota, Oregon, Wyoming
21. Blue hen chicken; Delaware
22. American goldfinch; Iowa, New Jersey, Washington
23. Brown thrasher; Georgia
24. Hermit thrush; Vermont
25. Purple finch; New Hampshire
26. Chinese ring-necked pheasant; South Dakota
27. Scissor-tailed flycatcher; Oklahoma
28. Ruffed grouse; Pennsylvania ☐☐

The Old Farmer's
General Store

BEEKEEPING HANDBOOK

BEER & WINE MAKING

BOOKS/PUBLICATIONS/CATALOGS

BUILDING

BUSINESS OPPORTUNITIES

CANNING/BUTCHERING

EDUCATION/INSTRUCTION

FARM & GARDEN

FINANCIAL/LOANS BY MAIL

FOOD & RECIPES

Classifieds

SHRUBS & TREES

SPRUCE, FIR, PINE SEEDLINGS
for reforestation, Christmas trees, landscaping, windbreaks. Wholesale prices. Free catalog. Flickingers' Nursery, Box 245, Sagamore PA 16250
www.flicknursery.com
800-368-7381

STAGE SINGING SECRETS

DISCOVER THE SIMPLE SECRET TECHNIQUES that give you "star" quality and charisma. Web site: www.stagesingingsecrets.com

WANTED TO BUY

CASH FOR 78-RPM RECORDS!
Send $2 (refundable) for illustrated booklet
identifying collectible labels, numbers,
with actual prices I pay.
Docks, Box 780218(FA),
San Antonio TX 78278-0218

WINE & BEER MAKING

FREE ILLUSTRATED CATALOG
Fast service. Since 1967.
Kraus, PO Box 7850-YB,
Independence MO 64054
www.eckraus.com/offers/fd.asp
800-841-7404

ADVERTISING INFORMATION

The Old Farmer's Almanac consistently reaches a proven, responsive audience and is known for delivering readers who are active buyers. The 2011 edition closes on May 9, 2010. Ad opportunities are also available in the 2010 *All-Seasons Garden Guide,* which closes on December 1, 2009, and on our Web site, Almanac.com. For ad rates, Web classifieds, or ad information, please contact Bernie Gallagher by e-mail at OFAads@aol.com, by phone at 203-263-7171, by fax at 203-263-7174, or by mail at The Old Farmer's Almanac, PO Box 959, Woodbury CT 06798.

Advertisements and statements contained herein are the sole responsibility of the persons or entities that post the advertisement, and *The Old Farmer's Almanac* does not make any warranty as to the accuracy, completeness, truthfulness, or reliability of such advertisements. *The Old Farmer's Almanac* has no liability whatsoever for any third-party claims arising in connection with such advertisements or any products or services mentioned therein.

Index to Advertisers

Anecdotes & Pleasantries

A sampling from the hundreds of letters, clippings, articles, and e-mails sent to us by Almanac readers from all over the United States and Canada during the past year.

Three Things You Can Still Count On . . . or Can You?

–courtesy of J. W., St. Louis, Missouri

Old Faithful

Old, yes. But faithful?

Records indicate that in 1870, when the geyser was discovered and named, it blew reliably every 65 minutes. A century later, it began erupting at irregular intervals. Today, the pause between outbursts can range from 30 minutes up to 2 hours, 3 minutes. After each eruption (but only during visiting hours), rangers use a fairly complex formula to predict when she will spout off again, but the calculation is only good for the next "show." New numbers must be crunched at every point.

This is not all that's unpredictable about this great gusher. The duration of each eruption varies: A blow can last from 1 minute, 30 seconds to 5 minutes. The height of a steam plume varies from 106 feet to 184 feet. (Old Faithful is not the highest plume in the park or the world. Nearby Steamboat geyser holds the world plume height record, rising up to 400 feet when it blows, which can happen at any rate from 20 times per year to once every 50 years.)

None of this should shake your faith in this grand old geyser. It's still as beautiful as ever—just a little unfaithful.

The Annual Return of the Swallows to Capistrano

They return to the area, yes—but not to Capistrano.

Documents written by the missionaries in the 1700s indicate that each year during the third week of March, the sky above San Juan Capistrano, California, would be "blackened with [cliff] swallows." In 1776, when Mission San Juan Capistrano was completed, the thousands of birds began to take shelter under the eaves of the new church. The phenomenon continued for centuries.

Now, it seems, the swallows have flown the coop. Steady development of the land surrounding the mission and work in 1985 to make it less prone to damage from earthquakes forced the birds to find new perches under highway overpasses near farm fields. The bridges offer protection, the traffic generates a supply of dead bugs for food, and the fields provide an infinite source of mud for their nests.

Innovative attempts have been made to lure the swallows back to the mission: Mud was made available in "swallows' wallows," ceramic nests were placed under the eaves, and thousands of ladybugs, a favorite food, were released.

Nothing worked. These days, only about 20 swallows migrate to the mission each year; it is people who flock every spring. The annual migration of the birds is observed at the mission with a festival held around March 19.

Niagara Falls

Surely it can never change. Wrong. Not only can it change, but it can disappear. During the last ice age (about 12,000 years ago), glacial movement and melting ice created what we know as Niagara Falls. Today, rain and snowmelt from four of the five Great Lakes drain into the Niagara River. It would appear to the casual observer that the geological wonder has not changed since it was formed.

But appearances are deceiving. The cataract has eroded the falls to seven miles behind its original location, the river rarely runs at full strength, and the cliffs are now braced against collapse. Since 1957, when a power plant was built on the river's edge, half of the water (750,000 gallons per second) that would have spilled over the falls between April 1 and October 31 (the tourist season) has been diverted to the plant. The falls fairly trickle water in winter between 10:00 P.M. and 8:00 A.M., when most of the remaining 375,000 gallons per second is siphoned into power plant intakes. This is all part of an agreement between the United States and Canada, which share the river as a natural boundary.

Today, the falls erode at a rate of less than one inch per year because of increased water diversion and stabilization efforts by the U.S. Army Corps of Engineers. In 1967, huge staples and bolts were placed in the bedrock to solidify and stabilize it as much as possible. In addition, the current face layer of limestone is quite hard, which slows the natural destruction. Despite this, experts believe that over the next 50,000 years the brink could retreat another 20 miles (to Lake Erie), eroding all the while until the falls cease to exist.

(c o n t i n u e d)

Why We Yawn

The real reason is pretty cool. And, no, it isn't because we're sleepy or bored.

–adapted from a New York Times *article by Eric Nagourney, courtesy of F.D.L., Albany, New York*

There have been many theories about why people yawn, citing such reasons as sleepiness, boredom, and, incorrectly, low oxygen levels in the blood.

"No one knows why we yawn," says Andrew C. Gallup, a researcher from Binghamton University, Binghamton, New York.

Gallup and fellow investigators have a new explanation: Yawning, they say, is a way for the body to cool the brain.

Writing in *Evolutionary Psychology*, they report that volunteers yawned more often in situations in which their brains were likely to be warmer than normal. To prove their theory, the researchers took advantage of the tendency of people to

If You Love Dogs . . .

Over the years, famous people have said some memorable things about our canine companions. –courtesy of F.R.S., Chicago, Illinois

"If there are no dogs in heaven, then when I die, I want to go where they went." *–Will Rogers, humorist (1879–1935)*

"The average dog is a nicer person than the average person."
–Andy Rooney, journalist (b. 1919)

"A dog teaches a boy fidelity, perseverance, and to turn around three times before lying down."
–Robert Benchley, humorist (1889–1945)

"My goal in life is to be as good a person as my dog already thinks I am."
–Unknown

"If your dog is fat, you aren't getting enough exercise." *–Unknown*

"Happiness is a warm puppy."
–Charles M. Schulz, cartoonist (1922–2000)

"Dogs are not our whole life, but they make our lives whole."
–Roger Caras, former president of the American Society for the Prevention of Cruelty to Animals (1928–2001)

"You can say any foolish thing to a dog, and the dog will give you a look that says, 'Wow, you're right! I never would've thought of that.'"
–Dave Barry, humorist (b. 1947)

"I wonder if other dogs think that poodles are members of a weird religious cult."
–Rita Rudner, comedienne (b. 1953)

"Women and cats will do as they please, and men and dogs should relax and get used to the idea."
–Robert A. Heinlein, writer (1907–88)

yawn when those around them do—the so-called contagious yawn.

Volunteers were asked to step into a room by themselves and watch a video showing people behaving neutrally, laughing, or yawning. Observers counted how many times the volunteers yawned.

Some volunteers were asked to breathe only through their noses as they watched. Later, volunteers were asked to press warm or cold packs on their foreheads.

"The two conditions thought to promote brain cooling (nasal breathing and forehead cooling) practically eliminated contagious yawning," the researchers wrote.

Editor's note: So?

How My Grandpa Made a Good Living

–courtesy of J. N., Twin Falls, Idaho

In the early days of the United States, when cars were still an oddity, highways were nonexistent. Pavement usually ended at the city limits, and drivers were on their own to find their way down rutted lanes and across open fields.

One day, a driver of one of the new gas buggies was making his way down a narrow lane and came to a large fence-to-fence mud hole. After some hesitation, he raced his motor and made a run at the puddle, hoping that his momentum would carry him to solid ground. Halfway across, his vehicle stalled and sank up to its running boards.

As he sat deciding what to do, my grandfather showed up driving a tractor. Grandpa yelled, "Hey, you wanna get pulled out? I'll do it for five dollars!"

The driver thought that this was highway robbery, but having no choice, he responded, "Okay."

Grandpa waded into the hole, hooked a chain to the stalled vehicle, and pulled it onto solid ground. As the driver handed him the five-dollar bill, he said, "It looks like you have found an easy way to make a living."

Grandpa replied, "Well, I wouldn't agree that it's easy. I have to haul the water for this mud hole all the way from the river." ☐☐

Vinegar Can Be Used For WHAT?

A Reference Compendium

R
E
F
E
R
E
N
C
E

compiled by Mare-Anne Jarvela

A Table Foretelling the Weather Through All the Lunations of Each Year, or Forever

■ This table is the result of many years of actual observation and shows what sort of weather will probably follow the Moon's entrance into any of its quarters. For example, the table shows that the week following January 23, 2010, will be rainy, because the Moon enters the first quarter that day at 5:53 A.M. EST. (See the **Left-Hand Calendar Pages, 110–136,** for 2010 Moon phases.)

Editor's note: Although the data in this table is taken into consideration in the yearlong process of compiling the annual long-range weather forecasts for *The Old Farmer's Almanac*, we rely far more on our projections of solar activity.

Time of Change	Summer	Winter
Midnight to 2 A.M.	Fair	Hard frost, unless wind is south or west
2 A.M. to 4 A.M.	Cold, with frequent showers	Snow and stormy
4 A.M. to 6 A.M.	Rain	Rain
6 A.M. to 8 A.M.	Wind and rain	Stormy
8 A.M. to 10 A.M.	Changeable	Cold rain if wind is west; snow, if east
10 A.M. to noon	Frequent showers	Cold with high winds
Noon to 2 P.M.	Very rainy	Snow or rain
2 P.M. to 4 P.M.	Changeable	Fair and mild
4 P.M. to 6 P.M.	Fair	Fair
6 P.M. to 10 P.M.	Fair if wind is northwest; rain if wind is south or southwest	Fair and frosty if wind is north or northeast; rain or snow if wind is south or southwest
10 P.M. to midnight	Fair	Fair and frosty

This table was created more than 175 years ago by Dr. Herschell for the Boston Courier; *it first appeared in* The Old Farmer's Almanac *in 1834.*

Safe Ice Thickness*

Ice Thickness	Permissible Load	Ice Thickness	Permissible Load
3 inches	Single person on foot	12 inches	Heavy truck (8-ton gross)
4 inches	Group in single file	15 inches	10 tons
7½ inches	Passenger car (2-ton gross)	20 inches	25 tons
8 inches	Light truck (2½-ton gross)	30 inches	70 tons
10 inches	Medium truck (3½-ton gross)	36 inches	110 tons

*Solid, clear, blue/black pond and lake ice

Slush ice has only half the strength of blue ice. The strength value of river ice is 15 percent less.

The UV Index for Measuring Ultraviolet Radiation Risk

The U.S. National Weather Service's daily forecasts of ultraviolet levels use these numbers for various exposure levels:

UV Index Number	Exposure Level	Time to Burn	Actions to Take
0, 1, 2	Minimal	60 minutes	Apply SPF 15 sunscreen
3, 4	Low	45 minutes	Apply SPF 15 sunscreen; wear a hat
5, 6	Moderate	30 minutes	Apply SPF 15 sunscreen; wear a hat
7, 8, 9	High	15–25 minutes	Apply SPF 15 to 30 sunscreen; wear a hat and sunglasses
10 or higher	Very high	10 minutes	Apply SPF 30 sunscreen; wear a hat, sunglasses, and protective clothing

"Time to Burn" and "Actions to Take" apply to people with fair skin that sometimes tans but usually burns. People with lighter skin need to be more cautious. People with darker skin may be able to tolerate more exposure.

What Are Cooling/ Heating Degree Days?

■ Each degree of a day's average temperature above 65°F is considered one cooling degree day, an attempt to measure the need for air-conditioning. If the average of the day's high and low temperatures is 75°, that's ten cooling degree days.

Similarly, each degree of a day's average temperature below 65°F is considered one heating degree and is an attempt to measure the need for fuel consumption. For example, a day with temperatures ranging from 60°F to 40°F results in an average of 50°, or 15 degrees less than 65°. Hence, that day would be credited as 15 heating degree days.

How to Measure Earthquakes

■ Seismologists have developed a new measurement of earthquake size, called Moment Magnitude, that is more accurate than the previously used Richter scale, which is precise only for earthquakes of a certain size and at a certain distance from a seismometer. All earthquakes can now be compared on the same scale.

Magnitude	Effect
Less than 3	Micro
3–3.9	Minor
4–4.9	Light
5–5.9	Moderate
6–6.9	Strong
7–7.9	Major
8 or more	Great

REFERENCE

Heat Index °F (°C)

TEMPERATURE °F (°C)	RELATIVE HUMIDITY (%)								
	40	**45**	**50**	**55**	**60**	**65**	**70**	**75**	**80**
100 (38)	109 (43)	114 (46)	118 (48)	124 (51)	129 (54)	136 (58)			
98 (37)	105 (41)	109 (43)	113 (45)	117 (47)	123 (51)	128 (53)	134 (57)		
96 (36)	101 (38)	104 (40)	108 (42)	112 (44)	116 (47)	121 (49)	126 (52)	132 (56)	
94 (34)	97 (36)	100 (38)	103 (39)	106 (41)	110 (43)	114 (46)	119 (48)	124 (51)	129 (54)
92 (33)	94 (34)	96 (36)	99 (37)	101 (38)	105 (41)	108 (42)	112 (44)	116 (47)	121 (49)
90 (32)	91 (33)	93 (34)	95 (35)	97 (36)	100 (38)	103 (39)	106 (41)	109 (43)	113 (45)
88 (31)	88 (31)	89 (32)	91 (33)	93 (34)	95 (35)	98 (37)	100 (38)	103 (39)	106 (41)
86 (30)	85 (29)	87 (31)	88 (31)	89 (32)	91 (33)	93 (34)	95 (35)	97 (36)	100 (38)
84 (29)	83 (28)	84 (29)	85 (29)	86 (30)	88 (31)	89 (32)	90 (32)	92 (33)	94 (34)
82 (28)	81 (27)	82 (28)	83 (28)	84 (29)	84 (29)	85 (29)	86 (30)	88 (31)	89 (32)
80 (27)	80 (27)	80 (27)	81 (27)	81 (27)	82 (28)	82 (28)	83 (28)	84 (29)	84 (29)

EXAMPLE: *When the temperature is 88°F (31°C) and the relative humidity is 60 percent, the heat index*

Clouds have many characteristics and are classified by altitude and typ

HIGH CLOUDS
(bases start above 20,000 feet, on average)

Cirrus: Thin, featherlike, crystal clouds.

Cirrocumulus: Thin clouds that appear as small "cotton patches."

Cirrostratus: Thin white clouds that resemble veils.

MIDDLE CLOUDS
(bases start at between 6,500 and 20,000 feet)

Altocumulus: Gray or white layer or patches of solid clouds with rounded shapes.

Altostratus: Grayish or bluish layer of clouds that can obscure the Sun.

LOW CLOUDS
(bases start below 6,500 feet)

Stratus: Thin, gray, sheet-like clouds with low bases; may bring drizzle or snow.

Stratocumulus: Rounded cloud masses that form in a layer.

Nimbostratus: Dark, gray, shapeless cloud layers containing rain, snow, or ice pellets.

85	90	95	100
35 (57)			
26 (52)	131 (55)		
17 (47)	122 (50)	127 (53)	132 (56)
10 (43)	113 (45)	117 (47)	121 (49)
02 (39)	105 (41)	108 (42)	112 (44)
96 (36)	98 (37)	100 (38)	103 (39)
90 (32)	91 (33)	93 (34)	95 (35)
85 (29)	86 (30)	86 (30)	87 (31)

w hot it feels, is 95°F (35°C).

**CLOUDS WITH VERTICAL
DEVELOPMENT
form at almost any altitude
and can reach to more than
9,000 feet)**

Cumulus: Fair-weather clouds
with flat bases and dome-shape
ops.

Cumulonimbus: Large, dark,
ertical clouds with bulging
ops that bring showers, thun-
er, and lightning.

How to Measure Hail

■ The **Torro Hailstorm Intensity Scale** was introduced by
Jonathan Webb of Oxford, England, in 1986 as a means
of categorizing hailstorms. The name derives from the
private and mostly British research body named the
TORnado and storm Research Organisation.

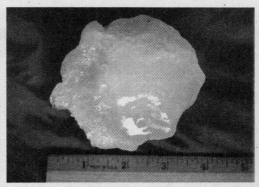

INTENSITY/DESCRIPTION OF HAIL DAMAGE	
H0	True hail of pea size causes no damage
H1	Leaves and flower petals are punctured and torn
H2	Leaves are stripped from trees and plants
H3	Panes of glass are broken; auto bodies are dented
H4	Some house windows are broken; small tree branches are broken off; birds are killed
H5	Many windows are smashed; small animals are injured; large tree branches are broken off
H6	Shingle roofs are breached; metal roofs are scored; wooden window frames are broken away
H7	Roofs are shattered to expose rafters; cars are seriously damaged
H8	Shingle and tile roofs are destroyed; small tree trunks are split; people are seriously injured
H9	Concrete roofs are broken; large tree trunks are split and knocked down; people are at risk of fatal injuries
H10	Brick houses are damaged; people are at risk of fatal injuries

R
E
F
E
R
E
N
C
E

How to Measure Wind Speed

■ The **Beaufort Wind Force Scale** is a common way of estimating wind speed. It was developed in 1805 by Admiral Sir Francis Beaufort of the British Navy to measure wind at sea. We can also use it to measure wind on land.

Admiral Beaufort arranged the numbers 0 to 12 to indicate the strength of the wind from calm, force 0, to hurricane, force 12. Here's a scale adapted to land.

"Used Mostly at Sea but of Help to All Who Are Interested in the Weather"

Beaufort Force	Description	When You See or Feel This Effect	Wind Speed (mph)	(km/h)
0	Calm	Smoke goes straight up	less than 1	less than 2
1	Light air	Wind direction is shown by smoke drift but not by wind vane	1–3	2–5
2	Light breeze	Wind is felt on the face; leaves rustle; wind vanes move	4–7	6–11
3	Gentle breeze	Leaves and small twigs move steadily; wind extends small flags straight out	8–12	12–19
4	Moderate breeze	Wind raises dust and loose paper; small branches move	13–18	20–29
5	Fresh breeze	Small trees sway; waves form on lakes	19–24	30–39
6	Strong breeze	Large branches move; wires whistle; umbrellas are difficult to use	25–31	40–50
7	Moderate gale	Whole trees are in motion; walking against the wind is difficult	32–38	51–61
8	Fresh gale	Twigs break from trees; walking against the wind is very difficult	39–46	62–74
9	Strong gale	Buildings suffer minimal damage; roof shingles are removed	47–54	75–87
10	Whole gale	Trees are uprooted	55–63	88–101
11	Violent storm	Widespread damage	64–72	102–116
12	Hurricane	Widespread destruction	73+	117+

Retired Atlantic Hurricane Names

These storms have been some of the most destructive and costly; as a result, their names have been retired from the six-year rotating list of names.

NAME	YEAR	NAME	YEAR	NAME	YEAR
Jeanne	2004	Stan	2005	Noel	2007
Dennis	2005	Wilma	2005	Gustav	2008
Katrina	2005	Dean	2007	Ike	2008
Rita	2005	Felix	2007	Paloma	2008

Get your local forecast at Almanac.com.

Atlantic Tropical (and Subtropical) Storm Names for 2010			Eastern North-Pacific Tropical (and Subtropical) Storm Names for 2010		
Alex	Julia	Tomas	Agatha	Javier	Tina
Bonnie	Karl	Virginie	Blas	Kay	Virgil
Colin	Lisa	Walter	Celia	Lester	Winifred
Danielle	Matthew		Darby	Madeline	Xavier
Earl	Nicole		Estelle	Newton	Yolanda
Fiona	Otto		Frank	Orlene	Zeke
Gaston	Paula		Georgette	Paine	
Hermine	Richard		Howard	Roslyn	
Igor	Shary		Isis	Seymour	

How to Measure Hurricane Strength

■ The **Saffir-Simpson Hurricane Scale** assigns a rating from 1 to 5 based on a hurricane's intensity. It is used to give an estimate of the potential property damage and flooding expected along the coast from a hurricane landfall. Wind speed is the determining factor in the scale, as storm surge values are highly dependent on the slope of the continental shelf in the landfall region. Wind speeds are measured using a 1-minute average.

CATEGORY ONE. Average wind: 74–95 mph. No real damage to building structures. Damage primarily to unanchored mobile homes, shrubbery, and trees. Also, some coastal road flooding and minor pier damage.

CATEGORY TWO. Average wind: 96–110 mph. Some roofing material, door, and window damage to buildings. Considerable damage to vegetation, mobile homes, and piers. Coastal and low-lying escape routes flood 2 to 4 hours before arrival of center. Small craft in unprotected anchorages break moorings.

CATEGORY THREE. Average wind: 111–130 mph. Some structural damage to small residences and utility buildings; minor amount of

curtainwall failures. Mobile homes destroyed. Flooding near coast destroys smaller structures; larger structures damaged by floating debris.

CATEGORY FOUR. Average wind: 131–155 mph. More extensive curtainwall failures with some complete roof failures on small residences. Major beach erosion. Major damage to lower floors near the shore.

CATEGORY FIVE. Average wind: 156+ mph. Complete roof failures on many residences and industrial buildings. Some complete building failures; small buildings blown over or away. Major damage to lower floors located less than 15 feet above sea level (ASL) and within 500 yards of the shoreline.

How to Measure a Tornado

■ The original **Fujita Scale** (or F Scale) was developed by Dr. Theodore Fujita to classify tornadoes based on wind damage. All tornadoes, and other severe local windstorms, were assigned a number according to the most intense damage caused by the storm. An enhanced F scale (EF) was implemented in the United States on February 1, 2007. The new EF scale uses three-second gust estimates based on a more detailed system for assessing damage, taking into account different building materials.

F SCALE		EF SCALE (U.S.)
F0 • 40–72 mph (64–116 km/h)	light damage	EF0 • 65–85 mph (105–137 km/h)
F1 • 73–112 mph (117–180 km/h)	moderate damage	EF1 • 86–110 mph (138–178 km/h)
F2 • 113–157 mph (181–253 km/h)	considerable damage	EF2 • 111–135 mph (179–218 km/h)
F3 • 158–207 mph (254–332 km/h)	severe damage	EF3 • 136–165 mph (219–266 km/h)
F4 • 208–260 mph (333–419 km/h)	devastating damage	EF4 • 166–200 mph (267–322 km/h)
F5 • 261–318 mph (420–512 km/h)	incredible damage	EF5 • over 200 mph (over 322 km/h)

Wind/Barometer Table

Barometer (Reduced to Sea Level)	Wind Direction	Character of Weather Indicated
30.00 to 30.20, and steady	westerly	Fair, with slight changes in temperature, for one to two days.
30.00 to 30.20, and rising rapidly	westerly	Fair, followed within two days by warmer and rain.
30.00 to 30.20, and falling rapidly	south to east	Warmer, and rain within 24 hours.
30.20 or above, and falling rapidly	south to east	Warmer, and rain within 36 hours.
30.20 or above, and falling rapidly	west to north	Cold and clear, quickly followed by warmer and rain.
30.20 or above, and steady	variable	No early change.
30.00 or below, and falling slowly	south to east	Rain within 18 hours that will continue a day or two.
30.00 or below, and falling rapidly	southeast to northeast	Rain, with high wind, followed within two days by clearing, colder.
30.00 or below, and rising	south to west	Clearing and colder within 12 hours.
29.80 or below, and falling rapidly	south to east	Severe storm of wind and rain imminent. In winter, snow or cold wave within 24 hours.
29.80 or below, and falling rapidly	east to north	Severe northeast gales and heavy rain or snow, followed in winter by cold wave.
29.80 or below, and rising rapidly	going to west	Clearing and colder.

Note: *A barometer should be adjusted to show equivalent sea-level pressure for the altitude at which it is to be used. A change of 100 feet in elevation will cause a decrease of $\frac{1}{10}$ inch in the reading.*

R
E
F
E
R
E
N
C
E

Windchill Table

■ As wind speed increases, your body loses heat more rapidly, making the air feel colder than it really is. The combination of cold temperature and high wind can create a cooling effect so severe that exposed flesh can freeze.

							TEMPERATURE (°F)								
Calm	**35**	**30**	**25**	**20**	**15**	**10**	**5**	**0**	**−5**	**−10**	**−15**	**−20**	**−25**	**−30**	**−35**
5	31	25	19	13	7	1	−5	−11	−16	−22	−28	−34	−40	−46	−52
10	27	21	15	9	3	−4	−10	−16	−22	−28	−35	−41	−47	−53	−59
15	25	19	13	6	0	−7	−13	−19	−26	−32	−39	−45	−51	−58	−64
20	24	17	11	4	−2	−9	−15	−22	−29	−35	−42	−48	−55	−61	−68
25	23	16	9	3	−4	−11	−17	−24	−31	−37	−44	−51	−58	−64	−71
30	22	15	8	1	−5	−12	−19	−26	−33	−39	−46	−53	−60	−67	−73
35	21	14	7	0	−7	−14	−21	−27	−34	−41	−48	−55	−62	−69	−76
40	20	13	6	−1	−8	−15	−22	−29	−36	−43	−50	−57	−64	−71	−78
45	19	12	5	−2	−9	−16	−23	−30	−37	−44	−51	−58	−65	−72	−79
50	19	12	4	−3	−10	−17	−24	−31	−38	−45	−52	−60	−67	−74	−81
55	18	11	4	−3	−11	−18	−25	−32	−39	−46	−54	−61	−68	−75	−82
60	17	10	3	−4	−11	−19	−26	−33	−40	−48	−55	−62	−69	−76	−84

(WIND SPEED (mph))

Frostbite occurs in ▮ 30 minutes ▮ 10 minutes ▮ 5 minutes

EXAMPLE: When the temperature is 15°F and the wind speed is 30 miles per hour, the windchill, or how cold it feels, is −5°F. For a Celsius version of this table, visit Almanac.com/Windchill.

–*courtesy National Weather Service*

How to Measure Volcanic Eruptions

The Volcanic Explosivity Index (VEI)

VEI/Description	Plume	Volume Height	Classification	Frequency
0 Nonexplosive	<100 m	1,000 m³	Hawaiian	Daily
1 Gentle	100–1,000 m	10,000 m³	Hawaiian/Strombolian	Daily
2 Explosive	1–5 km	1,000,000 m³	Strombolian/Vulcanian	Weekly
3 Severe	3–15 km	10,000,000 m³	Vulcanian	Yearly
4 Cataclysmic	10–25 km	100,000,000 m³	Vulcanian/Plinian	10 years
5 Paroxysmal	>25 km	1 km³	Plinian	100 years
6 Colossal	>25 km	10 km³	Plinian/Ultra-Plinian	100 years
7 Supercolossal	>25 km	100 km³	Ultra-Plinian	1,000 years
8 Megacolossal	>25 km	1,000 km³	Ultra-Plinian	10,000 years

REFERENCE

Weather Lore Calendar

■ For centuries, farmers and sailors—people whose livelihoods depended on the weather—relied on lore to forecast the weather. They quickly connected changes in nature with rhythms or patterns of the weather. Here is a collection of proverbs relating to months, weeks, and days.

January

■ *Fog in January brings a wet spring.*

■ [13th] *St. Hilary, the coldest day of the year.*

■ [22nd] *If the Sun shine on St. Vincent, there shall be much wind.*

February

■ *There is always one fine week in February.*

■ *If bees get out in February, the next day will be windy and rainy.*

■ *Fogs in February mean frosts in May.*

■ *Winter's back breaks about the middle of February.*

March

■ *When March has April weather, April will have March weather.*

■ *Thunder in March betokens a fruitful year.*

■ *Dust in March brings grass and foliage.*

■ *A March Sun sticks like a lock of wool.*

April

■ *If it thunders on All Fools' Day, it brings good crops of corn and hay.*

■ *Moist April, clear June.*

■ *Cloudy April, dewy May.*

■ *Snow in April is manure.*

May

■ *Hoar frost on May 1st indicates a good harvest.*

■ *A swarm of bees in May is worth a load of hay.*

■ *In the middle of May comes the tail of winter.*

June

■ *A good leak in June, sets all in tune.*

■ *When it is hottest in June, it will be coldest in the corresponding days of the next February.*

■ [24th] *Rain on St. John's Day, and we may expect a wet harvest.*

July

■ *If the 1st of July be rainy weather, it will rain more or less for three weeks together.*

■ *Ne'er trust a July sky.*

■ [3rd] *Dog days bright and clear, indicate a happy year.*

August

■ *If the first week in August is unusually warm, the winter will be white and long.*

■ [24th] *Thunderstorms after St. Bartholomew are mostly violent.*

■ *When it rains in August, it rains honey and wine.*

September

■ *Fair on September 1st, fair for the month.*

■ *Heavy September rains bring drought.*

■ *If on September 19th there is a storm from the south, a mild winter may be expected.*

■ [29th] *If St. Michael's brings many acorns, Christmas will cover the fields with snow.*

October

■ *Much rain in October, much wind in December.*

■ *For every fog in October, a snow in the winter.*

■ *Full Moon in October without frost, no frost till full Moon in November.*

November

■ *A heavy November snow will last till April.*

■ *Thunder in November, a fertile year to come.*

■ *Flowers in bloom late in autumn indicate a bad winter.*

December

■ *Thunder in December presages fine weather.*

■ *A green Christmas, a white Easter.*

■ *As the days lengthen, so the cold strengthens.*

■ *If it rains much during the twelve days after Christmas, it will be a wet year.*

Animal Signs of the Chinese Zodiac

■ The animal designations of the Chinese zodiac follow a 12-year cycle and are always used in the same sequence. The Chinese year of 354 days begins three to seven weeks into the western 365-day year, so the animal designation changes at that time, rather than on January 1. **See page 109** for the exact date of the start of the Chinese New Year.

Rat

Ambitious and sincere, you can be generous with your money. Compatible with the dragon and the monkey. Your opposite is the horse.

1900	1936	1984
1912	1948	1996
1924	1960	2008
1972		

Dragon

Robust and passionate, your life is filled with complexity. Compatible with the monkey and the rat. Your opposite is the dog.

1904	1940	1988
1916	1952	2000
1928	1964	2012
1976		

Monkey

Persuasive, skillful, and intelligent, you strive to excel. Compatible with the dragon and the rat. Your opposite is the tiger.

1908	1944	1992
1920	1956	2004
1932	1968	2016
1980		

Ox or Buffalo

A leader, you are bright, patient, and cheerful. Compatible with the snake and the rooster. Your opposite is the sheep.

1901	1937	1985
1913	1949	1997
1925	1961	2009
1973		

Snake

Strong-willed and intense, you display great wisdom. Compatible with the rooster and the ox. Your opposite is the pig.

1905	1941	1989
1917	1953	2001
1929	1965	2013
1977		

Rooster or Cock

Seeking wisdom and truth, you have a pioneering spirit. Compatible with the snake and the ox. Your opposite is the rabbit.

1909	1945	1993
1921	1957	2005
1933	1969	2017
1981		

Tiger

Forthright and sensitive, you possess great courage. Compatible with the horse and the dog. Your opposite is the monkey.

1902	1938	1986
1914	1950	1998
1926	1962	2010
1974		

Horse

Physically attractive and popular, you like the company of others. Compatible with the tiger and the dog. Your opposite is the rat.

1906	1942	1990
1918	1954	2002
1930	1966	2014
1978		

Dog

Generous and loyal, you have the ability to work well with others. Compatible with the horse and the tiger. Your opposite is the dragon.

1910	1946	1994
1922	1958	2006
1934	1970	2018
1982		

Rabbit or Hare

Talented and affectionate, you are a seeker of tranquility. Compatible with the sheep and the pig. Your opposite is the rooster.

1903	1939	1987
1915	1951	1999
1927	1963	2011
1975		

Sheep or Goat

Aesthetic and stylish, you enjoy being a private person. Compatible with the pig and the rabbit. Your opposite is the ox.

1907	1943	1991
1919	1955	2003
1931	1967	2015
1979		

Pig or Boar

Gallant and noble, your friends will remain at your side. Compatible with the rabbit and the sheep. Your opposite is the snake.

1911	1947	1995
1923	1959	2007
1935	1971	2019
1983		

REFERENCE

PHASES OF THE MOON

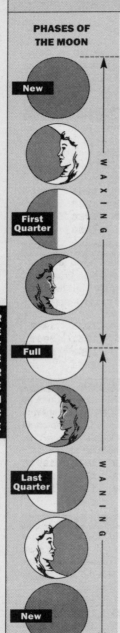

New

WAXING

First Quarter

Full

Last Quarter

WANING

New

The Origin of Full-Moon Names

■ Historically, the Native Americans who lived in the area that is now the northern and eastern United States kept track of the seasons by giving a distinctive name to each recurring full Moon. This name was applied to the entire month in which it occurred. These names, and some variations, were used by the Algonquin tribes from New England to Lake Superior.

Name	Month	Variations
Full Wolf Moon	January	Full Old Moon
Full Snow Moon	February	Full Hunger Moon
Full Worm Moon	March	Full Crow Moon Full Crust Moon Full Sugar Moon Full Sap Moon
Full Pink Moon	April	Full Sprouting Grass Moon Full Egg Moon Full Fish Moon
Full Flower Moon	May	Full Corn Planting Moon Full Milk Moon
Full Strawberry Moon	June	Full Rose Moon Full Hot Moon
Full Buck Moon	July	Full Thunder Moon Full Hay Moon
Full Sturgeon Moon	August	Full Red Moon Full Green Corn Moon
Full Harvest Moon*	September	Full Corn Moon Full Barley Moon
Full Hunter's Moon	October	Full Travel Moon Full Dying Grass Moon
Full Beaver Moon	November	Full Frost Moon
Full Cold Moon	December	Full Long Nights Moon

The Harvest Moon is always the full Moon closest to the autumnal equinox. If the Harvest Moon occurs in October, the September full Moon is usually called the Corn Moon.

REFERENCE

Many Moons Ago

January's full Moon was called the **Wolf Moon** because it appeared when wolves howled in hunger outside the villages.

February's full Moon was called the **Snow Moon** because it was a time of heavy snow. It was also called the **Hunger Moon** because hunting was difficult and hunger often resulted.

March's full Moon was called the **Worm Moon** because, as the Sun increasingly warmed the soil, earthworms became active and their castings (excrement) began to appear.

April's full Moon was called the **Pink Moon** because it heralded the appearance of the grass pink, or wild ground phlox—one of the first spring flowers.

May's full Moon was called the **Flower Moon** because blossoms were abundant everywhere at this time.

June's full Moon was called the **Strawberry Moon** because it appeared when the strawberry harvest took place.

July's full Moon was called the **Buck Moon** because it arrived when male deer started growing new antlers.

August's full Moon was called the **Sturgeon Moon** because that large fish, which is found in the Great Lakes and Lake Champlain, was caught easily at this time.

September's full Moon was called the **Corn Moon** because this was the time to harvest corn.

The **Harvest Moon** is the full Moon that occurs closest to the autumnal equinox. It can occur in either **September** or **October.** At this time, crops such as corn, pumpkins, squash, and wild rice are ready for gathering.

October's full Moon was called the **Hunter's Moon** because this was the time to hunt in preparation for winter.

November's full Moon was called the **Beaver Moon** because it was the time to set beaver traps, before the waters froze over.

December's full Moon was called the **Cold Moon.** It was also called the **Long Nights Moon** because nights at this time of year were the longest.

When Will the Moon Rise Today?

■ A lunar puzzle involves the timing of moonrise. If you enjoy the out-of-doors and the wonders of nature, you may wish to commit to memory the following gem:

 The new Moon always rises at sunrise

 And the first quarter at noon.

 The full Moon always rises at sunset

 And the last quarter at midnight.

■ Moonrise occurs about 50 minutes later each day.

■ The new Moon is invisible because its illuminated side faces away from Earth, which occurs when the Moon lines up between Earth and the Sun.

■ One or two days after the date of the new Moon, you can see a thin crescent setting just after sunset in the western sky as the lunar cycle continues. (**See pages 110–136** for exact **rise and set times.**)

The Origin of Month Names

JANUARY. Named for the Roman god Janus, protector of gates and doorways. Janus is depicted with two faces, one looking into the past, the other into the future.

FEBRUARY. From the Latin word *februa,* "to cleanse." The Roman Februalia was a month of purification and atonement.

 **MARCH.** Named for the Roman god of war, Mars. This was the time of year to resume military campaigns that had been interrupted by winter.

APRIL. From the Latin word *aperio,* "to open (bud)," because plants begin to grow in this month.

MAY. Named for the Roman goddess Maia, who oversaw the growth of plants. Also from the Latin word *maiores,* "elders," who were celebrated during this month.

JUNE. Named for the Roman goddess Juno, patroness of marriage and the well-being of women. Also from the Latin word *juvenis,* "young people."

JULY. Named to honor Roman dictator Julius Caesar (100 B.C.–44 B.C.). In 46 B.C., Julius Caesar made one of his greatest contributions to history: With the help of Sosigenes, he developed the Julian calendar, the precursor to the Gregorian calendar we use today.

AUGUST. Named to honor the first Roman emperor (and grandnephew of Julius Caesar), Augustus Caesar (63 B.C.–A.D. 14).

SEPTEMBER. From the Latin word *septem,* "seven," because this had been the seventh month of the early Roman calendar.

OCTOBER. From the Latin word *octo,* "eight," because this had been the eighth month of the early Roman calendar.

NOVEMBER. From the Latin word *novem,* "nine," because this had been the ninth month of the early Roman calendar.

DECEMBER. From the Latin word *decem,* "ten," because this had been the tenth month of the early Roman calendar.

The Origin of Day Names

■ The days of the week were named by ancient Romans with the Latin words for the Sun, the Moon, and the five known planets. These names have survived in European languages, but English names also reflect Anglo-Saxon and Norse influences.

English	Latin	French	Italian	Spanish	Anglo-Saxon and Norse
SUNDAY	dies Solis (Sol's day)	dimanche	domenica	domingo	Sunnandaeg (Sun's day)
		from the Latin for "Lord's day"			
MONDAY	dies Lunae (Luna's day)	lundi	lunedı	lunes	Monandaeg (Moon's day)
TUESDAY	dies Martis (Mars's day)	mardi	martedı	martes	Tiwesdaeg (Tiw's day)
WEDNESDAY	dies Mercurii (Mercury's day)	mercredi	mercoledı	miércoles	Wodnesdaeg (Woden's day)
THURSDAY	dies Jovis (Jupiter's day)	jeudi	giovedı	jueves	Thursdaeg (Thor's day)
FRIDAY	dies Veneris (Venus's day)	vendredi	venerdı	viernes	Frigedaeg (Frigga's day)
SATURDAY	dies Saturni (Saturn's day)	samedi	sabato	sábado	Saeterndaeg (Saturn's day)
		from the Latin for "Sabbath"			

Best Planetary Encounters of the 21st Century

Me = Mercury   V = Venus   Mn = Moon   Ma = Mars   J = Jupiter   S = Saturn

In all of these cases, face west between twilight and 10 P.M. to see the conjunction.

DATE	OBJECTS	DATE	OBJECTS
August 6, 2010	V, Ma, S	June 27, 2074	V, Mn, J
February 20, 2015	V, Mn, Ma	June 28, 2076	Ma, J
June 30–July 1, 2015	V, J	October 31, 2076	Mn, Ma, S
July 18, 2015	V, Mn, J	February 27, 2079	V, Ma
December 20, 2020	J, S	November 7, 2080	Ma, J, S
March 1, 2023	V, J	November 15, 2080	Ma, J, S
December 1–2, 2033	Ma, J	November 17, 2080	Mn, Ma, J, S
February 23, 2047	V, Ma	December 24, 2080	V, J
March 7, 2047	V, J	March 6, 2082	V, J
May 13, 2066	V, Ma	April 28, 2085	Mn, Ma, J
July 1, 2066	V, S	June 13, 2085	Me, V, J
March 14, 2071	V, J	May 15, 2098	V, Ma
June 21, 2074	V, J	June 29, 2098	V, J

How to Find the Day of the Week for Any Given Date

To compute the day of the week for any given date as far back as the mid–18th century, proceed as follows:

■ Add the last two digits of the year to one-quarter of the last two digits (discard any remainder), the day of the month, and the month key from the key box below. Divide the sum by 7; the remainder is the day of the week (1 is Sunday, 2 is Monday, and so on). If there is no remainder, the day is Saturday. If you're searching for a weekday prior to 1900, add 2 to the sum before dividing; prior to 1800, add 4. The formula doesn't work for days prior to 1753. From 2000 to 2099, subtract 1 from the sum before dividing.

Example:
The Dayton Flood was on March 25, 1913.

Last two digits of year:	13
One-quarter of these two digits:	3
Given day of month:	25
Key number for March:	4
Sum:	45

45 ÷ 7 = 6, with a remainder of 3. The flood took place on Tuesday, the third day of the week.

KEY

January	1
leap year	0
February	4
leap year	3
March	4
April	0
May	2
June	5
July	0
August	3
September	6
October	1
November	4
December	6

Easter Dates (2010–14)

■ Christian churches that follow the Gregorian calendar celebrate Easter on the first Sunday after the paschal full Moon on or just after the vernal equinox.

YEAR	EASTER
2010.	April 4
2011.	April 24
2012.	April 8
2013.	March 31
2014.	April 20

■ Eastern Orthodox churches follow the Julian calendar.

YEAR	EASTER
2010.	April 4
2011.	April 24
2012.	April 15
2013	May 5
2014.	April 20

Friggatriskaidekaphobia Trivia

Here are a few facts about Friday the 13th:

■ In the 14 possible configurations for the annual calendar (see any perpetual calendar), the occurrence of Friday the 13th is this:

6 of 14 years have one Friday the 13th.
6 of 14 years have two Fridays the 13th.
2 of 14 years have three Fridays the 13th.

■ There is no year without one Friday the 13th, and no year with more than three.

■ There is one Friday the 13th in 2010, in August.

■ We say "Fridays the 13th" because it is hard to say "Friday the 13ths."

Sowing Vegetable Seeds

Sow or plant in cool weather	Beets, broccoli, brussels sprouts, cabbage, lettuce, onions, parsley, peas, radishes, spinach, Swiss chard, turnips
Sow or plant in warm weather	Beans, carrots, corn, cucumbers, eggplant, melons, okra, peppers, squash, tomatoes
Sow or plant for one crop per season	Corn, eggplant, leeks, melons, peppers, potatoes, spinach (New Zealand), squash, tomatoes
Resow for additional crops	Beans, beets, cabbage, carrots, kohlrabi, lettuce, radishes, rutabagas, spinach, turnips

A Beginner's Vegetable Garden

■ A good size for a beginner's vegetable garden is 10x16 feet. It should have crops that are easy to grow. A plot this size, planted as suggested below, can feed a family of four for one summer, with a little extra for canning and freezing (or giving away).

Make 11 rows, 10 feet long, with 6 inches between them. Ideally, the rows should run north and south to take full advantage of the sunlight. Plant the following:

ROW
1 Zucchini (4 plants)
2 Tomatoes (5 plants, staked)
3 Peppers (6 plants)
4 Cabbage

ROW
5 Bush beans
6 Lettuce
7 Beets
8 Carrots
9 Chard
10 Radishes
11 Marigolds (to discourage rabbits!)

REFERENCE

Traditional Planting Times

■ Plant **corn** when elm leaves are the size of a squirrel's ear, when oak leaves are the size of a mouse's ear, when apple blossoms begin to fall, or when the dogwoods are in full bloom.

■ Plant **lettuce, spinach, peas,** and other cool-weather vegetables when the lilacs show their first leaves or when daffodils begin to bloom.

■ Plant **tomatoes, early corn,** and **peppers** when dogwoods are in peak bloom or when daylilies start to bloom.

■ Plant **cucumbers** and **squashes** when lilac flowers fade.

■ Plant **perennials** when maple leaves begin to unfurl.

■ Plant **morning glories** when maple trees have full-size leaves.

■ Plant **pansies, snapdragons,** and other hardy annuals after the aspen and chokecherry trees leaf out.

■ Plant **beets** and **carrots** when dandelions are blooming.

Flowers and Herbs That Attract Butterflies

Allium. . . . . *Allium*	Mallow . . . . *Malva*
Aster . . . . *Aster*	Mealycup sage . . . . *Salvia farinacea*
Bee balm. . . . . *Monarda*	Milkweed . . . . *Asclepias*
Butterfly bush . . . . . . *Buddleia*	Mint . . . . *Mentha*
Catmint . . . . *Nepeta*	Oregano. . . . . *Origanum vulgare*
Clove pink. . . . . *Dianthus*	Pansy. . . . . *Viola*
Cornflower . . . . *Centaurea*	Parsley. . . . . *Petroselinum*
Creeping thyme . . . . . *Thymus serpyllum*	crispum
Daylily . . . . *Hemerocallis*	Phlox . . . . *Phlox*
Dill. . . . . *Anethum graveolens*	Privet. . . . . *Ligustrum*
False indigo . . . . *Baptisia*	Purple coneflower. . *Echinacea purpurea*
Fleabane . . . . *Erigeron*	Purple loosestrife. . . . . *Lythrum*
Floss flower . . . . *Ageratum*	Rock cress. . . . . *Arabis*
Globe thistle . . . . *Echinops*	Sea holly . . . . *Eryngium*
Goldenrod . . . . *Solidago*	Shasta daisy . . . . *Chrysanthemum*
Helen's flower . . . . *Helenium*	Snapdragon . . . . *Antirrhinum*
Hollyhock. . . . . *Alcea*	Stonecrop . . . . *Sedum*
Honeysuckle . . . . *Lonicera*	Sweet alyssum . . . . *Lobularia*
Lavender. . . . . *Lavendula*	Sweet marjoram. . . *Origanum majorana*
Lilac . . . . *Syringa*	Sweet rocket . . . . *Hesperis*
Lupine. . . . . *Lupinus*	Tickseed . . . . *Coreopsis*
Lychnis . . . . *Lychnis*	Zinnia . . . . *Zinnia*

Flowers* That Attract Hummingbirds

Beard tongue . . . . *Penstemon*	Summer phlox . . . . . . *Phlox paniculata*
Bee balm. . . . . *Monarda*	Trumpet honeysuckle . . . . *Lonicera*
Butterfly bush . . . . *Buddleia*	sempervirens
Catmint. . . . . *Nepeta*	Verbena . . . . *Verbena*
Clove pink. . . . . *Dianthus*	Weigela. . . . . *Weigela*
Columbine . . . . *Aquilegia*	
Coral bells . . . . *Heuchera*	
Daylily . . . . *Hemerocallis*	
Desert candle . . . . *Yucca*	
Flag iris . . . . *Iris*	
Flowering tobacco. . . . . *Nicotiana alata*	
Foxglove . . . . *Digitalis*	
Larkspur . . . . *Delphinium*	
Lily . . . . *Lilium*	
Lupine. . . . . *Lupinus*	
Petunia. . . . . *Petunia*	
Pincushion flower . . . . *Scabiosa*	
Red-hot poker . . . . *Kniphofia*	
Scarlet sage . . . . *Salvia splendens*	
Soapwort . . . . *Saponaria*	

*Note: Choose varieties in red and orange shades.

pH Preferences of Trees, Shrubs, Vegetables, and Flowers

■ An accurate soil test will tell you your soil pH and will specify the amount of lime or sulfur that is needed to bring it up or down to the appropriate level. A pH of 6.5 is just about right for most home gardens, since most plants thrive in the 6.0 to 7.0 (slightly acidic to neutral) range. Some plants (azaleas, blueberries) prefer more strongly acidic soil in the 4.0 to 6.0 range, while a few (asparagus, plums) do best in soil that is neutral to slightly alkaline. Acidic (sour, below 7.0) soil is counteracted by applying finely ground limestone, and alkaline (sweet, above 7.0) soil is treated with gypsum (calcium sulfate) or ground sulfur.

Common Name	Optimum pH Range	Common Name	Optimum pH Range	Common Name	Optimum pH Range
TREES AND SHRUBS		Spruce	5.0–6.0	Canna	6.0–8.0
Apple	5.0–6.5	Walnut, black	6.0–8.0	Carnation	6.0–7.0
Ash	6.0–7.5	Willow	6.0–8.0	Chrysanthemum	6.0–7.5
Azalea	4.5–6.0			Clematis	5.5–7.0
Basswood	6.0–7.5	**VEGETABLES**		Coleus	6.0–7.0
Beautybush	6.0–7.5	Asparagus	6.0–8.0	Coneflower, purple	5.0–7.5
Birch	5.0–6.5	Bean, pole	6.0–7.5	Cosmos	5.0–8.0
Blackberry	5.0–6.0	Beet	6.0–7.5	Crocus	6.0–8.0
Blueberry	4.0–6.0	Broccoli	6.0–7.0	Daffodil	6.0–6.5
Boxwood	6.0–7.5	Brussels sprout	6.0–7.5	Dahlia	6.0–7.5
Cherry, sour	6.0–7.0	Carrot	5.5–7.0	Daisy, Shasta	6.0–8.0
Chestnut	5.0–6.5	Cauliflower	5.5–7.5	Daylily	6.0–8.0
Crab apple	6.0–7.5	Celery	5.8–7.0	Delphinium	6.0–7.5
Dogwood	5.0–7.0	Chive	6.0–7.0	Foxglove	6.0–7.5
Elder, box	6.0–8.0	Cucumber	5.5–7.0	Geranium	6.0–8.0
Fir, balsam	5.0–6.0	Garlic	5.5–8.0	Gladiolus	5.0–7.0
Fir, Douglas	6.0–7.0	Kale	6.0–7.5	Hibiscus	6.0–8.0
Hemlock	5.0–6.0	Lettuce	6.0–7.0	Hollyhock	6.0–8.0
Hydrangea, blue-flowered	4.0–5.0	Pea, sweet	6.0–7.5	Hyacinth	6.5–7.5
Hydrangea, pink-flowered	6.0–7.0	Pepper, sweet	5.5–7.0	Iris, blue flag	5.0–7.5
Juniper	5.0–6.0	Potato	4.8–6.5	Lily-of-the-valley	4.5–6.0
Laurel, mountain	4.5–6.0	Pumpkin	5.5–7.5	Lupine	5.0–6.5
Lemon	6.0–7.5	Radish	6.0–7.0	Marigold	5.5–7.5
Lilac	6.0–7.5	Spinach	6.0–7.5	Morning glory	6.0–7.5
Maple, sugar	6.0–7.5	Squash, crookneck	6.0–7.5	Narcissus, trumpet	5.5–6.5
Oak, white	5.0–6.5	Squash, Hubbard	5.5–7.0	Nasturtium	5.5–7.5
Orange	6.0–7.5	Tomato	5.5–7.5	Pansy	5.5–6.5
Peach	6.0–7.0			Peony	6.0–7.5
Pear	6.0–7.5	**FLOWERS**		Petunia	6.0–7.5
Pecan	6.4–8.0	Alyssum	6.0–7.5	Phlox, summer	6.0–8.0
Pine, red	5.0–6.0	Aster, New England	6.0–8.0	Poppy, oriental	6.0–7.5
Pine, white	4.5–6.0	Baby's breath	6.0–7.0	Rose, hybrid tea	5.5–7.0
Plum	6.0–8.0	Bachelor's button	6.0–7.5	Rose, rugosa	6.0–7.0
Raspberry, red	5.5–7.0	Bee balm	6.0–7.5	Snapdragon	5.5–7.0
Rhododendron	4.5–6.0	Begonia	5.5–7.0	Sunflower	6.0–7.5
		Black-eyed Susan	5.5–7.0	Tulip	6.0–7.0
		Bleeding heart	6.0–7.5	Zinnia	5.5–7.0

R
E
F
E
R
E
N
C
E

How to Grow Vegetables

VEGETABLE	START SEEDS INDOORS (weeks before last spring frost)	START SEEDS OUTDOORS (weeks before or after last spring frost)	MINIMUM SOIL TEMPERATURE TO TO GERMINATE (°F)	COLD HARDINESS
Beans		Anytime after	48–50	Tender
Beets		4 before to 4 after	39–41	Half-hardy
Broccoli	6–8	4 before	55–75	Hardy
Brussels sprouts	6–8		55–75	Hardy
Cabbage	6–8	Anytime after	38–40	Hardy
Carrots		4–6 before	39–41	Half-hardy
Cauliflower	6–8	4 before	65–75	Half-hardy
Celery	6–8		60–70	Tender
Corn		2 after	46–50	Tender
Cucumbers	3–4	1–2 after	65–70	Very tender
Lettuce	4–6	2–3 after	40–75	Half-hardy
Melons	3–4	2 after	55–60	Very tender
Onion sets		4 before	34–36	Hardy
Parsnips		2–4 before	55–70	Hardy
Peas		4–6 before	34–36	Hardy
Peppers	8–10		70–80	Very tender
Potato tubers		2–4 before	55–70	Half-hardy
Pumpkins	3–4	1 after	55–60	Tender
Radishes		4–6 before	39–41	Hardy
Spinach		4–6 before	55–65	Hardy
Squash, summer	3–4	1 after	55–60	Very tender
Squash, winter	3–4	1 after	55–60	Tender
Tomatoes	6–8		50–55	Tender

REFERENCE

WHEN TO FERTILIZE	WHEN TO WATER
After heavy bloom and set of pods	Regularly, from start of pod to set
At time of planting	Only during drought conditions
Three weeks after transplanting	Only during drought conditions
Three weeks after transplanting	At transplanting
Three weeks after transplanting	Two to three weeks before harvest
Preferably in the fall for the following spring	Only during drought conditions
Three weeks after transplanting	Once, three weeks before harvest
At time of transplanting	Once a week
When eight to ten inches tall, and again when first silk appears	When tassels appear and cobs start to swell
One week after bloom, and again three weeks later	Frequently, especially when fruits form
Two to three weeks after transplanting	Once a week
One week after bloom, and again three weeks later	Once a week
When bulbs begin to swell, and again when plants are one foot tall	Only during drought conditions
One year before planting	Only during drought conditions
After heavy bloom and set of pods	Regularly, from start of pod to set
After first fruit-set	Once a week
At bloom time or time of second hilling	Regularly, when tubers start to form
Just before vines start to run, when plants are about one foot tall	Only during drought conditions
Before spring planting	Once a week
When plants are one-third grown	Once a week
Just before vines start to run, when plants are about one foot tall	Only during drought conditions
Just before vines start to run, when plants are about one foot tall	Only during drought conditions
Two weeks before, and after first picking	Twice a week

Lawn-Growing Tips

- Test your soil: The pH balance should be 7.0 or more; 6.2 to 6.7 puts your lawn at risk for fungal diseases. If the pH is too low, correct it with liming, best done in the fall.

- The best time to apply fertilizer is just before it rains.

- If you put lime and fertilizer on your lawn, spread half of it as you walk north to south, the other half as you walk east to west to cut down on missed areas.

- Any feeding of lawns in the fall should be done with a low-nitrogen, slow-acting fertilizer.

- In areas of your lawn where tree roots compete with the grass, apply some extra fertilizer to benefit both.

- Moss and sorrel in lawns usually means poor soil, poor aeration or drainage, or excessive acidity.

- Control weeds by promoting healthy lawn growth with natural fertilizers in spring and early fall.

- Raise the level of your lawnmower blades during the hot summer days. Taller grass resists drought better than short.

- You can reduce mowing time by redesigning your lawn, reducing sharp corners and adding sweeping curves.

- During a drought, let the grass grow longer between mowings, and reduce fertilizer.

- Water your lawn early in the morning or in the evening.

Herbs to Plant in Lawns

Choose plants that suit your soil and your climate. All these can withstand mowing and considerable foot traffic.

Ajuga or bugleweed (*Ajuga reptans*)
Corsican mint (*Mentha requienii*)
Dwarf cinquefoil (*Potentilla tabernaemontani*)
English pennyroyal (*Mentha pulegium*)
Green Irish moss (*Sagina subulata*)
Pearly everlasting (*Anaphalis margaritacea*)
Roman chamomile (*Chamaemelum nobile*)
Rupturewort (*Herniaria glabra*)
Speedwell (*Veronica officinalis*)
Stonecrop (*Sedum ternatum*)
Sweet violets (*Viola odorata* or
  V. tricolor)
Thyme (*Thymus serpyllum*)
White clover (*Trifolium
  repens*)
Wild strawberries
  (*Fragaria virginiana*)
Wintergreen or
  partridgeberry
  (*Mitchella repens*)

A Gardener's Worst Phobias

Name of Fear	Object Feared
Alliumphobia	Garlic
Anthophobia	Flowers
Apiphobia	Bees
Arachnophobia	Spiders
Batonophobia	Plants
Bufonophobia	Toads
Dendrophobia	Trees
Entomophobia	Insects
Lachanophobia	Vegetables
Melissophobia	Bees
Mottephobia	Moths
Myrmecophobia	Ants
Ornithophobia	Birds
Ranidaphobia	Frogs
Rupophobia	Dirt
Scoleciphobia	Worms
Spheksophobia	Wasps

REFERENCE

Cooperative Extension Services

■ Contact your local state cooperative extension Web site to get help with tricky insect problems, best varieties to plant in your area, or general maintenance of your garden.

Alabama
www.aces.edu

Alaska
www.uaf.edu/coop-ext

Arizona
www.ag.arizona.edu/
extension

Arkansas
www.uaex.edu

California
www.ucanr.org

Colorado
www.ext.colostate.edu

Connecticut
www.extension.uconn.edu

Delaware
ag.udel.edu/extension

Florida
www.solutionsforyourlife
.ufl.edu

Georgia
www.caes.uga.edu/extension

Hawaii
www.ctahr.hawaii.edu/ext

Idaho
www.extension.uidaho.edu

Illinois
web.extension.uiuc.edu/
state/index.html

Indiana
www.ces.purdue.edu

Iowa
www.extension.iastate.edu

Kansas
www.oznet.ksu.edu

Kentucky
www.ca.uky.edu/ces

Louisiana
www.lsuagcenter.com

Maine
www.umext.maine.edu

Maryland
extension.umd.edu

Massachusetts
www.umassextension.org

Michigan
www.msue.msu.edu

Minnesota
www.extension.umn.edu

Mississippi
www.msucares.com

Missouri
www.extension.missouri.edu

Montana
www.extn.msu.montana.edu

Nebraska
www.extension.unl.edu

Nevada
www.unce.unr.edu

New Hampshire
www.extension.unh.edu

New Jersey
www.njaes.rutgers.edu

New Mexico
www.cahe.nmsu.edu/ces

New York
www.cce.cornell.edu

North Carolina
www.ces.ncsu.edu

North Dakota
www.ext.nodak.edu

Ohio
extension.osu.edu

Oklahoma
www.oces.okstate.edu

Oregon
www.extension
.oregonstate.edu

Pennsylvania
www.extension.psu.edu

Rhode Island
www.uri.edu/ce

South Carolina
www.clemson.edu/
extension

South Dakota
sdces.sdstate.edu

Tennessee
www.utextension.utk.edu

Texas
texasextension.tamu.edu

Utah
www.extension.usu.edu

Vermont
www.uvm.edu/~uvmext

Virginia
www.ext.vt.edu

Washington
ext.wsu.edu

West Virginia
www.wvu.edu/~exten

Wisconsin
www.uwex.edu/ces

Wyoming
ces.uwyo.edu

REFERENCE

How to Grow Herbs

HERB	PROPAGATION METHOD	START SEEDS INDOORS (weeks before last spring frost)	START SEEDS OUTDOORS (weeks before or after last spring frost)	MINIMUM SOIL TEMPERATURE TO GERMINATE (°F)	HEIGHT (inches)
Basil	Seeds, transplants	6–8	Anytime after	70	12–24
Borage	Seeds, division, cuttings	Not recommended	Anytime after	70	12–36
Chervil	Seeds	Not recommended	3–4 before	55	12–24
Chives	Seeds, division	8–10	3–4 before	60–70	12–18
Cilantro/coriander	Seeds	Not recommended	Anytime after	60	12–36
Dill	Seeds	Not recommended	4–5 before	60–70	36–48
Fennel	Seeds	4–6	Anytime after	60–70	48–80
Lavender, English	Seeds, cuttings	8–12	1–2 before	70–75	18–36
Lavender, French	Transplants	Not recommended	Not recommended	—	18–36
Lemon balm	Seeds, division, cuttings	6–10	2–3 before	70	12–24
Lovage	Seeds, division	6–8	2–3 before	70	36–72
Oregano	Seeds, division, cuttings	6–10	Anytime after	70	12–24
Parsley	Seeds	10–12	3–4 before	70	18–24
Rosemary	Seeds, division, cuttings	8–10	Anytime after	70	48–72
Sage	Seeds, division, cuttings	6–10	1–2 before	60–70	12–48
Sorrel	Seeds, division	6–10	2–3 after	60–70	20–48
Spearmint	Division, cuttings	Not recommended	Not recommended	—	12–24
Summer savory	Seeds	4–6	Anytime after	60–70	4–15
Sweet cicely	Seeds, division	6–8	2–3 after	60–70	36–72
Tarragon, French	Cuttings, transplants	Not recommended	Not recommended	—	24–36
Thyme, common	Seeds, division, cuttings	6–10	2–3 before	70	2–12

REFERENCE

SPREAD (inches)	BLOOMING SEASON	USES	SOIL	LIGHT*	GROWTH TYPE
12	Midsummer	Culinary	Rich, moist	○	Annual
12	Early to midsummer	Culinary	Rich, well-drained, dry	○	Annual, biennial
8	Early to midsummer	Culinary	Rich, moist	◑	Annual, biennial
18	Early summer	Culinary	Rich, moist	○	Perennial
4	Midsummer	Culinary	Light	○◑	Annual
12	Early summer	Culinary	Rich	○	Annual
18	Mid- to late summer	Culinary	Rich	○	Annual
24	Early to late summer	Ornamental, medicinal	Moderately fertile, well-drained	○	Perennial
24	Early to late summer	Ornamental, medicinal	Moderately fertile, well-drained	○	Tender perennial
18	Midsummer to early fall	Culinary, ornamental	Rich, well-drained	○◑	Perennial
36	Early to late summer	Culinary	Fertile, sandy	○◑	Perennial
18	Mid- to late summer	Culinary	Poor	○	Tender perennial
6–8	Mid- to late summer	Culinary	Medium-rich	◑	Biennial
48	Early summer	Culinary	Not too acid	○	Tender perennial
30	Early to late summer	Culinary, ornamental	Well-drained	○	Perennial
12–14	Late spring to early summer	Culinary, medicinal	Rich, organic	○	Perennial
18	Early to midsummer	Culinary, medicinal, ornamental	Rich, moist	◑	Perennial
6	Early summer	Culinary	Medium rich	○	Annual
36	Late spring	Culinary	Moderately fertile, well-drained	○◑	Perennial
12	Late summer	Culinary, medicinal	Well-drained	○◑	Perennial
7–12	Early to midsummer	Culinary	Fertile, well-drained	○◑	Perennial

REFERENCE

How to Grow Bulbs

SPRING-PLANTED BULBS

COMMON NAME	LATIN NAME	HARDINESS ZONE	SOIL	SUN/ SHADE*	SPACING (Inches)
Allium	Allium	3–10	Well-drained/moist	○	12
Begonia, tuberous	Begonia	10–11	Well-drained/moist	◑●	12–15
Blazing star/ gayfeather	Liatris	7–10	Well-drained	○	6
Caladium	Caladium	10–11	Well-drained/moist	◑●	8–12
Calla lily	Zantedeschia	8–10	Well-drained/moist	○◑	8–24
Canna	Canna	8–11	Well-drained/moist	○	12–24
Cyclamen	Cyclamen	7–9	Well-drained/moist	◑	4
Dahlia	Dahlia	9–11	Well-drained/fertile	○	12–36
Daylily	Hemerocallis	3–10	Adaptable to most soils	○◑	12–24
Freesia	Freesia	9–11	Well-drained/moist/sandy	○◑	2–4
Garden gloxinia	Incarvillea	4–8	Well-drained/moist	○	12
Gladiolus	Gladiolus	4–11	Well-drained/fertile	○◑	4–9
Iris	Iris	3–10	Well-drained/sandy	○	3–6
Lily, Asiatic/Oriental	Lilium	3–8	Well-drained	○◑	8–12
Peacock flower	Tigridia	8–10	Well-drained	○	5–6
Shamrock/sorrel	Oxalis	5–9	Well-drained	○◑	4–6
Windflower	Anemone	3–9	Well-drained/moist	○◑	3–6

FALL-PLANTED BULBS

COMMON NAME	LATIN NAME	HARDINESS ZONE	SOIL	SUN/ SHADE*	SPACING (Inches)
Bluebell	Hyacinthoides	4–9	Well-drained/fertile	○◑	4
Christmas rose/ hellebore	Helleborus	4–8	Neutral–alkaline	○◑	18
Crocus	Crocus	3–8	Well-drained/moist/fertile	○◑	4
Daffodil	Narcissus	3–10	Well-drained/moist/fertile	○◑	6
Fritillary	Fritillaria	3–9	Well-drained/sandy	○◐	3
Glory of the snow	Chionodoxa	3–9	Well-drained/moist	○◑	3
Grape hyacinth	Muscari	4–10	Well-drained/moist/fertile	○◑	3–4
Iris, bearded	Iris	3–9	Well-drained	○◑	4
Iris, Siberian	Iris	4–9	Well-drained	○◑	4
Ornamental onion	Allium	3–10	Well-drained/moist/fertile	○	12
Snowdrop	Galanthus	3–9	Well-drained/moist/fertile	○◑	3
Snowflake	Leucojum	5–9	Well-drained/moist/sandy	○◑	4
Spring starflower	Ipheion uniflorum	6–9	Well-drained loam	○◑	3–6
Star of Bethlehem	Ornithogalum	5–10	Well-drained/moist	○◑	2–5
Striped squill	Puschkinia scilloides	3–9	Well-drained	○◐	6
Tulip	Tulipa	4–8	Well-drained/fertile	○◑	3–6
Winter aconite	Eranthis	4–9	Well-drained/moist/fertile	○◐	3

REFERENCE

DEPTH (inches)	BLOOMING SEASON	HEIGHT (inches)	NOTES
3–4	Spring to summer	6–60	Usually pest-free; a great cut flower
1–2	Summer to fall	8–18	North of Zone 10, lift in fall
4	Summer to fall	8–20	An excellent flower for drying; north of Zone 7, plant in spring, lift in fall
2	Summer	8–24	North of Zone 10, plant in spring, lift in fall
1–4	Summer	24–36	Fragrant; north of Zone 8, plant in spring, lift in fall
Level	Summer	18–60	North of Zone 8, plant in spring, lift in fall
1–2	Spring to fall	3–12	Naturalizes well in warm areas; north of Zone 7, lift in fall
4–6	Late summer	12–60	North of Zone 9, lift in fall
2	Summer	12–36	Mulch in winter in Zones 3 to 6
2	Summer	12–24	Fragrant; can be grown outdoors in warm climates
3–4	Summer	6–20	Does well in woodland settings
3–6	Early summer to early fall	12–80	North of Zone 10, lift in fall
4	Spring to late summer	3–72	Divide and replant rhizomes every two to five years
4–6	Early summer	36	Fragrant; self-sows; requires excellent drainage
4	Summer	18–24	North of Zone 8, lift in fall
2	Summer	2–12	Plant in confined area to control
2	Early summer	3–18	North of Zone 6, lift in fall
3–4	Spring	8–20	Excellent for borders, rock gardens and naturalizing
1–2	Spring	12	Hardy, but requires shelter from strong, cold winds
3	Early spring	5	Naturalizes well in grass
6	Early spring	14–24	Plant under shrubs or in a border
3	Midspring	6–30	Different species can be planted in rock gardens, woodland gardens, or borders
3	Spring	4–10	Self-sows easily; plant in rock gardens, raised beds, or under shrubs
2–3	Late winter to spring	6–12	Use as a border plant or in wildflower and rock gardens; self-sows easily
4	Early spring to early summer	3–48	Naturalizes well; good cut flower
4	Early spring to midsummer	18–48	An excellent cut flower
3–4	Late spring to early summer	6–60	Usually pest-free; a great cut flower
3	Spring	6–12	Best when clustered and planted in an area that will not dry out in summer
4	Spring	6–18	Naturalizes well
3	Spring	4–6	Fragrant; naturalizes easily
4	Spring to summer	6–24	North of Zone 5, plant in spring, lift in fall
3	Spring	4–6	Naturalizes easily; makes an attractive edging
4–6	Early to late spring	8–30	Excellent for borders, rock gardens, and naturalizing
2–3	Late winter to spring	2–4	Self-sows and naturalizes easily

REFERENCE

Plastics

■ In your quest to go green, use this guide to use and sort plastic. The number, usually found with a triangle symbol on a container, indicates the type of resin used to produce the plastic. Call **1-800-CLEANUP** for recycling information in your state.

Number 1 • *PETE or PET (polyethylene terephthalate)*
IS USED IN . . . . microwavable food trays; salad dressing, soft drink, water, and beer bottles
STATUS . . . . hard to clean; absorbs bacteria and flavors; avoid reusing
IS RECYCLED TO MAKE . . carpet, furniture, new containers, Polar fleece

PETE

Number 2 • *HDPE (high-density polyethylene)*
IS USED IN . . . . household cleaner and shampoo bottles, milk jugs, yogurt tubs
STATUS . . . . transmits no known chemicals into food
IS RECYCLED TO MAKE . . detergent bottles, fencing, floor tiles, pens

HDPE

Number 3 • *V or PVC (vinyl)*
IS USED IN . . . . cooking oil bottles, clear food packaging, mouthwash bottles
STATUS . . . . is believed to contain phalates that interfere with hormonal development; avoid
IS RECYCLED TO MAKE . . cables, mudflaps, paneling, roadway gutters

V

Number 4 • *LDPE (low-density polyethylene)*
IS USED IN . . . . bread and shopping bags, carpet, clothing, furniture
STATUS . . . . transmits no known chemicals into food
IS RECYCLED TO MAKE . . envelopes, floor tiles, lumber, trash-can liners

LDPE

Number 5 • *PP (polypropylene)*
IS USED IN . . . . ketchup bottles, medicine and syrup bottles, drinking straws
STATUS . . . . transmits no known chemicals into food
IS RECYCLED TO MAKE . . battery cables, brooms, ice scrapers, rakes

PP

Number 6 • *PS (polystyrene)*
IS USED IN . . . . disposable cups and plates, egg cartons, take-out containers
STATUS . . . . is believed to leach styrene, a possible human carcinogen, into food; avoid
IS RECYCLED TO MAKE . . foam packaging, insulation, light switchplates, rulers

PS

Number 7 • *Other (miscellaneous)*
IS USED IN . . . . 3- and 5-gallon water jugs, nylon, some food containers
STATUS . . . . contains bisphenol A, which has been linked to heart disease and obesity; avoid
IS RECYCLED TO MAKE . . custom-made products

OTHER

Tile and Vinyl Flooring

■ Make a scale drawing of your room with all measurements clearly marked, and take it with you when you shop for tile flooring. Ask the salespeople to help you calculate your needs if you have rooms that feature bay windows, unusual jogs or turns, or if you plan to use special floor patterns or tiles with designs.

Ceramic Tile

■ Ceramic tiles for floors and walls come in a range of sizes, from 1x1-inch mosaics up to 12x12-inch (or larger) squares. The most popular size is the 4¼-inch-square tile, but there is a trend toward larger tiles (8x8s, 10x10s, 12x12s). Installing these larger tiles can be a challenge because the underlayment must be absolutely even and level.

■ Small, one-inch mosaic tiles are usually joined together in 12x12-inch or 12x24-inch sheets to make them easier to install. You can have a custom pattern made, or you can mix different-color tiles to create your own mosaic borders, patterns, and pictures.

Sheet Vinyl

■ Sheet vinyl typically comes in 6- and 12-foot widths. If your floor requires two or more pieces, your estimate must include enough overlap to allow you to match the pattern.

Vinyl Tile

■ Vinyl tiles generally come in 9- and 12-inch squares. To find the number of 12-inch tiles you need, just multiply the length of the room by the width in feet (rounding fractions up to the next foot) to get the number of tiles you need. Add 5 percent extra for cutting and waste. Measure any obstructions on the floor that you will be tiling around (such as appliances and cabinets), and subtract that square footage from the total. To calculate the number of 9-inch tiles, divide the room's length (in inches) by 9, then divide the room's width by 9. Multiply those two numbers together to get the number of tiles you need, and then add 5 percent extra for cutting and waste.

Wallpaper

■ Before choosing your wallpaper, keep in mind that wallpaper with little or no pattern to match at the seams and the ceiling will be the easiest to apply, thus resulting in the least amount of wasted wallpaper. If you choose a patterned wallpaper, a small repeating pattern will result in less waste than a large repeating pattern. And a pattern that is aligned horizontally (matching on each column of paper) will waste less than one that drops or alternates its pattern (matching on every other column).

To determine the amount of wall space you're covering:

■ Measure the length of each wall, add these figures together, and multiply by the height of the walls to get the area (square footage) of the room's walls.

■ Calculate the square footage of each door, window, and other opening in the room. Add these figures together and subtract the total from the area of the room's walls.

■ Take that figure and multiply by 1.15, to account for a waste rate of about 15 percent in your wallpaper project. You'll end up with a target amount to purchase when you shop.

■ Wallpaper is sold in single, double, and triple rolls. Coverage can vary, so be

R
E
F
E
R
E
N
C
E

sure to refer to the roll's label for the proper square footage. (The average coverage for a double roll, for example, is 56 square feet.) After choosing a paper, divide the coverage figure (from the label) into the total square footage of the walls of the room you're papering. Round the answer up to the nearest whole number. This is the number of rolls you need to buy.

■ Save leftover wallpaper rolls, carefully wrapped to keep clean.

HOW MUCH DO YOU NEED?

Interior Paint

■ Estimate your room size and paint needs before you go to the store. Running out of a custom color halfway through the job could mean disaster. For the sake of the following exercise, assume that you have a 10x15-foot room with an 8-foot ceiling. The room has two doors and two windows.

For Walls

■ Measure the total distance (perimeter) around the room:

(10 ft. + 15 ft.) x 2 = 50 ft.

■ Multiply the perimeter by the ceiling height to get the total wall area:

50 ft. x 8 ft. = 400 sq. ft.

■ Doors are usually 21 square feet (there are two in this exercise):

21 sq. ft. x 2 = 42 sq. ft.

■ Windows average 15 square feet (there are two in this exercise):

15 sq. ft. x 2 = 30 sq. ft.

■ Take the total wall area and subtract the area for the doors and windows to get the wall surface to be painted:

```
 400 sq. ft. (wall area)
- 42 sq. ft. (doors)
- 30 sq. ft. (windows)
 328 sq. ft.
```

■ As a rule of thumb, one gallon of quality paint will usually cover 400 square feet. One quart will cover 100 square feet. Because you need to cover 328 square feet in this example, one gallon will be adequate to give one coat of paint to the walls. (Coverage will be affected by the porosity and texture of the surface. In addition, bright colors may require a minimum of two coats.)

For Ceilings

■ Using the rule of thumb for coverage above, you can calculate the quantity of paint needed for the ceiling by multiplying the width by the length:

10 ft. x 15 ft. = 150 sq. ft.

This ceiling will require approximately two quarts of paint. (A flat finish is recommended to minimize surface imperfections.)

For Doors, Windows, and Trim

■ The area for the doors and windows has been calculated above. (The windowpane area that does not get painted should allow for enough paint for any trim around doors and windows.) Determine the baseboard trim by taking the perimeter of the room, less 3 feet per door (3 ft. x 2 = 6 ft.), and multiplying this by the average trim width of your baseboard, which in this example is 6 inches (or 0.5 feet).

50 ft. (perimeter) − 6 ft. = 44 ft.
44 ft. x 0.5 ft. = 22 sq. ft.

■ Add the area for doors, windows, and baseboard trim.

```
 42 sq. ft. (doors)
+30 sq. ft. (windows)
+22 sq. ft. (baseboard trim)
 94 sq. ft.
```

One quart will be sufficient to cover the doors, windows, and trim in this example.

—courtesy M.A.B. Paints

Lumber and Nails

The amount of lumber and nails you need will depend on your project, but these guidelines will help you determine quantities of each.

Lumber Width and Thickness (in inches)

Nominal Size	Actual Size DRY OR SEASONED	Nominal Size	Actual Size DRY OR SEASONED
1 x 3	¾ x 2½	2 x 3	1½ x 2½
1 x 4	¾ x 3½	2 x 4	1½ x 3½
1 x 6	¾ x 5½	2 x 6	1½ x 5½
1 x 8	¾ x 7¼	2 x 8	1½ x 7¼
1 x 10	¾ x 9¼	2 x 10	1½ x 9¼
1 x 12	¾ x 11¼	2 x 12	1½ x 11¼

Nail Sizes

The nail on the left is a 5d (five-penny) finish nail; on the right, 20d common. The numbers below the nail sizes indicate the approximate number of nails per pound.

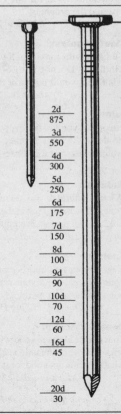

2d
875
3d
550
4d
300
5d
250
6d
175
7d
150
8d
100
9d
90
10d
70
12d
60
16d
45
20d
30

Lumber Measure in Board Feet

Size in Inches	LENGTH 12 ft.	14 ft.	16 ft.	18 ft.	20 ft.
1 x 4	4	4⅔	5⅓	6	6⅔
1 x 6	6	7	8	9	10
1 x 8	8	9⅓	10⅔	12	13⅓
1 x 10	10	11⅔	13⅓	15	16⅔
1 x 12	12	14	16	18	20
2 x 3	6	7	8	9	10
2 x 4	8	9⅓	10⅔	12	13⅓
2 x 6	12	14	16	18	20
2 x 8	16	18⅔	21⅓	24	26⅔
2 x 10	20	23⅓	26⅔	30	33⅓
2 x 12	24	28	32	36	40
4 x 4	16	18⅔	21⅓	24	26⅔
6 x 6	36	42	48	54	60
8 x 8	64	74⅔	85⅓	96	106⅔
10 x 10	100	116⅔	133⅓	150	166⅔
12 x 12	144	168	192	216	240

R E F E R E N C E

The Golden Rule

(It's true in all faiths.)

Brahmanism:
This is the sum of duty: Do naught unto others which would cause you pain if done to you.
Mahabharata 5:1517

Buddhism:
Hurt not others in ways that you yourself would find hurtful.
Udana-Varga 5:18

Christianity:
All things whatsoever ye would that men should do to you, do ye even so to them; for this is the law and the prophets.
Matthew 7:12

Confucianism:
Surely it is the maxim of loving-kindness: Do not unto others what you would not have them do unto you. *Analects 15:23*

Islam:
No one of you is a believer until he desires for his brother that which he desires for himself.
Sunnah

Judaism:
What is hateful to you, do not to your fellowman. That is the entire Law; all the rest is commentary. *Talmud, Shabbat 31a*

Taoism:
Regard your neighbor's gain as your own gain and your neighbor's loss as your own loss.
T'ai Shang Kan Ying P'ien

Zoroastrianism:
That nature alone is good which refrains from doing unto another whatsoever is not good for itself.
Dadistan-i-dinik 94:5

–courtesy Elizabeth Pool

Famous Last Words

■ **Waiting, are they? Waiting, are they? Well—let 'em wait.**
(To an attending doctor who attempted to comfort him by saying, "General, I fear the angels are waiting for you.")
–Ethan Allen, American Revolutionary general, d. February 12, 1789

■ **A dying man can do nothing easy.**
—Benjamin Franklin, American statesman, d. April 17, 1790

■ **Now I shall go to sleep. Good night.**
—Lord George Byron, English writer, d. April 19, 1824

■ **Is it the Fourth?**
—Thomas Jefferson, 3rd U.S. president, d. July 4, 1826

■ **Thomas Jefferson—still survives . . .**
(Actually, Jefferson had died earlier that same day.)
–John Adams, 2nd U.S. president, d. July 4, 1826

■ **Friends, applaud. The comedy is finished.**
—Ludwig van Beethoven, German-Austrian composer, d. March 26, 1827

■ **Moose . . . Indian . . .**
—Henry David Thoreau, American writer, d. May 6, 1862

■ **Go on, get out—last words are for fools who haven't said enough.**
(To his housekeeper, who urged him to tell her his last words so she could write them down for posterity.)
—Karl Marx, German political philosopher, d. March 14, 1883

■ **Is it not meningitis?**
—Louisa M. Alcott, American writer, d. March 6, 1888

■ **How were the receipts today at Madison Square Garden?**
–P. T. Barnum, American entrepreneur, d. April 7, 1891

■ **Turn up the lights, I don't want to go home in the dark.**
–O. Henry (William Sidney Porter), American writer, d. June 4, 1910

■ **Get my swan costume ready.**
—Anna Pavlova, Russian ballerina, d. January 23, 1931

■ **Is everybody happy? I want everybody to be happy. I know I'm happy.**
—Ethel Barrymore, American actress, d. June 18, 1959

■ **I'm bored with it all.**
(Before slipping into a coma. He died nine days later.)
—Winston Churchill, English statesman, d. January 24, 1965

■ **You be good. You'll be in tomorrow. I love you.**
–Alex, highly intelligent African Gray parrot, d. September 6, 2007